SCHOOL LAW FOR TEACHERS

SCHOOL LAW
FOR
TEACHERS

M. Chester Nolte
Associate Professor of Education
University of Denver

John Phillip Linn
Assistant Dean, College of Law
University of Denver

Danville, Illinois: **THE INTERSTATE PRINTERS & PUBLISHERS, INC.**

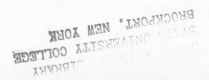

SCHOOL LAW FOR TEACHERS. Copyright © 1963 by The
Interstate Printers & Publishers, Inc., Danville, Illinois.
Printed in the United States of America.

Second Printing, December, 1964

Library of Congress Catalog Card Number: 63-13805

DEDICATED TO

Gwenneth and Marilynn

WITHOUT WHOSE INSPIRATION

AND UNDERSTANDING

THIS BOOK

WOULD NOT HAVE BEEN POSSIBLE

PREFACE

American colleges and universities have for many years recognized the need to develop among school administrators an understanding of laws governing school systems and personnel. Following World War II, a proliferation of legal courses at the college level was developed to acquaint school superintendents and principals with the law. There was, however, little recognition of the teacher's need for knowledge of legal principles underlying his day-to-day teaching activities and his role as a member of a group seeking to develop teaching as a profession.

Now there is growing awareness that teachers must be knowledgeable in the law if they are to effectively perform their professional duties. In today's schools, the teacher, in addition to perpetuating an appreciation of the American way of life, is expected to develop in the classroom a concept of world peace through international law. This *societal* function of teaching presupposes a perception of how the law operates, and how legal principles are developed. Furthermore, because the teacher's role has been substantially extended into broader teaching responsibilities and administrative duties, new legal relationships are arising which impose a greater obligation on the teacher to possess at least a fundamental knowledge of school law. Finally, as an active member of a united profession, the teacher is increasingly involved in activities related to the evaluation and promulgation of laws governing the teaching profession. Consequently, the teacher is more conscious than ever before of a need to know the law as it affects him in his vocation.

State legislatures and state boards of education, realizing the importance of having teachers well informed in the law, have begun to prescribe courses in school law as a prerequisite to teacher certification. Colleges and universities are responding with new courses designed to educate the teacher in legal fundamentals. The need for a school law textbook specifically designed for teachers became evident.

The purpose of this book, therefore, is to provide a textbook for American school teachers, both those in service and those in preparation, which will aid them in understanding and exercising their rights and responsibilities before the law and which will heighten their appreciation of law as it regulates the conduct of individuals in a modern democratic society. The approach of the authors has been to identify the problem areas out of which litigation involving school teachers arises, and to discuss the generally applicable principles of law.

For convenience to the reader, the materials in the book are arranged in five sections, representing categories of importance to the teacher in an initial study of school law. Section One contains preliminary materials of importance to the student in orienting to the American legal system, and to an understanding of the terminology and materials to be encountered in the following sections. Chapter I outlines the historical development of the more important legal principles undergirding the educational system of the United States. Chapter II contains an elemental explanation of the federal and state court structure, the conduct of a trial, and instructions in how to find the law. The authors have recognized that students beginning their study of school law need certain basic concepts before they attempt to take up the other categories contained in the book.

Section Two consists of two chapters relating to certification and contracting, the purpose being to explore these two major problem areas faced by teachers entering the profession for the first time. The importance of proper certification to valid contracting is explored fully in this section.

Section Three relates to the rights of teachers before the law, particularly tenure and retirement rights, employee welfare rights, and personal and political rights of teachers in the public schools. Section Four, on the other hand, pertains to teacher responsibility and liability, the chapters dealing with teacher dismissal, pupil discipline and control, and teacher liability for pupil injury. Emphasis throughout Sections Three and Four is on delineation of the dual rights-liabilities dichotomy incident to the teacher's day-to-day role under normal teaching conditions.

Section Five pertains to the student teacher in legal theory and to problems encountered in this phase of the modern educational enterprise. The Appendix contains information for the serious student whose interest in the subject of school law hopefully has been awakened by reading the earlier portions of the book.

The program of teacher preparation in the modern college or university is based upon the assumption that the teacher may teach in any state of the union. While school laws differ from state to state, there exists a very broad, fundamental body of law underlying the work of the public school teacher that is common to all the states. The authors anticipate that the teacher will become acquainted as soon as possible with the laws and court decisions of the particular state in which he wishes to teach. When the teacher is cognizant of the problem areas, he can readily ascertain the applicable law for a particular jurisdiction.

It is in the hope that this book may make a contribution to the professionalization of teaching that the authors have undertaken the work.

M. Chester Nolte
John Phillip Linn

Denver, Colorado

CONTENTS

Page

Preface _____ **vii**

Section One
SOURCES OF THE LAW

Chapter

I. Legal Foundations of the American Educational System _____ **3**

Prologue. Why Study School Law? Education a State
Function: Local school districts. An Evolving School
System. Early Educational Background: Private colleges
founded; State school system proposed; The Dartmouth
College case. The Federal Government in Education:
Constitution silent on education. Secondary Education in
America: The Kalamazoo case. The Common Schools:
The Olde Deluder Satan Act. The Supreme Court and
Education: Sectarian versus secular education; The Ore-
gon case; Released time; Other issues; The Supreme Court
and racial segregation; "Separate but equal." Suggested
Activities. Further Readings.

II. The American Legal System _____ **31**

Introduction. Sources of American Law. The Federal Court
Structure. The State Court Structure. Commencement
of a Civil Action. Conduct of a Trial. The Criminal
Case. Appellate Review of a Civil Action. The Case as
Reported by the Court: Name of the case; Docket number; Date of decision; Prefatory statement; Syllabus or headnote; Names of counsel; Synopsis of briefs of counsel; Opinion of the court; Decision. Finding the Law: Statutory
law; Case law; The National Reporter System; Other
sources of the law. Suggested Activities. Further Readings.

Section Two
LICENSING AND CONTRACTING

III. The Teaching Certificate _____ **55**

> Introduction. What is Certification? Limitations of the
> Certificate. Who May Teach? Is Certification a Prerequi-
> site to Contracting? Purposes of Certification. History of
> Certification. Changes in Preparation for Certification:
> Substandard certification; Hopeful signs. The State and
> Certification. Accreditation. Suggested Activities. Further
> Readings.

IV. The Teacher's Contract _____ **81**

> Introduction. The Contractual Relationship. Elements of
> a Valid Contract: Competency of the parties; Mutual as-
> sent; Valid consideration; Definite terms; Not prohibited
> by law. The Teacher's Contract: Colonial contracts;
> Today's teaching contract; Legislation; State department
> rules and regulations; School board rules and regulations;
> Court decisions. Earmarks of a Good Contract. Ratifica-
> tion of the Contract. Renewal of Contract. Breach of
> Contract. Suggested Activities. Further Readings.

Section Three
RIGHTS OF TEACHERS

 V. Tenure and Retirement Rights of Teachers _____ **111**

> Prologue. Tenure Laws and Continuing Contracts: The
> annual contract; Continuing contract; Tenure legislation.
> Purposes of Tenure Legislation. Validity of Tenure Laws.
> Probationary Period. Reduction in Salary, Demotion, and
> Transfer. Cancellation Grounds and Procedures. Rights
> of the Teacher Under Permanent Tenure. Right to Re-
> tirement Benefits. Suggested Activities. Further Readings.

VI. Employee Welfare Rights of Teachers _____ **137**

> Introduction. Importance of Teacher Welfare. Teachers
> Are Employees. The Salary Rights of Teachers: Right of
> boards to fix salaries; Salary schedules; Merit pay; Extra pay
> for extra work; Miscellaneous salary rights. Minimum
> Salary Laws. Duty-free Lunch Periods. Right to Leaves
> of Absence: Maternity leave; Sick leave; Other leaves of
> absence. Right to Hold Other Employment. Workmen's
> Compensation and Other Insurance. Suggested Activities.
> Further Readings.

VII. Political and Personal Rights of Teachers _____ **167**

Introduction. Teacher's Constitutional Rights. Academic
Freedom. Organizational Membership of Teachers. Loyalty.
Teacher's Political Rights: Right to hold legislative office;
Right to engage in political activity. Right to Bargain
Collectively: The union shop; Right to strike; The Con-
don-Wadlin Act; Teachers, public employees; National
Labor Relations Act; Right to non-membership. Right to
Speak and Write: Defamation of character; Communica-
tions by teachers about pupils; Communications between
board and superintendent; Communications from one teacher about another; Communications from third parties about
teachers. Right to Work: Anti-discrimination law; Rights
involved. Teacher's Right to a Redress of Grievances.
Suggested Activities. Further Readings.

Section Four
TEACHER RESPONSIBILITY AND LIABILITY

VIII. Pupil Discipline and Control _____ **205**

Introduction. In Loco Parentis. Right to Control Pupils
Outside School Hours. The Law Governing Pupil Attendance: Compulsory attendance; Home instruction; Entrance age; Vaccination; Right to assign pupils; Right of
the board to charge fees. Enforcement of School Board
Rules and Regulations: Corporal punishment; Assault and
battery; Suspension and expulsion; Regulation of the personal appearance of pupils; Requiring pupils or their parents
to pay for damage to school property; Pupil marriages;
Participation in athletics; Control of secret societies; Right
to withhold diploma. Constitutional Rights v. Police Power.
Parental Right to Control Children at School. Suggested
Activities. Further Readings.

IX. Teacher Liability for Pupil Injury _____ **241**

Torts. Tort Liability of Public School Districts. Liability
of the School's Employees: Negligence. Teacher Liability
for Inadequate Supervision. Defenses Against Charges of
Negligence: Student assumption of risk; Contributory neg-
ligence. Liability Waivers. School Safety Patrols. Field
Trips: Errands. Transportation in Privately Owned Cars.
Medical Treatment of Pupils. Avoidance of Tort Liability:
"Save harmless" legislation. Suggested Activities. Further
Readings.

Chapter *Page*

X. Dismissal of Teachers _____ **271**

    Dismissal in General. Board Limitations in Dismissal. Dismissal of the Tenure Teacher: List of charges; Prescribed procedure. Reasons for Dismissal: Insubordination; Immorality; Unprofessional conduct; Incompetency; Neglect of duty; Marriage; Justifiable decrease in teaching positions; Subversion; Miscellaneous reasons. Remedies of the Teacher Wrongfully Dismissed. Right of the Teacher to Resign. Suspension. Power of Boards to Assign and Transfer Teachers. Suggested Activities. Further Readings.

Section Five
EMERGING CONCEPTS OF SCHOOL LAW

XI. The Student Teacher in Legal Theory _____ **307**

    Introduction. History of Student Teaching. Character of Student Teaching Changing. Authority to Permit Practice Teaching. Statutory Provision for Student Teaching. Student Teacher Certification. Liability of Student Teacher for Tort. Legal Rights of the Student Teacher. Suggested Activities. Further Readings.

Appendix

Literature and Organizations in School Law _____ **329**

    Current Status of School Law: The literature; School law at the state level; School law in colleges and universities; Organizations; Publications.

Index of Cases Cited by State _____ **335**

Index of Topics _____ **337**

SOURCES OF THE LAW

*Legal Foundations of the
American Educational System*

The American Legal System

Chapter I

LEGAL FOUNDATIONS OF THE
AMERICAN EDUCATIONAL SYSTEM

Prologue

The children began arriving at 8:30, and soon the classroom was buzzing with talk and laughter. By 8:45, all the children had arrived, but Miss Jones, the teacher, was nowhere to be seen. The noise became louder. Among the group of students in the back of the room, one boy began brandishing a knife. Just before the 9:00 o'clock class bell, he stabbed another student in the hand. The teacher had not yet arrived.

✠ ✠ ✠

"Miss Smith, I don't like to make an issue of your lesson plans, but you know the board's rule concerning them. On Fridays, each teacher is required to file her plans for the following week with the principal. Unless you comply with the board's rule, I shall have no alternative but to report you to the superintendent."

✠ ✠ ✠

"Wouldn't you know it! My car's in the garage for repairs and I've got to get these five players to the football game this afternoon. Do you mind if I use yours just this once?" asked the coach. "The game's in Lynville, only fifteen miles away, and since it's an afternoon game, I'll have it home in plenty of time for your date tonight. Of course, I'll pay all gas and oil expense out of football receipts." The teacher hesitated, then said, "Sure, go ahead. But watch the right front tire. It may need a little air."

✠ ✠ ✠

For ease of moving it from room to room, the school piano was mounted on a low platform on wheels. As the piano was shaky, the teacher had to be careful not to rock it too violently, because it might fall from the dolly. The piano was usually kept in the gymnasium. One day, the physical education teacher was leading a game in the gymnasium in which

3

the girls were jumping up and down. Suddenly the piano fell backwards without warning, pinning a girl's ankle to the floor.

⌘ ⌘ ⌘

Miss Jamison opened the note quickly. She wondered why the Board President had sent the note to school with his son. She read:

> Dear Miss Jamison:
>
> The Board has considered your case very carefully, and we conclude that you are not a suitable teacher for our school. You are hereby notified that your contract is declared null and void.
>
> Yours truly,
(Names of the Board members)

The cases briefly described here are not at all novel. They are real-life dramas, all with one thing in common: in each case the teacher found himself in court. In the case of Miss Jones, the court found that her presence in the classroom was vital to her case. The boy brandishing the knife was visible to all the pupils in the room, and would have been seen by Miss Jones had she been present. Therefore, the court concluded, the teacher's absence from the room was the proximate cause of the injuries suffered, and liability resulted from her negligence.

In the second incident, Miss Smith remained adamant; she refused to comply with the board's rule to file lesson plans each Friday with her principal. When the board dismissed her, she brought suit to compel them to reinstate her. The court, however, held the board rule was reasonable, and concluded that Miss Smith had been legally dismissed for not complying with it.

What of the teacher who loaned his car? Enroute to the game, the coach had an accident, and one of the boys was severely injured. The state in which the school was located had a guest statute, which provided that no person injured while riding in another's car could hold the owner or operator liable, except where the accident was intentional, or resulted from intoxication or recklessness, conditions not present in this instance. The court, however, held that the boys were not "guests" within the meaning of the statute, inasmuch as they had been instructed to ride in that particular vehicle. The teacher was liable for the injury, since the driver-coach was held to be an agent of the teacher-owner.

The physical education teacher was held responsible for the girl's injured ankle, even though she was present in the gymnasium at the time of the injury. The court ruled that maintaining the piano in a hazardous condition constituted a nuisance. If the teacher was aware of the hazard, she was negligent in failing to avoid the accident. If unaware of the hazard, she was negligent in being unobservant. In either event, her lack of proper care for those in her custody made her liable to the full extent of the injury.

In the final case, Miss Jamison consulted an attorney to determine her rights under the contract. Upon the advice of her attorney, she brought suit to recover the balance of her salary, contending that the board had acted in an arbitrary, capricious, and illegal manner in removing her from her teaching position without cause. The court ruled that she was legally entitled to the balance due her under the contract, and entered judgment in her favor.

Litigation involving teachers is not a new phenomenon, but such litigation is rapidly increasing as the number of teachers in America's classrooms rises and the educational enterprise grows more complex. It seems appropriate, therefore, to examine in detail the reasons why teachers now find it advisable to study school law.

Why Study School Law?

The college student preparing for a career in education raises the question, "Why study school law?" Did teachers of an earlier era feel the need for the subject? Is not the present program of preparation at the collegiate level already overburdened with courses in methods, psychology, content subjects, and student teaching? Are not teachers of today better prepared than those of any other generation in our nation's history? Why, then, spend valuable time studying school law? Of what importance is the subject to the prospective public school teacher?

The preparation of teachers today bears little resemblance to the hasty, often sketchy, preparation of teachers over most of our educational history. The prospective teacher attends college for a longer period of time, studying more subjects, than those of any other era. Most of the states require, or have plans for requiring, four years of collegiate preparation for initial certification of teachers, and a few require five years of study for entrance into the field. The predictable result: schools of education are producing teachers who are superior in every way to those of previous generations. And the current trend is toward even longer periods of preparation.

Sophisticated though he may be, the graduate teacher of today is little prepared in a field of knowledge which is of growing importance to him and his profession—the study of the law, that set of principles

5

and regulations which governs every social and individual action. In a society in which people live, work, and play ever more closely together, and in which roles are constantly changing, the study of the law is of increasing importance to every citizen, especially to teachers in our public elementary and secondary schools.

There are many reasons why teachers need a knowledge of the law, but the most compelling of these are the four which follow. First, ours is a nation founded upon a *government under law*. Our national security, our leadership in world affairs—in fact, our very national existence—depend upon each citizen knowing and discharging his rights and responsibilities before the law. The unique place of the public schools in transmitting our culture makes it imperative that teachers know and appreciate the qualities of citizenship which have made America great. Only then can our priceless heritage be safely imparted to the rising generations of youngsters upon whom America will depend for its future strength.

Teachers play a key role in conveying to our youth an appreciation of the American ideal of democratic government. The importance of the teacher's knowledge of the law, therefore, cannot be overemphasized. The schools of America are truly the "laboratories of democracy." The cherished premise that every individual is expected to discharge his obligations to society, just as his rights are protected by that society, is one of the important lessons each citizen must learn. Unless pupils have an opportunity to participate in the democratic process, they will gain little appreciation of its worth. Unless they learn that knowledge of the law is the price a good citizen pays for the privilege of living in a democracy, our American way of life is in constant danger.

Just as the rule of law is important to our domestic relationships, so is it important to a world community. The growing influence of the law in resolving international problems must not be overlooked. The key role of the teacher in developing, among pupils, an appreciation of law and order in world affairs will expand in importance as our concept of world peace through international law progresses. The "law of nations" concept becomes more meaningful to pupils and teachers when they appreciate the law's effect in their everyday lives.

Secondly, teachers need to know the law because our national system of schools is based on an intricate partnership plan among local, county, state, and national governments. Our *partnership system* of education has no parallel anywhere. In order for the teacher to understand it fully, he must have an opportunity to study the legal structure of the system, and become familiar with it. The teacher who lacks a knowledge of the political, historical, and legal foundations of our system of education is handicapped in his classroom and as an influential member of his community.

Legal concepts surrounding American education are quite different from psychological concepts. Most teachers are well schooled in the psychological concepts pertaining to individual development through modern American education. The typical program of teacher preparation stresses an understanding of individual differences among pupils in the public schools. There is a strong emphasis on psychology, particularly that branch of psychology which deals with the individual and how he develops. Therefore, the student teacher may perceive only the individual and his problems, ignoring the equal importance of the contribution of the school to society.

Under the legal concept, however, public schools exist primarily for the good of the society, not the individual. Under compulsory attendance laws, parents are required to yield their children for educational purposes because it is believed that an enlightened citizenry makes a strong society; under public health acts, children are required to submit themselves to programs in hygiene and vaccination because it is believed that healthy persons are most productive; and under the taxation laws, the general adult population must support the public school system because it is believed that the general public benefits from well educated individuals. While there is no inherent incompatibility between the legal and psychological approaches to the study of education, familiarity with only one point of view will result in a lack of appreciation of the other, a condition all too prevalent in the schools today. The study of school law presents the societal perspective, broadening the insight of the teacher into the importance of our schools in the American social order.

Thirdly, knowledge of the law will advance the professional growth of teachers. Educators may differ regarding many aspects of teaching, but they share one common goal: to obtain for teaching the recognition which it deserves as a significant profession, an objective which depends to a large extent upon the establishment of legal sanctions and controls surrounding the profession's members. Teachers as a class are provided for in the constitutions and statutes of the various states, but the rights and responsibilities of teachers as individuals are constantly being hammered out in legislative chambers and courtrooms. As teaching changes, the rights and responsibilities of the individual teacher change, both legislatively and judicially.

As a group, teachers are becoming more and more involved in the passage of legislation affecting their profession, and the educational opportunities of children. Teachers' groups have urged the passage of laws such as those relating to attendance, public school finance, and the organizational structure and improvement of school districts. Under circumstances in which teachers are increasingly active in improving education through legislative channels, a wide and comprehensive knowledge of the law is essential to every member of the teaching profession.

Lastly, teachers will be better able to avoid involvement in *needless litigation* when they possess a thorough knowledge of the law. One can only conjecture at the number of cases which might be termed "needless," but hundreds of cases involving teachers could have been avoided had the teachers known their rights and responsibilities before the law. This is not to say that the individual teacher should become an "expert" in school law. Such a proficiency is neither necessary nor generally possible. Suffice it to say that the teacher should understand our system of public schools, and have an appreciation of their historical and legal development. He should be able to form sound judgments on specific legal problems where he or his profession is involved. He should be able to recognize the circumstances surrounding potential litigation in order to avoid unnecessary actions at law. And he should know that consulting counsel *before* the trouble starts is preferable to waiting until called upon to respond in court.

Education a State Function

Let us begin our study of school law by examining the American educational system as we know it in the twentieth century. That system, if indeed it may be called a system, is unlike any school system in the sense that the term is used in other countries, especially those of Europe, the U.S.S.R., and South America. In contrast to the highly-centralized, government-controlled-and-supported school systems in those lands, our own system is unique in its de-centralization, its various levels of financial support, and the control which exists over education at the local level. The American educational system is not modeled after the systems of any other country, but is cut entirely from new cloth to satisfy the felt needs of the people in the various states.

The federal constitution makes no mention of education, although the framers of the constitution were mindful of the need for general education. The power for establishing and maintaining the public schools is, by implication, reserved to the several states. Thus, because Congress is powerless to make laws controlling education in the separate states, education is said to be *a function of the state* government.

Every state constitution provides for a system of state-supported schools. As each state was admitted to the union, a clause in its state constitution was inserted to provide for the public schools. Under each constitutional provision, the legislature is made responsible for the operation and maintenance of this intra-state school system. For example, section 2 of article IX of the constitution of the State of Colorado provides for a state-wide system of schools using the following language:

> Section 2. *Establishment and maintenance of public schools.* The general assembly shall, as soon as practicable, provide for the establishment and maintenance of a thorough and uniform system of free public schools throughout the state, wherein all residents of the state, between the ages of six and twenty-one years, may be educated gratuitously. One or more public schools shall be maintained in each school district within the state, at least three months in each year; any school district failing to have such school shall not be entitled to receive any portion of the school fund for that year.

In effect, then, instead of a single, centrally-controlled "system" of schools in America, there are actually fifty separate and distinct school systems, controlled by the people in each of the respective states. This control is exercised through the state legislative body, which is acknowledged to have *plenary* control over educational matters within the state. While this control is subject, of course, to constitutional limitations, *the state is the unit of education.* It remains for the legislative body to decide in what way and to what extent it shall exercise its power. Commonly, each legislature has seen fit to establish a state educational agency, usually called the state department of education, as an intermediary administrative entity for the maintenance of the public schools. Each state has also provided for the subdivision of the state into school districts, and enacted statutes governing the election or appointment of school board members in each of the several districts. To these school boards, the legislature has delegated, through the state educational agency, certain administrative duties involving some discretionary powers in the conduct of the public schools of the state. It is this "local control in a state-wide setting" which has been generally accepted as the true strength of our system of education. By this system, more than any other, can the people of a local community develop educational hopes and aspirations through control "at the grass roots" over the destiny of school facilities and programs. Those states in which legislatures have allowed the people to strongly control educational policy at the local level have been most successful in developing outstanding public school systems.

Local school districts. While legislatures could, if desired, abolish all school districts and operate the schools directly, legislative fiat is peculiarly void of any such directive. The legislatures in their wisdom have seen the importance of a high level of local involvement in policy-making to financial and moral support of public education. The soundness of their judgment is verified when one considers that many school districts today are supporting public education to the very limit of the financial ability of the districts to support schools. When people are given the control of their schools to a large extent, more public participation in school matters at the local level results, and educational affairs prosper. Much of this participation funnels through the local board of education.

School districts belong to a class of corporations known, in legal terminology, as "quasi-corporations," a class of organizations having limited powers. As agents of the school districts, carrying out a state function, *i.e.,* education of the young, local school boards possess only such powers as are expressly or impliedly delegated to them by the legislature, or necessary for the conduct of their involuntary function. Thus, it depends upon the will of the legislature as to what extent local boards may be free to make decisions concerning the schools under their jurisidiction.

Because of their special status as "quasi-corporations," school districts come under special rules relating to this class of corporations. School board members are state officers; even though their work is in a local setting, the members of the board are legally state and not local officers. They hold in trust the property of the school district in the name of the state. Their powers are derived from the constitution and statutes of the state, and are subject only to limitations placed upon them by the state legislature. In the absence of a statute dealing with a particular matter in which a decision must be made by a local board, the board may exercise its power of discretion in any way it wishes, so long as its acts are reasonable, within the power of the board to enact, and not arbitrary, capricious, or illegal. The courts have made a practice of non-interference with boards in the exercise of their discretionary powers, unless there is evidence that they have acted outside their powers or in an arbitrary or capricious manner.

Legislatures have thrown around school boards, as agents of the state, an immunity from the consequences of their acts not otherwise available to private corporations. The so-called "doctrine of sovereign immunity" arose in English law under the principle that "the King can do no wrong," and was incorporated into the early colonial charters. Except in the few states where legislatures have taken steps to limit or abolish the immunity doctrine, the rule is that school districts may not be held legally liable for their wrongful acts. The trend seems to be towards abrogation of the immunity rule in more and more states, but this trend is slow in developing. The majority of the states continue to operate under almost complete immunity from tort liability on the part of school districts.

The doctrine of district immunity does not extend, however, to school employees, who may be held individually liable in damages if negligence is evident in their acts. In Chapter IX, teacher liability for negligence is explored in considerable detail. Let us turn now to the historical events which led to the evolution of our American educational system as we know it today.

An Evolving School System

The American educational system is portrayed in the preceding pages essentially as it appears today. But the element of change is an ever-present phenomenon in our culture, and in no aspect of our national life is change more evident than in the public schools of the land. More than three hundred years were needed to develop the distinctively American educational system we know today. In the evolutionary process, conflicting conceptions of education had to be compromised, and divergent currents of educational thought brought into agreement. The conflicts which arose were resolved in many ways —through legislation and litigation, trial and error, debate and compromise—until our present system emerged. Many of the educational problems which concerned Americans of an earlier day remain to challenge us as a people. These are knotty problems and not susceptible of easy solution. The process by which our schools evolved is still in operation, indicative of the will of the people to fit the schools to our emerging needs as a growing, changing nation.

As the various conflicts relating to education arose and were debated, certain *landmarks* emerged, some of which were in the school codes of the day, and some of which were enunciations of judicial opinion. These are the *legal foundations* on which rest our present concept of education in America. A chronological evaluation of the *landmark cases and laws* is one of the most interesting stories of our times.[1] Let us turn to the story as it evolved from earliest colonial times to the present, resulting, as Hansen has noted, in a school system which is free, publicly-supported, state-controlled-and-managed, compulsory, and non-sectarian in character.[2]

Early Educational Background

Schools arose in colonial times as adjuncts of the churches, their purpose being to prepare boys and girls to read so that they might become acquainted with the Word of God and learn what was demanded of them. Cubberley[3] noted that the first schools in the New World were influenced by the Protestant Revolt in Europe, a movement which emphasized the necessity of the Gospels as a means to personal salvation. Prohibited from realizing their religious and educational aspirations in Europe, the early colonists left their native lands and journeyed to the New World. Hence, the earliest beginnings of American education were strongly influenced by European standards of religion, morals, and ideas about the upbringing of children.

The original ideal of *religious literacy* was augmented in the waning years of the eighteenth century by the addition of *humanitarian ideals* born of the French Revolution, the Enlightenment, and Declaration of the Rights of Man. Supporting and paralleling these influences was the gradual awakening of *scientific inquiry*, resulting in the industrial development of the new country. Later, the growth of nationalism and westward expansion blended with other influences to shape the educational system along lines to fit the needs of a polyglot people in a changing, maturing nation. According to Cubberley, our forefathers fought seven *strategic battles* in order that the public schools might be free, non-sectarian, tax-supported and locally controlled, and available to all. The seven battles were as follows:

To obtain tax support
To eliminate the pauper-school idea

---

[1]See R. Freeman Butts and Lawrence A. Cremin. *A History of Education in American Culture* (New York: Henry Holt and Company, 1953).

[2]Kenneth H. Hansen. *Public Education in the United States* (Englewood Cliffs, N. J.: Prentice-Hall, 1956), p. 18.

[3]Ellwood P. Cubberley. *Public Education in the United States* (Boston: Houghton Mifflin Company, 1919), p. 13.

To make the schools entirely free
To establish state supervision
To eliminate sectarianism
To extend the system upward
To add the state university as the crown of the system.[4]

A complete development of the historical background underlying each of these battles for schools to better serve the growing nation would require more space than is available here. Therefore, only those legal concepts resulting in original legislation or landmark court decisions will be treated in the remaining portion of Chapter I.

Private colleges founded. The threads which were to become the warp and woof of the present educational system were already beginning to appear in the colonies as early as 1636. In that year, an appropriation of £ 400 was made by the Massachusetts Bay Colony for the establishment of a college. This modest sum, together with one-half the estate of Mr. Harvard, and other private gifts, produced the first of the institutions of higher learning which today are representative of private colleges and universities in America. The 1636 appropriation of public moneys for higher education was undoubtedly the earliest school finance act of consequence in the New World.[5]

An expenditure of *public* money for the establishment of a college was justified by the colonists on the grounds that a combined civil and religious form of government would contribute most to the furtherance of the Puritan way of life in the Massachusetts Bay Colony. The purpose for which Harvard College was founded was presented in a pamphlet issued in London in 1643.

The pamphlet, entitled *New England's First Fruits*, was in effect an appeal for funds, and affords the student an insight into the attitude of the early Puritans toward the dual ideals of religion and learning.

> After God had carried us safe to New-England, and wee had builded our houses, provided necessaries for our livelihood, rear'd convenient places for Gods worship, and setled the Civill Government: One of the next things we longed for, and looked after was to advance Learning and perpetuate it to Posterity; dreading to leave an illiterate Ministery to the Churches, when our present Ministers shall lie in the Dust.[6]

---

[4]National Education Association. "The State and Sectarian Education" *NEA Research Bulletin* (December, 1956), p. 169.

[5]Harold C. Syrett (ed). *American Historical Documents* (New York: Barnes and Noble, 1960), pp. 34-35.

[6]*Ibid.*

The practice of using combined public tax and private endowment funds for founding and operating colonial colleges persisted until well into the middle of the eighteenth century. Civil government officials usually were represented on the board of control of the early colleges. In several instances, public officials made up the entire board. After 1750, however, when the question of using public funds to support private colleges became an issue, private boards of control became more common and funds for supporting colleges and universities tended to be almost entirely of the endowment variety.

Conflict inevitably arose between those who favored religious sectarian higher education under the control of the church, and those who favored a broader, more secular curriculum. As with Harvard, the colonial colleges were intended principally for the preparation of ministers. To this early theological curriculum in time was added the study of medicine, and later, law. Instruction in medicine depended upon the study of sciences and mathematics. Thus, the need for a gradual inclusion in the curriculum of subjects not strictly religious in nature was evident to those who saw the university as serving the state as well as the church.

State school system proposed. Among the latter was Thomas Jefferson, who in 1779 proposed a complete system of public education based on state organization. A stout advocate of French humanitarian ideas, Jefferson recommended many of the French revolutionary ideas, including a public school system tailored to French conceptions. At the base of the state educational system, or pyramid, Jefferson advocated the establishment of the "common" school for the teaching of reading, writing, and arithmetic in each "hundred" (district). Instruction in the common school was to be free for three years, and children might attend longer if the parents were willing to pay school costs.

Grammar schools for the teaching of Latin, Greek, geography, and the higher branches of mathematics were to be provided above the common schools. Several of these were to be scattered throughout the state, and were open to those boys who were selected annually as "the best genius in the (lower) school." At the apex of the educational pyramid was the state university. Instead of the narrow, predominantly religious curriculum of the time, Jefferson envisioned a course of study "extended to include all the useful sciences." But this scheme was too far in advance of the time to be readily and generally accepted.

The state university, said Jefferson, should be under the control of a public board of visitors responsible to the public good. Only to the extent that enlightened civil leadership was provided could the new nation expect to take its place among the nations of the world. Writing from Monticello in 1816, Jefferson emphasized this belief in the following words:

> If a nation expects to be ignorant and free in a state of civilization it expects what never was and never will be. . . . There is no safe deposit for the functions of government, but with the people themselves; nor can they be safe with them without information.[7]

Jefferson advocated that the state should assume control of existing private colleges and place them in the state educational systems. In his proposal of 1779, commonly referred to as his First Plan, he urged changing the board of visitors of William and Mary College from a private body to a public board of control "appointed by joint ballot of both houses of the Assembly." Such a group, he maintained, would be more responsive to the public welfare than would a private body narrowly sectarian in its orientation.

Subsequently, similar attempts were made to transfer King's College in New York, the College of Philadelphia, Yale, and Harvard to state control. These attempts, however, met with stiff resistance from church groups and certain legislators. Not until 1819, in the famous *Dartmouth College* case, did the courts shed some light on the relationship between church and state in higher education.

The Dartmouth College case. In 1816, the legislature of New Hampshire enacted a law which changed the name of Dartmouth College, a private institution under a charter from the state, to Dartmouth University, and placed it under the control of a board of overseers composed principally of public appointees and *ex-officio* officers of the state government. Under the terms of the statute, Dartmouth College became, in effect, a state university. The Supreme Court of New Hampshire upheld the legislation. On appeal, the Supreme Court of the United States reversed the state court's decision, and declared the statute unconstitutional inasmuch as it subverted the original contract extended to the college by the State of New Hampshire.

The argument that state funds were being used to support the college, and therefore a public body should control it, did not satisfy the court. The necessity of protecting the original contract under which

---

[7]Cubberley, *op. cit.*, p. 57.

the college was founded far outweighed the fact that public funds were utilized in its operation.[8]

Said the Court:

> The will of the state is substituted for the will of the donors in every essential operation of the college. . . . The charter of 1769 exists no longer. It is reorganized; and reorganized in such a manner as to convert a literary institution, molded according to the will of its founders and placed under the control of private literary men, into a machine entirely subservient to the will of government. This may be for the advantage of this college in particular, and may be for the advantage of literature in general; but it is not according to the will of the donors, and is subversive of that contract on the faith of which their property was given. . . . The judgment of the state court must, therefore, be reversed.

Thus, it was established that the state's authority over private institutions is not unlimited. A charter granted to a private institution is in the nature of a contract, and cannot be altered or revoked without the consent of those to whom it is granted. The way was now open for a parallel system of higher education alongside the state systems.

The importance of the *Dartmouth College* case on higher education in the United States can hardly be overemphasized. One effect of the decision was that the permanency of endowment funds was assured, and a great proliferation of endowed colleges and universities followed. Another, and perhaps just as important, effect was that states now turned their attention to the founding of colleges and universities supported and controlled by the respective states, since they were prevented from taking over private institutions without the consent of those involved.

The resulting growth in state universities was dramatic. In all, twenty-one state-supported institutions of higher education were established in twenty states between the close of the Revolution and the Civil War. By 1860, there were 246 colleges and universities in this country, of which 17 were state universities.[9]

The Federal Government in Education

The idea of federal responsibility for education is older than the Constitution. Although, as noted earlier, the federal government

---

[8]Trustees of Dartmouth College v. Woodward, 17 U.S. (4 Wheat.) 518 (1819).
[9]Roald F. Campbell, John E. Corbally, Jr., and John A. Ramseyer. *Introduction to Educational Administration* (Boston: Allyn and Bacon, 1958), p. 41.

left the educational issue to the states, the new government found it impossible to avoid the problem of federal assistance to the states in their early efforts to support education. The first mention of education as a national rather than a state issue appeared in the Ordinance of 1787 establishing the government for the Northwest Territory. Realizing that some inducement was necessary to draw settlers into the territory, a group of land speculators convinced the Continental Congress that the act should contain a guarantee of rights to be expected in the new western area. Educationally, the Ordinance of 1787 was undoubtedly the most important act passed by the Continental Congress. Its effect upon public education over the subsequent century and a half was tremendous.

The inhabitants of the new territory were guaranteed writs of *habeas corpus* and trial by jury, as well as a long list of personal freedoms, among them freedom of worship. The act also stipulated, "Religion, morality and knowledge being necessary to good government and the happiness of mankind, schools and the means of education shall forever be encouraged."

The first "encouragement" was in the form of grants of public land—section 16 of each congressional township—for the maintenance of schools within the township. The practice of federal grants of land was expanded after the Morrill Act of 1862, which granted 30,000 acres of public land or its equivalent in scrip for each Congressman from the state, for the establishment of colleges of agriculture and mechanic arts. In 1850, when California was admitted to the union, the grant was raised to two sections in each township for schools. These grants of land—and later money—for public schools and colleges had a tremendous impact on the life of the westerner and did much to create a sentiment for state schools instead of the parochial schools transplanted from the older states.

As new states entered the union, provisions for public school systems were written into their constitutions as a condition of statehood. Following the early public land grants and the land-grant college acts, the federal government continued to support specific educational programs through appropriations of land and money to the states. The Vocational Education Acts of 1917, 1929, 1936, 1946, and 1956 promoted vocational training for teachers and students in the public schools. The School Lunch Act of 1946, the Veterans Education (GI) Acts of 1944, 1952, and 1956, as well as Public Laws 815 and 874 (providing assistance to federally impacted areas due to the activities of the federal government), proved again the concern of Congress for education. In all, more than 160 different federal aid laws in support of education have been passed by the Congress since 1785.

In 1958, the National Defense Education Act alone authorized the spending of $887 million in federal funds over a period of four years to strengthen critical areas related to science, mathematics, and modern foreign languages. Millions of dollars have been spent, and will continue to be spent by the Congress, for support of public education. With few exceptions, fiscal control over federal funds has remained firmly in the hands of state educational officials.

Constitution silent on education. Although education was not referred to in the Constitution of the United States, certainly the matter was not omitted from deliberation at the Constitutional Convention in 1787. There were other more pressing issues vying for the attention of the constitution makers. Apparently, the delegates were convinced that the Constitution, as finally drafted, contained an implied measure of power sufficient to cover educational purposes. With the passage of the tenth amendment in 1791, reserving to the several states the powers not delegated to the central government by the Constitution, much of the doubt about the place of education in the national scheme was removed. The tenth amendment stated, "The powers not delegated to the United States by the Constitution, nor prohibited by it to the States, are reserved to the States respectively, or to the people."

The division of power over education between the federal government and the states was thus clarified, being somewhat as follows: Congress, in exercising its legislative powers, must look to the Constitution for a grant of its authority. If there is no express or implied authority inherent in the Constitution, Congress is to that extent limited in its law-making power. With the states, the case is quite different. States have complete power unless the power has been delegated to the federal government, or unless it has been denied to the states in the Constitution. An example of the latter limitation upon the states is the fourteenth amendment, ratified following the Civil War, which courts have ruled applies to the public schools:

> . . . No state shall make or enforce any law which shall abridge the privileges or immunities of citizens of the United States; nor shall any State deprive any person of life, liberty, or property, without due process of law; nor deny to any person within its jurisdiction the equal protection of the laws.

The first amendment also applies to education:

> Congress shall make no law respecting an establishment of religion, or prohibiting the free exercise thereof; or abridging

the freedom of speech, or of the press; or the right of the people peaceably to assemble, and to petition the government for a redress of grievances.

Upon these amendments rests our present concept of the role of government in education. Under the tenth amendment, the courts have ruled that education is *impliedly* a function of state government. In addition, they have ruled that the federal government, under its "general welfare" clause, may aid education from time to time. The extent to which central government should go in supporting education is, of course, not a settled issue. Under the fourteenth amendment, individuals are guaranteed *individual* rights, such as the right to due process of law, and equal protection of the laws. Under the first amendment, courts will allow no establishment of religion, nor an abridgement of the freedom of speech, press, or the right of assembly. Upon these constitutional guarantees have turned many of the leading cases involving educational issues in our nation's history.

Secondary Education in America

Paralleling the struggle to establish higher education in this country was an equally interesting struggle over secondary education. As early as 1647, a Massachusetts law provided that when a town reached one hundred householders, a Latin grammar school should be established. This early precursor of the American high school stood between the common school and the college and university, and was for the exclusive purpose of preparing boys for college.

Cubberley[10] noted that "the colonial Latin grammar school had been almost entirely an English institution, and never well suited to American needs." Also, it was never widely adopted outside the New England colonies, where the attitude toward classical studies was most prevalent. About the middle of the eighteenth century, a movement arose to establish secondary schools with a more practical curriculum than that possessed by the Latin grammar schools. The result was the rise of the academy. Benjamin Franklin's academy was founded in Philadelphia in 1751, and later became the University of Pennsylvania. It was the first of the academies to be founded. By 1800, there were 17 academies, 36 by 1820, and 403 by 1850.[11]

The academy was characterized by its semi-public control, its broader curriculum, and the extension of its services to girls. The

---

[10]Cubberley, *op. cit., p.* 78.
[11]*Ibid.,* p. 185.

higher education of women in the United States, in fact, dates from the early academies. But the question of public control over this means of education, together with the settlement of the tax question in the *Kalamazoo* case, tended to bring the academy into question. The American academy was actually a transitional step between the early Latin grammar schools and the American high school as we know it today.

The first *public* high school was established in 1821 in Boston. A Massachusetts law six years later set the pattern for the American high school. The 1827 law provided that in every town having 500 families or more a high school should be established. United States history, algebra, bookkeeping, geometry, and surveying were to be offered. In addition, each town having 4,000 inhabitants or more was required to include the study of Greek, Latin, history, rhetoric, and logic. A penalty was provided for those towns which refused, or neglected, to provide a high school. The Massachusetts law of 1827 was followed by similar laws in other states.

The Kalamazoo case. Whereas the Massachusetts high school law was mandatory, several of the states passed permissive legislation relating to high schools. One such state was Michigan, where the legislature opened the door for local school districts to establish high schools if they so desired. Objection was brought by one Stuart, a taxpayer, on the grounds that paying taxes for the support of a high school and the employment of a superintendent of schools violated the Michigan constitution.[12] While not doubting the power of the state to tax for common schools, Stuart maintained that the high school was not necessarily a part of the state public school system, and that education beyond the common school was a luxury to be paid for privately. The Supreme Court of Michigan held otherwise.

After noting with approval that the state had provided not only for common schools but also for a state university, the court pointed out that failure to provide for secondary education would seem inconsistent indeed. To the argument that classical and foreign languages were the accomplishment of the few, the court expressed surprise that anyone should question the right of the state to bring a liberal education within the grasp of youth of all classes within the state.

The *Kalamazoo* case had an immediate effect upon the growth of high schools in this country, particularly among those boards of education which previously had hesitated to set up a high school for legal

---

[12]Stuart v. School Dist. No. 1 of Kalamazoo, 30 Mich. 69 (1874).

reasons. Between 1870 and 1890, the number of high schools increased fivefold.[13] Beginning in 1890, high school enrollments doubled each decade until 1920. In 1960, the number of high school graduates in this country exceeded 1,627,000, an all-time high. State aid was available in all the states for the support of high schools, an integral part of state educational systems. It is unlikely that anyone today would question the legality of a board's action in levying a tax for the support of a high school. The *Kalamazoo* decision stands as a landmark on the educational horizon, because it settled the issue of a state's right to permit boards to establish high schools and to employ a superintendent of schools.

The Common Schools

Six years after the founding of Harvard College, the Massachusetts Bay Colony passed the first law dealing with general education in the New World. Through the Massachusetts School Law of 1642, the people of that colony placed upon the town council in each village the responsibility of providing common schools in which all the children of the village might learn reading, writing, and arithmetic. The following quotation is from the law itself:

> Ye chosen men appointed for managing the prudentiall affaires of the same shall henceforth stand charged with the care of the redresse of this evill . . .

the "evill" being

> . . . that great neglect of many parents & masters in training up their children in learning & labor, & other implyments which may be proffitable to the common wealth. . . .

Town councils were given the responsibility of taking account from time to time of all parents and masters, and their children, concerning their calling and "implyments," and especially of their ability to read and understand the principles of religion "& the capitall lawes of the country." Fines were assessed upon those parents and masters who refused to render suitable accounts to the town council when required to do so.[14]

The modern trend toward assigning to the schools the task of conserving human resources need not appear strange to anyone reading the Massachusetts Bay School Law of 1642!

---

[13]John S. Brubacher. *A History of the Problems of Education* (New York: McGraw-Hill Company, 1947), p. 435.

[14]Syrett, *op. cit.*, pp. 33-34.

The Olde Deluder Satan Act. Perhaps the best known of all the early education acts was the so-called *Olde Deluder Satan Act* passed in Massachusetts in 1647 to correct an oversight in the act of five years earlier.[15] Nowhere in the school act of 1642 was specific provision made for the establishment of *schools* by the town councils. Therefore, this second act was passed to remedy the error. The act gets its name from its opening words:

> It being one chief project of that old deluder, Satan, to keep men from the knowledge of the Scriptures . . . (by) keeping them in an unknown tongue . . . (in order that) learning may not be buried in the grave of our fathers, . . . The Lord assisting our endeavors, . . .
>
> IT IS THEREFORE ORDERED, that every township in this jurisdiction, after the Lord hath increased your number to 50 householders, shall then forthwith appoint one of your number to teach all such children as shall resort to him to write and read . . .

In towns which increased to 100 householders, the law directed that a Grammar school should be set up to instruct youth for the university. The wages of the teachers were to be paid by the parents and masters of the children and/or by the inhabitants of the town in general, "by way of supply."

Although these early laws were quite forward-looking, their indefiniteness left much to be desired. Nevertheless, the courts insisted that the laws of 1642 and 1647 be enforced. In 1668, a court order was issued by the Quarterly Court of Essex County directing the Selectmen of Topsfield, Massachusetts, to appear in court and show reason why they were allegedly negligent in enforcing these early school laws.[16]

School laws of a nature similar to those in Massachusetts were enacted in Connecticut in 1650 and the Plymouth Colony in 1658 and 1663. Pennsylvania Colony enacted a school law in 1683 which provided that the poor were to be instructed as well as the rich in "good and commendable learning, which is to be preferred before wealth."

The first school established under the Pennsylvania law of 1683 was opened in October of that year in Philadelphia. Governor William Penn and the Colonial Council, mindful of the serious need for "instruction & Sober Education of youth in the towne of Philadelphia," entered into a contract with one Enoch Flower, a man of some 20

---

[15] Ellwood P. Cubberley (ed). *Readings in the History of Education* (Boston: Houghton Mifflin Company, 1920), p. 299.

[16] *Ibid.*, pp. 299-300.

years' teaching experience in England. Mr. Flower agreed under the terms of the contract[17] to teach the school with the approval of the Council of the following rates per pupil:

> . . . to Learne to read English 4s by ye Quarter, to Learne to read and write 6s by ye Quarter, to learne to read, Write and Cast account 8s by ye Quarter; for Boarding a Scholler, that is to say, dyet, Washing, Lodging, & Schooling, Tenn pounds for one whole year.

Unlike its modern counterpart, the contract of Mr. Flower gave no assurance that the Council would provide the money; it merely set the rates which Mr. Flower was allowed to charge his pupils for services rendered. In fact, the Pennsylvania School Law of 1683 placed the responsibility for the education of the child squarely upon "all persons, guardians and trustees of orphans, and others in this Province and Territory."

Parents or masters who were found deficient in fulfilling the terms of the law were assessed a fine of five pounds. "Fulfillment" standards were defined under this legislation as the ability of the child to read the scriptures and write by the time he had attained the age of twelve years, except in cases where there "appeared an incapacity in body or understanding to hinder it."

For the time, the Pennsylvania School Law of 1683 indicated a forward-looking attitude on the part of members of the colony. But it must be remembered that their motivations were religious, rather than secular. The teachers were "ecclesiastically" acceptable, having had little formal education themselves, but being chosen for their religious conformity and orthodoxy rather than their wide knowledge of the subject matter. Their schools were places where Christian prayers, commandments, catechism, and scriptures were central to the curriculum. Their duties quite often included, in addition to the teaching of religious matters, the cleaning of the church, assisting the minister in church services, digging the grave in the event of a death, sending out death notices, tolling the bell, and other similar duties. Support of the schools, said Hansen,[18] was a matter of Christian charity, rather than a civic duty fulfilled by the payment of school taxes.

The Supreme Court and Education

The role of the Supreme Court of the United States will be examined further in Chapter II of this book. However, at this point it will be

[17]*Ibid.*, p. 307.
[18]Hansen, *op. cit.*, p. 9.

useful to the student to examine the developing role of the Supreme Court as it applied to legal interpretation at the turn of the century. A dramatic change between 1900 and 1908 is of interest in assessing educational issues referred to in the future.

Prior to the Civil War, the Supreme Court practiced a policy of non-interference in matters involving the exercise of police powers by the states, except in cases in which the legislation in question impared the obligation of contracts, or where the regulation of foreign and interstate commerce was at issue. Following 1868, when the fourteenth amendment giving Negroes constitutional rights following the Civil War was adopted, a pressure arose to broaden the scope of the civil liberties guaranteed in this amendment. The Supreme Court, however, resisted changing from its non-interference policy on the grounds that to interfere in the affairs of the states would be to assert its right to review the social and economic factors underlying state legislation. In the famous *Slaughter-house cases*, the court narrowly limited the application of the fourteenth amendment, on the grounds that it had been framed for protecting the Negro and was not intended as a general guarantee of civil rights.[19]

The period between the Civil War and 1908 has been referred to by Edwards[20] as a period of "judicial ruthlessness." The constitutionality of laws was regarded as a legal matter, and the court refused to take into account the social and economic factors which motivated the legislature in formulating the law.

A case involving an Oregon law relating to a ten-hour work day for women came before the Supreme Court of the United States in 1907. In ruling on the case, the Court finally abandoned its policy of legalistic adjudication, and for the first time based its decision on the physiological and sociological factors of the case. Following *Muller v. Oregon*,[21] the Supreme Court has taken the stand that legislation which seems to be necessary to the public welfare should be sustained, and that which is inimical to the public morals, health, and welfare of the people should be declared unconstitutional. Essentially, this is the present policy of the Court.

Sectarian versus secular education. Most of the colonists came from countries where the church and state were not separated. The

---

[19]Slaughter-house Cases, 83 U.S. (16 Wall) 36(1873); Munn v. Illinois, 94 U.S. (4 Otto) 113, 24 L. Ed. 77 (1877).
[20]Newton Edwards. *The Courts and the Public Schools* (Chicago: University of Chicago Press, 1947), pp. 32-33.
[21]208 U.S. 412, 28 Sup. Ct. 324, 52 L. Ed. 551 (1907).

settlers, in seeking religious freedom in the New World, set up colonial governments which were a union of church and state. The arrangement, while affording to the particular church group religious freedom, nevertheless limited the rights of those who chose to differ religiously from the dominant group. Thus, intolerance and provincialism were evident colony by colony according to which group was in control. As the desirability of separation of church and state became more and more evident, religious and political quarrels arose. By the time of the adoption of the Constitution, the basic human rights were recognized for what they were, and adopted in the first ten amendments. Among the foremost of these rights was that embodied in the first amendment, that of freedom of worship. Congress in the first amendment, as we have seen, was prohibited from passing any law respecting an establishment of religion, or prohibiting the free exercise thereof. This has come to mean that *states* as well as Congress shall not pass any law compelling the financial support, through taxation or otherwise, of religious sectarian education, nor may the state compel attendance at any religious worship. Several leading cases in which separation of church and state have been the central issue are worthy of note.

The Oregon case. In 1922, the Oregon legislature enacted a statute which required school children between the ages of eight and sixteen to attend a public school. The law was to become effective in 1926. Obviously, the net effect of the legislation would have been to eliminate private elementary schools entirely. Before the law went into effect, two private corporations, the Society of Sisters of the Holy Names of Jesus and Mary, and the Hill Military Academy, sought an injunction restraining enforcement of the law. The district court issued the injunction. On appeal, the Supreme Court of the United States upheld the lower court.[22] The Court said:

> The manifest purpose is to compel attendance at public schools by normal children, between eight and sixteen, who have not completed the eighth grade. . . . enforcement of the statute would seriously impair, perhaps destroy, the profitable features of appellees' business and greatly diminish the value of their property.
> The fundamental theory of liberty upon which all governments in this Union repose excludes any general power of the State to standardize its children by forcing them to accept instruction from public teachers only. The child is not the mere creature of the State; those who nurture him and direct his

[22]Pierce v. Society of Sisters of the Holy Names of Jesus and Mary, 268 U.S. 510, 45 Sup. Ct. 571, 69 L. Ed. 1070 (1925).

destiny have the right, coupled with the high duty, to recognize and prepare him for additional obligations.

This case was important because it made clear the right of parents to educate their children in non-public schools if they choose, providing, of course, that the latter meet state educational standards.

The Supreme Court in 1930 ruled that the use of public funds to purchase school books and distribute them free to parochial school children in Louisiana was not in violation of the fourteenth amendment, inasmuch as the benefit was directly to the child and only incidentally to the school.[23] In a later case, the Court enlarged upon the "child benefit theory," by upholding a New Jersey law permitting public transportation of parochial school children.[24] Since these two opinions are in accord, one might expect their effect to be cumulative, but the evidence is that a reversal of the theory is inevitable. No single state court in interpreting its constitution has supported the principle involved in the "child benefit theory," and some of the Justices of the Supreme Court of the United States appear to have changed their attitude on this issue. There seems to be little logic in the false distinction between a "benefit" to the child or to his school. It appears likely that the states' resistance to full acceptance of this theory will eventually prevail.

Released time. Widely debated in relation to the issue of separation of church and state is the practice of "released time" for religious instruction. In the so-called *Champaign* case, the Supreme Court of the United States ruled that the use of school buildings by the board of education for religious instruction during school time was in violation of the doctrine of separation of church and state,[25] and amounted to an establishment of religion. However, within four years, the Court ruled that a released time arrangement off the school premises during school hours for the public school children was constitutional.[26] Students under the latter plan were released for religious instruction on the written consent of their parents. Apparently, released time arrangements which are carried on in public schools and with particular administrative cooperation are an unconstitutional establishment of religion, whereas those held outside the school and with only a minimum

---

[23]Cochran v. Louisiana State Board of Educ., 281 U.S. 370, 50 Sup. Ct. 335, 74 L. Ed. 913 (1930).
[24]Everson v. Board of Educ., 330 U.S. 1, 67 Sup. Ct. 504, 91 L. Ed. 711 (1947).
[25]Illinois ex rel. McCollum v. Board of Educ. of School Dist. No. 71, Champaign County, 333 U.S. 203, 68 Sup. Ct. 461, 92 L. Ed. 649, 2 A.L.R.2d 1338 (1948).
[26]Zorach v. Clauson, 343 U.S. 306, 72 Sup. Ct. 679, 92 L. Ed. 964 (1952).

of administrative cooperation are within the rights of a board of education to provide.

Other issues. Several other issues involving school teachers and administrators have been before the highest Court of the land. In conflict are two decisions involving the flag salute as a condition of attendance at a public school. In the *Gobitis* case in Pennsylvania,[27] the Court sustained a school board rule that students should salute the flag as a condition of attendance. Three years later, the Court reversed itself and held that a similar law in West Virginia violated the first amendment of the Constitution.[28]

The flag salute cases, the status of Bible reading and offering of prayers, religious instruction, and other issues will be taken up in the appropriate portions of this book. The student should acquaint himself with the further readings following this chapter dealing with those issues considered by the Supreme Court. Many of these issues are being closely examined and re-examined by the Supreme Court and other courts of the land. There is no guarantee that a court holding of today must apply tomorrow. The applicable law in each case rests upon the peculiar set of circumstances that is before the court and the arguments raised by counsel for the court's consideration as well as upon sociological, economic, and philosophical issues in relation to the overall public weal.

The Supreme Court and racial segregation. Today, another battle ensues to provide equal education for all. The Supreme Court of the United States has had to decide questions focusing on the problems arising out of racial segregation in the schools. It is not the objective of the authors to present an exhaustive review of the extensive literature on this subject. It is, however, important to show that certain concepts about the education of minorities have changed in our society.

"Separate but equal." Racial segregation in the public schools of the nation was permitted prior to 1954, provided that separate facilities of an "equal" nature were maintained for Negroes. The concept arose in our history in Massachusetts, in a case in which the supreme court of that state sustained the validity of "separate but equal" schools for Negroes in Boston.[29] The concept later was strengthened by the Su-

---

[27]Minersville School Dist. v. Gobitis, 310 U.S. 586, 60 Sup. Ct. 1010, 84 L. Ed. 1375, 127 A.L.R. 1493 (1940).

[28]West Virginia State Bd. of Educ. v. Barnette, 319 U.S. 624, 63 Sup. Ct. 1178, 87 L. Ed. 1628, 147 A.L.R. 674 (1943).

[29]Roberts v. City of Boston, 59 Mass. 198 (1849).

preme Court in the famous case of *Plessy v. Ferguson*,[30] which upheld a Louisiana statute requiring separate railroad accommodations for Negroes and whites. The Court denied the pleas of a Negro plaintiff who maintained that his personal rights guaranteed him under the thirteenth and fourteenth amendments had been violated. Said the Court:

> Laws permitting, and even requiring (separation of the races) in places where they are liable to be brought in contact do not necessarily imply the inferiority of either race to the other and have been generally, if not universally, recognized as within the competency of the state legislatures in the exercise of their police power. The most common instance of this is connected with the establishment of separate schools for white and colored children which has been held a valid exercise of the legislative power, even by the courts of states where the political rights of the colored race have been longest and most earnestly enforced.

The "separate but equal" concept was held to be the rule until May 17, 1954. On that date, the Court said:

> We conclude that in the field of public education the doctrine of "separate but equal" has no place. Separate educational facilities are inherently unequal. Therefore we hold that the plaintiffs and others similarly situated for whom the actions have been brought are, by reason of the segregation complained of, deprived of the equal protection of the laws guaranteed by the Fourteenth Amendment. This disposition makes unnecessary any discussion whether such segregation also violates the Due Process Clause of the Fourteenth Amendment.[31]

Realizing that the decision would be far-reaching in its implications, the high Court, in an unprecedented move, postponed the implementation of the decision pending further study. On May 31, 1955, the Court handed down a directive implementing the May 17, 1954, decision.[32] Responsibility for placing in effect the decision rested with the appropriate federal district courts, which were ordered to take steps *with all deliberate speed* toward entering orders and decrees designed to admit on a nondiscriminatory basis the parties to these cases. The courts were further ordered to take into account the circumstances under which the decision was to be carried out, including problems

---

[30]163 U.S. 537, 16 Sup. Ct. 1138, 41 L. Ed. 256 (1896).
[31]Brown v. Board of Educ. of Topeka, 347 U.S. 483, 74 Sup. Ct. 686, 97 L. Ed. 790, 38 A.L.R.2d 1180 (1954).
[32]Brown v. Board of Educ. of Topeka, 349 U.S. 294, 75 Sup. Ct. 753, 99 L. Ed. 1083 (1955).

related to administration and redistricting in each of the several states affected. Burden of proof that more time was necessary for full integration was placed upon the defendant school districts "in the public interest and consistent with good faith."

As might be expected, considerable litigation arose as a result of the Court's two decisions. Some of the litigation was aimed at knocking down legislation violating the spirit of the decisions. It remains to be seen what meaning the term "with all deliberate speed" may have in each of the states affected by the ruling.

Suggested Activities

DISCUSSION:

1. What is the purpose of the American public schools?
2. Should the Supreme Court of the United States be limited in the exercise of its power over education since education is a state function?
3. Do public school teachers need a knowledge of the law in order to be fully prepared for teaching in a modern society?
4. What is the role of the administrator in assisting his teachers to become aware of their legal rights and liabilities?
5. Do the parallel sectarian and secular systems in our culture make for an enhanced and strengthened system of education? Illustrate.
6. Is the Supreme Court of the United States right in taking into account the sociological, psychological, and philosophical backgrounds involved in educational cases to come before it?

ROLE PLAYING:

1. Assume you are Enoch Flower, schoolmaster in Philadelphia in 1683. Outline for the Colonial Council your qualifications to teach the first school in the colony under the new law of that year.
2. Assume you are a modern-day teacher. Present to the board of education an outline of your qualifications to assume your teaching duties.
3. Dramatize your own personal experiences in which a knowledge of the law might have been of assistance to you in solving an educational problem.

SUMMARIZATION:

1. Summarize the growth of common schools from Olde Deluder Satan days to the present in the United States.
2. Summarize the important court cases highlighting the various "battles" as outlined in Chapter I.
3. Summarize the rights guaranteed you as a teacher under the Constitution of the United States.

RESEARCH:

1. In what article of your state constitution is provision made for

a system of free public education? What are the terms of this constitutional provision?

2. Discover historically what problems, if any, were presented as a result of (a) the constitutional silence on education, and (b) education's being thus an implied power of state government.

3. From colonial history, find why a formal system of higher education was forthcoming ahead of such important educational needs as common schools.

4. What factors in our society have caused the American people recently to become "sue conscious"?

Further Readings

Burrup, Percy E. *The Teacher and the Public School System* (New York: Harper and Brothers, 1960), Ch. 6.

Butts, R. Freeman. "Search for Freedom—the Story of American Education," *National Education Association Journal*, (March, 1960), pp, 33-48.

Edwards, Newton. *The Courts and the Public Schools* (Chicago: University of Chicago Press, 1955), Chs. II and III.

Fellman, David. *The Supreme Court and Education* (New York: Teachers College, Columbia University, 1960).

Gauerke, Warren E. *Legal and Ethical Responsibilities of School Personnel* (Englewood Cliffs, N. J.: Prentice-Hall, 1959), Ch. 2.

Good, H. G. *A History of Western Education, Second Edition* (New York: The Macmillan Company, 1960), Ch. 17.

O'Leary, Rt. Rev. Msgr. Timothy F. "Government Aid to Catholic Schools: Social and Legal Basis," *The Catholic Educator*, (September, 1960).

Remmlein, Madaline Kinter. *School Law, Second Edition* (Danville, Illinois: Interstate Printers and Publishers, 1962).

Shoemaker, Don (ed). *With All Deliberate Speed* (New York: Harper and Brothers, 1957), pp. 1-14.

Spurlock, Clark. *Education and the Supreme Court* (Urbana, Illinois: University of Illinois Press, 1955), pp. 54, 150, and 222.

United States Office of Education. *State and Education; Structure and Control of Public Education at the State Level*, Bulletin No. 23, 1955.

Chapter II

THE AMERICAN LEGAL SYSTEM

Introduction

One purpose of the course in school law is to acquaint the student with the federal and state *legislation* and *case* law governing the activities of teachers. Both of these forms of law are a vital part of our American legal system. Although the types of legislation are generally known and understood by teachers, the complexities of judicial systems make a similar familiarity with, and understanding of, the case law of the courts much more difficult.

This chapter is designed to introduce the student to the American legal system, especially as it has developed in the courts of the land. The cases handed down by these courts will be meaningful to the student only to the extent that he understands the sources of the law, sees the relationship between the federal and the state court structures, learns something of the procedures followed in the conduct of a case in the courts, and gains some familiarity with the technical terminology of the legal profession.

Sources of American Law

Law is generally regarded in our modern society as a set of enforceable rules of external conduct. We contrast the law, on the one hand, with the non-legal principles or customs which govern our behavior, on the other. Simple societies have been controlled almost exclusively by custom. In more complex societies, governments enact an increasing amount of legislation, combining it with common law and custom to provide a superstructure for societal order.

The term "legislation" is frequently considered synonymous with "statute," but in the broadest sense legislation may include all law that originates in an official body having power to make general rules. These rules are reduced to an official textual form and constitute the *written law*.

America has several types of legislation. Article VI, paragraph two, of the Constitution of the United States provides in part: "This Constitution, and the Laws of the United States which shall be made in Pursuance thereof, and all Treaties made, or which shall be made, under the Authority of the United States, shall be the Supreme Law of the Land." Thus, the federal constitution, treaties, and federal statutes which are passed by the Congress of the United States pursuant to the Constitution, are the highest forms of legislation and are a part of the law of every state. The executive orders of the President of the United States, and the rules and regulations of federal administrative officials and agencies are additional types of legislation on the federal level. Similarly, state constitutions, state statutes, state administrative rules and regulations, and municipal codes or ordinances are legislative in character.

The *common law* is the second form of American law. The term is used in varying senses, but is here intended to include the case decisions of courts and administrative agencies, as distinguished from enacted legislation. This law may be termed *case law* or *unwritten law;* the latter term is misleading because the decisions of the most important federal and state courts and agencies are reduced to writing and "reported," *i. e.*, officially published. The volumes of unwritten law far outnumber the volumes of written law.

The legislation and common law of England played a most important part in the development of American law. Early Americans were familiar with the manner of conduct imposed by English law. They were best able to read and interpret the English language, and the books available to them were usually written in English. Consequently, the English law set the pattern for life among the colonies, and was later adopted by the states as their own when they broke away from the mother country. Every state, except Louisiana, adopted the common law of England to the extent that it was applicable to the situation in that state. Louisiana based its criminal law on the English common law, but its civil law was based upon Roman law as modified by the French. Roman law, commonly known as the Civil Law, is the basis of law in all European countries except England.

The common law, as it developed in England, became quite rigid in structure. Particular fact situations gave rise to particular forms of actions at law, with specific and limited forms of relief available in the courts. For example, one whose property was continually trespassed by another could bring an action in trespass each time against the wrongdoer and recover money damages, but the court would not order the trespasser to refrain from trespassing or be held in contempt of court. The wrongdoer could not be enjoined from his action and the property owner could not practically bring an action in court each time a trespass occurred. Thus the inflexibility of the common law court procedures prevented litigants in those courts from obtaining justice. As a result, the King, whose judicial power was supreme, authorized his Chancellor to make other equitable remedies available where none then existed at law. The procedures and remedies that became applicable to the chancery courts were known as *equity*, which developed as a separate system of justice and functioned to supplement the common law. Both the common law and equity of England became a part of the law in every state of the United States. Although the distinction between common law and equity is not as significant today as it once was, its importance remains substantial and some states still have separate courts to handle actions at law and suits in equity.

In settling disputes between individual persons or groups of persons, judges will be called upon to interpret legislation considered applicable to the case; where there is no controlling legislation, the common law will be examined. A sense of justice requires that litigants be treated alike in "like" controversies. Consequently, a judge may feel bound to follow the common law previously established in a case decided by a higher court in the same jurisdiction. Adherence to precedents makes for stability and predictability in the law and, for that reason, is more desirable, but courts sometimes refuse to follow precedents when it is determined that the legal principle has no further usefulness.

When an American judge can find no applicable legislation and no applicable American or English common law, he may have to apply the law as he believes it should be. Such *judge made law* then becomes a part of the common law in that jurisdiction. The matter of jurisdiction is much better understood when one is familiar with the American dual court structure, federal and state, that exists as a unique judicial system. An examination of the court structure follows.

The Federal Court Structure

Article III, sections 1 and 2, of the Constitution of the United States establishes the judicial powers on the federal level. Section 1 provides in part: "The judicial Power of the United States, shall be vested in one Supreme Court, and in such inferior Courts as the Congress may from time to time ordain and establish." Section 2 (1) provides:

> The judicial Power shall extend to all Cases, in Law and Equity, arising under this Constitution, the Laws of the United States, and Treaties made, or which shall be made, under their Authority;—to all cases affecting Ambassadors, other public Ministers and Consuls—to all Cases of Admiralty and maritime jurisdiction;—to Controversies to which the United States shall be a Party;—to Controversies between two or more states; —between citizens of different states.

Thus, the Supreme Court of the United States is a constitutional court in the sense that it is specifically established by virtue of the Constitution. Except for the power to change the number of justices sitting on the Supreme Court, the Congress has no power over that Court. The other federal courts were established by the first session of the First Congress with the passing of the "Judiciary Act of 1789." As creatures of the Congress, these federal courts may be changed, or conceivably abolished, by that legislative body. Numerous special courts have been established by the Congress, *e.g.*, the United States Court of Claims, the United States Customs Court, the United States Court of Customs and Patent Appeals, but we shall not concern ourselves with these courts.

The three-tier system of federal courts as we now have it, was brought about by the enactment of the Judicial Code in 1911. On the bottom tier is the United States District Court, a court of original jurisdiction, or trial court. Each state has at least one United States District Court, with one or more judges to hear both civil and criminal cases. The great majority of civil cases arise because of diversity of citizenship between the litigants, *e.g.*, the citizen of one state is involved in a legal dispute with the citizen of another state. Historically, persons felt that if such diversity of citizenship cases were brought in the state courts, the litigant, who was also a citizen of the state in which the court was sitting, would receive more favorable treatment. Consequently, the early colonists insisted on federal court jurisdiction over such cases. The validity of this theory no longer exists, and Congress has imposed greater and greater limitations to prevent the exercise of jurisdiction by the United States District Court. Whereas these courts were once available to diversity of citizenship cases whenever an amount in excess of $1,500 was involved, today the amount must exceed $10,000. When less than $10,000 is involved, exclusive of interest and cost of the proceedings, the litigants must usually bring their actions in a state court.

When a case has been tried in a United States District Court and a final judgment has been rendered by the court, the loser to the action has a right to have that judgment considered by an appellate court. Except in very special cases, the appeal will be to the United States Court of Appeals of the circuit in which the District Court is located. The United States Court of Appeals is solely a court of review; it has no original jurisdiction.

There are eleven judicial circuits serving all of the states, the District of Columbia, the Commonwealth of Puerto Rico and the territories of the United States—Canal Zone, Guam, and the Virgin Islands (see figure 2-1). Each circuit includes the United States District Courts and the United States Courts of Appeals.

The Supreme Court of the United States, with its limited original and broad appellate jurisdiction, stands at the apex of the federal judicial system. The Court's original and exclusive jurisdiction provided for in the Constitution over disputes between two or more states, or actions in which a foreign ambassador or minister, or one of their domestic servants is being sued, is rarely exercised. Cases usually go to the Supreme Court of the United States on review. Although the high Court must review cases on appeal by a party from a lower federal court or from the highest state court in which a decision could be had wherein a state or federal statute is claimed to be contrary to the Constitution of the United States, the great majority of cases are heard by the Court through the exercise of its discretion, and not as a matter of right. To invoke this discretion, a party must petition the Supreme Court for a *writ of certiorari*. The Supreme Court will hear the case only if the issue presented is of broad and general interest to the nation's welfare. For this reason, most decisions of the United States Courts of Appeals are final and binding on the parties. The weekly opinions of the Supreme Court are read each Monday during its eight-month term from October to May, and are published unofficially in *United States Law Week* magazine and some newspapers, notably the *New York Times*.

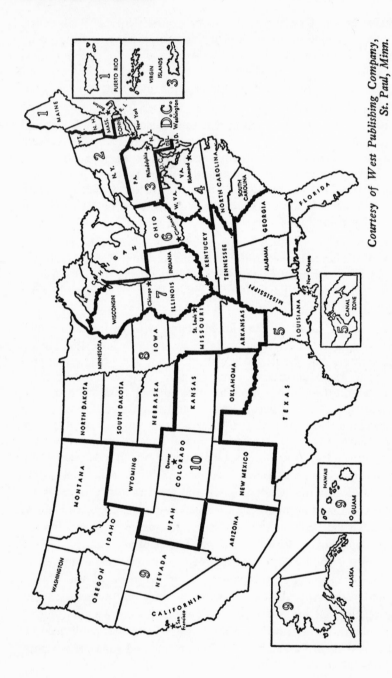

Courtesy of West Publishing Company,
St. Paul, Minn.

Figure 2-1
THE ELEVEN FEDERAL JUDICIAL CIRCUITS

The State Court Structure

Every state constitution, except that of New Hampshire,[1] provides for one court of ultimate review, usually called the Supreme Court,[2] at the apex of the state court structure. These courts have state-wide jurisdiction and ultimate jurisdiction over controversies involving the interpretation of the state constitution and statutes.

In numerous states, intermediate appellate courts have been created to help reduce the caseloads of the highest state courts. There is little uniformity in the names of these intermediate appellate courts or in the jurisdiction exercised by them. Generally, they exercise appellate jurisdiction, sometimes limited as to the types of cases they may hear or to cases involving a certain maximum monetary amount.

The trial courts are variously known as circuit, county, district, superior, or common pleas courts. The New York trial court of original and general jurisdiction is named the Supreme Court. These courts generally handle civil litigation, criminal prosecutions, and suits in equity. The more populated states have separate probate or surrogate courts to dispose of decedents' estate matters, and there may be separate criminal courts, domestic relations courts, and juvenile courts. Procedure in juvenile courts is usually quite informal, and extensive use is made of auxiliary services such as are provided by social welfare workers and probation officers. Reference must be made to the constitutions and statutes of the states to determine the specific jurisdiction of a particular trial court.

The states often have a number of inferior or minor courts that dispose of small civil claims and petty criminal cases. The justice of the peace, municipal, small claims, magistrate, and traffic courts handle many minor cases by using relatively simple procedures. They are not generally courts of record; that is, they do not record the proceedings of the trial, so a review of the case is impossible. Consequently, an appeal from these inferior courts results in a new trial, a trial *de novo*, in an upper court, often a trial court of general jurisdiction, which may be followed by appellate review of the trial court's judgment in a court of intermediate appeal or court of ultimate review.

Many administrative agencies exist on both the federal and state

---

[1] In New Hampshire, the legislature established the highest court.

[2] Called the Supreme Court of Errors in Connecticut; the Supreme Judicial Court in Maine and Massachusetts; the Court of Appeals in Kentucky, Maryland and New York; and the Supreme Court of Appeals in Virginia and West Virginia. Texas and Oklahoma each has a Supreme Court for civil cases but also has a separate Court of Criminal Appeals.

levels. The administrative boards and commissions have been empowered by statute to make decisions as to the rights or privileges of persons within a limited class of cases. Some administrative tribunals explain their decisions in written opinions not unlike the opinions of appellate courts, *e.g.*, Interstate Commerce Commission, National Labor Relations Board, and Workmen's Compensation Commission; others make decisions without explaining them and are often primarily licensing bodies.

Where an administrative agency has been established to determine controversies, it is generally necessary that one exhaust all possible relief through the administrative tribunal before relief is available to him through the courts.

Commencement of a Civil Action[3]

Actions at law may be classified as *criminal* and *civil* actions. In a criminal action, a defendant is charged with violating a law and a prosecution follows, in the name of the government or people for the punishment of the crime.

A *civil action* may be brought in a court of law to enforce or protect rights of private persons, or to secure a remedy for the invasion of such rights of persons or property. An action in *contract* concerns rights arising under an agreement of the parties. A *tort* is a violation of a duty fixed by law, independent of any contract or will of the parties. The person against whom an injury or wrong is committed may seek *damages,* a sum of money recoverable as compensation, from the wrongdoer.

The injured person will first consult an attorney-at-law to determine the strength of his case and whether litigation is justified. If the attorney determines that court action is required, he will prepare a *summons* and *complaint* so that an action may be instituted for his client, the *plaintiff*. A summons is the writ of process used to notify the person to be sued, the *defendant*, of the nature of the charge against him. Under modern procedure, in most jurisdictions, no specific cause of action must be brought, but the plaintiff must set out in the

---

[3]The authors wish to express their deep appreciation to their colleague and mentor, Professor Vance R. Dittman, Jr., of the University of Denver College of Law, author of *Cases and Materials on Civil Procedure* (Denver: University of Denver Law Center, 1962), and co-author with Karl P. Warden of *Cases and Materials on Trial and Appellate Procedure* (Denver: University of Denver Law Center, 1961), and *Cases and Materials on Procedure After Judgment and Decree* (Denver: University of Denver Law Center, 1961), from whose work we have extensively borrowed.

complaint sufficient facts to show that he is entitled to relief. The court gains *jurisdiction* over the plaintiff and defendant, the parties to the action, when the summons, or the summons together with the complaint, is served on the defendant or filed with the court.

After service of process has been made on the defendant, the defendant's attorney may make any number of motions in an effort to have the action dismissed, or to get additional information to help him answer the complaint. The filing of such a motion by the defendant will delay the necessity of his filing an *answer* until the plaintiff sets a time for a hearing on the motions by the judge. Unless the action is dismissed, the defendant must eventually file an answer to the allegations in the plaintiff's complaint. In the answer, the defendant may deny or admit the allegations, or he may set up as an affirmative defense any fact which may act as a bar to defeat the plaintiff's action. If an affirmative defense is established in the answer, the plaintiff will have to admit or deny the defense in his reply. Thus, an issue will be established from the controverted facts as presented in the plaintiff's and defendant's pleadings.

At any time after the action commences, the attorneys for the plaintiff or defendant may enter upon discovery proceedings to secure additional facts, admissions, and other evidence. The attorneys will seek to obtain written or oral depositions, mental and physical examinations, affidavits, and documents.

In many state courts, and in the federal courts, a preliminary trial conference is held in the judge's chambers to decide what issues exist and must be tried, and whether a settlement or compromise can be reached. If the case is not settled at this pre-trial conference, it will be placed on the active trial calendar, to be heard at the earliest possible time.

Conduct of a Trial

Sessions of the court are usually open to the public; however, when the nature of the case may be such as to injure public morals, or make an orderly procedure difficult, the judge may, in his discretion, exclude the public from the courtroom.

One or both of the parties may make a demand for a *jury*, whose function is to determine the *issues of fact* when the factual circumstances are in dispute. A jury in a civil action is usually composed of six persons, but there may be as few as three or as many as twelve jurors. A unanimous finding by the jurors is usually required, unless the parties stipulate to a finding by a stated majority of the jurors.

From those persons called to the court for jury duty, a number will be called to compose a *jury panel,* from which the *petit jurors* are selected through a system of challenges. The attorneys for the parties question the prospective jurors to determine whether they are qualified to fairly try the questions of fact in the case. The attorney for the plaintiff will first make a brief statement to familiarize the jurors with counsel, the parties, and the type of case so that any bias or prejudice felt by the jurors may be discovered. The attorney next questions the jurors in an effort to determine their ability to impartially sit as jurors in the case. If any of the prospective jurors are found unqualified, the attorney *challenges* that juror "for cause" by stating to the judge the exact grounds for his challenge.

It then becomes the duty of the judge to determine whether the challenge for cause is well founded, and to overrule or sustain the challenge. If the plaintiff's attorney is satisfied with the jurors, he passes the jury for cause and the attorney for the defendant questions the jury. Any challenges for cause that he may have are disposed of by the court in the same way, until the defendant's attorney also passes all of the prospective jurors for cause.

The attorneys will next exercise their *peremptory challenges,* which are made without stating any grounds or reasons. In turn, each attorney will strike the name of one of the jurors until he has exercised all of the peremptory challenges to which he is entitled. These named jurors leave the jury box, and the remaining jurors are sworn to constitute the jury to truly try the matter at issue and render a verdict according to the evidence.

To aid the jury in understanding the significance of the evidence, each attorney may make an opening statement, outlining the facts he expects to prove. Then, because the plaintiff has the *burden of proof,* he will introduce evidence to prove his case. The plaintiff's attorney questions the plaintiff and other witnesses. After each witness testifies, on *direct examination,* the defendant's attorney will question that witness, on *cross-examination,* concerning matters brought out during direct examination. This may lead to *re-direct examination* by plaintiff's attorney and *re-cross-examination* by defendant's attorney. The purpose of direct examination is to secure testimony from plaintiff's own witness as to his knowledge of the facts to be proved. The purpose of cross-examination is to discredit the testimony of that witness or to attack his credibility as a witness. When all of the plaintiff's witnesses have been questioned on direct examination and cross-examination, and the plaintiff's exhibits and documentary evidence have been submitted, the plaintiff *rests* his case.

At the termination of the plaintiff's case, the attorney for the defendant will move for a *directed verdict*. This motion will test the adequacy of the plaintiff's proof, because the court must decide whether, giving the plaintiff the benefit of every doubt, and believing all of his evidence to be true, the plaintiff has shown sufficient facts to entitle him to a favorable jury verdict. If the judge believes the plaintiff has not produced sufficient facts, has not established a *prima facie case*, the defendant's motion will be granted, the jury will be instructed to bring in a verdict for the defendant, and the judge will enter a judgment for the defendant upon that verdict. If the judge believes a *prima facie* case has been made, the motion will be denied, and the examination of defense witnesses follows. The defendant's witnesses are questioned on direct and cross-examination as in the case of plaintiff's witnesses.

Throughout the trial, *objections* may be made as to the admissibility of evidence. The judge usually rules immediately that the proffered evidence is or is not admissible, according to the law of evidence.

When the defendant's attorney has called all of his witnesses, he rests his case and the presentation of evidence ends, unless the plaintiff's attorney wishes to call witnesses to give rebutting evidence in regard to new points presented by defendant's witnesses. Similarly, the defendant may call witnesses on surrebuttal to controvert plaintiff's evidence produced in rebuttal.

A *motion for a directed verdict* may be made by the plaintiff or the defendant after all the evidence is presented and both sides have rested. The judge may *sustain* or *deny* the motion, or *reserve his ruling* on the motion until the verdict has come in from the jury.

The judge instructs the jury as to the law in the case so that the jury may properly apply the facts and arrive at a verdict. The attorneys request the judge to make special *instructions to the jury* according to their theories as to the law applicable to the facts. The judge may then reject, modify, or grant the requested instructions.

After the jury has been instructed, arguments summarizing the evidence are made by each attorney and the jury is asked to find a verdict in favor of his client. The plaintiff's counsel makes the *opening argument*, the defendant's counsel follows, and the *closing argument* is again made by the plaintiff's attorney. When the plaintiff bears the *burden of proof*, as is generally the case, he is entitled to make the *opening statement* at the beginning of the trial, and the opening and closing arguments at the end of the trial.

When the *charge to the jury* is given before the closing arguments, the attorneys have an opportunity to comment upon the judge's instructions to the jury, but the orthodox practice is for the court to give the jury instructions just before the jury retires to the juryroom for deliberations. The bailiff is placed in charge of the jury until a verdict is reached. The verdict is read in open court, and either party may ask the judge to *poll* the jury to determine whether it is the verdict of each individual juror. The verdict is then recorded and the jury is discharged.

The party against whom the verdict was rendered may make a *motion in arrest of judgment,* or a *motion for a judgment notwithstanding the verdict* (a motion for judgment *non obstante veredicto,* or simply a motion for judgment *n.o.v.*). If a judgment is entered on the verdict, the losing party may move the court to set aside the verdict and judgment entered thereon, or a motion for a new trial may be made.

The Criminal Case

Teachers are not often involved in criminal cases; they are usually concerned with those matters that give rise to a civil action only. But the same acts which are the grounds for civil litigation may also constitute a crime. For example, a teacher who unnecessarily places a child in fear of bodily harm and, in fact, unreasonably strikes the child, has committed an assault and battery against the child for which a civil action for damages may lie. The child, or a person acting on behalf of the child, may bring an action to recover an amount of money to compensate for the tortious conduct. The teacher's act against the child, however, is also an act against the people of the city or state, because it is an act of violence forbidden by the criminal laws. As such, a separate criminal action may be prosecuted against the teacher, for which a fine or imprisonment may be imposed upon a finding of guilty.

The procedure differs somewhat in a criminal prosecution. The action is begun by an *indictment* by a grand jury, or by an *information* filed by the prosecutor. Arrest is the substitute for the summons, and appearance is required by coercion rather than volition.

A plea of guilty or not guilty is entered by the defendant, and a jury is waived or selected. Generally the trial and the judgment proceed upon lines similar to those of a civil case. The prosecution, however, may not appeal from the acquittal of the defendant so as to change the result. Once found innocent, the defendant is secure from further prosecution for the same offense.

Appellate Review of a Civil Action

After the judge has ruled on all motions with respect to the jury's verdict, *judgment* is ordinarily entered forthwith. The defeated party may seek review of this judgment by an appellate court. This was done by an *appeal* in equity and by a *writ of error* at common law. Today, the writ of error is generally the single form of proceeding for appellate review.

The party seeking the appellate review because of dissatisfaction with the final judgment of the lower court becomes the *plaintiff-in-error*, or the *appellant*. The party against whom a cause is appealed from a lower court to a higher one becomes the *defendant-in-error*, *appellee*, or the *respondent*. The attorney for the appellant prepares a document specifying the errors he maintains were committed by the trial court in the conduct of the trial. The appellate court will review *questions of law* only; it will generally accept the *findings of fact* of the trial court, because the facts can best be understood and evaluated in the trial court, where the credibility of witnesses is determined. The appeal to the high court is for a holding in accordance with the evidence as elicited during the trial. Attorneys for both appellant and appellee will prepare briefs to be submitted to the appellate court. These briefs are intended to help the court in its understanding and disposition of the case. Most appellate courts also provide a limited time when the attorneys may orally argue the important issues presented for the court's consideration. The appellate court may *affirm* the finding of fact and holding of law of the trial court, may *reverse* the finding and holding of the trial court and *order a new trial*, or reverse and *remand* the case to the trial court—instructing that court to do a specific thing in disposing of the case.

The decision of the highest appellate court having jurisdiction over the case, the *court of last resort*, is a final adjudication of the rights and duties of the parties arising out of the facts in litigation. The decision is binding on the parties; it is *res ajudicata*, because neither party can have the case tried again. The principle of *res ajudicata* prohibits a vindictive litigant from having a particular dispute adjudicated more than once.

Our common law system is one of *law by precedent*. This means that whenever a principle of law is presented to a court of authority for consideration and determination, and such a determination is then made, the resulting rule of law may serve as a rule for guidance in other similar controversies.

Precedent is regarded by other courts as either *binding* authority, which must be followed, or as merely *persuasive* in nature. For instance, a decision by the Supreme Court of the United States is binding precedent for all lower federal courts and state courts; a decision by a state supreme court is binding only upon the lower courts of that particular state, and may be persuasive precedent for a state court in another state. The persuasive nature of the precedent, however, might be given great weight.

The concept of binding precedent is also known as the doctrine of *stare decisis*. It must be noted that the courts are not absolutely bound to follow the prior legal principle even in their own jurisdictions. Public policy, historical evolution, resulting injustice, and other extenuating circumstances may force the court to break with precedent, ignore *stare decisis*, and formulate a different principle of law. Such a deviation is much more the exception than the rule.

The Case as Reported by the Court

Very few trial courts write opinions, but when an appellate court has determined a dispute, it will usually write an opinion of the case. These court cases are subsequently published in appropriate reporter systems. Because the student may have occasion to examine and *brief*, *i.e.*, abstract or summarize, these reported cases, we shall now examine the elements of an American court case.

Name of the case. Usually a case is identified by the names of the parties to the lawsuit. The parties are not consistently listed in any particular order so one may not be certain who was the plaintiff or defendant from the name of the case alone. The *name* of the case is also referred to as the *title* of the case or the *style* of the case.

Docket number. As each case is filed with the clerk of the court, it is assigned a numerical designation by the clerk to aid in identification of the case. The docket number usually appears just after the name of the reported case.

Date of decision. Immediately following the docket number is the date on which the decision was rendered by the court.

Prefatory statement. To aid one in understanding a reported case, the prefatory statement or summary will usually explain the nature of the case, the identity of the lower court and its judge, the disposition of the case in the lower court, and the action taken by the appellate court.

Syllabus or headnote. The syllabus or headnote is a brief summary of the legal rule or significant facts about the case. Because most cases are concerned with more than a single principle of law, there will be several syllabi or headnotes, one for each legal principle embodied in the case.

Names of counsel. The names of the attorneys representing the parties to the suit precede the court's opinion.

Synopsis of briefs of counsel. The synopsis of the briefs of counsel reveals the contentions of the parties and the theories supporting the arguments made by their attorneys. Only a few reported cases now provide this element of the case.

Opinion of the court. After a majority of the judges of the court agree upon the *decision* in a case, that is the *conclusion or result* in a case, a member of the *majority* will write the opinion of the court. The *opinion* usually contains the salient facts of the case, the rule of law applied by the court to govern the case, and the *reasoning* of the court in explanation or support of its decision. The name of the authoring judge precedes the opinion, and the names of the concurring judges follow the opinion.

When a member of the majority agrees with the conclusion or result in the case but disagrees with the applicable law or reasoning of the majority of the court, he may write a *concurring opinion* in which he states his reasons for the decision. Members of the minority may state their views in a *dissenting opinion.*

A *per curiam* opinion is considered to be the opinion of the whole court with no specific judge taking the responsibility for the written opinion.

It is not uncommon for opinions to include statements which do not relate directly to issues raised in the case, or are unnecessary to the decision of the case. Such statements are considered to be *dicta* and have no binding effect as precedent.

Decision. The decision is the court's disposition of the case.

Finding the Law

The task of finding the law under the American system of juris-prudence is made difficult because of the plethora of laws which have been, and continue to be, produced by the various forms of legal machinery. Each year, state legislatures and the Congress of the United States enact new laws, and amend or repeal many others. The people vote to amend basic constitutional provisions. Judges hand down thousands upon thousands of written opinions. Administrative tribunals adopt and change rules and regulations. Some of this law directly affects the teacher and the teaching profession. All of this law must be published and indexed so that it will be readily accessible to the legal profession and to the general public.

A large modern law school library may house several hundred thousand volumes. Law office buildings often have libraries housing thousands of volumes. Unless the teacher has access to such libraries, however, his research may be limited to the sources found at the public library. In any event, a brief description of the more commonly used legal research materials will prove helpful to the teacher in his re-search and in his reading appreciation.

Statutory law. Laws passed by the state legislatures, often called general assemblies, are ordinarily published in chronological order, by date of passage, in bound volumes known as *session laws,* with a subject index made at the end of each legislative session. The session laws are later compiled with a subject or form arrangement and pub-lished as statutes or *codes.* The laws are numbered so that they may be easily located in the code volumes, and the series is indexed. A typical citation of a state statute would be: Mass. Gen. Laws ch. 41 §95 (1932). This refers to the law in the official statute codification of Massachusetts, the Massachusetts General Laws compiled in 1932. The statute cited is the 95th section of chapter 41.

Volumes of the session laws or supplemental materials, placed in the back of each volume of the statutes from time to time, keep the compiled statutes up to date. When checking any particular law, it is necessary to examine the session laws and the supplemental materials to determine whether the compiled law has been repealed or amended.

One volume of the state statutes will usually contain the federal and state constitutions, and other basic laws. These laws and the statutes may be *annotated,* which means that digest paragraphs from cited cases will immediately follow that section of the law which has been interpreted by a court of law.

The acts passed by the Congress of the United States each session are published in the *United States Statutes at Large*, chronologically arranged by date of passage. Congress has authorized a compilation of the federal legislation; the *United States Code*, 1952 edition (cited "U.S.C.") is the current official compilation. Two unofficial compilations of federal laws, published without statutory directive, are the *United States Code Annotated* (Cited "U.S.C.A."), and the *Federal Code Annotated* (cited "F.C.A.").

Case law. The written decisions by the highest appellate courts in the various states are usually reported as authorized by state statutes, and are thus published as "official reports." Unofficial reports are published without statutory authorization by private publishing houses. For example, the decisions of the Supreme Court of the United States are officially published as the *United States Reports* (cited "U.S."), but they are unofficially published by the West Publishing Company as the *Supreme Court Reporter* (cited "Sup. Ct."), and by the Lawyers Co-operative Publishing Company as the *United States Supreme Court Reports* or *Lawyers Edition* (cited "L. Ed."). Consequently, reference to a Supreme Court case may cite its location in each of these official and unofficial reporters, *e.g.*, *Cochran v. Louisiana State Bd. of Educ.*, 281 U.S. 370, 50 Sup. Ct. 335, 74 L. Ed. 913 (1930). The number preceding the reporter citation refers to the volume of the reporter, and the number immediately following the reporter citation is the page number where the case is located, *e.g.*, this case is found in volume 281, page 370, of the *United States Reports*.

Throughout much of the nineteenth century, the cases of the Supreme Court of the United States, and of a few state courts, were published by private reporters, and the reports were cited by the name of the reporter. The seven early reporters of the Supreme Court of the United States were: Dallas, Cranch, Wheaton, Peters, Howard, Black, and Wallace. It is customary to parenthetically indicate the name of the report editor and the volume of his series in addition to the official citation, *e.g.*, *Green v. Biddle*, 21 U.S. (8 Wheat.) 1 (1823).

It should be noted that the unofficial reporter is just as accurate and complete as the official reporter, and many states have discontinued the publication of official state reports because such publications are very expensive and the unofficial reports alone have proved to be most satisfactory.

The National Reporter System. The most comprehensive unofficial reporter system is the *National Reporter System* of the West Publishing

Company. In addition to the *Supreme Court Reporter*, the *National Reporter System* includes opinions from the lower federal courts in the *Federal Reporter* (cited "Fed."), the *Federal Supplement* (cited "F. Supp."), and the *Federal Rules Decisions* (cited "F.R.D."). The New York state court opinions are published in the *New York Supplement* (cited "N.Y. Supp."). California state court opinions since 1960 are published in the *California Reporter* (cited "Cal. Rptr."). The opinions of the other state courts have been arranged roughly by geographical divisions into seven regional units of the *National Reporter System* known as the *Atlantic Reporter* (cited "Atl."), *North Eastern Reporter* (cited "N.E."), *North Western Reporter* (cited "N.W."), *Pacific Reporter* (cited "Pac."), *South Eastern Reporter* (cited "S.E."), *South Western Reporter* (cited "S.W."), and *Southern Reporter* (cited ("So.") (see figure 2-2). This system of state courts reporting was begun in 1879. Because so many volumes of the regional reporters have been published since that time, the publisher has begun numbering them in a second series, *e.g.*, the second series of the Pacific Reporter is a continuation of the first series and is cited "P.2d."

Citations to case opinions will usually show the official reporter citation immediately following the title or name of the case, the regional unofficial reporter citation, and the year in which the case was decided, *e.g.*, *State v. Haworth*, 122 Ind. 462, 23 N.E. 946 (1890). This 1890 case is found in volume 122, page 462, of the official *Indiana Reporter*, and in volume 23, page 946, of the unofficial regional *North Eastern Reporter*.

Because the cases are published in the *National Reporter System* in chronological order as they are handed down by the courts, the West Publishing Company has published an index to those cases which is called the *American Digest System*. The *American Digest System* purports to cover every reported case from 1658 to date. It consists of a *Century Digest*, covering cases from 1658 to 1896, and six *Decennials*, each covering ten year periods from 1897. The *Sixth Decennial* covered cases from 1946 to 1956. Cases since 1957 are included in the bound volumes of the *General Digest*, 3rd series. Digest paragraphs are arranged alphabetically under a subject or topic heading with a key-number. The key-number is essentially a section number. Anyone interested in locating all reported cases on a particular point of common law needs to be familiar with the West key-number system as employed in all of the units of *American Digest System*, except the *Century Digest*, and the *National Reporter System*, in addition to other West publications.

National Reporter System Map.

Showing the States included in each Reporter group

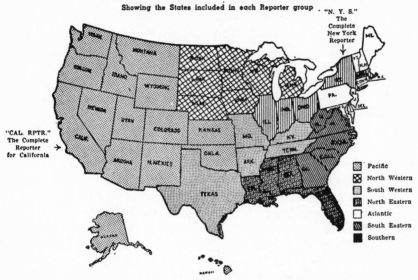

The National Reporter System also includes the Supreme Court Reporter, the Federal Reporter, the Federal Supplement, Federal Rules Decisions, the New York Supplement, and West's California Reporter.

Courtesy of West Publishing Company, St. Paul, Minn.

Figure 2-2

Other sources of the law. The more important federal and state cases are reported and annotated currently in the *American Law Reports, Annotated* (cited "A.L.R."). This publication is now in its second series, a continuation of the first series. Decisions of the Supreme Court of the United States are annotated in the *United States Supreme Court Reports,* Lawyers' Edition. The annotations are encyclopedic essays on significant legal topics embodied in the reprinted cases. These discussions on detailed points of law facilitate research because they obviate the need to individually locate and analyze all cases in point.

Definitions and correct pronunciations of legal words and phrases may be found in special law dictionaries, and frequently in other English language dictionaries. Cases in law often turn on the definition of a particular word or phrase as it is applied in a special situation.

Judges are regularly called upon to define legal and non-legal terms. More than 300,000 of these judicial definitions have been compiled in the comprehensive 45 volume set of *Words and Phrases*.

Corpus Juris Secundum (cited "C.J.S.") and *American Jurisprudence* (cited "Am. Jur.") are legal encyclopedias which serve the researcher as an excellent index and introductory guide to the general law on any topic. *Corpus Juris Secundum* superseded the earlier encyclopedia *Corpus Juris; American Jurisprudence 2d* began in 1962, and will eventually supersede *American Jurisprudence*.

Shepard's Citations is a useful service to determine the current status of the various forms of legislation, citations to judicial interpretations of that legislation, and citations to subsequent judicial rulings on established case law. *Shepard's Citations* consists of the following units: *United States Citations, Federal Reporter Citations, State Citations* (a separate citator for each state), and *National Reporter System Citations* (a separate citator for each of the units of the *National Reporter System*).

When the researcher has a citation to a case involving a legal principle and wants to know how courts have ruled subsequently on that proposition, he may refer to the appropriate citator. Thus, if you wish to determine whether the rule in the case *Houghton v. School Comm. of Somerville*, 306 Mass. 542, 28 N.E.2d 1001 (1940), has been treated in subsequent cases, you may use the volume and page numbers of the official reporter citation to refer to *Shepard's Massachusetts Citations*, or use the volume and page numbers of the regional reporter citation to refer to *Shepard's North Eastern Citations*. As a matter of practice, the authors recommend the use of the *National Reporter System Citations* over the *State Citations*.

There are, of course, many other sources of the law which must be used daily by practicing attorneys. The publications discussed here are the basic research tools in law, and the educator who learns to use them will be able to further his understanding of the law as it relates to himself and to the teaching profession.

Suggested Activities

DISCUSSION:
1. Organizations that attempt to influence school legislation.
2. The impact of the philosophies of judges in the development of American Law.
3. The activities of the courts and agencies established by law to handle juvenile problems.

4. The functions of a state agency empowered by statute to administer public school policies.
5. *Marbury* v. *Madison,* 5 U. S. (1 Cranch) 137, 2 L. Ed. 60 (1803).
6. A state Teacher's Tenure Law provided in part that any person who, after having served in any school corporation under contract as a teacher for five successive years, and who shall enter into a teacher's contract for further service with such corporation, shall thereupon become a permanent teacher of such school corporation whose contract shall continue in effect for an indefinite period and be known as an indefinite contract. The indefinite contract was to remain in force unless succeeded by a new contract signed by both parties, or unless canceled, upon notice and hearing, for incompetency, insubordination, neglect of duty, immorality, justifiable decrease in the number of teaching positions, or other good and just cause, but not for political or personal reasons. Miss Jones, a teacher in a township school corporation in the state, acquired the permanent teacher's status under the provisions of this state law.

Several years later the act was amended and made to apply to city and town school corporations only. The township school officers noted that townships, to which the act originally applied, were omitted in the amendment, which had the effect of repealing the law so far as townships, schools, and the teachers therein were concerned, so they notified Miss Jones that her teaching contract would not be renewed.

Miss Jones contends that having become a permanent teacher under the act before the amendment, she has a vested property right in her indefinite contract, which cannot be impaired under article I, section 10, of the Constitution of the United States which provides: "No state shall pass any law impairing the obligation of contracts."

What steps may Miss Jones take in protecting her alleged rights? What arguments can be made in support of the school officers' actions?

Indiana ex rel. Anderson v. Brand, 303 U.S. 95, 58 Sup. Ct. 443, 82 L. Ed. 685 (1937).

DEFINE:
1. "Supreme Law of the Land"
2. Original and appellate jurisdiction
3. Due process of law
4. Plenary power
5. Police power.

BRIEF A COURT CASE:
Examine a case of your choice or select one of the cases cited in the footnotes throughout this textbook. Your *brief* should include:
(1) The title of the case

(2) The citation and date of the case
(3) A brief statement of the facts of the case
(4) The issue(s) or question(s) of law raised for the court's consideration
(5) The rule(s) of law applied by the court to resolve the issue(s)
(6) The reasons given by the court to support its decision.

Further Readings

Edwards, Newton. *The Courts and the Public Schools* (Chicago: University of Chicago Press, 1955).

Fryer, William T., and Carville D. Benson. *Legal Method and Legal System* (St. Paul: West Publishing Company, 1950).

Gavit, Bernard C., et al. *Cases and Materials on an Introduction to Law and the Judicial Process, Second Edition* (Chicago: Callaghan & Company, 1952).

Jones, Harry W. (ed). *Materials for Legal Method, Second Edition* (Brooklyn: Foundation Press, 1952).

Plucknett, Theodore F. T. *A Concise History of the Common Law, Fifth Edition* (Boston: Little, Brown and Company, 1956).

Pollack, Ervin H. *Fundamentals of Legal Research, Second Edition* (Brooklyn: Foundation Press, 1962).

Price, Miles Oscar, and Harry Bitner. *Effective Legal Research* (New York: Prentice-Hall, 1953).

Syrett, Harold C. (ed.) *American Historical Documents* (New York: Barnes and Noble, 1960).

Section Two

LICENSING AND CONTRACTING

The Teaching Certificate

The Teacher's Contract

Chapter III

THE TEACHING CERTIFICATE

Introduction

At the time the U.S.S.R. orbited its first Sputnik a wave of apprehension seized the American people. Was our educational system equal to the new challenge? Were schools producing enough well-trained scientists, mathematicians, and linguists to assure America of continuing leadership in world affairs? If not, what should be done to accomplish this all-important task?

In the late 1950's and early 1960's, the attention of educators and laymen was thus turned to the development of a higher level of effectiveness in the public schools. Extensive studies were undertaken to re-define *quality* in education; ways and means were explored for bringing to bear the collective forces of our society upon problems pertaining to excellence in educational matters. Among the means were two which lie within the powers of state government: certification and accreditation. It is worthy of note that both means have been utilized more fully since the implications of Sputnik turned our attention to the necessity of upgrading the school program.

Certification differs from *accreditation* in that it pertains to the individual, rather than the institution. Certification is the legal device by which the state assures that all who teach shall possess certain minimum personal and professional qualifications. Accreditation, on the other hand, is a control exercised by the state, and some regional and national voluntary organizations, for the overall improvement of school programs.

There are many indications that states are diligently seeking ways to further utilize both these legal means to improve the general quality of American schools. For example, in a nation-wide study conducted in 1959, thirty-three states reported that intensive studies of certification practices were being undertaken.[1] In several of the states, plans for raising certification standards were underway, with certification bills being prepared for introduction into legislative hoppers.

What Is Certification?

Persons entering the teaching profession for the first time often become bewildered by the legal prerequisites to their employment. Their confusion arises chiefly because statutes governing these matters vary considerably from state to state. Adding to the confusion, certification requirements are subject to revision with such rapidity that even those who work constantly in the field of teacher preparation find it difficult, if not impossible, to keep abreast of the changes. This chapter and the next contain information for those entering the field of teaching, or those who may wish to acquaint themselves with the legal background necessary to understand the principles involved in entering upon a career in teaching.

Any person wishing to begin teaching in a particular state should first become acquainted with the laws pertaining to schools in that state. An initial point of contact is the state department of education, located in the state capitol city. A letter of inquiry addressed to this department will be sufficient to obtain the necessary forms on which to make application for a certificate and instructions for becoming fully "certificated."

What, then, is certification? Huggett and Stinnett[2] present the following definition:

> Certification is the process of giving legal sanction to teach. It includes all types of licenses whether permanent or temporary in character, whether short-term or long-term, and whether issued on the basis of several years of study or as a result of a few weeks or months of preparation or even on the basis of having passed an examination. It includes those of an emergency nature as well as those which meet regular requirements.

---

[1]W. Earl Armstrong and T. M. Stinnett. *A Manual on Certification Requirements* (Washington: National Commission on Teacher Education and Professional Standards, 1959), p. 4.

[2]Albert J. Huggett and T. M. Stinnett. *Professional Problems of Teachers* (New York: Macmillan Company, 1956), p. 412.

The certificate to teach should be considered within its legal framework. Its nature is determined by the statutory details which govern its issuance. It is necessary in each state to determine how closely the provisions of the governing statute must be followed in order to assure the validity of the teaching certificate. Whether the statute is mandatory or directory is a question often before the courts. When it is a mandatory statute, failure to follow its provisions will render the certification procedure illegal and void. In general, the rule is that such details are merely directory, and the failure to follow them exactly does not invalidate the certificate.

Douglas reported in 1950 that a nationwide study disclosed about two-hundred fifty court cases of record on the problem of teacher certification.[3] The study revealed that even though this is not a major problem area in the same category with actions involving contracts, corporal punishment, and the like, certification is, nevertheless, an area deserving of the careful attention of teachers everywhere.

The mere number of available certificates gives rise to some confusion among educators. Stinnett reported, in 1959, a total of 630 different types or separate-name certificates in the United States. The numerical range in the states was from one in West Virginia (with several forms) to 65 in New Jersey. Three-hundred twelve certificates were based on requirements equal to the bachelor's degree, while forty-five were based on more than four years, but less than five years, of college attendance. One-hundred sixty-one certificates were based on the master's degree, six on the doctor's degree, while another eighty-eight were based on requirements of preparation below the bachelor's level.[4]

Limitations of the Certificate

The teaching certificate is by nature a "limited" legal document issued by the state, which may be revoked under whatever conditions the state wishes to impose. The certificate is merely a *license* to teach in a given state, attesting to the fact that the holder possesses, at the time of issuance, the required qualifications. No absolute rights, such as guaranteed employment, or tenure rights, are conferred by the certificate upon the holder. Indeed, its continuing validity is often

---

[3]Lawrence M. Douglas. "Legal Issues in Teacher Certification as Shown by an Analysis of American Court Decisions," (Pittsburgh: University of Pittsburgh, 1950), unpublished doctoral dissertation, p. 10.

[4]T. M. Stinnett. "Certification Requirements and Procedures Among the States in 1960," *Journal of Teacher Education* (June, 1960), pp. 173-184.

dependent upon successful, continuous employment in school work. Should the holder fail to secure employment, or teach only intermittently, the certificate may be terminated according to rules laid down by the legislature or the state department of education. Upon its termination, the certificate is completely annulled and is subject to renewal only upon full compliance with certification standards in effect at the time of renewal.

The certificate, furthermore, is a *prerequisite to employment*, since one who teaches without a certificate is considered a mere *volunteer* before the law. No matter how well he may teach, one who lacks the certificate may not recover salary for his work, for the certificate is necessary before he may legally be paid from public funds. The certificate has none of the elements of a contract, under which the teacher is protected by due process of law under the provisions of federal or state constitutions.

The certificate is a *personal privilege* granted by the state to an individual, and may not be transferred, sold, or bartered to another person. It is valid for certain specified grades, levels, or subjects only, or for certain kinds of work, such as that performed by the school psychologist, speech therapist, or social worker. One cannot be allowed to teach at any level other than that allowed by his certificate, nor may he perform duties essentially different from those for which he is qualified.

The holder of a teaching certificate is impliedly bound by the rules and regulations of the employing board of education, even when the rules and regulations are made subsequent to the signing of the contract. In the same way, the holder of a certificate is subject to all operative certification legislation which the legislature has enacted in the past and enacts in the future, and to the rules and regulations affecting certification of the state department of education.

Although this may indicate that the limitations of the certificate tend to render it of little value, quite the opposite is true. Certain definite rights and privileges attach to the holder of the teaching certificate. Since one who obtains the certificate must meet certain qualifications, the certificate is *prima facie* evidence of the holder's competency to perform the work in question. The board of education which seeks to dismiss the teacher on the basis of incompetency, therefore, is given the burden of proving that the teacher is indeed incompetent; the holder is considered competent until the court is convinced otherwise.

A certificate, being in the nature of a commission from the state, *is not open to collateral attack*. Since there exists a presumption that the certificate was legally issued, and the teacher qualified to hold it, a school board may not dismiss a teacher on the pretense that his certificate was illegally issued. Any action to test the validity of the certificate must be done directly, rather than by indirectly attempting to destroy or evade its effect. Its immunity to collateral attack is one of the principal strengths of the teaching certificate.

Furthermore, a certificate protects the holder in most cases *from demotion and a reduction in salary*. It entitles the teacher to contract within the state in the manner and mode designated by the school laws of that state and to collect salary for his labors. Unless the local board of education requires additional qualifications of its teachers, the certificated teacher is considered qualified in any school district in the state wherein he holds certification.

Who May Teach?

No person has an *inherent right* to teach in the public schools. Rather, it is a *privilege* granted to a select number of individuals, *viz.*, those who possess the qualifications specified by the state. When specific qualifications are met, the state issues, or directs one of its agencies to issue, the teaching license, sometimes referred to as the credential or teaching certificate. Thus, the individual wishing to enter upon a career in teaching must first prepare himself to meet the specific qualifications of the state in which he wishes to teach. Then he must acquire, or be reasonably certain of acquiring, prior to taking up his work, the license to teach in that state.

The personal and professional qualifications established for certificated teachers vary from state to state. In 1959, thirty-one of the states required teaching candidates to be United States citizens, or to have filed preliminary citizenship papers. Twenty-eight states required candidates to ascribe to an oath of allegiance. Forty-two states required that candidates be endorsed by their respective preparatory college or university.

With respect to the health of candidates, in 1959 twenty-four of the states required a general health certificate for certification, and fifteen states required a chest X-ray. Some states had enabling legislation permitting local boards to require health examinations as a prerequisite to employment. Two of the states, North Carolina and

South Carolina, required an examination for tuberculosis and other communicable diseases for certification.

Sixteen states had no age requirements for teachers; two required candidates to be at least 17 years of age, twenty-nine required 18 years, three, 19 and two, 20 years of age. Some of the states reported that teachers must have formally studied the state history and constitution for certification, but this requirement was being waived in areas where teacher shortages existed.

Not all school personnel must be certificated, but it is well established in all the states that school administrators, special school services personnel, and public elementary and secondary teachers must hold a certificate. In 1959, fifteen of the states required public nursery school teachers to be certificated, while forty states required it of public kindergarten teachers. A total of sixteen states made it requisite that junior college teachers be certificated, and, in five states, teachers in the state teachers' colleges needed certificates. Twelve states required private or parochial school teachers to be certificated at some school level.[5]

There was some evidence that the states were experimenting with standardized teachers' examinations as a basis for certification. In some instances, such examinations were being utilized for certificating liberal arts college graduates, and for authorizing experienced teachers to function in additional subject areas. Most states demanded that teachers continue to teach in order to keep the certificate in force. For example, several state statutes specified that the certificate might not be renewed for any person who allowed a three-year lapse in his teaching experience.[6]

Even when a teacher possesses all of the qualifications for certification by the state, he must be assured that he is certificated in that particular school district in which he performs his work. A factually interesting Colorado case emphasizes this legal principle. In that case,[7] a teacher was employed under a certificate from a neighboring school district. The employing district was consolidated with the same superintendent and directors as the neighboring first-class district under which the teacher was certified. The board dismissed the teacher, who brought suit to recover her position. The Supreme Court of Colorado ruled that the certificate held by the plaintiff teacher was

[5]Armstrong and Stinnett, *op. cit.,* p. 7.
[6]*Ibid.*
[7]Union High School Dist. v. Paul, 105 Colo. 93, 95 P.2d 5 (1939).

valid only in the issuing district, regardless of that district's affiliation with the district employing the teacher.

The teacher asked the Colorado Court to take into consideration a state statute which provided that no teacher should be discharged without a hearing and good cause shown. In ruling that the teacher was not entitled to regain her position, the court pointed out that inasmuch as her certificate was void, she was not entitled to a contract or to the benefits of the statutory provisions because they were available only to regularly licensed teachers. No benefits were available to one whose license and contract were void *ab initio* (from the beginning).

A school board may impose certification standards upon a teacher in addition to the certification requirements set by the state, to qualify the teacher for employment in its school district. For example, the board may require teachers to reside in the employing school district, a requirement which, in at least two instances, has been declared by the courts to be a reasonable exercise of board power.[8] Similarly, the board may choose to employ married women only, or just those teachers with advanced degrees. As long as the rule appears reasonable, the courts will not interfere with a board's decision to require special qualifications of its teachers.

Is Certification a Prerequisite to Contracting?

The principle of law governing legal prerequisites to teaching may be illustrated by two cases, an 1867 Minnesota case, and a recent case from Kentucky. In the Minnesota case, the plaintiff, a teacher named Jennes, contracted for a three-month term of teaching starting on December 24. Although he had no certificate when the contract was made, he later obtained a certificate dated December 24 of the same year.

In ruling that the teacher could not recover on the contract, the court said:

> It is plain that the sections of the statute confer no power or authority on the board of trustees to contract with or hire a teacher before he has obtained the requisite certificate of qualification, and that the contract sued upon in this case is therefore void. The statute confers and measures the power of the board, and its affirmative language, that the board shall hire "such teachers as have procured a certificate," implies a

---

[8]Stuart v. Board of Educ. of City and County of San Francisco, 118 Pac. 712 (Cal. 1911); Appeal of Sinton, 35 A.2d 542 (Pa. 1944).

negative—that it shall not hire any other. Every person is presumed to know the law and is bound at his peril to take notice of the public statutes. It must be supposed, therefore, the plaintiff knew that the board had power only to contract with a class of persons to which he did not belong—those having certificates of qualification to teach.

If he has no remedy he cannot say he was misled or deceived, or that the district is in equity bound to perform a contract that the parties contracting knew they had no right to make.[9]

A similar case before the Court of Appeals of Kentucky concerned a Miss Slone, who was assigned as a teacher, although she had no teaching certificate, as was required by statute, and was not eligible for certification under the statute until she reached the age of eighteen. She taught from September 3 until November 18, when she became eighteen years of age, then brought an action to recover wages for her work prior to her eighteenth birthday, those wages having been refused her by the school board.

The trial court found for the teacher ruling that where parties to an illegal contract for services are not in equal fault and the contract is only *malum prohibitum* (a wrong prohibited), the innocent party may recover for the value of the services rendered. This ruling of the trial court, however, was reversed by the Court of Appeals, which held that the rule is valid only as to contracts between individuals; the case before the court was one involving payment by public agencies to employees, in which ". . . the rights of employees to compensation are incident to and dependent upon their right to . . . employment." The court based its refusal to grant the teacher wages for the period between September 3 and November 18 on the grounds that ". . . one who is ineligible for a public office and therefore holds it without title is a volunteer and cannot recover for services."[10]

In yet another case, a contract of employment made between a teacher and a school district was void because the teacher did not have a certificate and so was not qualified to teach when the contract was consummated. Thereafter, however, the teacher entered upon the performance of her duties under a new arrangement made by the school board, by which a temporary certificate was procured by the teacher before she commenced her services, and a proper certificate was later obtained by her. Under those circumstances, it was held:

---

[9]Jennes v. School Dist. No. 31, Washington County, 12 Minn. 337 (1867).
[10]Floyd County Bd. of Educ. v. Slone, 307 S.W.2d 912 (Ky. 1957).

The commencement of the school term by the teacher with the knowledge and consent of the board, after she had received a certificate of qualification, was equivalent to the making of a new contract upon the terms of the one into which they attempted to enter [earlier].[11]

It appears from other cases that, in instances where the teacher begins to teach, and the board pays her for services rendered, an *implied contract* is established, even though the original contract was void; provided, however, that the teacher cannot be reimbursed for services performed during the time she was devoid of a valid certificate. Where the contract is one that the board could not legally make at the outset, the teacher cannot recover the value of services rendered under it.

Even though the board of education may wish to compensate a teacher who lacks a certificate, it cannot do so whenever a valid certificate is a prerequisite to an enforceable contract. In some instances, board members have been held personally liable for illegal payment of public moneys to unauthorized persons. The board may accept the free services of the uncertificated teacher, but it is clearly prohibited from paying public money to any teacher other than one who holds a valid teaching certificate. The law presupposes the judicious use and zealous guarding of public moneys, and the proper accounting thereof. No statutes are more clearly written than those which limit the boards of education in exercising discretion with respect to the public treasury. In Ohio, for example, it is unlawful for the clerk of the board of education to pay any compensation whatsoever for services rendered by a teacher until the clerk has received from the superintendent in the district a written statement certifying that a valid certificate has been filed with the superintendent. Numerous other states have similar restrictions.

All states agree that a person who wishes employment as a teacher must possess the appropriate certificate of the particular state in which he wishes to teach. Lack of agreement exists, however, as to *when* a teacher must obtain the certificate in order to enter into a valid contract with a board of education. In some states, as has been noted, the teacher must possess the certificate *at the time* of initial contracting, that is, at the time when the teacher and board reach an agreement. In other states, a teacher who lacks the necessary license may still enter into a contract that will be binding if the teacher obtains the necessary certificate *by the time he begins his work*. In other states,

---

[11]Hotz v. School Dist. No. 1, 1 Colo. App. 40, 27 Pac. 15 (1891).

it is sufficient if the teacher obtains the certificate *prior to his receipt of any salary*. The student should, of course, consult the school code in his respective state to determine the conditions under which contracting for teaching services may be legally consummated.

A Nebraska case illustrates that legal principle requiring teachers to possess the certificate by the time work begins. The case is interesting, too, in the particular action taken by the court when the teacher, who failed to be certificated at the time her work began, secured the certificate before the board declared her contract void and of no effect. In this case, Miss Johnson, the teacher, contracted on October 20, 1954, to teach school for seven months, beginning on November 1 of that year. The board dismissed Miss Johnson on January 26, 1955, paying her for that part of the contract already completed. The teacher brought an action against the school board, maintaining that she had been illegally dismissed. The board contended that the contract was void because the teacher had not complied with the statutory requirements for holding and registering a valid teaching certificate.

Controlling parts of the Nebraska statute provided that a teaching contract should contain a provision whereby the employed person affirmed that he held, or would hold at the beginning of the term of employment, a valid certificate properly registered in the office of the superintendent of the county in which the teaching would take place; no certificate to teach or contract for a school should be valid until the certificate was so registered. The statute further provided that a teacher violating the certificate and registration provisions of the statute should not recover any money for services rendered during the time that such contract and certificate were invalid. Said the Supreme Court of Nebraska:

> It is plain . . . that a teacher may enter into a valid contract with a school district who does not then have a teacher's certificate. In other words, such a contract is not void because a teacher does not hold a teacher's certificate. She may properly contract to have such a certificate and to register it with the county superintendent at the beginning of the term of the contract. The contract in the instant case is clearly within the purview of the statutes on the subject. . . .
>
> Such contracts under the cited sections of the statutes are valid when entered into and are voidable when statutory requirements are not met. The effect of existing statutes is that a teacher must have a certificate registered with the county superintendent before she begins to teach. If the teacher does

not have such certificate on file the contract is voidable and may be terminated by the school district. If the contract is not terminated during the time the teacher is in default in not having a teacher's certificate registered with the county superintendent before beginning to teach, the statute provides that such teacher shall not recover any money for teaching during the period of such default. In other words, if the contract is not terminated by the proper authority during the period of the default, and the teacher subsequently meets the requirements of the statute as to holding and registering her certificate, the contract is valid, even though the teacher is precluded from recovering compensation during the period of the default.[12]

What of the teacher who holds a certificate, but allows it to expire? This question of law arose in a case in Colorado. A teacher legally contracted to teach; at the time of contracting, she had a certificate authorizing her to teach, but it expired soon after the term of school began. The board continued to pay the teacher, and she continued to teach without the certificate. In an attempt to recover the amount paid the teacher, the board contended that the teacher was not certificated, and was, therefore, not entitled to the money. The court could not agree with this contention, and held in favor of the teacher, using the following language:

> The teacher having been qualified at the time the contract was entered into, and the board having accepted her services without objection and paid for the same, there are few, if any, authorities, and no good reasons, which would permit the district to recover for money already paid, notwithstanding the terms of the statute, which provide that, if the term of school for which the teacher is employed extends more than one month after the expiration of such certificate, the teacher shall secure a new certificate, or a renewal of the one held, while it is in force. So far as that contract of employment was concerned . . . the parties were *in pari delicto* (in equal fault). Money paid under an agreement which is executed, whether paid as the consideration or in performance of the promise, cannot be recovered back, where the parties are *in pari delicto* (emphasis supplied).[13]

---

[12]Johnson v. School Dist. No. 3 of Clay County, 168 Neb. 547, 96 N.W.2d 623 (1959).

[13]School Dist. No. 46 of Sedgwick County v. Johnson, 26 Colo. App. 433, 143 Pac. 264 (1914).

Purposes of Certification

The power of the state to control licensing of occupational groups is implied in the state's power to protect the health, morals, and general well being of its people. The ability to protect the general welfare is termed the *police power* of the state. Thus, the state may enact laws relating to marriage, divorce, public health, gambling, and a host of other general welfare measures. The right to control education is one of the police powers of the state. Inasmuch as the public schools contribute to the betterment of society, educational legislation often reflects the hopes and aspirations of the legislative branch of government in exercising control over the health, morals, and general welfare of the social order. To assist the courts in interpreting the laws, state legislatures may express underlying purposes for the legislation in the law itself. An illustration of this expression of purpose is contained in section 2 of the Colorado State Teacher Certification Act of 1961, passed by the General Assembly of that state. Here the purposes are set forth clearly and unequivocally:

> Legislative declaration—(1) It is hereby declared to be the policy of the state of Colorado to provide quality education in the schools of the state and to this end further to raise the standards for the certification of teachers and to encourage the professional development of those presently certificated. It is further the policy of the state that teachers in Colorado be of good moral character, have a thorough grounding in the moral, ethical, and philosophical roots of our civilization, have a broad educational background in the liberal arts, hold at least a bachelor's degree, have a thorough and up-to-date knowledge in depth of their subject matter, and have an adequate foundation of professional education including *student teaching or its equivalent* (emphasis supplied).
>
> (2) It is also declared to be the policy of the state to safeguard the welfare of our children against unqualified, incompetent, and immoral teachers, to improve the instructional programs in the schools of the state, to encourage wiser use of the services of teachers, and to permit maximum flexibility of standards for the certification of teachers in accordance with changing educational concepts and programs. To these ends (the certification laws) shall be liberally construed.[14]

Need for the legislative intent to "safeguard the welfare of our children against unqualified, incompetent, and immoral teachers" arises as our society grows increasingly more complex, and the number of

---

[14]Colo. Rev. Stat. § 123-17-19 (Supp. 1961).

certificated teachers becomes larger. Other occupational groups coming under licensing requirements at the state level are becoming more numerous and now include doctors, perhaps the first group to be generally licensed, dentists, lawyers, morticians, pharmacists, engineers, architects, insurance agents, and several dozen others. The trend is in the direction of the state licensing more occupational groups, one obvious purpose being to protect the people from charlatans who prey upon the gullibility of the public.

The chief purpose of teacher certification is to make certain that only duly qualified persons come in contact with children of young and tender years. However, there are additional purposes advanced for certification. Certification statutes protect the public treasury, fulfilling the rule that public moneys shall be paid only to persons who possess the license to teach. This stewardship function has as its motive the prevention of illegal dissipation of public funds to unauthorized persons. Furthermore, certification helps to maintain a school system designed to improve society, in that teachers must meet a *minimum* level of quality before the certificate will be issued. Finally, certification protects the profession of teaching by establishing criteria for membership in the profession. Under ideal conditions, certification may also insure the continuing growth of the individual teacher. Thus, certification is seen as protecting (1) the child's right to an education under qualified persons, (2) the public fisc, (3) society, by establishing minimum standards for teachers, and (4) the profession of teaching. Through its certification laws, the people of the state implement their educational hopes and aspirations for the improvement of educational opportunities for all.

The development of our certification laws has been slow and halting. Through trial and error, through professional and legislative concern, certification advanced to its present status. Because the general public aspired to higher standards for its teachers, there were placed upon the statute books the laws necessary to achieve improved certification standards. The long steps taken have not produced ideal certification legislation, for much remains to be done in all the states before certification will produce the desired results. Some insight into the historical development in this area, however, will increase the teacher's appreciation for what has been accomplished and what remains to be effected. A brief review of certification as it developed in the United States is contained in the next few pages of this chapter.

History of Certification

LaBue noted that there were four distinct periods in the development of American certification.[15] The first period, terminating in 1789, was concerned with regulating the licensing of teachers, but there was virtually no interest in teacher education or competencies. The second period, from 1789 to 1860, was characterized by a shift of the licensing function from local boards to state educational agencies, and the establishment of the first normal schools. From 1860 to 1910, the third period, the normal schools expanded, teachers' colleges were established, and schools of education began in the universities and liberal arts colleges. The final period, from 1910 to the present, was a period of significant development and influence on the movement to improve standards for teacher certification. In this later period came several important innovations, among them—state reciprocity, standardized teachers' examinations, the use of college transcripts to replace oral and written examinations, and similar steps in the upgrading of certification standards.

During the second period, in 1839, William A. Alcott, a schoolmaster, described an oral examination before the Board of School Visitors in a New England village.[16] The local minister and two laymen comprised the board's membership. The object of the examination was to determine Mr. Alcott's fitness for a teaching certificate. Members of the board questioned the candidate on his knowledge of educational matters in general and of "schoolmastering" in particular. "How many sounds has the letter B? the letter C? Two is to four as seven is to what number?" they asked. A sample of Mr. Alcott's handwriting was requested. He read aloud for the group, answered questions put to him on such subjects as grammar and geography, and pronounced words given by the board members. He successfully spelled common words contained in the *Introduction to the Spelling Book*. Curiously, the members of the board said nothing about the management and discipline of the school, presumably, as Mr. Alcott noted later, upon the erroneous opinion prevailing at the time, that these were a "gift, or rather as some seemed to regard it, a matter of mere haphazard." At the conclusion of the examination, said Mr. Alcott with relief, ". . . they wrote me a certificate."

---

[15] Anthony C. LaBue. "Teacher Certification in the United States; A Brief History," *Journal of Teacher Education* (June, 1960), p. 147.

[16] William A. Alcott. *Confessions of a Schoolmaster.* (Andover: Newman and Saxton, 1839), quoted in Marjorie Smiley and John Diekhoff. *Prologue to Teaching* (New York: Oxford University Press, 1959), pp. 113-115.

The case of Mr. Alcott illustrates the prevailing method of licensing teachers in the United States until the latter part of the nineteenth century. Throughout most of our nation's history, the granting of licenses to teach was a function of local boards of education, who often left the matter to the only educated man in town, the local minister. Such factors as the religious orthodoxy of the candidate, his ability to influence the board members through oratory or a display of knowledge, as well as the abundance or shortage of available teachers, influenced the decisions of local boards. Persons might, and often did, "set themselves up in business" merely by convincing a local board of their knowledge, orthodoxy, or facility in ciphering to the "rule of three." An itinerant schoolmaster, unable to obtain a teaching license in one community, might travel about until he discovered a board willing to issue a teaching certificate and employ him.

Because there were no public normal schools for the preparation of teachers in this country before 1839, there was a scarcity of teachers. Boards could not, therefore, be highly selective in their examination of candidates. Consequently, examinations were held only as the need arose. States did not interfere with local board functions, but gradually began to question some of the practices used by the boards. For example, less than five months after he assumed the office of Secretary to the Massachusetts State Board of Education in 1837, Horace Mann presented a comprehensive survey of the conditions in the public schools of that state. This "first of the superintendent's reports" revealed many things of interest to the state board. Under the heading, "The Manner in Which the School Committees Performed Their Duties," Horace Mann reported that the school committees of that time, unled by professional administrators, were neglectful in regard to the time of examining teachers, the character of the examinations, and the reluctance to reject incompetent candidates for teaching positions.[17]

Successful candidates were issued certificates to teach, and boards of education entered into contractual agreements with those whom the board had certificated. Should the board look unfavorably upon a candidate, it might make the examination so difficult as to preclude the issuance of the certificate. Indeed, there was considerable leeway for this practice, inasmuch as there were no statutes governing subjects to be covered. Theology, philosophy, classical languages, litera-

---

[17]Henry Barnard. *American Journal of Education* (Hartford: F. C. Brownell, 1856), Volume V, pp. 654-656.

ture, grammar, geography, and similar fields were often included. The examinations were at times lengthy and quite unpredictable as to content. Since the certificate was good for only a short time, usually for no longer than a year, the examinations had to be repeated frequently. Furthermore, there was no assurance that the certificate issued by one board would prove acceptable to a board in any other district of the state.

These shortcomings of the certification function led the states, in the 1880's, to begin withdrawing certification authority from local boards, and gradually vesting it in other agencies, chiefly county boards, state colleges, and universities. While generally accepting the state's plenary power over educational matters, including the granting of teaching certificates, the states nonetheless resisted removing the licensing of teachers or contracting therefor from the local boards as long as possible. However, since 1900, the trend has been in the direction of placing teacher certification under the direct control of state departments of education or state boards of educational examiners.

Gauerke reported that certification was first made a matter of state statute in the Midwest. It was in 1837 that Indiana passed a law permitting state circuit courts to appoint certification examiners, but full enforcement at the state level was not forthcoming until 1850.[18]

Burrup related that Massachusetts, in 1951, was the last state to require state certification of all teachers.[19] Slightly more than one hundred years intervened between the first issuance of certificates by a state and the completion of this phase of certification, yet many changes took place. The written "teacher's examination" came into general usage to replace the oral examination. It was often taken in the county superintendent's office, and covered such subject matter as orthography, didactics, pedagogy, and similar subjects. As certification gradually became the prerogative of the state, examinations were replaced by an official transcript of the student's college record. Now it is unusual to find a state in which local boards of education are empowered to issue the teaching certificate, although it is common practice for local boards to administer examinations such as the National Teacher Examinations to candidates for teaching positions.

---

[18]Warren E. Gauerke. *Legal and Ethical Responsibilities of School Personnel* (Englewood Cliffs, N.J.: Prentice-Hall, 1959), pp. 36-37.
[19]Percy E. Burrup. *The Teacher and the Public School System* (New York: Harper and Brothers, 1960), pp. 219-220.

A statute in Florida provides that no teacher who makes a score of less than 500 on the National Teacher Examination will be issued a certificate to teach in that state. Additional provisions of the Florida law include annual evaluations for teachers and the requirement that teachers teach within their fields of competency. A California law effective July 1, 1963, provides that all elementary teachers are required to have five years of college education or its equivalent for initial certification. A similar law in Wisconsin requires all teachers who have taught in the state seven years to obtain the bachelor's degree for certificate renewal. Certification standards are being raised in many other states of the union.

Changes in Preparation for Certification

Following World War II, some rather important changes developed regarding the amount of collegiate preparation for initial teacher certification. By 1960, forty states required at least four years of college preparation for initial certification of elementary teachers; forty-eight states required this level of preparation for beginning high school teachers. Three states required five years of college preparation for the initial high school teaching certificate.

A so-called *life certificate* permits the holder to teach during his entire life as long as he is on good behavior. Recently, there has been a substantial decrease in the number of states issuing the life certificate, from 28 states in 1957 to 20 in 1959. The life certificate made no demands upon the teacher to meet additional standards in order to continue teaching. The decrease in the number of states having life certificates undoubtedly represents a desire on the part of the states and the teaching profession to continue to re-evaluate the qualifications of certificated teachers.

Sub-standard certification. The practice of issuing *emergency certificates* or sub-standard "letters of authorization" became necessary because of teacher shortages resulting from the war, and the increased enrollments occasioned by the post-war population explosion. Emergency certificates to teach numbered more than 92,000 in 1962, and represented one of every fifteen classroom teachers in the nation. In spite of rising initial standards in most of the states, the practice of issuing emergency certificates has not declined. In 1960, there was an annual need for 110,000 teachers to replace those leaving, another 30,000 to serve increased enrollments, 30,000 to relieve overcrowding and eliminate half-day sessions, 20,000 to give instruction and services not currently provided, and at least 40,000 to replace the unprepared.[20] Thus, the annual need for 230,000 teachers reflects one of the major obstacles to advancing state certification requirements.

Hopeful signs. Several hopeful signs for the improvement of certification standards presage better things to come in American education. Emphasis by teacher preparation institutions upon greater depth, balance, and scholarship in subject-matter areas, a trend toward accreditation of teacher preparation institutions, and certification of non-public school and college teachers seem to promise substantially improved standards. A tendency toward *reciprocity* in certification, by which persons moving from one state to another may more easily obtain certification in the second state is noteworthy. Also under discussion by some professional groups is a certification requirement recommendation from the applicant's training institution. Although several of these practices are only in their initial stages, their potential influence promises to be enormous on upgrading certification programs in the several states.

Another trend affording promise of improved services to children is evidenced in the increased standards for certification renewal. Technological and sociological advances clearly indicate that educators must keep abreast of societal progress if they are to properly perform as teachers of children in a changing world. What better method can the state employ to upgrade teaching services than that of improved certification standards?

No certificated person ought to assume he is fully and forever qualified to teach, and without need to periodically add to his existing body of knowledge and skills. Teaching methods and materials change, making it imperative that in-service teachers seek personal and professional growth. In spite of the so-called *grandfather clauses*, guaranteeing that teachers shall not lose their rights established under existing licenses without due process of law, several states are adopting standards which require further university study, travel, or research for renewal of the teaching certificate. Thousands of school boards have similar regulations for continuing employment. As noted earlier, the gradual disappearance of life certificates may be considered in support of the idea that states intend to require teachers to continue to grow in order to keep their certificates in force.

---

[20]National Education Association. "The Teacher Shortage Analyzed," *Research Bulletin* (October, 1960), p. 74.

The State and Certification

The courts have consistently ruled that states have plenary power over educational matters, including the formulation of certification standards, the examination of teachers, and the issuance of certificates. As long as these functions are performed in a reasonable manner, the courts will not interfere. However, instances have often arisen in which persons seeking certificates, believing themselves qualified, have brought court action to force the issuance of a certificate. Such cases frequently depend upon whether the issuance of the certificate is a *ministerial* or *discretionary* function of the issuing agency or official. The former term indicates that the official *merely issues the certificate when all of a predetermined set of qualifications have been met*. The latter indicates that the official is called upon *to exercise judgment as to whether all the qualifications have been met*.

The question of whether school authorities may deny teachers a certificate will be controlled to a large extent by the terms of the applicable statute. Ordinarily, school authorities have discretion to determine whether an applicant possesses the qualifications made necessary by the statute, but once that determination is made by the authorities, their power of discretion is exhausted. If it is found that the applicant possesses the qualifications, the performance of the ministerial act of issuing a certificate becomes mandatory. The case of *Northington v. Sublette* is in point.

In that case, a teaching applicant took the required examination, but was denied a certificate, and instituted a proceeding in *mandamus* in a Kentucky court. Mandamus is a judicial investigation, the object of which is to secure or enforce a legal right through the performance of an act which the law specially enjoins as a duty. After hearing all of the evidence, the court held:

> It is true mandamus does not lie to control a discretion. It only lies to compel ministerial action. It lies against a board of examiners to compel them to decide what grade a teacher has made, but it does not lie to compel them to give the teacher a certain grade. In other words, if they made a mistake in grading the teacher that mistake cannot be corrected by mandamus; for in grading the teacher they must exercise their own judgment, and this cannot be controlled by the court. But when they have graded the teacher they have no further discretion. . . . if a teacher makes the required grade he is entitled to a . . . certificate, and the board, without special cause . . . has no right to withhold it from him.[21]

---

[21]Northington v. Sublette, 114 Ky. 72, 69 S.W. 1076, 121 A.L.R. 1472 (1902).

The court awarded the mandamus as prayed for by the teacher.

A teacher in San Francisco sought to renew her credential, presenting as evidence of successful experience her employment in the schools of that city for eleven years. A California law contained the provision that a tenure teacher must show verification of at least five years of *successful experience* as a basis for renewal of the certificate. Her credential had previously been renewed. The principal of the school in which the teacher was employed submitted a letter in which he stated that her work had been *unsatisfactory*. The Commission on Credentials denied her request for a renewal of her credential, whereupon she was dismissed from her position by the district board of education.

The teacher sought restoration, by mandamus, of her position in the school system, maintaining that since no charge of incompetency had been lodged against her in the eleven years of employment in the district, her legal rights were being violated. The court agreed with the teacher, and reinstated her. "Successful experience," said the court, "must be taken to mean a . . . period without charges of unfitness or incompetency ever having been filed against the teacher."[22] The renewal of the certificate was not a matter of discretion on the part of the Commission on Credentials, but was ministerial in nature.

Another legal principle is illustrated by the above case, *viz.*, that courts of law have consistently accepted the certificate as *prima facie* evidence of the competency of the teacher until such time as it has been proved to be otherwise. In cases where incompetency is given as a cause for dismissal of the teacher, or non-renewal of the certificate, it is not necessary for the teacher to prove his competency. The presence of a valid certificate is *ipso facto* an evidence of such competency. On the contrary, the burden of proof rests with those who initiate the charge of incompetency.

Whenever school authorities act in good faith in granting or withholding a certificate or in denying renewal of a certificate, they are not liable in damages for their error in judgment. If, however, such authorities act maliciously in withholding a certificate from an applicant lawfully entitled to it, an action in damages will lie.

Inasmuch as the state possesses the power to issue certificates, it follows that the state also possesses the power to revoke them. A license is, in the very nature of things, revocable. One who holds a license to teach does so at the pleasure of the issuing agency.

---

[22]Matteson v. State Bd. of Educ., 57 Cal. App. 2d 991, 136 P.2d 120 (1943).

State statutes may be silent as to the causes for which the state will revoke the certificate, or they may list the causes. The Nevada statute pertaining to the suspension or revocation of teaching certificates is typical of a class of legislation found in most states. In Nevada, the

> . . . state board of education shall have power to revoke any state diploma or any state certificate of any teacher, after notice and an opportunity for hearing before the state board of education, for:
> 1. Immoral or unprofessional conduct.
> 2. Evident unfitness for teaching.
> 3. Persistent defiance of or refusal to obey the laws of this state, the rules and regulations of the state board of education, or the rules and regulations of the superintendent of public instruction, defining and governing the duties of teachers.[23]

Another section of the Nevada statute provides for forfeiture or revocation of the teacher's certificate if the teacher knowingly reports, causes to be reported, or permits to be reported the presence of any pupil or pupils at school when such pupil or pupils were absent or when school is not in session.[24]

It is well settled, however, that where a statute authorizes revocation of the certificate for stated reasons, the certificate may be revoked for those reasons, and those reasons alone.

As a general principle of law, statutes must be narrowly construed, and, by implication, all other "reasons" not specifically enumerated in the statute will not constitute legal grounds for revocation of the certificate. The student should become familiar with the laws governing revocation in the state in which he wishes to teach and learn the causes for which the state may revoke the teaching certificate. An examination of revocation of the certificate, when the teacher wilfully breaches the contract, follows in the next chapter.

Accreditation

As indicated earlier in this chapter, accreditation as well as certification affords an avenue through which a state and voluntary organizations may improve educational opportunities. These avenues are important because they allow a state to meet the guarantee to provide equal educational opportunity to all children regardless of where they

---

[23]Nev. Rev. Stat. § 391.330 (1956).
[24]Nev. Rev. Stat. § 391.340 (1956).

live within the state. State constitutions invariably contain, either in writing or impliedly, some variation of this educational guarantee. The courts have specified that such a constitutional provision is a first lien upon the resources of the state. While such provisions do not necessarily mean *identical* facilities for all children, they do place upon the state government the responsibility of maintaining a *uniform* system of education.

To improve educational offerings in general, and to assist the state in its guarantee of equal educational opportunities, the legislatures have delegated to state departments of education the authority to evaluate the schools and to report the condition of the educational system from time to time. One method of evaluation takes the form of accreditation.

Accreditation is a designation applied to an educational institution to indicate that certain required standards have been met. The accrediting agency may be the state itself, through one of its subdivisions, or it may be a non-governmental, voluntary accrediting agency. Various types of the latter exist—a regional association of colleges and secondary schools, such as the North Central Association of Colleges and Secondary Schools; an association of practitioners, such as the American Medical Association or the American Bar Association; or a council composed of several groups or associations, such as the Council on Dental Education.

Considerable practical value has resulted from the use of accreditation in American education. The pioneer regional associations began operations as early as 1885, with the inception of the New England Association of Colleges and Secondary Schools. Initially, standards for accreditation of educational institutions were limited to qualifications of teachers, length of class periods, physical equipment and plant, and the morale of the staff. From time to time, various other standards were added—minimum salaries for teachers, professional preparation of administrative and supervisory personnel, and the financial adequacy of the institution's support. Bent and McCann[25] noted that the regional accreditation associations had exercised a very powerful influence upon the character of the American high school.

The practice of withholding state financial aid from unaccredited high schools until such time as these institutions met the accreditation standards was used in an earlier era of raising secondary school stand-

---

[25]Rudyard K. Bent and Lloyd E. McCann. *Administration of Secondary Schools* (New York: McGraw-Hill Book Company, 1960), p. 92.

ards. Recently, however, state departments have tended to be less directive and more permissive in exercising their accreditation authority. The upgrading of educational standards should be voluntary insofar as possible. In this respect, the six regional accrediting associations have made a unique contribution to the quality of American education.

There seem to be no court cases bearing directly on accreditation. The material contained in this section is presented to show the *extralegal nature* of the accreditation function in American education. Like numerous other cooperative efforts in education, accreditation has had its greatest effect through the concern and voluntary involvement of those interested in better schools.

Suggested Activities

DISCUSSION:

1. Why is teacher supply and demand frequently a controlling factor in the state's certification standards? Should this be so? If not, what may be done to remedy the situation?
2. What recourse has a teacher who, possessing an elementary credential, is nevertheless assigned to teach in the secondary school?
3. Resolved: That certification should be an exclusive function of state departments of education.
4. The following practices have been suggested to upgrade the certification program. Discuss the implications if each were adopted in your state.
   (a) State requires institutional approval for certification.
   (b) Colleges require greater breadth and depth in the liberal arts for prospective teachers.
   (c) All teacher preparation institutions must meet national accreditation standards.
   (d) Complete reciprocity of certification from one state to the next.

RESEARCH:

1. What types of certificates are issued in the state in which you are now teaching, or in which you wish to teach?
2. Who has the authority to revoke certificates in the above states?
3. Must a substitute teacher hold a valid certificate in the aforementioned state? Is this a state law, or simply common practice among most boards of education?

ROLE PLAYING:

1. With two classmates, imagine you are the Board of School Visitors interviewing William A. Alcott for a teaching certificate. Adapt your questioning to 1839.
2. Imagine you are a member of a modern board of education having

the privilege of issuing a certificate. What questions would you ask a candidate for the certificate?

SUMMARIZE:

1. The requirements for initial certification in the state in which you wish to teach.
2. The leading principles of law illustrated in this chapter.

CASE STUDY:

Case #1. A man who failed in college had "an overpowering desire to become a teacher." He taught three years in a large midwestern city on a teaching certificate obtained through false records which enabled him to pass as a teacher. His salary amounted to $15,000, of which $1,100 went into the pension fund. His deception was discovered and he was arrested. What recourse has the board of education to recover the money illegally paid him?

Case #2. A board of education refused to pay a teacher the first month's salary until the teacher had filed a valid certificate in the county superintendent's office, and signed an oath of allegiance, as required by state law. The teacher filed a valid certificate, but refused to sign the loyalty oath. May the board legally (a) pay the teacher for her work? (b) discharge the teacher?

Case #3. A college graduate, concerned by the teacher shortage, volunteered to teach free of charge if the district would accept his services. He did not possess the certificate to teach, nor was he eligible for one in that particular state. May the board legally accept his services *gratis* and assign him to classroom duty?

Further Readings

Burrup, Percy E. *The Teacher and the Public School System* (New York: Harper and Brothers, 1960), pp. 219-221.

Cubberley, Ellwood P. "The Certification of Teachers," *Fifth Yearbook of the National Society for the Scientific Study of Education* (Chicago: University of Chicago Press, 1906), pp. 7-88.

Edwards, Newton. *The Courts and the Public Schools* (Chicago: The University of Chicago Press, 1947), Ch. XIV.

Garber, Lee O., et al. *The Law and the Ohio Teacher* (Danville, Illinois: Interstate Printers and Publishers, 1956), pp. 49-53.

Gauerke, Warren E. *Legal and Ethical Responsibilities of School Personnel* (Englewood Cliffs, N.J.: Prentice-Hall, 1959), pp. 62-65.

Hamilton, Robert R. *Legal Rights and Liabilities of Teachers* (Laramie, Wyoming: School Law Publications, 1956), pp. 6-9.

Huggett, Albert J., and T. M. Stinnett. *Professional Problems of Teachers* (New York: Macmillan Company, 1956), Ch. 16.

National Education Association. *The Teacher and the Law.* Research Monograph, 1959-M3 (September, 1959).

Wellemeyer, J. Fletcher. *The Education of Teachers: Certification* (Washington: National Commission on Teacher Education and Professional Standards, November, 1960), 32 pp.

Wingo, G. Max, and Raleigh Schorling. *Elementary School Student Teaching* (New York: McGraw-Hill Book Company, 1960), Ch. 16.

Woellner, Robert C., and M. Aurilla Wood. *Requirements for Certification* (Chicago: University of Chicago Press, 1959), 134 pp.

Chapter IV

THE TEACHER'S CONTRACT

Introduction

In 1958, the National Education Association reviewed 715 court cases in which teachers were litigants between 1942 and 1957. Half of the cases were concerned with questions related to teachers' contracts and tenure rights. Another 90 cases related to contractual eligibility, certification, and appointment of teachers.[1] The comparatively large number of cases involving the contractual relationship of teachers and boards of education marks this as one of the most significant legal problem areas confronting the public school teacher. Clearly, teachers do not comprehend the nature, value, and limitations of their contracts of employment. It is also apparent that those administrators and school board members who contract with teachers are unaware of their duties and legal limitations in contract-making.

Contracting is seldom a simple matter, but the peculiar laws governing the teacher's contract create significantly special problems. Many legal questions face the teacher. Is the school superintendent a proper party with whom to contract? Must the contract be in writing? Are all mandatory clauses, such as relate to teacher loyalty or contract termination, included in the contract document? Can the rules and regulations of the board of education be changed and affect an existing contract of employment? This chapter concerns itself with those questions and the many principles of law governing the teacher's rights and liabilities in contracting.

---

[1]National Education Association. *Plaintiffs and Defendants—School Teachers in Court* (Washington: Research Division, NEA, April, 1958), p. 58.

The Contractual Relationship

The relationship between a teacher and the school authorities is created by contract. A contract may be defined as an agreement between two parties to do or not to do certain things. The teacher's contract of employment or contract of hire is an agreement whereby the services or labor of a teacher are stipulated to be given over a specific period of time for a certain salary and other fringe benefits. From a valid teaching contract, reciprocal obligations arise which are recognized and enforceable under the law. One whose contractual rights are threatened or ignored may seek the aid of the courts to enforce the fulfillment of the employment agreement.

The rules of law governing the ordinary contracts of the business world also apply to contracts for the employment of teachers except to the extent that state constitutions or statutes regulate such contracts. As might be expected, most legal problems stem from the contract areas controlled by constitutional and statutory provisions. Teachers and board members have great difficulty keeping informed of statutory changes governing teaching contracts because statutes vary from state to state, are subject to frequent change, are often mandatory in nature, and usually cannot be waived. A violation of the statutory provision may void the contract of employment and abrogate the attempted contractual relationship entirely. Consequently, the teacher must learn the law governing contracts and act in accordance therewith.

The language of the Colorado Court of Appeals serves to illustrate the legal principle that teachers will not be excused for ignorance of the controlling statutory law in contractual arrangements. In the case of *School District No. 46 of Sedgwick County v. Johnson*,[2] the court said:

> The teacher is required to have special training as to the school law, upon which she must pass an examination, and it must be assumed that, knowing the law, she . . . violated it, and . . . neither law nor equity affords her redress.

Elements of a Valid Contract

All contracts under the common law possess certain essential elements upon which their validity depends. A valid contract, including the contract for teaching services, has five basic elements, the absence

---

[2]26 Colo. App. 433, 143 Pac. 264 (1914).

of any one of which will render the contract null and of no effect. These five elements are as follows:

1. The contract must be between competent parties;
2. The contract must be based upon mutual assent;
3. The contract must contain a valid consideration;
4. The contract must contain rights and liabilities sufficiently definite to be enforceable; and
5. The contract must be of such a nature as not to be prohibited by statute or common law.[3]

Since it is assumed that those who contract do so in full knowledge of their rights and limitations and in full knowledge of the law, a more detailed examination of these basic elements will follow. At the same time, consideration will be given to special statutory provisions that often regulate these basic elements in the teacher's contract of employment.

Competency of the parties. In general, the parties to the teaching contract are the teacher and a board of education. The legal *competency* of the contracting parties refers to the authority to contract which each must possess in order for the law to recognize the validity of the contract and enforce its provisions. Before the teacher is competent to contract for a teaching position in a school system, he must have eligibility and capacity to contract.

We have noted in Chapter III that the teaching certificate, while not a contract, is evidence that the teacher has eligibility to contract. Allen[4] described the distinction between *eligibility* to contract and *capacity* to contract in this way:

> Eligibility to contract should not be confused with capacity to contract. Eligibility to contract is a specialized condition or status prescribed by the state or its representative, while capacity to contract is one of the essential requisites of all simple contracts. One does not need to be eligible to contract for the purchase of a house or to rent a farm but one must be eligible to teach a school or to practice either law or medicine. In other words, a professional status or condition must precede or accompany the contractual status. The term usually applied to such professional status of the teacher is known as "eligibility."

---

[3]Newton Edwards. *The Courts and the Public Schools* (Chicago: University of Chicago Press, 1947), p. 171.

[4]Ira M. Allen. *The Teacher's Contractual Status as Revealed by an Analysis of American Court Decisions* (New York: Columbia University, 1928).

It is well established that teachers, lawyers, doctors, and others who perform their duties under a commission from the state must first become eligible to contract through possession of the necessary license or certificate. They must belong to a class of persons who possess the eligibility to contract as well as the capacity to contract. The majority of court cases involving teacher contracting have developed from the fundamental dependence of valid contracts on proper certification.

To have the capacity to contract, the teacher must meet the requirements as to age, citizenship, marital status, etc., as they are imposed by the state legislature. Few legal problems arise for teachers in this area.

The extent of the authority or competency of school districts, through their boards of education, to enter into contracts of employment with teachers depends on the terms of the statutory grant. The school district, as a quasi-corporation, has only such powers as are expressly or impliedly conferred upon it by the sovereign which created it. Hence, boards of education are limited in their capacity to contract by the amount of authority which has been delegated to them. The state constitution or statutes are the source of authority for the employment of public school teachers.

Persons dealing with a board of education are assumed to know the legal limitations under which the board operates. Teachers, as well as others, must realize that any contracts entered into by boards of education which go beyond the limits of the board's authority are *ultra vires*, outside the powers conferred upon the board by the statutes under which the board was instituted, and so the contract may be held to be of no legal effect.

This legal principle governing the teacher's responsibility to know the law has been stated by a Nebraska court in the following:

> The powers of the officers of the appellee [school district] are limited and can only be exercised as the statute provides. The appellant [teacher] is legally charged with notice of the extent of such power and the manner in which it must be exercised. . . . Therefore, under the express provisions of these statutes, the appellant was not qualified to enter into a contract with appellee nor was the appellee through its board, authorized to enter into a contract with the appellant and as provided in the statute such contract shall not be valid nor shall any recovery be had thereon.[5]

---

[5]Zevin v. School Dist. No. 11 of City of Cozad, Dawson County, 12 N.W.2d 634 (Neb. 1944).

Statutory authority to contract for teaching services is, with few exceptions, vested in the board of education of each school district, and not in one of its employees. The superintendent of schools, for example, may usually only recommend to the board that a teacher be issued a contract of employment. Because the superintendent is experienced in school matters and the selection of teachers, his recommendation is often controlling in the board's decision to contract with a teacher. But superintendents, as employees of the board, are not legally capable of consummating a contract because the board alone has been given that right. When the superintendent does contract with a teacher, the validity of that contract depends upon subsequent ratification by the members of the board. Cases often arise in which a teacher claims a contractual relationship because of agreements reached with the superintendent or a member of his staff, but because the superintendent lacks any power to contract, such cases are without merit.

In the absence of statutory restrictions, boards of education are not required to employ any particular person, and their reason for refusing to employ a teacher is not subject to legal inquiry. The board is generally free to exercise very broad discretion in hiring new teachers. In some jurisdictions, however, no person related to a board member within a certain specified degree of consanguinity may be employed by the school district. These statutes governing nepotism are mandatory and must be strictly observed in all instances of teacher employment. Similarly, a board of education may not employ one of its own members as a teacher.

Whenever a conflict of interests appears likely, the capacity to contract should be questioned. For example, a duly elected county superintendent of schools lacked the legal capacity to contract for a position as a teacher in the county, even though she volunteered to serve as county superintendent without compensation. She possessed the proper teaching certificate and was thus eligible to contract, but the state attorney general determined that an incompatibility existed in the two positions that denied the teacher's capacity to contract in that county. Citing a statutory provision that the duty of a county superintendent "includes the duty to exercise a careful supervision over the schools of his county" and to "fill vacancies on the school board," the attorney general said:

> It appears to me that the above-mentioned provisions of the statute clearly indicate that the duties of a county superinten-

dent of schools and a teacher are inconsistent and that it would not be proper for one person to hold both positions.[6]

The opinions of attorneys-general are advisory in nature, but they are ordinarily given the force and effect of law until they are overruled by court decision.

The manner and mode of contracting by boards of education may determine the validity of a contractual agreement. The state statutes are generally quite specific in the procedure that must be followed by the board in the conduct of its business. For example, the board meeting at which the business of a teacher's contract is conducted must be a legally convened meeting. Proper notice of the meeting must have been given; the meeting must be held within the territorial limits of the school district; a quorum of the board members must be present. Board members must act as a unit, not as individuals, when transacting district business. Action taken by individual members outside a legally convened meeting, or by a number less than a duly constituted quorum will not legally bind the district.

In the past half-century there have been few cases in which the board's capacity to contract has been in issue. One such case arose in Colorado in 1929 when the validity of several contracts was attacked on three grounds: (1) that one of the officers was not duly elected and was thus unlawfully acting in the capacity of board secretary (the election for secretary had resulted in a tie vote; the officer was the incumbent); (2) that the meeting at which the contracts were approved was not lawful because it was not a regular meeting nor properly a special meeting, since the board did not meet on the day prescribed by statute for regular meetings and had no rule of its own for holding special meetings; and (3) that the meeting was unlawful because one board member was not in attendance. (He had refused to attend.)

The court decided each of the important questions raised in the case in a manner favorable to uphold the validity of the contracts. The court reasoned that:

> (1) The acting secretary was without question either a *de jure* or *de facto* officer, and the act of a de facto officer is as binding as that of a de jure officer;
>
> (2) No formal action with reference to the calling of a special meeting of school directors is necessary in order to make a special meeting valid in the absence of a by-law or other board

---

[6]Colorado State Department of Education, *School News*, (October, 1960).

rule on the matter. By statute a special meeting informally called by two of three members of a board is a legal meeting; and

(3) One member of the board cannot be permitted to defeat or obstruct the transaction of business of a distict by refusal to attend a legally called meeting.[7]

Mutual assent. The second element of a valid contract is mutual assent. When two parties desire to bargain with each other, they normally negotiate until one or the other definitely promises to do or not to do something in return for a corresponding promise. This promise is called an *offer*; the response on the part of the other party is called *acceptance*. Acceptance validates the agreement, provided, of course, that the other elements essential to the formation of a contract are present.

The *offer and acceptance* aspects of contracts are many and varied. Fundamental to offer and acceptance is the rule that there exist a concurrence of assent on the part of both the offeror and the offeree, both in point of time and as regards the subject matter of the agreement. This assent is called a *meeting of the minds*, or mutual assent. The rule of mutuality was expressed by a North Carolina court in these words, "One of the essential elements of every contract is mutuality of agreement. There must be neither doubt nor difference between the parties."[8]

Similarly, concerning the need for each contracting party's clear intent, a Missouri court said:

> The meeting of the minds, which is essential to the formation of a contract, is not determined by the secret intentions of the parties, but by their expressed intention, which may be wholly at variance with the former.[9]

An offer may be withdrawn by the offeror at any time prior to its acceptance. Therefore, a board of education has the power to revoke or cancel its offer of employment at any time before the teacher accepts the offer. A valid acceptance of the offer must be within the terms of the offer as made by the board. If the teacher finds only a part of the offer acceptable, he may make a *counteroffer*. Under the rule of counteroffer, the parties change places—the offeree becomes the offeror, and vice versa.

---

[7]School Dist. v. Angus, 85 Colo. 505, 277 Pac. 466 (1929).
[8]Kirby v. Stokes County Bd. of Educ., 230 N.C. 619, 55 S.E.2d 322 (1949).
[9]Brewington v. Mesker, 51 Mo. App. 348, 356 (1892).

When an offer has been made, the offeree has the power to cause a contract to come into being. The exercise of the power constitutes the acceptance of the offer. Before a teaching contract may result, the offeree must either (1) communicate his acceptance to the offeror, or (2) act or speak in such a manner that it may reasonably be assumed that he has accepted the terms of the offer. In the first instance, the terms of the contract are usually reduced to writing. In the second, a contract may result, even though not reduced to writing, as an *implied contract*.

A teacher's contract of employment, like other contracts, need not be reduced to writing unless a statute requires a written contract. Even when no statute requires written contracts, nothing prohibits boards of education from insisting upon written contracts with new teachers and with permanent teachers in order that they may avoid the vexation of disputes arising over the substance of verbal agreements. Many state statutes expressly or by implication provide that contracts of employment must be in writing.[10] Generally, such requirements are mandatory and an oral contract of employment is unenforceable even though the teacher has partly performed the contract. Unless the requirement of writing is complied with, no valid contract exists, and the action taken by a board of education is subject to rescission or revocation by it.

Under the *statute of frauds,* usually a part of the law of each state, a contract that cannot be completely performed within one year from the date of its making is unenforceable unless it is in writing and properly signed. The mischief to be guarded against by the statute of frauds is the leaving of the proof of a contract, which is to run beyond a year, dependent on the memory of the parties to the contract or their witnesses. Many teaching contracts are not completed within the one year period and could be found invalid under this statutory requirement.

The desire for certainty as evidenced in the statute of frauds is also a part of the law which operates once the contract is in writing. The written contract should contain all of the terms agreed to by the parties. For that reason, courts will not permit the admission of parol (oral) testimony to alter a written contract in which the terms are plain and unambiguous.[11] This attitude on the part of courts affords protection to both parties, inasmuch as neither party may later claim,

---

[10]See Beach v. Ellis School, 68 S.D. 86, 298 N.W. 727 (1941).

[11]Wing v. Glick, 56 Iowa 473, 9 N.W. 384 (1881).

through the introduction of oral evidence, that the manifested and clearly ascertainable intentions of the parties as shown by the terms of the contract were otherwise than those contained within the written instrument itself. This evidentiary rule of courts is stated in a Pennsylvania case in this manner:

> . . . All negotiations leading up to the contract are presumed to be merged in the writing; moreover, oral testimony is not admissible to explain the written document in the absence of an ambiguity requiring such explanation.[12]

Whenever a contract is ambiguous or expressed in language that needs clarification, the courts will sometimes admit parol evidence to aid in the interpretation of the contract. The purpose of such admissibility of parol evidence is not to change the meaning of the contract or to add to it, but to enable the court to reach an understanding as to the rightful meaning of the written document. The courts will not do for a man what he has failed to do for himself, for as a man contracts, so is he bound. The intent of the contracting parties, as expressed in the written document, is the courts' only concern. Once that is established, provided that the contract is a valid one, the courts will not stand in the way of its enforcement.

In a 1955 case dealing with offer and acceptance, a district was negotiating with the plaintiff teacher for possible rehiring at a reduced rate in salary. The teacher was given fifteen days to consider the offer. Further consultation with the president of the board resulted in a conditional higher offer by him, but the plaintiff rejected his offer. The board was notified and another teacher was hired. The teacher, contending that she had accepted the board's offer, brought action to enforce the purported contract. The court found that there was no acceptance. One cannot accept an offer, said the court, yet take time to think it over. Acceptance is *in prasenti* (at the present time). The plaintiff's contention was inconsistent.[13]

An Iowa case illustrates the principle that *as a person contracts, so is he bound.* A teacher signed a contract containing a clause providing that if enrollment in the school became less than a specified number, the contract would be null and void. Later, before the year was completed, the school board closed the school when the enrollment dropped below the specified number. The teacher's suit to recover the salary for the remainder of the contractual period was unsuccessful. Said

---

[12]McCormack v. Jermyn, 351 Pa. 161, 40 A.2d 480 (1945).
[13]Delberra v. School Dist., 97 Colo. 517, 51 P.2d 350 (1935).

the Supreme Court of Iowa, in ruling on the validity of the contract:

> In any event, the second paragraph of the statute states, "Said contract shall remain in force . . . except as modified or terminated by mutual agreement of the board of directors and the teacher," thus clearly recognizing the right of the parties to the contract to terminate it by mutual agreement. If this may be done after the contract is entered into, it would seem the parties should be able to agree in the contract itself upon its termination upon the happening of a certain event such as a smaller enrollment than six. . . . If they may voluntarily abridge the length of time after the making of the contract, they necessarily had the same power in the making of the contract.[14]

The court denied the claim of the teacher, and held in favor of the board of directors.

A valid contract of employment, of course, must be free from fraud. Either party to a contract may avoid a contract which was induced by fraudulent misrepresentation so that the party agreed to something different than that which he intended. If a teacher makes a false representation of a material fact with the intent to cause a board of education to enter into a contract of employment, he may have his contract voided by the board.

A case based upon misrepresentations constituting fraud is that of *Guilford School Dist. v. Roberts*[15] in which the teacher stated, in her first interview with the school trustee, that she was not married and did not intend to be married during the school year. The trustee told the teacher that he would not employ a married woman as a teacher. Two months later, the teacher signed a contract in her maiden name, withholding the fact that she had been married four days earlier. When the marriage was discovered, the teacher was discharged. She sued for breach of contract and was awarded recovery in the lower court. The district offered as defense the argument that the contract was procured by fraudulent representations. The plaintiff had concealed her social status and had deceived the trustee. In ruling that the teacher could not enforce reinstatement of her position, the appellate court said:

> The condition of employment was that the plaintiff was unmarried, and would remain so for a limited time. Plaintiff made her employment conditional upon a promise not to

---

[14]Miner v. Lovilia Independent School Dist., 212 Iowa 973, 234 N.W. 817 (1931).
[15]28 Ind. App. 355, 62 N.E. 711 (1902).

marry. The verdict of the lower court, being without evidence to support it, is set aside. Judgment reversed.

Valid consideration. One of the essentials of any valid contract is a valid *consideration*, either a benefit to the promisor, or a loss or detriment to the promisee. This element of a contract is illustrated in a case which came before the Court of Appeals of Ohio. Superintendent Melvin was employed by the school board on July 15, 1938. On May 17, 1940, the board carried a motion to the effect that Melvin be "reappointed for a term of one year and eleven months beginning September 1, 1940." The superintendent did not come under the tenure laws of Ohio.

Some time later, a new board was appointed and received from the city solicitor the advice that, since the board had fixed no salary, the May 17 motion created no binding contract. The board thereupon passed a resolution that the position of superintendent was vacant.

Melvin immediately brought an action in mandamus to compel the board to recognize him as superintendent. The court stated:

> No inference as to the amount of compensation can be drawn from the language used by the respondent in the resolution of May 17, 1940. . . . As an appointment without compensation . . . would not be binding upon the relator, neither would it be binding upon the respondent. There would be no consideration for the promise and, therefore, no binding contract.[16]

Melvin's contention that the amount of salary was implied from past salaries held no weight with the court.

To the same effect as the *Melvin* case was one tried by a Kentucky court in 1902. The contract between the board of trustees and one Mingo stated that he (Mingo) would be principal for so many months "for the public money, which will be apportioned among them according to an agreement yet to be made by them and the teachers." Two other teachers were also appointed; the words "apportioned among them" evidently referred to the three parties.

The Kentucky statute required that the trustees agree as to compensation, and that the contract be in writing. Another principal was hired to serve, and Mingo brought action to recover damages for breach of contract. The Court of Appeals of Kentucky said:

> There was a failure to agree upon appellant's compensation; that was left for future agreement. . . . There was no

---

[16]State ex rel. Melvin v. Board of Educ. of City of St. Bernard, 670 Ohio App. 330, 34 N.E.2d 285 (1940).

written contract in contemplation of the law, and no cause of action exists.[17]

Definite terms. The fourth element of a valid contract relates to the *terms* thereof. It is a well settled principle of law that a contract lacks validity when the rights and liabilities of the contracting parties are not sufficiently definite as to be enforceable. A contract to pay a teacher "good wages" was held by one court to be invalid because of this defect.[18] Contracts which do not specify the beginning and ending of the term of employment have likewise been held to be unenforceable. In *Taylor v. School Town of Petersburg*,[19] a teacher filed an application for a position as a teacher. The school board met in regular session, and a motion was carried to hire the teacher for the ensuing year. The board's minutes were silent as to when the schools were to begin, the day and month and grade that the teacher was to teach, and the compensation to be paid. The teacher was not permitted to teach and brought suit to force the board to honor her contract. The court said, "A teacher cannot recover from a school corporation for the breach of an executory contract, [a contract in which a party binds himself to do a particular thing but which has not yet been performed], unless it is so full and definite as to be capable of specific enforcement." Therefore, since the resolution of the school board failed to state the terms of employment with particularity, the contract was declared by the court as so indefinite as to preclude the plaintiff teacher from recovering for its breach.

The case of a Mississippi teacher likewise failed because of a lack of definiteness of terms. Said the court in that case:

> Although it appears in the case before us that the appellant may have been unwilling to accept the position as principal of the school . . . except for the oral agreement that he should receive an increase in salary above the $120 per month, definitely specified, if the funds available should be sufficient for that purpose, and that he relied upon such agreement in good faith, nevertheless . . . the agreement for such increase was invalid and unenforceable against the county for the reason, first, that it rested entirely in parol, and second, it was void for uncertainty in that the amount of the extra compensation to be paid was not specified before the services were rendered.[20]

---

[17]Mingo v. Trustees of Colored Common-School Dist. No. A, Gerrard County, 113 Ky. 475, 68 So. 483 (1902).

[18]Fairplay School Township v. O'Neal, 127 Ind. 95, 26 N.E. 686 (1891).

[19]33 Ind. App. 675, 72 N.E. 159 (1904).

[20]Morris v. Robertson, 189 Miss. 592, 198 So. 290 (1940).

Teachers should carefully examine proffered contracts to determine whether the terms are sufficiently definite as to be legally enforceable. Should a question arise in this regard, an attorney should be consulted.

Not prohibited by the law. The courts will not enforce any agreement prohibited by legislation or the common law. Among the more common statutes barring or limiting the making of a valid contract are those concerning contracts which are made on Sunday, are in restraint of trade, are based on gambling or usurious interest rates. Any agreement which involves the commission of a tort or a crime is similarly contrary to public policy and unenforceable. Teachers are unlikely to be confronted with legal problems in this area when contracting for employment.

The Teacher's Contract

Since early colonial days, teaching in the United States has been an itinerant occupation.[21] Colonial schools were related to the church; a "slip" in orthodoxy on the part of the teacher might cause the church congregation to invite the teacher to seek employment elsewhere. School committees certificated and employed teachers for short periods of time. Teachers worked at agricultural tasks during the farming season and spent the winter in the classroom. Promotions ordinarily were gained by moving from one job to another slightly better until the top had been reached. Local control of education seemed to limit lengthy tenure in any one place, for as the board changed, so did the philosophy of the board, and with the philosophy, the school teacher. Lack of professional preparation tended to make teaching a sometime thing. Low salaries often caused teachers to move from one place to another in search of economic security. There was little incentive for teachers to stay long in one teaching situation.

As a teacher moved from one teaching position to another, he sought to contract under terms agreeable to his personal desires. It was an individual matter rather than an effort to gain job security and higher wages through profession-wide cooperative endeavor. Hence, contractual relationships historically were between the teacher as an individual, and the board of education itself, as contrasted with the group approach to contracting today. The arrangements were "talked out" and embodied in the original contractual agreement,

---

[21]Albert Huggett and T. M. Stinnett. *Professional Problems of Teachers* (New York: The Macmillan Company, 1956), p. 179.

whether oral or written. The contract was modified from year to year as the needs of the board and the teacher changed.

Gradually, administrators began to assist the board in the recruitment, employment, and assignment of teachers. As a consequence, a different contracting procedure developed. Whereas oral contracts between the teacher and board had once been common, the larger number of teachers and the intervening administrative corps led to the need for written contracts and more group-centered procedures. Contracting was further affected by the adoption of continuing contract and tenure statutes and other legislative regulations affecting the relationship of teacher and board. In addition, boards began to adopt written policies and by-laws on a wider scale, the conditions of which were included in the teacher's contract by implication. Finally, changes in the teacher's role and the lengthened school year made it necessary to change the mode of contracting.

Colonial contracts. The colonial teacher's contract contained detailed and specific duties required of the teacher. For example, a contract between a Dutch schoolmaster and the Board of Overseers of Flatbush, New York, in 1682, revealed the multiple nature of the schoolmaster's duties—teacher, chorister, janitor, and sexton. The hours of school and the responsibility of the schoolmaster for teaching the catechism, prayers, and psalms was clearly stated in the written document. The teacher was required to lead the children in reciting religious rites in the church on Sunday, a church which, under the terms of the contract, he was to keep clean, heated, and lighted. He rang the bell, read the Ten Commandments, and led the congregation in singing. When the regular minister was absent, he read a sermon on "the explanation of the catechism." He provided a basin with water for holy baptism, brought the bread and wine for holy communion, and stood by while the minister baptized infants. When a member of the congregation died, the schoolmaster dug the grave, issued funeral invitations, and tolled the bell to the limits of the town. However, the contract provided that additional money be paid for digging the grave and spreading the news beyond the limits of the town. The specified salary consisted of four hundred guilders, valued at Seewant and delivered at Brooklyn Ferry in grain, and the use of a dwelling house, barn, and meadow belonging to the school district.

In addition to his salary, the schoolmaster was entitled to receive from those who attended the school certain moneys in the form of tuition which he was allowed to keep. A day-school speller or reader paid three guilders a quarter; a writer paid four guilders. The contract further provided extra compensation for teaching adults in night classes.[22] Little wonder that colonial school masters were ever ready to move on.

A schoolmaster in New Amsterdam about the same date agreed under contract to teach gratuitously the poor and needy "who ask to be taught for God's sake."[23] A minister in Newburg, New York, in 1752, agreed to teach under an agreement that allowed no children incapable of studying the approved curriculum to be admitted, but which admitted children of poor parents *gratis*, so long as they exhibited strong natural ability in the Classics. The proceeds of certain public lands under the English patent were pledged for the payment of the minister-teacher.[24]

Today's teaching contract. Until recently, school boards attempted to include in the written contract document all of the duties which the teacher was expected to perform. The practice of including a comprehensive listing of duties inevitably resulted in a most lengthy document. Even then, it was virtually impossible to cover every exigency which might arise. Thus, the *long form* of the teaching contract was amended in the second quarter of the present century, and the *short form* took its place. This newer, more abbreviated form of contract is based on the understanding that all school board rules and regulations, as well as state statutes bearing on teachers' contracts, and all other extraneous limitations, are included *by implication* in the document in the interest of brevity. There is no attempt to include *all* the duties which the teacher will be called upon to perform: these are "read into" the short form and become implicit in it. The teacher, therefore, should not assume that the wording of the short form contains a comprehensive listing of the board's expectation of his work. Further examination of the rules and regulations which bear on the contract, and the statutes which control its implementation, are necessary before the full significance of the teacher's contract can be ascertained.

Figure 4-1 illustrates the short form of contract. Among other things, the contract refers to the state statutes, rules and regulations of the state board of education, and the rules and regulations of the board of education of the local district (paragraph 2 of the contract).

---

[22]Ellwood P. Cubberley. *Readings in Public Education in the United States* (Boston: Houghton Mifflin Company, 1934), pp. 67-68.

[23]*Ibid.*, pp. 66-67.

[24]*Ibid.*, p. 69.

BOULDER VALLEY PUBLIC SCHOOLS
BOULDER, COLORADO

PROFESSIONAL CONTRACT

The Board of Education of School District No. Re 2, Boulder County, Boulder, Colo., has appointed

you, ...to the staff of the said District for the term from

....to...at a salary

of..dollars

to be paid in ....equal monthly installments, as provided by said Board of Education.

YOUR APPOINTMENT IS SUBJECT TO THE FOLLOWING, TO WIT:

1   That you file in the office of the Superintendent of Schools an acceptance of your appointment within ten days from this date.

2.   The laws of the State of Colorado, including but not limited by the provisions of Chapter 123-17-17 Colorado Revised Statutes 1953, the rules and regulations of the State Board of Education of Colorado, and the rules and regulations of the Board of Education of said District.

3.   That you furnish said Board of Education, upon demand, an official birth certificate and a physician's certificate showing that you are in good health.

4.   That you are qualified and licensed to teach in the position for which you are employed, as provided by the laws of the State of Colorado, and that said qualifications and license remain in full force and effect during your employment by said School District.

Dated this the..................... day of.................................

Board of Education
School District No. Re 2, Boulder County
Boulder, Colorado

By..
President

ATTEST·
....
Secretary

BOARD OF EDUCATION, SCHOOL DISTRICT NO. Re 2
Boulder County, Boulder, Colorado
GENTLEMEN: ....19........
I hereby accept the above appointment and agree to the terms thereof.

....

....

Form c-100d 500 4/81

Figure 4-1

AN ILLUSTRATION OF THE SHORT FORM OF TEACHER'S CONTRACT

Each of these is a part of the contract under the legal *doctrine of incorporation by reference*. This doctrine was discussed by the Supreme Court of Delaware in these words:

> It is . . . axiomatic that a contract may incorporate by reference provisions contained in some other instrument. . . . However, one of the well settled exceptions to this rule is this:—that an agreement will not be deemed to incorporate matter in some other instrument or writing except to the extent that the same is specifically set forth or identified by reference.[25]

Because it is not necessary that the contract of employment be a single instrument, the teacher must become familiar with these other parts of the contract.

Legislation. As noted earlier in the chapter, it is essential that a teacher's contract of employment comply with all mandatory requisites prescribed by the state statutes. Through its legislative power, the state not only regulates the form of the contract, it also becomes a part of that contract. Even when the contract of employment is silent concerning existing constitutional and statutory provisions, such provisions are considered a part of the contract. Furthermore, the state legislature has the power to alter the school laws and the teacher's contract is subject to the operation of future amendments as well as the existing law.

A Pennsylvania court has considered this legal concept in the case of *Malone v. Hayden*[26] where it said:

> . . . The contract which the school teachers have with the state is a qualified contract. It is subject to delimitation of its operation by subsequent statutory change.
> . . . The constitutional requirement that the General Assembly shall provide for the maintenance and support of a thorough and efficient system of public schools demands that all matters, whether they be contracts bearing upon education, or legislative determinations of school policy, or the scope of educational activity, must at all times be subject to future legislative control.

Not only must the *form* of the contract accord with the state statute, but also the *mode* of contracting must comply. Where statutory provisions are ignored, or carelessly performed, chaos may sometimes result. A Missouri case is in point. A statute of that state

---

[25] Hirst v. Black, 46 Del. 295, 83 A.2d 678 (1951).
[26] 329 Pa. 213, 197 Atl. 344 (1938).

provided that failure to notify a teacher of his non-employment by April 15 would automatically constitute re-employment for the ensuing year. A board of education, not certain of finding another teacher, hesitated to dismiss a teacher, wishing to "remain on the fence." But in so doing, it neglected to notify the teacher by the appointed date. During the summer, another teacher was employed. On the first day of the fall term of school, both teachers appeared at the school, together with the members of the board of education! One can imagine the confusion which resulted.

The board members told the children to obey the second teacher, not the first. The board then sought an injunction against the first teacher to vacate the school, turning it over to the second. The court ruled that the first teacher was entitled to the position, inasmuch as the board had failed to follow the letter of the law in serving notice before the date specified. The court further noted that the plight in which the board members found themselves was "solely the result of their own failure to proceed in accordance with the statute hereinbefore referred to." To follow the statute in making the contract was mandatory, and was not a question open to the discretion of the board.[27]

Statutes which control the legal relationship between the board of education and the teacher are not often mentioned in the contract itself. It is taken for granted that the board and teacher are aware of such statutory provisions and conduct themselves accordingly. In some of the states, however, the statutes provide specifically that each teacher's contract shall contain on its face certain provisions, e.g., provisions concerning loyalty oaths, penalty for breach of contract, and health examination requirements. Thirty-three of the states in 1959 required the teacher to sign a loyalty oath before entering upon teaching duties. In nineteen of the thirty-three, the teacher must swear to discharge faithfully the duties of the teacher; in eight states, the teacher must swear to teach specific aspects of patriotism. In a few states, the teacher must swear to refrain from advocating overthrow of the government or from teaching specified theories of governmental organization.[28] It was not mandatory in each of the states that the loyalty oath explicitly appear in the teaching contract. Such provisions may be implied, but need not be included per se in the contract instrument. Other statutory provisions pertaining to membership in professional organizations, teacher tenure and retirement, the display

---

[27]Community School Dist. No. 27 of Gasconade County v. Brinkmann, 233 S.W.2d 768 (Mo. 1950).

[28]National Education Association. *Research Bulletin* (December, 1959), p. 116.

of the flag, and similar rules customarily are included in the contract by implication.

State department rules and regulations. By virtue of state statutes or state constitutional provisions, state departments of education are commonly charged with the responsibility of furnishing an efficient state-wide system of public education and enforcement of the school laws. These state groups are limited in their power by the legislative language creating them, but they usually possess explicit or implied power to prescribe rules and regulations for the government of the public schools. State departments of education have variously been given power to determine the general educational policies, particularly in respect to teachers' qualifications, the education curricula, and the public school supervision.

To determine the extent to which the rules and regulations of a state education department become binding on a teacher, if at all, it is necessary to examine the law of a particular state. A state department of education may be enjoined on the grounds that it has gone beyond the power conferred on it by the law of the state. Whenever the rule or regulation does not conform to statutory provisions, it will be of no effect.

In *State ex rel. Sights v. Edwards*,[29] a discharged teacher was trying to invoke a regulation of the State Board of Education of Indiana that established a form of discharge procedure that had not been followed by the school district. An Indiana statute made it the duty of every officer, or board, having power to make rules and regulations to submit such rules and regulations to the attorney general and governor who must then approve them to make them effective. Because the regulation in the case had not been so approved, it was ineffective and could not be invoked.

In the case of *State ex rel. Hirst v. Black*,[30] noted earlier in this chapter in its discussion of the doctrine of incorporation by reference, it was provided in a teaching contract that the teacher "agreed to observe and enforce the school laws of the State of Delaware, the Rules and Regulations of the State Board of Education, and the Mount Pleasant Special School District." At the time the teacher signed the contract of employment, she was handed a pamphlet containing the rules and regulations of the school district, but not a copy of the rules and regulations promulgated by the state board of education. The

---

[29]228 Ind. 13, 89 N.E.2d 443 (1950).
[30]46 Del. 295, 83 A.2d 678 (1951).

rules and regulations of the state board provided for the teacher's salary on a per diem basis but the teacher's contract clearly indicated that a monthly basis of payment was contemplated by the parties. In determining that the regulations of the state board were not a part of the teaching contract in this regard, the court said:

> . . . . Would a reasonable person in the light of such language and all the surrounding circumstances here mentioned, believe that she was being charged with knowledge of regulations of the State Board dealing with compensation not made available to her and which she had never seen? To me the use of the words "observe and enforce" connote an agreement bearing on the conduct of a school teacher in the execution of her duties as such—for instance, to agree to observe all regulations requiring teachers to behave themselves with decency both in and out of school, of those dealing with discipline, standards of teaching and a hundred and one other subjects which might readily come to mind; but not with those governing compensation already clearly set forth in the contract itself.

Whether the rules and regulations of the state board or department are a part of the teacher's contract of employment can be determined only after careful consideration of a particular factual situation, and in the light of the power of the board to make such rule or regulation as evidenced by the language of the particular state statute.

School board rules and regulations. Within reasonable limits, boards may adopt rules and regulations for the control of the schools under their charge. All rules and regulations in force at the time of the signing of the teacher's contract of employment become an integral part of the contractual agreement by implication. Some statutes provide that such rules and regulations are to be furnished to the teacher when the contract is made. Such a statute in Missouri provides that the rules and regulations of a school board shall be considered a part of a teacher's contract of employment, provided such rules and regulations are furnished to the teacher by the board when the contract is made. A Missouri teacher violated a board rule which was known to her even though she had not been given a copy of the board's rules and regulations. In a subsequent legal action, the court said:

> While the statute does not provide that a copy of the rules and regulations should be furnished to the teacher, in writing, yet this would be the safest method for the school board to pursue. However, it is our opinion that if a teacher has actual knowledge of a rule or regulation of a school board, before the contract is entered into, that the purpose of the statute

would be served and that the teacher who has actual knowledge of a rule or regulation and violates it cannot thereafter complain that the rules and regulations were not furnished.[31]

Some question may arise, however, as to whether rules and regulations adopted *after* the contract is drawn are binding on teachers in the absence of a statute. For example, in an Illinois case, a tenure teacher challenged a board regulation adopted subsequent to the attainment of tenure status by the teacher, which specified that all tenure teachers must take some graduate college work in order to advance on the salary scale. The teacher sued to force the board to give him a raise in salary, even though he had not met the requirement. The court held that the rules and regulations in effect at the time of the annual automatic renewal of the teacher's contract were part of the contract, and that the teacher on tenure was subject to all reasonable rules and regulations which might be adopted from time to time by the board.[32] The rule seems a reasonable one. Were it otherwise, school boards would be unable to promptly meet new situations and considerable damage to the school's educational program would inevitably result.

An Indiana case illustrates an application by the court of the same principle of law. A tenure teacher declared his candidacy for state representative. The board immediately passed a ruling that any school employee elected to a political office would be required to take a leave of absence without pay. The teacher brought action to recover wages lost through enforcement of the rule. Said the court, in declaring that the rule applied to the contract, even though made after the teacher had attained tenure:

> This rule, general in terms and applying to all teachers, does not to us seem such an unreasonable exercise of the board's powers as to warrant judicial interference. The board, not the courts, is charged with the duty of managing the school system and so long as it acts with fairness its decisions on matters within its discretion are not subject to judicial review.[33]

It is important for the teacher to note that board rules, statutes, or rulings of the state board of education passed subsequent to the signing of the contract of employment become effective immediately upon adoption by the respective body. Consequently, it is not necessary to

---

[31]Strayhorn v. Blodgett Consol. School Dist. No. 35, 86 S.W.2d 374 (Mo. 1935).
[32]Richards v. Board of Educ. of Twp. High School Dist. No. 201, 171 N.E.2d 37 (Ill. 1961).
[33]School City of E. Chicago v. Sigler, 219 Ind. 9, 36 N.E.2d 760 (1941).

wait until the anniversary of the contract for the governing body in question to put new rulings into effect. Of course, the teacher must have constructive knowledge of the new ruling, such as a general announcement or notification by letter, before he can be expected to comply.

Court decisions. Teacher's contracts may ultimately be subject to interpretation by the courts. Such interpretation may relate to the validity of the contract, or to a word, clause, or other part of the contract that establishes the rights or obligations of the parties. Teachers' contracts are construed under the general law of contracts which regulates the construction and operation of the ordinary contract. The court will examine the contract as a whole in its effort to determine the intention of the parties at the time they contracted. The words used by the parties in the contract will be considered in the sense of construction placed upon them by the parties themselves whenever possible, unless those words have been given statutory definition and it appears that they have been used in their statutory sense. If uncertainty or ambiguity exists, the courts will construe the terms of the contract in the light of conditions and circumstances surrounding the parties at the time the contract was executed.

When there is an alleged infraction of a rule or regulation that is a part of the contract, the court will use the test of reasonableness in examining that rule or regulation. What is considered reasonable in one factual situation, may not be equally reasonable in another. During the depression of the 1930's, a rule providing for automatic dismissal of female teachers who married during the school year was widely accepted. Under altered circumstances, as during a period of teacher shortage, such a rule might be considered unreasonable.

Earmarks of a Good Contract

Employment contracts for teachers received special attention following World War II, and the qualities of an ideal contract are still of consuming importance to teachers and school authorities. The result of this attention has been the refinement of the contracting process and all its ramifications, including the contractual document itself. The consensus seems to be that no ideal *single* contract is suitable to the needs of all school boards, but it is generally conceded that the better contracts contain certain desirable features. Indicative of the emphasis on better contracts was the work done in Michigan by Wesley E.

Thomas, who described the desirable features of the contract form as follows:

1. It is simple. It does not include clauses, terms, and phrases that are unnecessary.
2. The length of the school year and the opening date are clearly stated.
3. The salary and method of payment are clearly stated.
4. The services as a teacher are stated.
5. The rights of the school board or superintendent relative to teacher assignment or transfer are definite.
6. The sick leave plan is stated clearly.
7. Provision is made for signatures by authorized officers of the school district and the teacher.
8. The contract does not contain a detailed list of teaching duties.
9. It does not contain 15-day, 30-day, or some other cancellation clause.
10. It does not include a list of causes for dismissal. These usually are hard to define and difficult to enforce. The courts will uphold any just and reasonable cause for dismissal.[34]

The short form of the teacher's contract most nearly meets these criteria. When the short form is used, however, the teacher should request that he be furnished copies of the rules, regulations, and other laws that are considered a part of the contract and will govern his teaching. Boards of education may not furnish all of these documents, but they should be prepared to supply copies of their own rules and regulations. The other rules, regulations and laws may often be secured from the state department of education.

Ratification of the Contract

A contract invalid in its inception may become enforceable by subsequent board action. Such action is known as *ratification*. Where, for example, a teacher is employed under an invalid contract, and the board allows her to teach and actually pays her wages, the contract *may* become binding as if valid from the first. The general rule is that a school board may ratify any contract which it had the power to make in the beginning, but that no amount of action will suffice to ratify a contract which the board had no power to make in the first instance. Hence, contracts in excess of a constitutional debt limit, or

---

[34]Wesley E. Thomas. "A Good Contract for Teachers" *Michigan Education Journal* (January, 1958), p. 182.

those with teachers who do not possess the teaching certificate may not be ratified. Neither may a board validate through ratification contracts with one of its members, which is against public policy, or oral contracts when the statute clearly specifies that contracts must be in writing.

Ratification of a teacher's contract of employment may be expressed or implied; it is not necessary that a board take formal action to ratify a contract. The mere acceptance of a teacher's services, approval of the teacher's work, payment of the teacher's salary, or concurring or acquiescing therein, usually constitutes ratification in the legal meaning of the term.

Sometimes the courts will allow recovery on invalid contracts on the theory that, even though the contract is invalid, the board should pay for the services rendered. However, such ratification will ordinarily be allowed only to the extent of the degree of performance, and not to the full extent of the contract. Said an Oklahoma court in ruling on the question of the ratification of an oral contract, when the statute called for contracts to be in writing:

> We hold, therefore, that the ratification herein extends only to the period of performance and such oral contract cannot be enforced in its entirety. The plaintiff having been paid for the services actually rendered by him, the defendant's liability has been settled in full and the plaintiff cannot recover in this action.[35]

Renewal of Contract

Except to the extent that the state constitution or statutes provide for the renewal of the teacher's contract, there is no legal duty on the part of the board of education to re-employ a teacher after the expiration of his contract. The teacher has no right to re-employment even though his services have been satisfactory, no complaint or charge has been made against him, and he is qualified to continue teaching in the school district.

The decision of the board of education not to re-employ a teacher involves an unrestricted exercise of discretion. In the absence of statutory requirement, the board need not assign a cause or state its reasons for the decision, and a teacher is not entitled to a hearing on the matter. Even though the school authorities conspire to dispense with a teacher's services at the end of his contract, it is not unlawful.[36]

---

[35]Williamson v. Board of Educ. of Woodward, 189 Okla. 342, 117 P.2d 120 (1941).

[36]Morse v. San Diego High, 34 Cal. App. 134, 166 Pac. 839 (1917).

In many jurisdictions, state statutes provide for the renewal of teachers' contracts of employment. These are discussed more fully in Chapter V.

Breach of Contract

After the parties have bound themselves to a valid contract of employment, they must perform according to the contract terms or subject themselves to the legal consequences. The board of education may not terminate the teacher's services during the life of the contract, except on the grounds specifically set forth in the contract, so long as the teacher is able to perform his duties. When a contract provides for its termination "on reasonable grounds" or "for just cause," the test of reasonableness must be employed to determine whether a valid excuse for non-performance exists.

Several states have enacted legislation pertaining to breach of contract on the part of the teacher. The penalties for the teacher's refusal or failure to fulfill the terms of the contract range from censure or payment of a fine to suspension of the license to teach. For example, the Michigan School Code deals with this matter as follows:

> The State Board of Education shall have the authority to suspend for the reasons and in the manner herein provided any certificate issued to any teacher who refuses without sufficient cause, in the opinion of said board, to perform a lawful contract to teach. . . . Such suspension shall not be for a longer period of time than the end of the school year in the district in which such contract was violated. During the time such certificate is suspended, such a teacher shall not be qualified to teach in any school in this state in which teachers are required to hold a certificate.[37]

The statute further provides that a school board bringing charges of breach of contract against a teacher must follow specific procedures, including filing a signed complaint, providing for a hearing, allowing the teacher to answer charges, assignment of court costs, and the right of appeal. Similarly, upon a teacher's failure or refusal to fulfill a contract, without receiving a release from the board, or giving thirty days' notice of intention to cancel the contract, the Colorado School Code provides that:

> . . . It shall be the duty of said school board, upon the breach of said contract, to file a sworn affidavit setting forth

---

[37]Mich. School Code, Ch. 24-340.861.

the facts of such employment with the person or board who has authority to license teachers in Colorado. The licensing board shall notify said teacher to appear before said board within thirty days and show cause why the said teacher's license may not be suspended during the period of the contract. The licensing board shall thereupon hold a hearing, and if they find that the teacher has violated said contract without just cause therefor, they may suspend said teacher's license during the period of such contract.[38]

The object of the law obviously is to prevent "contract jumping" by those who may be holding a contract while looking for a more favorable contract elsewhere. Against those persons, the law will not permit willful breach of contract. The Colorado statute further provides:

It shall be lawful for a board of directors to assess a teacher up to and including one-twelfth of his annual salary for failure to complete his contract between August first and the close of the regular school term, unless release is granted by the board of directors of the school district. Every teacher's contract thereinafter entered into shall contain a clause that the same is subject to the provisions of this section, mentioning the chapter of the statutes wherein same appears.[39]

Consequently, all contracts of employment for Colorado teachers must contain, among other things, the provision for loss of pay equal to one-twelfth of the annual salary for breach of contract after August first, presumably to compensate the board of education for the loss of money occasioned by the necessity of obtaining another teacher.

In states where there is no statute bearing on the subject, the decision on a penalty for breach of the teaching contract devolves upon the courts. While courts do not have the power to cancel the teacher's certificate, in several instances they have assessed money damages against the teacher under a finding of breach of contract.

A recent nation-wide poll conducted by a leading educational magazine revealed that, of the superintendents responding, 81 per cent favored setting a date after which no teacher would be released from a signed contract in order to take a position in another school district.[40] The results of the poll undoubtedly reflect a reaction occasioned by the difficulty and added costs of recruiting able teachers at the last moment. The ethics of the teaching profession call for greater

---

[38]Colo. Rev. Stat. § 123-17-17 (1953).

[39]*Ibid.*

[40]Public Opinion Poll, *Nation's Schools* (September, 1958).

observance of the integrity of the teacher's contract. When teachers look upon the contract as "a mere scrap of paper," the state must take the necessary steps through legislative action to protect the sanctity of the contractual arrangement. Certainly the profession should be aware that when attempts to upgrade contractual practices through ethical means fail, legal avenues must be opened for the purpose. Each teacher, therefore, as a member of the profession, should adhere to the highest ethical standards in contracting. Only in this way will it remain unnecessary for the state to resort to legal channels for relief in breach of contract cases.

Suggested Activities

ROLE PLAYING:
1. As a principal, explain to the prospective teacher what extra duties other than classroom teaching will be expected which are not clearly stated in the contract document.
2. Assume you are a teacher making an application to the board of education in Ruralville. Discuss with the board of education members the conditions of the teaching contract.

RESOLVED:
1. That the *long* contract, as used in colonial times, is more effective in defining the duties of the teacher, than is the more recent short form.
2. That teachers' contracts should be in writing, even though the statute declares that oral contracts are binding.

DISCUSS:
1. What is the effect of a contract signed by board members individually at different times when prior corporate action has been taken in a legally-called meeting to employ a teacher?
2. What benefits to teachers in contracting might accrue from wider adoption of certification reciprocity agreements between the states?
3. Are there conditions under which a teacher is justified in breaching the contract?
4. What penalities should attach to breach of contract on the part of the teacher who accepts a more lucrative position elsewhere?
5. Why do the courts take the point of view that teachers and board members contract with a full knowledge of the laws affecting contracting?

SUMMARIZE:
1. The elements of a valid contract.
2. The statutes governing contracting in the state in which you wish to teach, as to prescribed form of the contract; whether oral or

written; board action necessary; date of notification of non-renewal; and the effect of outside forces on the contract, such as the inclusion of board of education rules and regulations.
3. The rules relating to *quantum meruit.*
4. Possible defects in the contract document.

Further Readings

Allen, Ira M. *The Teacher's Contractual Status as Revealed by an Analysis of American Court Decisions* (New York: Teachers College, Columbia University, 1928), pp. 44-88.

Burrup, Percy E. *The Teacher and the Public School System* (New York: Harper and Brothers, 1960), pp. 221-225.

Cubberley, Ellwood P. *Readings in Public Education in the United States* (Boston: Houghton Mifflin Company, 1934), Ch. III.

Edwards, Newton. *The Courts and the Public Schools* (Chicago: University of Chicago Press, 1955), Ch. XXI.

Gauerke, Warren E. *Legal and Ethical Responsibilities of School Personnel* (Englewood Cliffs, N. J.: Prentice-Hall, 1959), pp. 67-76.

Grismore, Grover C. *Principles of the Law of Contracts* (Indianapolis: The Bobbs-Merrill Company, 1947).

Hamilton, Robert R. *Legal Rights and Liabilities of Teachers* (Laramie: School Law Publications, 1956), Ch. II.

Henson, Ray D. (ed). *Landmarks of Law* (New York: Harper and Brothers, 1960).

Huggett, Albert J., and T. M. Stinnett. *Professional Problems of Teachers* (New York: The Macmillan Company, 1956), Ch. 8.

Kearney, Nolan C. *A Teacher's Professional Guide* (Englewood Cliffs, N. J.: Prentice-Hall, 1958), Chs. 10 and 11.

Messick, John D. *The Discretionary Powers of School Boards* (Durham, N. C.: Duke University Press, 1949), Ch. X.

Moore, Harold E., and Newell B. Walters. *Personnel Administration in Education* (New York: Harper and Brothers, 1955).

National Education Association. *The Teacher and the Law* (Washington: Research Division, NEA, 1959).

Remmlein, Madaline Kinter. *School Law, Second Edition* (Danville, Illinois: Interstate Printers and Publishers, 1962).

RIGHTS OF TEACHERS

*Tenure and Retirement Rights
of Teachers*

*Employee Welfare Rights
of Teachers*

*Political and Personal Rights
of Teachers*

Chapter V

TENURE AND RETIREMENT RIGHTS
OF TEACHERS

Prologue

WHEREAS, there are pending before the Legislature of the State of Minnesota, certain bills which, if enacted into law, would materially decrease the amount of income for said school district for the ensuing years, and

WHEREAS, the School Board of Independent School District No. 9, Itasca County, Minnesota, will be unable to determine until on or about the 22nd day of April, 1939, whether such measures will become laws, and

WHEREAS, under Chapter 161, Law of Minnesota for 1937, commonly known as the Teacher Tenure Act, the School Board of said school district must make any changes in teachers' contracts which are to take effect for the next school year on or before April 1st of each year, or must discharge teachers by terminating their contracts before April 1st, which said contracts would then remain in force to the end of the school year, 1938-1939, and

WHEREAS, the said School Board wish in fairness to all their employees who come under the provisions of the Teacher Tenure Act to make no adjustments in salaries which are unwarranted by the final circumstances which will be determined on the basis of whether or not the aforementioned bills become laws;

NOW, THEREFORE, be it resolved, by the School Board of Independent School District No. 9, Itasca County, Minnesota, at a meeting thereof duly called and legally held in the Nashwauk High School, at 7:00 p.m., on the 8th day of March, 1939, all members being present, that the assistant superinten-

> dent and all teachers now in the employ of said Independent School District No. 9, Itasca County, Minnesota, be discharged, effective at the close of the school year of 1938-1939, it being the intent of the said School Board that all teachers and other employees coming within the provisions of Chapter 161 of the Law of Minnesota for 1937, be discharged so that all such contracts will terminate at the close of the school year in 1939.[1]

So read a resolution by a Minnesota board of education in 1939. Some teachers affected by the resolution brought suit to enjoin the board from its enforcement. The Supreme Court of Minnesota was called upon to decide whether there had been a valid determination to discharge the teachers under and pursuant to the 1937 act referred to in the resolution.

In examining the case, the majority of that court said:

> The purpose of that [teacher tenure] act (L. 1937, c. 161) was to do away with the then existing chaotic conditions in respect to termination of teachers' contracts. Until then, in many cases teachers would be left in a state of uncertainty as to whether they would be re-elected for the ensuing year. In many instances this state of uncertainty ran over a period of months. The later in the year that a school board acted, the greater the teachers' disadvantage in finding vacancies elsewhere. That was the situation sought to be remedied. Under it a deadline of April 1 was fixed. If no termination had been made prior thereto and adequate notice given to the teacher, absent mutual consent by the teacher and the board, the contract continued in full force and effect.[2]

On the grounds that a public body may not be permitted to do indirectly what it was prohibited from doing directly, the court ruled that the board had acted illegally in discharging the teachers, and ordered them reinstated. Since the board obviously acted arbitrarily, and "before it was hurt," it should not be permitted to destroy the rights of those teachers who because of no failure or incompetency on their part would be gravely injured by the implementation of the resolution. A court order re-instituting the status quo was issued.

Tenure Laws and Continuing Contracts

Basic to an understanding of employment practices is an explanation of the three types of teachers' contracts: (1) the annual, or limited

---

[1]Downing v. Independent School Dist. No. 9, 207 Minn. 292, 291 N. W. 613 (1940).
[2]*Ibid.*

contract; (2) the continuing contract, sometimes referred to as the spring notification type; and (3) the tenure, or permanent contract. A description of each of these types of contracts follows.

The annual contract. Under the annual contract, the teacher is subject to non-renewal of the contract upon its completion. In the eyes of the law, non-renewal of an annual contract does not constitute dismissal in the same sense as non-renewal of contract of a teacher who is on tenure. The board merely has not found it expedient to offer the teacher another contract. Boards of education, furthermore, are under no legal compulsion to show cause for non-renewal of an annual contract. Although some boards, because of public relations and their concern for ethical principles, may choose to provide a hearing and show cause for non-renewal of an annual contract, they are generally not required by law to do so. As a rule, therefore, relief through administrative procedure or the courts is not available to the teacher under annual contract to compel renewal of contract, in the absence of a statute guaranteeing such procedures.

As a probationary teacher, or one of those who teach in a state utilizing the annual contract of employment exclusively, one's rights under the law are limited. Many thousands of educators teach under the annual contract, and their re-employment is solely at the pleasure of the board of education.

Continuing contract. The second contractual arrangement recognized in law is the continuing or spring notification contract. Of the thirteen states lacking tenure laws in 1959, five had mandatory continuing contract statutes of the spring notification variety. In another state, Virginia, the continuing contractual arrangement was optional with local boards. Seven of the states in 1959 utilized the annual contract exclusively in contracting with teaching personnel.

Statutes in the six states which utilized the continuing contract for teachers provided that the contract was automatically renewed for the ensuing year when notice to the contrary was not received by the teacher on or before a specified date, usually April 1 or 15. In Virginia, if neither party served notice by April 1 of intention not to renew, the contract was automatically renewed for another year.

In the continuing contractual arrangement, there are none of the elements of notice, statement of charges preferred, or guaranteed right to a hearing which characterize the true tenure statute. The teacher has little more security than under the annual contract, inasmuch as ordinarily no causes for non-renewal of the contract need be given by the board. However, the continuing contract affords a certain measure of protection to the teacher following the cut-off date, because the contract binds the board which fails to notify a teacher of non-renewal before the date specified in the statute.

Tenure legislation. In 1959, at least thirty-seven of the states and the District of Columbia had some variation of the tenure principle in force. In six of the states, tenure was optional with local boards of education, while in thirty-one, tenure statutes applied at some levels or all levels in a mandatory manner to the entire state. A few states made a practice of exempting smaller districts, or extending local option to the smaller districts, while making tenure mandatory for the larger districts.

The following pages contain an explanation of tenure laws as they affect the teacher in the classroom. The purposes of tenure legislation, the validity of such law, and cases illustrative of the protective nature of tenure legislation are given. The procedure by which a board may legally dismiss the teacher who has attained "tenure status" is likewise treated in some detail. The first section concludes with a perusal of the rights of the teacher under permanent tenure.

Purposes of Tenure Legislation

A traditional objection to teaching as a lifetime career prior to the late nineteenth century was that it offered the teacher little job security. Several practices were cited in support of this view. Under common law, a board could refuse to renew a teacher's contract for any reason or for no reason at all. Sometimes political favors were repaid by employing those who were relatives or friends of influential citizens. A board might save money by dismissing higher paid teachers and employing those who would work for lower salaries. In most cases, the discharged teachers had no recourse to law; the system allowed their dismissal not because of incompetency in teaching, but because ability to hold the teaching position depended at all times upon full acceptance at the hands of the board of education.

Tenure legislation began through an adaptation of the federal civil service laws of 1883 to the teaching profession. The first state to adopt a tenure law for teachers was Massachusetts, in 1886. Other states followed slowly, and by 1959, more than three-fourths of the states had some variation of tenure, continuing contract, or fair dismissal legislation. Chief among the promoters of tenure laws were teachers' professional organizations, which looked upon tenure legislation as providing improved services to children, in addition to affording job security to the teaching fraternity.

Tenure legislation changed the common law right of boards to dismiss teachers at pleasure, and substituted a permanent basis for contracting. The courts consistently upheld tenure legislation. In doing so, judges advanced some of the most cogent reasons for tenure laws to be found anywhere.

For example, the Supreme Court of Minnesota, in discussing the purposes of tenure legislation in 1938, said:

> Teachers' tenure, like civil service and other similar movements, dates back now over a period of many years. The abuses existing by reason of the "spoils system" which came into prominence during Jackson's administration, later followed by national and other administrations, led to much-deserved criticism. That is why on January 16, 1883 ("An act to regulate and improve the civil service of the United States," 22 Stat. 403), the first civil service act was passed. In 1885, the National Education Association brought forth the question of tenure of school officials. A committee of that association studied the matter and later submitted a report. Generally speaking, the tenure so sought was interpreted to mean, in substance, the application of principles of civil service to the teaching profession. It was thought that for the good of the schools and the general public the profession should be made independent of personal or political influence, and made free from the malignant power of spoils and patronage. In 1886 the state of Massachusetts enacted a law "relating to the tenure of office of teachers." (St. Mass. 1886, c. 313). Thereunder school districts were permitted to enter into contracts with teachers for a longer period than one year. In 1889 the committee on rules of the Boston School Community suggested a tenure law providing for a probationary period of one year, four years of annual elections, and thereafter permanent tenure subject to removal for cause after proper hearing. The bases for recommendations were that better talent would be attracted to the teaching profession; that annual contracts theretofore in vogue had not resulted in the elimination of poor, incompetent, and inefficient teachers; that the principle of annual election or appointment was not generally applied to policemen, firemen, or judicial officers, and in the very nature of things should not apply to teachers; that not infrequently the best teachers were discharged for inadequate reasons. . . .
>
> Foreign countries have long recognized the principle of teachers' tenure. . . . Since 1900 the principle of teachers' tenure in this country has developed more rapidly. In a general way it has followed the civil service pattern. The objec-

tives sought have been to protect the teachers against unjust removal after having undergone an adequate probationary period; that the movement itself has for its basis public interest, in that most advantages go to the youth of the land and to the schools themselves, rather than the interest of the teachers as such.[3]

A tenure law is defined as a statute which (1) provides for continuing employment of the teacher who has acquired tenure status, so long as service rendered remains satisfactory, and (2) contains a specific procedure to be followed if there is just cause for dismissal. Both provisions must be present in order for a statute to be properly called a tenure law. The purpose of the first provision, continuing employment based on good behavior, is obviously to protect the teacher from arbitrary and dictatorial dismissal where performance is acceptable. The purpose of a specified procedure is to provide an orderly sequence of steps by which a board may dismiss the teacher who is incompetent, immoral, or lacking in professional sensitiveness to his job. In those states having good tenure legislation, the result has been to protect competent and qualified teachers during good behavior against removal for unfounded, flimsy, or political reasons. Viewed in this light, tenure legislation has been in the public interest, inasmuch as it benefits teachers and affords to children a better educational opportunity. Hence, the courts have been reluctant to interfere in the exercise of board power in actions involving tenure of public school teachers, where the board has acted within its powers.

Said a Louisiana court in 1938:

> The teacher tenure act was designed to accomplish a laudable purpose. If sanely and impartially administered, the beneficent results to inevitably follow will vindicate the persistent efforts of its champions in procuring its adoption. It was intended, inter alia, to protect the worthy instructors of the youth of the parish from enforced yielding to the political preferences of those theretofore having the power to grant or withhold employment and to vouchsafe to such teachers employment, after a long term of satisfactory service to the public, regardless of the vicissitudes of politics or the likes or dislikes of those charged with the administration of school affairs.[4]

A Pennsylvania court gave the following purposes for teacher tenure legislation:

---

[3]McSherry v. City of St. Paul, 202 Minn. 102, 277 N.W. 541 (1938).
[4]Andrews v. Union Parish School Bd., 184 So. 574 (La. 1938).

To maintain an adequate and competent teaching staff, free from political and personal and arbitrary interference, whereby capable and competent teachers might feel secure, and more efficiently perform their duty of instruction.[5]

Among the many groups advocating the adoption of teacher tenure laws was the National Education Association. The objectives of tenure were announced by the Committee on Tenure and Academic Freedom of the NEA as follows:

1. To protect the classroom teacher and other members of the teaching profession against unjust dismissal of any kind—political, religious, or personal;
2. To prevent the management or domination of the schools by political or non-educational groups for selfish and other improper reasons;
3. To secure for the teacher employment conditions which will encourage him to grow in the full practice of his profession, unharried by constant pressure and fear;
4. To encourage competent, independent thinkers to enter and to remain in the teaching profession;
5. To encourage school management, which might have to sacrifice the welfare of the schools to fear and favor, to devote itself to the cause of education;
6. To set up honest, orderly, and definite procedures by which undesirable people may be removed from the teaching profession;
7. To protect educators in their efforts to promote the financial and educational interests of public school children;
8. To protect teachers in the exercise of their rights and duties of American citizenship; and
9. To enable teachers, in spite of reactionary minorities, to prepare children for life in a republic under changing conditions.[6]

With respect to the procedure to be included in the tenure laws of each state, the same NEA committee recommended a nine-point program of essentials to be guaranteed each tenure teacher as standard procedure to be followed upon his discharge:

1. Adequate notice would be given and a written statement of charges provided;
2. The teacher would be represented by counsel in all cases;

---

[5]Bragg v. School Dist. of Swarthmore, 337 Pa. 363, 11 A.2d 152 (1940).
[6]National Education Association. *Trends in Teacher Tenure Through Legislation and Court Decisions* (Washington: The Association, 1957), p. 8.

3. Testimony of witnesses at the hearing would be taken under oath or affirmation;
4. The teacher would have the right to subpoena witnesses;
5. Admissible evidence would be restricted to that bearing directly on the charges presented;
6. The teacher would have the right to argument on evidence and the law;
7. Stenographic transcripts of evidence and argument would be available;
8. The hearing would be held before the entire school board and arguments would be presented before the board as a whole; and
9. A vote of at least a majority of the entire board would be necessary before any action to dismiss would be final.[7]

Not all these guarantees were present in the tenure laws at the time of the statement in 1959. As legislatures become more aware of the value of tenure legislation, more orderly and equitable procedures for the conduct of hearings affecting teachers on tenure in this country are being adopted.

Illustrative of the protective purposes of tenure legislation was a case which arose in California in 1935. There a board of education was unanimously opposed to the policy of the state's teacher tenure law, and therefore knowingly re-employed no teachers for more than three consecutive school years so as to deny them the attainment of tenure. A teacher in the district taught successfully for three consecutive years, whereupon the superintendent asked her if she wished to be re-employed. She replied affirmatively. In response to this, the superintendent wrote the teacher a letter dated May 24, 1931, which read in part:

> I find only one fly in the ointment and that is the question of tenure. Members of the high school board have expressed themselves as opposed to placing any more teachers under tenure and the board passed a resolution by unanimous vote, with all members present, memorializing our representatives in the Legislature to repeal the tenure law.
> The new tenure law will not go into effect until August and specifically provides that all teachers under tenure at the time that it goes into effect shall retain their tenure so the only way out that I can see would be for you to tender your resignation and let it be accepted at the next regular

---

[7]National Education Association. "Teacher Tenure Laws," *Research Bulletin* (October, 1960), pp. 84-85.

meeting of the board prior to June 10, because if you were re-employed for a fourth year you would become a permanent teacher under the existing tenure law and unless you resign, even failure on the part of the board to notify you by June 10 that your services will not be required for the ensuing year, would amount to re-employment.

When your resignation is accepted, you will be entirely free to accept employment elsewhere and the board will be entirely free to employ someone in your place. If no one were employed in your place before the new law goes into effect, then I think that the board could select you as well as any one of the other applicants that might be candidates for the position and not be compelled to give you the status or classi-fication of a permanent teacher.

. . . I would suggest that you file your resignation because in any event it would be better to have the records show the acceptance of your resignation than to have them show re-fusal to re-employ you even though the reason might be the tenure law.[8]

After receipt of the letter, the teacher had a conference with the superintendent, at which he positively assured her that if she filed the formal resignation she would be re-employed. Being anxious to retain her position, she consented to this procedure and signed a printed form of resignation prepared by the board. Her resignation was promptly accepted; in August she applied for re-appointment and on the 24th of that month a board minute order was adopted re-employing her for the following year as a probationary teacher. She continued to serve for the entire year, and sought through court action to determine her tenure status under the California law. The court held that she had attained permanent status. Said the court:

Even though it be deemed that the members of the board did not deliberately procure her purported resignation for the purpose of avoiding the tenure law, one of the members of the board had full knowledge of the promise of re-instate-ment by the superintendent and had immediately followed his recommendation by re-appointing her; we must assume that the board at least acquiesced in the purpose and the promise of re-instatement by means of which her resignation was procured. This would amount to a circumvention of the purpose of the law, and the status of a permanent teacher may not be thus denied.[9]

---

[8]Sherman v. Board of Trustees of Siskiyou Union High School, 9 Cal. App. 2d 262, 49 P.2d 350 (1935).
[9]*Ibid.*

Validity of Tenure Laws

Tenure legislation has been consistently upheld by the majority of courts. The legislature, having complete power over schools and school district employees, has plenary power over the question of teacher tenure based on satisfactory service. Early objections that tenure laws were class legislation, that they interfered with the freedom to contract, or violated certain constitutional provisions have been rejected by the courts. Even where the legislature has failed to exercise its power to pass tenure legislation, a board of education has been held to have the power to adopt a resolution providing for tenure for its teachers.[10]

In six of the thirty-seven states having tenure legislation in 1959, tenure was optional with local boards of education, while in thirty-one, the statutes applied at some level or all levels in a mandatory manner to the entire state. A few states had the practice of exempting smaller districts, or extending local option to smaller districts, while making tenure legislation mandatory for all larger districts.

A few statutes of this nature extended tenure to classroom teachers only, while others included superintendents, principals, and supervisory personnel. In five states, superintendents were explicitly excluded by statute from attaining tenure; in twelve states they were explicitly included. A few statutes defined the word "teacher" to include all persons regularly certificated by the state. Under this type of legislation, an administrator was implied to have gained tenure when statutory provisions covering teachers had been met. In one or two states, tenure provisions extended only to those who taught for a major portion of the day. In several of the states where administrators were covered by tenure laws, the statute provided that these persons were not covered if they taught less than a major portion of the school day.

Probationary Period

All but two of the states require that teachers serve a probationary period, usually three years, before attaining tenure status. During this period, the teacher is on an annual contractual basis, and is subject to non-renewal of the contract at the discretion of the board. In practice, tenure is attained when the teacher has served continuously on a regular full-time basis for the specified period of time, then is appointed for the year immediately following the probationary period. Service as a

---

[10]Ironside v. Tead, 28 N.E.2d 399 (N.Y. 1940).

substitute, special teacher, part-time, or supply teacher ordinarily will not qualify one for tenure status. Should the teacher move to a new position in another district, the statutes almost unanimously provide that he must serve the full probationary period in that district before being admitted to permanent status.

In California, a teacher was notified that she would not be re-appointed at the end of the regular probationary period, in this case, at the end of the third year. During the following year, she served for a few days as a substitute teacher and for a short period of time in the summer school. The following year she was re-employed, and served as a full-time teacher for three years. She was again notified that she would not be employed for the fourth year. The teacher challenged the board's right to dismiss her at the end of the probationary period, and re-hire her as a probationary teacher. The court ruled that the board had acted legally in dismissing the teacher. She was not entitled to tenure status on the basis of having been employed for intervening short periods of time as a substitute teacher or part-time instructor.[11]

In a few states, the tenure statutes provide that no teacher may be advanced to tenure status without the recommendation of the superintendent. If the superintendent fails to make such a recommendation, the board has no legal right to re-employ the teacher and place the teacher on tenure. The board must at all times follow closely the limitations of the tenure law, no matter what those stipulations may be, e.g., in some states, the probationary teacher gains tenure status automatically, if he is rated satisfactory within the last four months of the probationary period, or if refused tenure status, the board must file specific reasons for such action.

It has been held in some jurisdictions that a teacher not on full-time contract may attain tenure status. Here the distinction seems to be related to whether the teacher is a *regular* teacher, as contrasted with a casual or temporary teacher. The test is upon the scope and purpose of the employment, rather than upon the length or regularity of time. In Indiana, for example, a teacher had been employed for six years at a fixed salary even though she taught only twelve days per month. The Supreme Court of Indiana held that she was entitled to tenure. The fact that she taught less than every hour of every school day did not prevent her from being regarded as a "regular" teacher.[12]

---

[11]Baldwin v. Fresno City Unified School Dist., 125 Cal. App. 44, 269 P.2d 942 (1954).

[12]Sherrod v. Lawrenceburg, 213 Ind. 392, 12 N.E.2d 944 (1938).

In Montana, a teacher who had taught full-time for 2⅓ years, and part-time for another five years, was ruled to have attained tenure status, although the statutes of that state provide that any teacher who shall be elected for a third consecutive year in a school district of the state shall be deemed to have been re-elected from year to year thereafter. The court pointed out that the work of this teacher was not essentially different from that of any other teacher of the district, although it was not equal in amount to a full-time teacher's load.[13]

Reduction in Salary, Demotion, and Transfer

May the tenure teacher be transferred, demoted, or suffer a reduction in salary? This question has often been before the courts for interpretation. Under some of the statutes, teachers have no protection against these changes; that is, the teacher has no vested right to the particular position or the salary which he holds. Generally speaking, tenure legislation does not entitle a teacher to a vested right to a *particular* position in the school system, or a particular *step* on the salary scale. Rather, the law merely provides that the teacher has the right to continuing employment so long as service is satisfactory, and when he is dismissed, it shall be according to a specified procedure. It seems well settled that the teacher may be transferred from one position within the district to another, so long as it does not amount to a demotion. Just what constitutes a demotion is, of course, different in each case, and a matter for the court to ultimately decide.

Restrictions on the lowering of a tenure teacher's individual salary may be included in the tenure statute, but this does not prevent the board from lowering all teachers, or lowering all elementary or secondary teachers as a class. Some laws provide that an individual teacher's salary may be reduced when a proportion of all teachers, such as seventy per cent, are lowered. The restriction is upon the board's lowering an individual's salary without cause. So long as it acts reasonably, and without discrimination among teachers, a board may change salary schedules from time to time, either upward or downward. The Supreme Court of Indiana, in ruling on this matter, said:

> By the great weight of authority, the rule seems to be that a tenure act does not preclude the employing agency from reducing the teacher's compensation below what it was be-

---

[13]State ex rel. Saxtorph v. District Court of Fergus County, 128 Mont. 353, 275 P.2d 209 (1954).

fore the breach occurred, so long as the salary to be paid equals or exceeds the minimum fixed by law and the teacher's classification for that purpose is not arbitrary nor unreasonable. This is necessary in order that administrative officers may be free to exercise the sound discretion with which they are charged. . . .[14]

With respect to demotion, the same court, in ruling on a case in which a superintendent had been transferred from that position to a position as principal, stated:

> There is nothing in the act specifying a particular position for any teacher. The act provides that a teacher who has been employed continuously for five successive years, and thereafter enters into a teacher contract for further service, shall become a permanent teacher in such corporation. It does not specify that the teacher must hold the same position, but only that he is a permanent teacher in the school corporation.[15]

Similarly, in a Minnesota case, the supreme court of that state declared:

> Notwithstanding a teacher has acquired tenure status, he may be . . . transferred from class to class, or building to building, or division to division without a resulting "discontinuance of position," and without seeming loss of caste, provided he is not thereby demoted. But though the power so to transfer teachers unquestionably exists, it must be exercised in good faith and for the best interest of the school district.[16]

Courts will not permit a board to transfer a teacher to a position in which the teacher is not qualified, then dismiss her for lack of qualification. Neither will they permit a transfer to a location where the teacher cannot find lodging, or where he would be forced to travel long distances to reach the school. The teacher is protected from transfers involving an entirely different kind of position, where in effect the transfer is tantamount to dismissal. Courts have ruled consistently that such transfers amounting to dismissal are an unreasonable exercise of board power, and not to be permitted.

A Negro teacher who possessed the same qualifications as similarly situated white teachers was declared by a circuit court of appeals to

---

[14]Haas v. Holder, 218 Ind. 263, 32 N.E.2d 590 (1941).

[15]School City of Peru v. State, 212 Ind. 255, 7 N.E.2d 176 (1937).

[16]State v. Board of Educ. of the City of Duluth, 213 Minn. 550, 7 N.W.2d 544 (1943).

have been discriminated against where the board paid lower salaries to Negroes than to whites, even though the teacher had signed a contract about which he complained. The court looked upon such action as violative of the *due process* and *equal protection* clauses of the fourteenth amendment. By refusing to review the findings of the circuit court, the Supreme Court of the United States, in effect, upheld the lower court, and thereby affirmed its decision.[17]

Cancellation Grounds and Procedures

Once the teacher has attained tenure status, he may not be dismissed for causes other than those specifically enumerated in the enabling legislation. In Wisconsin, for example, the tenure law provides for security of employment by teachers in populous counties with these words:

> No teacher on permanent contract . . . shall be refused employment, dismissed, removed or discharged, except for inefficiency or immorality, for wilful and persistent violation of reasonable regulations of the governing body of such school or for other good and just cause . . .[18]

An illustration of a suit brought by a tenure teacher to regain her position where the board had sought to dismiss her on grounds other than those specified in the tenure law is a New Mexico case which arose in 1955. A teacher was informed by the local board that her services would be discontinued at the end of the term due to closing of the high school department in which the teacher was employed. She was not re-employed in another position, although she had been continuously employed for nine years previously, and although there was evidence of several available positions held by non-tenure teachers in other schools of the district. The teacher brought an action in mandamus to compel the board to issue her a teaching contract as a tenure teacher.

The teacher's suit was successful. Said the Supreme Court of New Mexico in upholding the decision of the state board of education that the teacher's contract was in full force and effect:

> . . . according to its [the state board's] interpretation of the law, four grounds existed for discharge of a tenure teacher . . . none of which was assigned as cause for appellee's discharge.[19]

---

[17]Alston v. School Bd. of the City of Norfolk, 311 U.S. 693, 61 Sup. Ct. 75, 85 L. Ed. 448 (1940).

[18]Wisc. Stat. Ann. 40.42.

[19]Swisher v. Darden, 59 N.M. 511, 287 P.2d 73 (1955).

Occasionally, the courts have been called upon to decide whether the marriage of a woman teacher on tenure constitutes grounds for dismissal. The courts are divided on this issue. Some courts have held that marriage does not constitute just cause for dismissal in the absence of proof that marriage contributes to the lessening of efficiency on the part of the teacher. A board rule which summarily dismisses a teacher upon her marriage is considered by these courts to be an unreasonable exercise of the board's power, or *ultra vires* the power of the board. Other courts have taken the opposite view, ruling that marriage is a sufficient reason for dismissal where the statute provides for dismissal for "just cause."

Several of the state tenure laws contain no specific causes for dismissal beyond the statement that a teacher may be dismissed *for just cause*. When this is the case, the court is called upon to interpret the causes which rightfully fall into this category. When, however, a specification "for other good and just cause" is included in the statute, along with a list of specific causes, such as incompetency, neglect of duty, and the like, the courts have consistently held that "good and just cause" must be *related to the other specific causes* included in the act. In other words, "other good and just cause" must be of the same general nature as the list of specific causes contained in the statute.

In Ohio, the statute provided for dismissal of a tenure teacher for "gross inefficiency or immorality, for willful and persistent violations of reasonable regulations of the board of education, or for other good and just cause." The board had a rule that the contract of a female teacher would be terminated if she married. A tenure teacher who was married with full knowledge of the rule was dismissed by the board. Said the Supreme Court of Ohio in sustaining the dismissal as a reasonable exercise of the board's power:

> It will thus be seen that the General Assembly has granted boards of education wide latitude and discretion in the particulars mentioned and if, as a matter of policy, a board adopts a rule that upon the marriage of a woman teacher her contract will terminate, can it properly be said that the deliberate violation of such a rule does not constitute "good and just cause" for the cancellation of the contract?
>
> A rule of the kind described may have a sound basis in the particular school district and may bear a reasonable relationship to the responsibility of a board of education to build up and maintain an efficient and harmonious school system. Within the discretion conferred, a board may act on the theory that married women as a class will be absorbed with home

duties and cares to the detriment of their school work, or on the theory that married women generally have husbands who can support them and that such women should give way to unmarried women qualified to teach and who must support themselves.[20]

Boards of education, in bringing dismissal charges against a teacher on tenure, must take note not only of the grounds specified in the tenure law, but must also follow closely the *procedure* specified in the statute. Generally speaking, no deviation, however slight, will be permitted by a court of law. The statute is the measure of the board's power to dismiss, and any departure from the manner prescribed is without legal foundation. Were it otherwise, the tenure law would lose much of its power to protect the teacher from wrongful dismissal.

Usually, tenure laws prescribe the procedure to be followed by a board in dismissing a teacher. These may include the guarantees noted earlier—service of notice, right to a hearing and a statement of charges, right of appeal, and the like. The principle of law is well settled that the board must act substantially, if not entirely, in compliance with statutory procedure if it is to successfully discharge a tenure teacher.[21] An Indiana case will serve to illustrate this principle.

By Indiana statute, written notice to the teacher of the exact date, time, and place when the termination of a contract would be considered was required. Notice was given the plaintiff teacher that her termination would be considered at 4:00 p.m. on a named date at a named place. She was there with her attorney at 4:00. A quorum of trustees was not present until 4:30. The last of the five members arrived at 5:20. The teacher and her counsel left at 5:40, at which time the board had not convened, gone into session, or notified the teacher of a postponement. At 5:45 the board convened and terminated her contract.

The Supreme Court of Indiana, in holding such a termination illegal, said: "When the manner in which granted powers may be exercised are by statute restricted to a definite course of procedure, such procedure must be followed."[22] The fact that the board did not convene at 4:00 was not a factor influencing the decision. If the board had convened at the time a quorum was present, or within a reasonable time thereafter, their subsequent action would have been legal.

---

[20]Greco v. Roper, 145 Ohio St. 243, 61 N.E.2d 307 (1945).
[21]School Dist. No. 6 of Pima County v. Barber, 85 Ariz. 95, 332 P.2d 496 (1958).
[22]State v. School City of Anderson, 236 Ind. 649, 142 N.E.2d 914 (1957).

But the court failed to find even a substantial compliance with the statute; thus, the action of the board was illegal, and the teacher was reinstated.

Rights of the Teacher Under Permanent Tenure

The right of a teacher who has been admitted to permanent tenure in the district where such right has been secured, subject to reasonable rules of the board of education thereof, is held to be a *vested* right. Thus, the teacher who has attained tenure has a vested right to employment in the district, and cannot be deprived of this right except through an exercise of due process of law. The permanent teacher has preference over a probationary teacher where the former is qualified to perform certain tasks currently being performed by the latter. Furthermore, the tenure teacher retains his rights gained under tenure until duly dismissed according to the tenure law, much as the civil service employee continues in office until removed according to legal procedures outlined in the law.

Tenure teachers are in effect employed under a continuing contract, and need not be re-appointed annually as are probationary teachers. A permanent teacher is thus entitled to a succession of contracts for an indefinite period of time during good behavior. The execution of a contract for a definite period by the board will not deprive the teacher of his vested right to continuing employment under the state's tenure laws.

The right of the tenure teacher to continuing employment, however, is not unlimited and may be altered by the legislature. Since this right is statutory in origin, rather than contractual, it is not protected by the federal constitution, unless the legislature expressly or impliedly intends it to be so.

The federal constitution prohibits the enactment of a statute impairing the obligation of contracts. The legislature of the State of Indiana amended its tenure law to exclude teachers in township school districts. A teacher in a township school district brought an action in mandamus to compel the school board to continue her employment under tenure. She had taught for eight years in the district, and was a tenure teacher under the original law. The question before the court was whether the teacher's right to continuing employment was destroyed by the amendment or existed as a contractual right that could not be impaired.

The case reached the Supreme Court of the United States. Said that Court, in ruling that the teacher was entitled to indefinite employment during good behavior:

> In 1927 the State adopted the Teachers' Tenure Act under which the present controversy arises. . . . By an amendatory Act of 1933 township school corporations were omitted from the provisions of the Act of 1927. The court below construed this Act as repealing the Act of 1927 so far as township schools and teachers are concerned and as leaving the respondent free to terminate the petitioner's employment. But we are of the opinion that the petitioner had a valid contract with the respondent, the obligation of which would be impaired by the termination of her employment.[23]

The Court based its refusal to overthrow the teacher's right to tenure on the question of whether the legislature had intended to destroy or support the contractual obligations inherent in the original tenure act. Said the Court:

> The title of the Act is couched in terms of contract. It speaks of the making and canceling of indefinite contracts. In the body the word "contract" appears ten times in Section 1, defining the relationship; 11 times in Section 2, relating to the termination of employment by the employer, and four times in Section 4, stating the conditions of termination by the teacher.
>
> The tenor of the Act indicates that the word "contracts" was not used inadvertently or in other than its usual legal meaning . . . . Examination of the entire Act convinces us that the teacher was by it assured of the possession of a binding and enforceable contract against school districts.[24]

Thus, a tenure law is legislative policy only, and can be overcome by subsequent amendments. But where the legislative intent is to honor the sanctity of prior contracts, the courts will uphold the legislature in its right to so legislate.

Does the tenure teacher who accepts an administrative position in the same district abandon his right to tenure by such change of position? It is a general rule that one may assume an administrative post and still retain his vested right as a classroom teacher in the district. A classroom teacher on tenure in Minneapolis was offered and accepted the position of administrative assistant to the superintendent of

---

[23]Indiana ex rel. Anderson v. Brand, 303 U.S. 95, 58 Sup. Ct. 443, 82 L. Ed. 685, 113 ALR 1482 (1938).

[24]*Ibid.*

schools, the duties of which included no classroom teaching and which involved research and statistical work incidental to school administration. The position of administrative assistant to the superintendent was later abolished, and the teacher requested assignment to his former duties. The Supreme Court of Minnesota ruled that he could not gain tenure in the administrative position, inasmuch as it was not expressly named in the Teacher Tenure Act. However, he was entitled to return to his position as a teacher with full tenure rights. Said the court:

> While one entitled to tenure rights may abandon them, whether he does so in a particular case depends upon his intention with respect to the matter. Absent manifestation of intention to abandon tenure rights, acceptance by a classroom teacher from the school authority employing him to work involving the performance of administrative duties to the exclusion of classroom teaching does not constitute abandonment of his tenure rights.[25]

May the tenure teacher retain his tenure while on leave of absence? In at least one case, a court has ruled that he may. A teacher on permanent tenure in the District of Columbia requested and was granted a leave of absence in order to teach illiterate soldiers at an army camp in Maryland. During his absence, the teacher received no salary from the school district. The court ruled that the teacher retained his permanent status with the school district, so that upon the assumption of his duties he was entitled to his statutory rights and privileges attendant upon such tenure status, including an increased salary undiminished by his temporary absence.[26]

Right to Retirement Benefits

Seventy-two cases related to teacher retirement were litigated in the higher courts of the land between 1942 and 1957. The average number of such cases was thus slightly less than five per year during the sixteen-year period. The earlier cases were concerned principally with the constitutionality of retirement statutes. Out of these cases came a legal distinction between a *pension* and a *retirement plan*.[27] In the former, the teacher is not required to contribute a part of his

---

[25]Board of Educ. of City of Minneapolis v. Sand, 227 Minn. 202, 34 N.W.2d 689 (1948).

[26]Cooke v. Board of Educ., 161 F.2d 877 (D.C. 1947).

[27]Dodge v. Board of Educ. of Chicago, 302 U.S. 74, 58 Sup. Ct. 98, 82 L. Ed. 57 (1937).

salary to the system. In the latter, the teacher, and usually the school district or the state, contribute to a retirement plan.

The state has no obligation to pay a pension, but may do so legally if the people so desire. Some of the states, for example, have enacted emeritus teacher pension plans, which provide specified amounts for teachers who have served a certain number of years in the public schools of the state, and who have reached a designated age. It goes without saying that a teacher must meet the requirements set forth in the enabling statute in order to participate in a pension plan. He has no vested right to the pension, such as that arising out of a contract.

On the other hand, a retirement plan is an annuity, whereby a contractual relationship between the state and the teacher, who has made contributions to the fund, arises. A legal obligation has been established on which the teacher may depend. The teacher is said to have a *vested interest* in the retirement fund. Consequently, when questions arise with respect to a teacher's rights under a retirement system, the court will first attempt to determine whether the teacher has established a right to the retirement benefits. Although the cases are not in agreement, the weight of authority supports the view that teachers have vested rights in annuity systems to which they contribute, which rights cannot be abrogated or changed, inasmuch as such action would impair the obligation of contracts.

A Montana case is in point. A statute of that state provided that a teacher who quit teaching before retirement was entitled to the amount he had personally contributed to the retirement plan, plus a specified rate of interest. A later statute provided such a teacher should receive only the amount he had paid into the fund, without interest. A teacher challenged the latter statute, maintaining that her rights were contractual, and not subject to change. The Supreme Court of Montana held that her rights were indeed contractual, and that any law which purported to change them was unconstitutional as impairing the obligation of a prior contract.[28]

A board of education may not deduct an amount from a teacher's salary for retirement purposes, unless there is a statutory provision granting this deduction. In a leading case tried before the Supreme Court of Minnesota in 1902, that august body declared:

> The conviction cannot be avoided that the effect of such
> a requirement, when applied to all teachers employed, must

---

[28]Clarke v. Ireland, 122 Mont. 191, 199 P.2d 965 (1948).

be to compel some of them, at least, to enter into the contract upon compulsion and without any expectation of receiving any personal benefit therefrom. It is difficult, therefore, to sustain the validity of the act on the part of the board of education in thus withholding the 1 per cent of the salaries upon the ground that such a plan was voluntarily entered into by the teachers in the signing of the contract.[29]

New Jersey in 1896 was the first state to adopt a statewide system of teacher retirement. Following the Minnesota ruling in 1902, the states began to adopt legislation permitting boards to deduct from teachers' salaries for retirement purposes. By 1961, all of the states had such legislation.

Occasionally, the question of the *eligibility* of the teacher to receive retirement benefits arises. Two cases, one in New Mexico and the other in Iowa, will serve to illustrate the problem.

In New Mexico, a teacher who was receiving retirement benefits continued to teach and receive a salary. Said the Supreme Court of New Mexico in ruling on the case:

> The decisive question is whether the Educational Retirement Board may withhold retirement benefits from retired or emeritus employees during the time such employees are holding positions in the public schools of the state and drawing salaries for such services.
>
> The question requires an affirmative answer. The benefits under the retirement act are for those teachers who "retire from active service." A teacher, by accepting the benefits, removes himself completely from the public school system of the state.[30]

Of course, had the statute read otherwise, an entirely different conclusion might have been reached by the court. Teachers should become familiar with the contents of the retirement statutes, some of which permit teachers to continue to teach in other states after beginning to receive retirement benefits.

In Iowa, a statute provided that any person reaching the age of sixty-five, who had been an employee, holding a valid teaching certificate with twenty-five years of service in the public schools of the state, was entitled to receive retirement benefits. A teacher had more than twenty-seven years of service in the state, including fifteen years of actual teaching, and four years each as county superintendent and

---

[29]State ex rel. Jennison v. Rogers. 87 Minn. 130, 91 N.W. 430 (1902).
[30]State ex rel. Bernal v. Foraker, 64 N.M. 71, 323 P.2d 1107 (1958).

state superintendent of public instruction. When she was denied retirement benefits, the teacher sued to recover. The case came before the Supreme Court of Iowa, which held:

> . . . while Miss Francis was acting as county superintendent of schools and as state superintendent of public instruction she was a public officer rather than an employee. Each of the positions was created by statute, with duties prescribed by statute or which perforce inhered in the administration of the office itself. The individual holding the office was delegated some of the sovereign functions of government which he, or she, would perform without control of a superior officer. The office in each case had a fixed term; while the petitioner was holding them, each office was elective and was for a set term. An oath of office was required, and a bond was provided for.[31]

Such a position, the court ruled, was conclusively one of a public officer, and not of a public employee. Therefore, the plaintiff had not been "an employee . . . in the public schools of the state with a record of service of twenty-five years or more" as the statute required. She was, therefore, not entitled to retirement benefits.

The courts seem to be in agreement on the proposition that retirement statutes may be changed without violating the teacher's rights. Two cases are in point. In Iowa, the Des Moines school board raised the retirement age from fifty-five to sixty. A teacher who had reached age fifty-five, but who had not applied for retirement, brought suit to compel the board to pay her the amount due her under the older rule. She argued that her right to retire became vested upon her having reached age fifty-five, and that the board had no legal right to change the retirement age. She had contributed to the annuity, and there was no question of her right to retirement.

The teacher's suit failed. Said the Supreme Court of Iowa in explaining its decision:

> The [retirement] systems are seldom actuarially sound. It is usually several years before this is fully realized. And when attempts are then made to strengthen the plan and to put it on a sounder financial basis either by decreasing the contributions, raising the retirement age, or decreasing the allowances, the beneficiaries feel that their rights, present or prospective, are being impaired, when in fact what they think they have lost or will lose, is something impossible to obtain under the plan.[32]

---

[31] Francis v. Iowa Employment Security Comm., 250 Iowa 1300, 98 N.W.2d 733 (1959).

[32] Talbott v. Independent School Dist. of Des Moines, 230 Iowa 949, 299 N.W. 556 (1941).

An earlier case tried before the Supreme Court of the United States in 1937 was to the same effect.[33] An Illinois statute provided for an annual retirement payment to teachers who had reached age sixty-five, and who had retired voluntarily. Later, the law was amended to reduce the benefits. Some Chicago teachers sued the board challenging the constitutionality of the later statute. The teachers argued that their rights were vested, and not subject to amendment. But the Supreme Court of the United States rejected their pleas, maintaining instead that retirement laws are merely *declarations of intent* of the legislature, and may be changed under reasonable conditions when the legislature chooses to do so. Perhaps the fact that the case was tried during the depths of the Depression when retrenchment was necessary all along the line was an extenuating circumstance of the case. At any rate, it is well settled that, in spite of the earned rights which teachers may obtain through their contributions to the retirement system, and in spite of the fact that teachers come to rely on the retirement act for security in their later years, the courts will not permit such vested rights to prevent changes in retirement legislation when conditions warrant. Exactly what constitutes "reasonable changes" is, of course, subject to the decision of the courts, acting on current data.

One clue may be gathered from the case of *Meyer v. Board of Trustees of Teachers Pension and Annuity Fund*,[34] which arose in New Jersey in 1958. A teacher in that case, who was a member of the pension and annuity fund, nominated his wife as beneficiary to recover accumulated deductions on his death. The statute providing for payment of such deductions was repealed and a new statute enacted providing for payment of death benefits to a designated beneficiary. The teacher died without designating his wife the beneficiary, and the wife sued to recover the accumulated deductions. The court ruled, as a matter of statutory construction, that the original nomination of the wife to receive the accumulated deductions did not entitle her to the death benefit.

Teachers should be aware that their rights under retirement legislation may be limited. Teachers' organizations should apprise legislators of the best possible statutory law in this area. Certainly, the conclusion is inescapable that retirement systems are subject to actuarial contingencies and the will of the legislature acting in good faith. Unless

---

[33]Dodge v. Board of Educ. of Chicago, 302 U.S. 74, 58 Sup. Ct. 98, 82 L. Ed. 57 (1937).
[34]49 N.J. Super. 255, 139 A.2d 420 (1958).

the statutes clearly state that a contractual guarantee exists, the teacher would do well to go slowly in "counting her chickens" under present state retirement laws.

The final case in this section illustrates what may happen when compulsory provisions of a retirement statute are not observed. A New Jersey teacher taught from 1910 to 1914, and contributed to the state retirement fund then in force. In 1926, she returned to teaching in the same state, and continued to teach until 1956. Under New Jersey law, membership in the retirement system was compulsory. Nevertheless, on her return, the school board did not withhold money from the teacher's salary for the purpose, nor did it contribute matching funds as required by law.

When the teacher applied for retirement benefits, the Pension Fund advised the school board that all back payments in the amount of several thousand dollars were due in order to establish a credit in favor of the teacher. When the board refused to pay the amount, the state board of education withheld the amount from state school moneys due. In New Jersey, the state board of education is authorized to withhold state school funds from those school districts which did not make the deductions. The school board brought suit to compel the state to pay over the state funds in question.

The superior court of New Jersey held that in spite of the board's failure to deduct from the teacher's salary for pension purposes, the teacher nonetheless was entitled to retirement benefits. However, she was required to pay her half of the total contribution due, plus interest. The court reasoned that she must have known that she would be required to make payments to the retirement fund in order to reap benefits from it. The board of education was likewise required to pay its share, with interest. Failure to pay the district's share was merely a default, and subjected the board to withholding of state funds from the school district. Had the state law controlling retirement funds for teachers been otherwise, a different interpretation might have been handed down by the court.[35]

This and other cases treated in this section serve to illustrate the principle that teachers should know—in fact, are assumed to know—the law with respect to their rights and privileges under the state's retirement system. Where there is any question of such rights, the teacher should consult an attorney for advice.

---

[35]Board of Educ. of City of Linden v. Liebman, 57 N.J. Super. 556, 153 A.2d 385 (1959).

Finally, the question of *when* one must retire is an area of possible litigation. In several of the states, tenure protection against dismissal or involuntary retirement ceases when the teacher reaches the age of sixty-five or some other specified age. Usually, the statutes provide that contracts must be drawn on a year-to-year basis beyond the specified age.

Suggested Activities

SUMMARIZE:

1. The legal safeguards which surround teachers on tenure as presented in this chapter.
2. The purposes of tenure legislation.

DISCUSS:

1. These objections to tenure laws in general
   (a) They violate the Constitution of the United States;
   (b) They are against public policy;
   (c) They result in the expenditure of public moneys for private purposes;
   (d) They are special laws for the management of the public schools.
2. The relative merits of pension grants paid entirely by the state; annuities in which beneficiaries pay the total cost; reserve joint-contributory systems in which beneficiaries and school boards share costs.
3. The advantages and disadvantages to be gained if teachers were placed on permanent tenure after the first year of successful teaching experience in the district.

RESEARCH:

1. The term "grandfather clause" is sometimes heard in connection with tenure legislation. What is the meaning of the term, and how does it apply in your state?
2. What advantages and disadvantages might be noted where tenure laws in a state permit a principal or superintendent to obtain permanent tenure?
3. What are the specific causes for cancellation of a tenure teacher's contract in the state in which you plan to teach? Does the enabling statute specify "for other good and just cause"?
4. What is meant by saying that a state retirement system is "actuarily sound?"
5. What are the possible advantages and disadvantages in state-to state reciprocity in retirement benefits for teachers?

Further Readings

Burrup, Percy E. *The Teacher and the Public School System* (New York: Harper and Brothers, 1960), pp. 514-517.

Edwards, Newton. *The Courts and the Public Schools* (Chicago: University of Chicago Press, 1955), Ch. XVIII.

Garber, Lee O. *The Yearbook of School Law* (Danville, Illinois: Interstate Printers and Publishers, 1957).

Gauerke, Warren E. *Legal and Ethical Responsibilities of School Personnel* (Englewood Cliffs, N. J.: Prentice-Hall, 1959), pp. 94-95.

Grieder, Calvin, Truman M. Pierce, and William Rosenstengel. *Public School Administration* (New York: Ronald Press, 1961), pp. 247-250.

Hamilton, Robert R. *The Bi-Weekly School Law Letter* (Laramie, Wyoming: R. R. Hamilton, publisher, December 25, 1952 and January 8, 1953).

_____. *Legal Rights and Liabilities of Teachers* (Laramie, Wyoming: School Law Publications, 1956), pp. 70-74.

Hugett, Albert J., and T. M. Stinnett. *Professional Problems of Teachers* (New York: Macmillan, 1956), Ch. 7.

Kearney, Nolan C. *A Teacher's Professional Guide* (Englewood Cliffs, N. J.: Prentice-Hall, 1958), Ch. 13.

Moore, Harold E., and Newell B. Walters. *Personnel Administration in Education* (New York: Harper and Brothers, 1955).

National Education Association. *The Teacher's Day in Court: Review of 1959* (Washington: Research Division, NEA, April, 1960), Research Report 1960-R5.

Remmlein, Madaline Kinter. *School Law, Second Edition* (Danville, Illinois: Interstate Printers and Publishers, 1962).

Chapter VI

EMPLOYEE WELFARE RIGHTS
OF TEACHERS

Introduction

Classroom teachers in the public schools of America numbered more than 1,500,000 in 1963. In that year, to service an enrollment of 40,000,000 students in some 35,000 basic administrative units, presided over by 165,000 lay school board members, it was necessary to provide financial support in excess of $21,000,000,000. More than half of this financial sum was budgeted for staff salaries, an amount in itself larger than the entire national expenditure for public education a decade earlier. Public school costs were expected to continue to rise during the 1960's as new personnel were added at a rate in excess of 100,000 teachers annually.

Competition for qualified workers was keen following World War II, and school boards found it advantageous to offer fringe benefits and improved conditions of work to school personnel in order to staff the schools. Teachers, aware of the shortage of qualified personnel, influenced by the success of labor, and united by a sense of professional solidarity, sought rights for collective bargaining, better conditions of work, more liberal leave policies, and other fringe benefits not theretofore open to them. While some of these benefits were won by mutual agreement, others evolved as constructs of the courts and legislative arms of government. It is not the purpose of the authors to chronicle here these developments. Rather, it is their purpose in this chapter to acquaint the reader with some of the legal rights of the classroom teacher in the public schools, particularly those rights associated with teacher welfare in the current meaning of that term. More specifically, the chapter deals with the salary rights of teachers, the right of teachers to leaves of absence, and other fringe benefits which have arisen in recent years in connection with their work.

Importance of Teacher Welfare

School administrators recognize the importance of improving conditions under which teachers work as a means of improving instructional services to children. The rationale for this point of view can be explained briefly as follows:

1. Teachers work better when their personal welfare problems have been solved.
2. Teachers are enticed by the employee welfare benefits to be found in industry, business, and the semi-professional categories; hence, educational administrators must take cognizance of the competition for talented manpower in formulating their employee welfare policies.
3. A complex social setting such as that in which the modern teacher works demands a clearer delineation of the teacher's rights as an employee of the board.
4. A growing number of cases involving teachers' rights is evidence of the need for emphasis on this phase of school administration.
5. The growth of professionalization among school administrators, the increased number of larger districts, as well as the standardization of personnel practices show the need for faculty job descriptions.
6. The organized profession, some 800,000 strong, has brought the prestige of the profession to bear on teacher welfare. The establishment of the National Commission on Professional Rights and Responsibilities by the National Education Association in June, 1961, is evidence of a growing awareness of this phase of employee welfare.

Teachers Are Employees

The legal status of public school teachers is generally explained by referring to them as *employees,* as distinguished from *school officials.*[1]

---

[1]Carr, William D. "Selected Aspects of the Legal Status of the Public School Teacher in Oklahoma." (Stillwater: Oklahoma State University, 1959), unpublished doctoral dissertation, p. 21.

The courts and educational authorities are in substantial agreement on this point; however, the employee-employer relationship of the teacher and the board of education is, in the main, little understood. The misunderstanding arises, no doubt, from utilizing the employee-employer relationship concept common to private enterprise and the business world without an understanding of the legal relationships of master-servant or principal-agent.

The relation of master and servant exists where a person, for pay or other valuable considerations, performs a service for another, *e.g.*, the housemaid is the servant of her employer, the master. A principal-agent relationship arises when the employee acts, on the expressed or implied authority of his employer, to bind the employer in an agreement with another, *e.g.*, the employer, as principal, authorizes his employee, as agent, to purchase supplies and charge them to the account of the principal. Of course, an employee may serve in the capacity of a servant at one time, and as an agent at another, depending upon the act he performs.

The teacher also serves as a servant or agent of the board of education. For the most part, the teacher acts as a servant, but on occasion, the teacher may be asked by his principal or superintendent to perform an act that will establish the principal-agent relationship. As an agent, the teacher's authority will be limited because of the statutory limitations relating to schools and school districts. Consequently, the teacher-agent may not bind the board of education or school district except to the extent of that statutory authority. Furthermore, the board of education cannot be bound by its agent, unless it has given express authority for the agent's acts or later ratifies his actions.

The law is well established that those who deal with boards of education and their agents are charged with the responsibility of knowing the district's powers and limitations. Thus, third parties dealing with teachers are assumed to know the law, and the extent to which a teacher may legally bind his employer.

The Salary Rights of Teachers

Instructional salaries have been consistently held by the courts to be primary obligations of boards of education, and must be paid in preference to all other claims against the public funds which boards hold in trust. On an individual basis, the teacher may bring suit for payment and recover the amount owed where compensation as agreed has not been paid under the contract of employment. But the right of the teacher to salary payment is conditioned upon the holding of a valid certificate in the state where the teacher works, and a valid contract of employment in the same state.

We have seen in another chapter how the teacher may legally contract in some states without holding the certificate at the time of signing the contract, but he may not be paid under the terms of the contract as long as he is devoid of the license to teach. He is not entitled to payment, since he does not belong to the class of persons who may be legally paid, namely, those teachers who hold the license to teach in the state in question.

The following pages contain materials relating to the right of the board to fix teachers' salaries, establish salary schedules including merit pay provisions, reimburse teachers beyond the terms of the contract for extra work, and pay the teacher while under suspension. As usual, appropriate case materials are cited to illustrate the points of law developed.

Right of boards to fix salaries. No teacher, even one who has attained tenure status, may acquire a vested right to a particular salary or to a periodic increase in pay. The courts will generally not interfere in the exercise of the power of the board to establish certain salaries, unless there is evidence that some statute has been violated, or that the board acted in an arbitrary or capricious manner.

It is a well established principle of law that the power to fix salaries within the above mentioned limitations is legally vested in the local board of education. Roach [2] pointed out that salaries are, for the most part, a local problem dependent upon many variable factors. The discretion of the board in this respect appears to be quite broad. When the board acts in good faith, and within its statutory limitations, its control over teachers' salaries is not susceptible to challenge.

A Florida case is in point. In 1953, the state legislature set aside funds for the purpose of increasing teachers' salaries, stipulating that "county school teacher salary schedules shall provide at least a $350 annual increase from state funds over the salary schedules for the previous year." The salary schedule for 1953-1954 was little changed from that in use in 1952-1953 in Duval County, whereupon some teachers brought suit for a declaration of their rights to salary increases under the state legislation.

---

[2]Stephen F. Roach. "Compensation," in *Law and the School Superintendent* (Cincinnati: W. H. Anderson Company, 1958), The National Organization on Legal Problems of Education, p. 84.

The trial court found that the 1952-1953 salary included a $250 raise for teachers from nonrecurrent funds, and that the 1953-1954 salary schedule applied the state aid moneys provided for under the statute almost entirely to instructional salaries. Without the state aid, the board would not have been able to raise salaries even the lesser amount. The court therefore concluded that the board had complied substantially with the provisions of state aid law. On appeal, the Supreme Court of Florida upheld the decision of the lower court.

Said the latter court in declaring the right of the board to fix teachers' salaries:

> . . . By providing the barest minimum for routine operation and maintenance, they were able to maintain their salary schedule for instructional personnel at the 1952-3 level using all available county, state and federal funds. The defendants did all that they could, and we do not see how they could be required to do more.[3]

It is well settled that legislative enactments take precedence over the actions of boards of education with respect to salaries for teachers. A board in Pennsylvania voted to give all teachers a ten per cent salary increase as of January 1, 1956. In June, the legislature of Pennsylvania enacted a statute which provided for a $200 increase for all teachers over the salary received in the 1955-1956 school year. When the board concluded that the two raises were not cumulative, some teachers sought court interpretation of their salary rights. The court ruled that the raises were cumulative, and that the teachers in question were entitled to the $200 raise provided for under the statute, in addition to the ten per cent raise which they had received through board action in January.[4]

Similarly, in Tennessee a court ruled that teachers who had signed contracts "for the amount of the state minimum salary," and who later brought suit to have their salaries increased to an amount equal to those received in the previous year, could not be estopped from making such demands, in the face of a statutory provision supporting such claims. Said the court:

> . . . the counties through their participation in the State funds use the State money in payment of teachers and operation of their schools. Any statutory provision made for this

---

[3]Harwell v. Sheffield, 112 So. 2d 377 (Fla. 1959).

[4]Raymond v. School Dist. of the City of Scranton, 186 Pa. Super. 352, 142 A.2d 749 (1958).

purpose should override and supercede anything in the contract which is repugnant to such statutory provisions. This being true the teachers are not estopped then to assert their rights to secure a higher salary which is provided by statute if it is necessary to assert such rights in court.

. . . This is because of the fact that the salary statute, since it is applicable to the contract of a teacher, enters into and forms a part of the contract as if it had actually been written or copied into the contract.[5]

Salary schedules. In the absence of a statute to the contrary, the board may provide for schedules which classify teachers according to salaries to be paid. Such schedules may be either subjective or objective in nature. In at least one case, a state supreme court has ruled that a salary schedule which placed inefficient, uncooperative, and uninterested teachers in one category and all other teachers in another was permissible.[6] The school authorities, said the court, had the right to weigh all factors in classifying teachers and fixing their compensation. Although such weighing of the factors sometimes lacks objectivity, the courts seem to be in agreement that a board may use *subjective* evaluative criteria in arriving at their classifications.

Authorities are not in complete agreement, however, on the legality of classifications built upon distinctions between male and female teachers, married and unmarried or Negro and white teachers, or teachers with and without dependents. The Supreme Court of Indiana ruled, for example, that a board acted illegally in stipulating that married women teachers were not entitled to increments provided under the adopted salary schedule. The court pointed out that such arbitrary classification bore no real relationship to the kind or character of work done in the classroom.[7]

The Supreme Court of Massachusetts reached an opposite conclusion in 1952. In the City of Chelsea, Massachusetts, married teachers who were the sole support of a spouse, child, or children were paid $300 per year more than those without such dependents. Said the court, in upholding the board's right to make this distinction in teachers' salaries:

School committees are not charged with the task of ironing out the inequities of life or setting up systems of social welfare. If the vote is to be held valid it must be because the committee could reasonably believe that it would be for the

[5]McMinn County Bd. of Educ. v. Anderson, 200 Tenn. 333, 292 S.W.2d 198 (1956).

[6]Board of School Trustees School City of Peru v. Moore, 218 Ind. 386, 33 N.E.2d 114 (1941).

[7]Hutton v. Gill, 212 Ind. 164, 8 N.E.2d 818 (1937).

good of the school system to pay more for teachers having dependents. . . . It is simply a question whether making the amount of salary depend to some small extent upon the situation of the teacher with respect to dependents can be thought by a reasonable school committeeman to have some effect in producing more efficient schools. On the whole, we incline to the view that the vote can be sustained.[8]

Also, the adoption of a salary schedule by a board of education does not vest the teacher with a right to increments contained in the schedule. Such increments are merely a declaration of policy, and do not constitute grounds for action by a teacher, inasmuch as salary schedules are subject to revision or even abolition at the discretion of the board. The salary schedule is not a contract between the teacher and the board, and should not be so considered.

A city board of education in New Jersey, by resolution, adopted a state statute providing for payment of a fixed annual salary increment until a stated maximum salary had been reached. The schedule remained in force from 1927 until 1932, when poorer economic conditions caused the board to reconsider the matter. Consequently, the board adopted a resolution to gradually reduce salaries, a practice which continued until 1937. Some teachers, principals, and supervisors brought suit against the board, alleging that the board had refused to conform to the earlier salary schedule, and alleging further that the board's adoption in 1927 of the schedule had created a contractual obligation, which, when rescinded, violated the Constitution of the United States which prohibits the passing of laws that impair the obligation of contracts.

The court, in dismissing the petition, held that such state statutes as pertain to tenure and salaries invest the teacher with mere legislative status, subject to legislative alteration and amendment not giving rise to an irrepealable legislative contract. The earlier by-law was repealed by implication by the later resolution. Said the court, in defining the board's right to regulate salaries:

> A city school board's regulation, providing for annual increments to teachers' salaries, is mere declaration of legislative policy subject at all times to abrogation by the board in the public interest. . . .
> Permanent tenure statutes prohibiting reduction of salaries give to the teacher mere legislative status subject to legislative alteration and amendment.[9]

[8]Cotter v. City of Chelsea, 329 Mass. 314, 108 N.E.2d 47 (1952).
[9]Offhouse v. State Bd. of Educ., 131 N.J.L. 391, 36 A.2d 884 (1944).

When individual teachers or small groups have been singled out for reductions in salary, the courts have generally concluded that such board rulings constituted *demotions,* and were therefore not allowable unless for just cause. The Colorado Teacher Tenure statute (several of the states have similar statutes) provides: "There shall be no reduction in the salary of any classroom teacher unless there is a general reduction in the salaries of fifty per cent or more of all teachers in the district."[10] Of course, the board may pay teachers salaries above the minimum fixed by law.

In assigning teachers to positions other than their original assignments, or in reducing their salaries, the board must not act in an arbitrary or unreasonable manner. An interpretation of the power of a board to transfer an employee and reduce his salary was before the court in a Colorado case which arose in 1958. In one school district, an administrator-teacher held tenure status as a teacher under the existing statute. The district eliminated the position of administrator-teacher held by the plaintiff, and offered the plaintiff a teaching job at a greatly reduced salary. The question before the court was whether the board had the power to transfer the plaintiff from one position to another, and if so, whether it was proper to adjust his salary in proportion to the change.

The court held that a district board may indeed transfer its employees, but that such a right is limited. It may not change the employee's position on the salary schedule to cause a reduction in pay, unless service in the prior position was unsatisfactory, a condition which was not alleged here. The plaintiff, said the court, had attained continuous tenure as a teacher after five years' continuous service. He could not be dismissed except under the provisions of the existing statute. Hence, the board's action was contrary to the Teacher Tenure act, and therefore unlawful.[11]

Merit pay. In recent discussions about salary schedules, the principle of merit pay has been given increased consideration. Although merit pay plans have not been generally accepted throughout the country, some boards, desirous of recognizing individual differences among teachers, have devised plans to compensate for these differences. Under some plans, the salaries of superior teachers may be raised, while under other plans, the salaries of less efficient teachers may be

---

[10] Colo. Rev. Stat. § 123-18-6 (1953).
[11] School Dist. No. 2 in the County of Fremont v. Brenton, 137 Colo. 247, 323 P.2d 899 (1958).

144

reduced. So long as the standards governing the merit pay plan appear to be on some reasonable basis, a court will not substitute its judgment for that of the administrative body promulgating the plan, and will not disturb the exercise of the board's power.

The problem of reasonableness in connection with a teachers' salary schedule was discussed in a California case in which two permanent teachers had their salaries reduced because their superintendent was dissatisfied with their work, while at the same time other teachers in the system were granted raises. The two teachers brought suit to require the board to restore their salaries to the previous level, contending that the action of the board was unreasonable, arbitrary, and discriminatory, and designed to force them to resign, since they were the only permanent teachers in the district. The superintendent testified that the teachers were not indifferent to their duties in any way, but that they did not seem to embrace wholeheartedly "the philosophy of teaching which I was trying to get over to them at that time." Said the Supreme Court of California in upholding the teachers, and ruling against the action of the board:

> It seems self-evident that such an indefinite and uncertain term as "philosophy of teaching" cannot be used as justification for the salary reduction and differentiation that is existent here. This court is admittedly not sufficiently enlightened to discuss or even recognize the different philosophies of teaching. It is common knowledge that even the authorities in the educational field differ violently not only as to the value of the various philosophies of teaching, but also as to the methods by which they should be carried out. If such generalities were to be used as justification for salary changes, then the actions of the administrative boards would not be discretionary but wholly arbitrary. The instant case is illustrative of the inadvisability of using such a method to test the value of a teacher.[12]

The court went on to say that it is entirely within the discretion of the board to increase the salary of the superior teacher, utilizing the following language:

> It is quite possible that a situation might exist in which one of two teachers of similar experience and service might be not only more capable, but also more industrious and willing than the other, who although sufficiently competent to prohibit dismissal, might be somewhat indolent and non-cooperative. In such a situation the school board should be permitted

---

[12]Kacsur v. Board of Trustees, 18 Cal. App. 2d 586, 116 P. 2d 593 (1941).

to exercise its reasonable discretion in raising the salary of the industrious teacher as a reward for her good work without at the same time having to increase the salary of the undeserving teacher.

In another California case, a plan which provided salary increases for those teachers who earned additional college hours and reductions for those who failed to earn such hours was alleged to be discriminatory and unreasonable. The court held that as long as the plan applied generally to all certificated employees, it was not illegal. Said the court:

> At his option, a teacher may, by obtaining additional educational credits, from time to time qualify for additional salary. If he does not choose to do so, the board of education rates his worth to the school district at a lesser amount than one who enlarges his educational experience. In short, the salary schedule merely provides that a teacher is to be compensated in accordance with training and experience.
>
> Certainly this is a desirable procedure. Miss Rible has not been singled out for particular or arbitrary action and the rules do not impose a penalty in the legal sense of that term but set up a standard of salary to be paid each year. . . . The fixing of a lower salary for one who has not taken a course of study during four years is not a dismissal without cause, nor do the rules impose training requirements upon permanent teachers, in addition to those prescribed by the State Board of Education, as a condition precedent to employment.[13]

Is the teacher who performs his services during only a part of the school year legally entitled to the proportionate part of the salary payments to be made during the summer months? The teacher who works approximately nine months may be paid on a twelve-equal-payments basis, a portion of the salary being paid during the summer after the work is performed. The authorities are in agreement that, even though he resigns or otherwise leaves the system, the teacher is entitled to the proportionate share of the summer salary represented by the length of his service in the district. The reasoning is quite logical in such decisions. The classroom teacher is not expected to perform any services during the summer months for the compensation specified in the contract. In other words, the services are to be performed during a period of approximately nine months, while the salary is to be paid upon the basis of twelve months. The teacher who performs, let us say, 8/9 of the work called for in the contract and

---

[13]Rible v. Hughes, 24 Cal. App. 2d 437, 150 P. 2d 455 (1944).

then resigns is therefore entitled to receive that proportion of the summer salary.[14]

Extra pay for extra work. The question of whether teachers are entitled to extra pay for extra work required of them has sometimes come before the courts. In New York, a board of education passed a resolution requiring teachers to give service outside of regular classroom hours. Considering that the new resolution constituted additional work on their part, the teachers brought suit to force the board to raise their salaries. The court said in ruling in favor of the board:

> The hours of service of its teachers may not necessarily coincide with the hours of classroom instruction, nor is it legally required that the hours fixed be the same for all teachers. . . . Of course, it is recognized that any bylaw of a board outlining teachers' duties must stand the test of reasonableness. . . . A board is not required to pay additional compensation for such services. The duty assigned must be within the scope of teachers' duties. Teachers may not be required, for instance, to perform janitor service, police service . . . school bus driving service, etc. These are not "teaching duties." The board may not impose upon a teacher a duty foreign to the field of instruction for which he is licensed or employed.[15]

At issue ostensibly was the question of whether rules and regulations passed by a board of education during the life of a teaching contract become binding upon the teachers involved. It is well settled that so long as they act in good faith, in a reasonable manner, and within their statutory rights, a board of education may enact such rules and regulations, the effect of which bears a similarity to enactments by state legislatures in that they are legally binding upon the teachers even though the teachers may not have acceded to the requirements in question.

To clarify this point, some boards of education include an *elastic clause* in the contractual document, in which the teacher agrees to perform, in addition to the general instructional duties, such "other reasonable duties as the board or superintendent may direct." The additional duties are considered to be included in the annual salary stipulation at no extra pay, unless, of course, provisions for extra pay are made in the contract.

Although available evidence does not indicate a fast developing trend, many boards now provide extra pay for extra work, and include

[14]State v. Black, 46 Del. 295, 83 A.2d 678 (1951).
[15]Parrish v. Moss, 106 N.Y.S.2d 577 (Sup. Ct. 1951).

provisions in their annual contracts to that effect. The legality of these provisions has not been questioned in a court of law.

An interesting case involving extra pay for extra work arose in Kansas, when a teacher shortage developed due to wartime drafts of teaching personnel. Being unable to recruit additional teachers, the board decided to solve the problem by paying the remaining teachers for carrying on the additional work. A taxpayer in the district objected to the board's action, and brought suit to enjoin the board from such payments. Plaintiff maintained that such payments constituted a gift, gratuity, or bonus, inasmuch as the teachers were legally obligated to carry on the work of the school without additional pay. The Supreme Court of Kansas, however, could not agree with the plaintiff, since the payments to teachers were made not under the original contracts, but under separate and independent agreements.[16]

In California, a teacher objected to a board rule which required that each male teacher supervise three football and three basketball games each year, for which there was no extra compensation. The purpose of the rule was to "protect the welfare of the students." The duties consisted of maintaining order in the stands, clearing the aisles on occasion, taking tickets, and preventing smoking in the gymnasium. In presenting his case, the plaintiff argued that the board's rule was not written in the teacher's handbook, nor was there anything in his contract or in the state laws to indicate that he must perform this duty. Furthermore, he argued, the duty was unprofessional in nature, outside his area of preparation, and imposed during unreasonable hours.

The court could not agree with the teacher's arguments. It pointed out that a board may make any reasonable rule not inconsistent with state law to promote the welfare of the student body; the fact that the rule was not written into the handbook was immaterial. Authority for the duty lay in a law which made principals responsible for the supervision and administration of their schools, and a published board rule which required "teachers to cooperate with their superiors."

Said the Supreme Court of California in denying relief to the teacher, and in holding for the board:

> Teachers are engaged in a professional employment. . . .
> The worth of a teacher is not measured in terms of a specific sum of money per hour. A teacher expects to and does perform a service. If that service from time to time requires additional hours of work, a teacher expects to and does perform it. . . .

---

[16]Joint Consol. School Dist. No. 2 v. Johnson, 166 Kan. 636, 203 P.2d 242 (1949).

A teacher's duties and obligations to students and the community are not satisfied by closing the classroom door at the conclusion of a class. . . . All of his duties are taken into consideration in his contract for employment at the annual salary. All of this is, of course, subject to the test of reasonableness. . . .[17]

Miscellaneous salary rights. Is a tenure teacher entitled to his salary during a period of suspension by the board? In a leading Pennsylvania case, a teacher brought court action to recover salary from the date of his suspension to the date of discharge, a period of some five weeks. The teacher did not question the right of the board to dismiss him, but did claim his right to compensation while under suspension. The lower court ruled for the teacher, but both the superior court and the Supreme Court of Pennsylvania upheld the board.

Said the supreme court, in reasoning in support of the board of education and against the teacher:

> Kaplan was suspended because of his refusal to cooperate with the school authorities. . . . The contract which he signed with the school district on July 12, 1948, assured him a salary provided he worked. It did not guarantee compensation if he was idle as the result of a situation which he voluntarily brought about. The law of contracts is as constant as the law of gravitation. No one is entitled to anything from anybody without consideration. One may obtain gratuities, he may be favored with special attention, but when he goes to law to collect money he must prove that he forewent some advantage which enured to the benefit of the person from whom he claims money.[18]

The weight of authority supports the rule that a teacher may not be penalized salary-wise because of temporary interruptions due to the closing of the school. While some earlier district defendants sought to make a distinction between closings occasioned by "an act of God" and other closings, the courts have generally held that, unless it was otherwise stipulated in the contract, the district was not relieved from liability to pay the teacher when the school was closed for reasons beyond the teacher's control. In an Illinois case, where the teacher was prevented from teaching because the schoolhouse was destroyed by a tornado, it was held that he could recover for the entire term.[19] Likewise, when a school was closed for two months because of an influenza

---

[17]McGrath v. Burkhard, 131 Cal. App. 2d 367, 280 P.2d 864 (1955).
[18]Kaplan v. School Dist. of Phila., 388 Pa. 213, 130 A.2d 672 (1957).
[19]Corn v. Board of Educ., 39 Ill. App. 446 (1891).

epidemic, the court ruled that the teacher could recover wages for the time lost. Said the court in the latter case:

> That the school might be closed on that account [an epidemic] was a contingency that might happen, and whether the school authorities took the initiative, or whether it was done by action of the board of health, does not alter the rights of the parties to the contract. It works no hardship on anyone to require school authorities to insert in the contract of employment a provision exempting them from liability in the event the school is closed on account of a contagious epidemic. As said by the Supreme Court of Ohio, courts will not insert by construction, for the benefit of one of the parties, a condition which they have omitted from their own contract.[20]

To the opposite effect was a 1921 case which arose in Indiana. The plaintiff teacher brought suit to recover pay for twenty-seven days' service. She was unable to teach for this period due to the closing of the schools by the health authorities. In holding that the plaintiff could not recover pay for the time lost, the court reasoned, "It is the rule that, when the performance of a contact becomes impossible, non-performance is excused, and no damages can be recovered."[21] The closing of the schools by the health officials because of an influenza epidemic was an exercise of statutory authority over which the township trustees had no control. The court held it was not necessary that the contract contain a clause expressly setting aside the conditions of the contract in the event of the closing of the schools. This rule, however, has been applied in only a minority of cases.

Many teachers' contracts of employment incorporate by reference the provisions of written board policies covering deductions from wages when schools are closed because of any epidemic, loss of the building, or observation of recognized holidays. Such written policies, as part of the contractual arrangement between board and teacher, enable both parties to better resolve the effect of such closings in computing the salary due. It is submitted that, in the light of a more complex personnel picture, larger schools, and increasing faculty numbers, the written board policy is apt to be increasingly used to provide solutions to problems associated with school closings.

May the teacher be required to make up time caused by interruptions in the school year resulting from epidemics and the like? In at

---

[20]Phelps v. School Dist. Number 109, Wayne County, 302 Ill. 193, 134 N.E. 312, 21 A.L.R. 737 (1922).
[21]Gregg School Township v. Hinshaw, 76 Ind. App. 503, 132 N.E. 586 (1921).

least one case a court has ruled that he may.[22] Subsequent cases, however, have ruled to the contrary.[23] Apparently, when the teacher holds himself in readiness even though the school is closed, he may be entitled to compensation for the period when school is suspended, and may also receive additional compensation when asked to teach additional days at the conclusion of the school year. Such a ruling takes into account the inability of the teacher to enter into another permanent contractual arrangement while school duties under his contract are temporarily suspended.

In an Illinois case, the question of the authority of the board to require participation in a professional growth program as a condition of salary increments arose.[24] A township high school board adopted a ruling that increases in teachers' salaries would be contingent upon the completion of additional college work or its equivalent by participation in accredited workshops. The usual procedure in the district had been to base such salary increases on a combination of years of experience in the district and college work completed.

The plaintiff, in this case a full-time tenure teacher with a master's degree and a life certificate, failed to obtain a raise under the new salary schedule because he had not met the professional growth requirements. The teacher brought an action for a declaratory judgment to compel the board to increase his salary. The court held that plaintiff was not entitled to the salary increase until he met the requirements; nor was he entitled to that amount he had not received when he later complied, *i.e.*, he was not entitled to retroactive pay.

Does a board have the right to "supplement" the teacher's salary? The general rule is that boards of education may not utilize public funds for other than "school purposes." The line between what constitutes "school" and "non-school" purposes cannot be clearly drawn. As a result, court action is frequently necessary to resolve controversies arising in this area.

The weight of judicial opinion throughout the years has been to the effect that boards may not provide transportation to teachers as a "fringe benefit" in the absence of a contrary declaration by the legislature. In Tennessee, the county trustees levied a fund for teacher transportation, and the county board of education sought to use the money to pay regular teachers' salaries. In refusing to allow the trans-

---

[22]Gear v. Gray, 10 Ind. App. 428, 37 N. E. 1059 (1894).

[23]McKay v. Barnett, 21 Utah 239, 60 Pac. 1100, 50 A.L.R. 371 (1900); Randolph v. Sanders, 22 Tex. Civ. App. 320, 54 S.W. 621 (1899).

[24]Richards v. Board, 21 Ill. 2d 104, 171 N.E.2d 37 (1960).

fer of funds for this purpose, the Supreme Court of Tennessee noted that the school statute pertaining to "public school transportation" did not include transportation of teachers. It is proper, in determining legislative intention, to look to the legislature. Said the court:

> If the Legislature wants to provide teacher transportation, the Legislature should and must say so in unmistakable terms, otherwise it seems to us that it is very clear from past Acts of the Legislature and from just common knowledge that the Legislature has never yet nor does not mean in the instant case to provide teacher transportation.[25]

On the other hand, school officials have been allowed to receive reimbursement for travel outside the state in order to recruit teachers.[26] The distinction was made clear in this case that the expenditure was obviously for a "school purpose."

Minimum Salary Laws

In 1959, approximately three of every four states in the nation had enacted so-called minimum salary laws. Such legislation was originally intended to provide stability for teachers as a professional group, the ultimate objective being better instructional services to the children of the state. For this reason, professional teachers' groups early adopted as one of their objectives the passage of minimum salary laws. In states without such legislative provisions, the united profession is still seeking their adoption. In states having such legislation, the upward revision of the minimums is one of the major goals of teachers' professional groups.

Minimum salary laws provide that local boards of education may not pay teachers annual salaries *below* a certain stated base prescribed in the statute. Generally speaking, the bases are lower than the actual base salary schedules in current usage by local boards, inasmuch as minimum salary laws do not prevent local boards from paying teachers more than the required minimums.

Sometimes minimum salary provisions are included as a part of the state school finance foundation act, and represent a certain proportion of the classroom unit, or other unit of state aid distribution. In such instances, local communities which do not pay teachers the minimum specified wage usually are not entitled to participate in the distribution of state aid funds. In this way, local boards are encouraged to raise

---

[25]State v. Davidson County, 198 Tenn. 24, 277 S.W.2d 396 (1954).
[26]School Dist. v. Bruck, 255 Ore. 496, 358 P.2d 283 (1960).

teachers' salaries to the specified figure. Very little litigation on the problem of minimum salaries for teachers has arisen in the United States.

Duty-free Lunch Periods

Four states, California, Illinois, Massachusetts, and Ohio, have statutes which prescribe a duty-free, minimum-length lunch period for classroom teachers. In Pennsylvania, the law applies to teachers and all women employed for more than five hours a day. To date, the validity of these statutes has not been challenged in the courts.

The portion of the Ohio statute dealing with duty-free lunch periods for classroom teachers states:

> Each teacher employed by the board of education of a school district shall be granted at least thirty minutes for lunch each school day, during which time he shall not be required to perform any school activity; except that in a one-teacher school where enforcement of the foregoing provisions shall work a hardship, the county board of education of the school district in which the one-teacher school is located may require the teacher to remain on duty.
>
> The granting of the lunch period to a teacher shall not be cause for lengthening the school day.[27]

The inclusion of duty-free lunch periods in the platform of teachers' groups could conceivably lead to a trend in legislation similar to that noted in the five states mentioned above.

Right to Leaves of Absence

Among the rules and regulations which boards are authorized to adopt are those providing for leaves of absence from teaching duties in such instances as maternity of the teacher, illness or death in the family, professional improvement, and health reasons. Recently, several state legislatures have provided leaves of absence for teachers. Of course, whenever rules and regulations of school boards conflict with state statutes in these matters, the state law is controlling.

In the absence of state legislation on the matter, it is a fairly well settled rule of law that boards have such power as seems necessary in providing for employee leaves of absence. Not only is such authority implied from the board's role as an employer, but also from its role as steward and trustee of the welfare of the children in the public

---

[27]*Page's Ohio Rev. Code* § 3319.111.

schools. The courts will construe as nearly as possible such board rules and regulations in the light of ultimate benefits to children, so long as the board acts judiciously in the handling of public moneys in its care.

In earlier times, the contract for performance of teaching duties was interpreted by the courts as performance *by the teacher* only and no other. Performance was of necessity a personal matter, and the employment of a substitute would not suffice to meet the conditions of the contract. Said a New York City court, in ruling on a case arising when a teacher who was ill sued the school board for pay while absent from the classroom:

> The salary of an employee not being an incident to the office but payment for service rendered, there would certainly be nothing illegal in a provision changing the conditions under which the salary is paid, so that it is payable only for the period for which services are actually rendered. The school board therefore has the right to reduce the salary of a teacher by providing that he is to receive no compensation for the days on which he is absent without leave.[28]

More recently, however, this problem has been solved by including in the contract, or in board rules and regulations, provisions for the teacher's absence from the job for short periods of time in the event such an eventuality becomes necessary. This seems to be the better interpretation of the teacher's rights. Terms of school are longer than formerly, there is more activity in professional organizations than before, and work pressures often make it desirable for the teacher to "stop a while and rest." Our society has readily accepted the idea of leaves of absence for employees in industry, business, and the military. What seems more logical, therefore, than that teachers should be provided for in board policy and legislative enactment in such matters?

The courts have ruled that deductions from salary for unauthorized leaves of absence must be "ratable deductions"; that is, they should be in due proportion to the salary that the teacher's time of absence from duty without leave bears to the entire time of duty.[29] Thus, boards may withhold 1/180 of the teacher's salary where the teacher absents himself from work for a day and the length of the contractual period is 180 days.

---

[28]Murphy v. Board of Educ. of City of N.Y., 87 App. Div. 277, 84 N.Y. Supp. 380 (1903).

[29]Glucksman v. Board of Educ. of City of New York, 101 Misc. 682, 167 N.Y. Supp. 1075 (1917).

Maternity leave. At one time, the majority of America's women teachers were single. Today, however, more than one-half of the female teaching force are married. Although courts have not always implied through their decisions that boards of education should expect pregnancy among married women teachers, and provide for such exigency through a maternity leave provision, several court decisions are to this effect. Some state legislatures have dealt with the problem, and most boards of education in larger school districts have formulated a controlling policy in one way or another. But it is in the courts that the reasonableness of maternity leave policies is finally decided.

A Pennsylvania teacher was absent from work for about three months due to physical disability resulting from pregnancy. The state statute specified that teachers were required to perform their duties unless prevented by a "personal illness or disease. . . ." The board had granted no formal leave, but proceeded to pay the teacher for five days' sick leave, and continued her normal salary during her absence. In ruling that the teacher was not entitled to count the time lost in computing seniority rights, the court pointed out that in that state, at least, pregnancy of a married teacher is not considered as an illness or disease, but a normal condition even though it may be accompanied by pathological developments. The period of the absence, short in duration though it was, must be taken into consideration in computing seniority rights of the teacher.[30]

Another Pennsylvania case is also in point. The court in this case was called upon to decide whether because of her pregnancy a teacher became *incompetent* to perform her duties. The board had so ruled, and had dismissed the teacher on the grounds of incompetency. There was general agreement that her incompetency, if indeed it were such, arose not from her educational qualifications, but entirely from her physical condition. The teacher sought reinstatement to her position by recourse to the courts.

The action of the board was upheld by the Supreme Court of Pennsylvania. Said that body in ruling on the case:

> We must bear in mind that Mrs. Brown was not being discriminated against because of her marriage. . . . Her dismissal was due neither to that fact nor to her legitimate pregnancy, but because she became incompetent due to her physical incapacity to discharge her duties.[31]

---

[30]West Mahanoy Township School Dist. v. Kelly, 156 Pa. Super. 601, 41 A.2d 344 (1945).

[31]Appeal of School Dist. of City of Bethlehem, 347 Pa. 418, 32 A.2d 565 (1943).

Following World War II, a serious teacher shortage developed, and housewives, many of whom had previous teaching experience, were called into teaching service to alleviate the shortage. In the interest of equity, it became apparent that married women should not be discriminated against in their employment because of motherhood, a natural consequence of their marital status. If and when pregnancy occurred, the married teacher should not be penalized therefor, but should be given reasonable leave.

Faced with the problem, several state legislatures enacted statutes outlining the rights of the married teacher to maternity leave. In the absence of such statutes, the majority of boards of education began to include in their written board policies provisions for maternity leaves. An example of such a policy is that adopted by the Boulder, Colorado, Board of Education in 1963:

> *6.5.5. Maternity Leave.* The school district will require leaves of absence to be taken or resignations to be submitted for maternity reasons, such leave or resignation to become effective at least four and one-half months prior to the anticipated birth of the child.
>
> Maternity leave, not to exceed two years in length, will be granted, without pay, to any fulltime certificated employee on tenure, upon the recommendation of the Superintendent of Schools and the approval of the Board of Education. A probationary teacher will not be given maternity leave but must resign.
>
> Sick leave allowances may not be applied toward a leave of absence for maternity reasons.
>
> · Neither sick leave nor salary increments will accrue to a teacher while she is on maternity leave, but she will retain any balance of these benefits that she had accumulated up to the effective date of the leave.
>
> Application for reinstatement after maternity leave must be made at least sixty days before the opening of the school year. As a rule, reinstatement will not be made at any time other than at the beginning of the school year. Exceptions may be made in cases of emergencies in the school system.
>
> A teacher who has taken leave or resigned for maternity reasons must have the written permission of her attending physician before reinstatement to her teaching duties. In no case may she return to duty before the child is three months old.[32]

---

[32]Boulder Valley School Board of Education. "Handbook of Policies and Procedures," (Boulder, Colorado: School District Number Re2, 1963), mimeo.

In Louisiana, a state statute provided that regularly employed teachers "shall be granted maternity leave for a reasonable time before and after childbirth." A board of education in that state accordingly adopted a rule requiring any married woman teacher in its employ who became pregnant to ask for a leave of absence immediately after having knowledge of her condition, and under no circumstances to remain at work after three months of pregnancy. The teacher was required by the board to remain at least fifteen months on leave, and there were other provisions similar to those adopted by the Boulder Board of Education. Later, the board adopted a resolution which provided that a teacher who became pregnant again while already on maternity leave must remain off the job until six months after the birth of the second child.

A Louisiana tenure teacher, while on maternity leave, notified the board that she was again pregnant, but that the second child would be born in time for her to resume her duties when school reopened in the fall of 1957. The second child was born on August 17, and the teacher requested in writing to be permitted to resume teaching on September 3rd. This request was denied by the board.

In bringing action for reinstatement, the teacher argued that the board's refusal to permit her to resume teaching was in effect a "removal from office." In Louisiana, a tenure teacher may be removed only on written and signed charges of willful neglect of duty, incompetency, or dishonesty. The board's action was therefore illegal, it was contended, and should be set aside.

The teacher's suit for reinstatement was dismissed. The board had not acted arbitrarily, nor was the teacher's failure to be reinstated a removal from office. Although there was nothing in the law to specify what constituted *a reasonable time*, the court said that the board had acted legally in considering the welfare not only of the teacher, but also of the school children and the school system. Reinstatement was rightfully a matter of discretion with the board so long as these conditions were present.[33]

To the same effect was a similar case in Pennsylvania in which the supreme court of that state held reasonable a board rule which required that female employees should apply for leaves of absence in cases of expected maternity. A teacher who refused to apply for such leave was legally discharged because of such refusal. The board rule stipu-

---

[33]State ex rel. Sepulvado v. Rapides Parish School Bd., 236 La. 482, 108 So. 2d 96 (1959).

lated that "failure to comply with the resolution shall be construed as an act of insubordination on the part of the employee, and shall be treated as such." This part of the rule was also sustained by the court.[34]

It seems apparent from these cases that boards of education may exercise wide discretionary powers in dealing with matters of maternity leave for teachers in their employ, in the absence of a statute directly bearing on the subject. A wise board of education will provide for such exigencies in written policy and employees will be notified accordingly.

Sick leave. The practice of making deductions from the teacher's salary for absences occasioned by sickness or personal injury seems to be disappearing. Boards of education are coming to realize that the granting of leave with full pay for a period of illness or injury has beneficial effects on teachers and the school system in general. Such payments are clearly within the authority of local boards to grant in the absence of statutes to the contrary. The board may choose to carry insurance covering such matters, or adopt a wage continuation plan for the period during which the teacher is absent on account of sickness or injury.

Local boards are not the only governing bodies to note the salutary effect of sick leave provisions on school personnel. By 1961, three-fourths of the legislatures had enacted some type of state-wide sick-leave provision, illustrating, no doubt, the desire of legislators to provide the same type of benefits for teachers as are received by workers in business and industry. In twenty-five of the states, such legislation made it mandatory for boards of education to provide sick-leave benefits; in the other states it was permissive legislation. In eleven of the twenty-five states where paid sick-leave for teachers was mandatory, boards of education were expressly granted the power to exceed the state minimum benefits if they so desired.

Furthermore, the United States Treasury Department has ruled that taxpayers, including teachers, are entitled to special sick leave benefits. Section 105 (d) of the Internal Revenue Code of 1954 excludes from a taxpayer's gross income all or a part of the wages, or payments in lieu of wages, which the teacher receives under his employer's wage continuation plan for a period during which he is absent from work on account of personal illness or injury.

---

[34]Board of School Directors v. Snyder, 346 Pa. 103, 29 A.2d 34 (1942).

In those states in which mandatory sick leave has been adopted, the statute generally provides for a certain specified number of days' pay to which the teacher is entitled, the average number of such days being ten. There are usually additional provisions pertaining to the number of unused sick leave days which may accumulate to the credit of the teacher. In Washington, the statute provides that unused sick leave may be cumulative up to 180 days, or one full school year. California, Hawaii, and New Jersey allow indefinite accumulation. By contrast, unused sick leave is not cumulative in Georgia, while a maximum of twenty days is allowed in three other states.

Other leaves of absence. The list of types of leaves to which teachers may be entitled is indeed long and varied. In some states, the legislature provides that all workers, including teachers, shall be excused from work for a certain limited period of time in order to visit the polls and vote. Leaves for jury duty, for active service in the armed forces, and for other community services may be provided. Short leaves for personal reasons, such as attending to business affairs, or for sickness or death in the immediate family may also be provided.

Perhaps the most common type of leave is for professional improvement. This may range from leave for teaching in a foreign country on an exchange basis to attending a one-day professional meeting. Sabbatical leave for professional study in at least one instance was declared to be the right of the teacher rather than a privilege.[35] Sabbatical leaves are usually available to a teacher only after he has completed a given number of years of service in the school district.

Whether teachers may be entitled to leave on religious holidays with or without pay is still an unsettled question. The teacher should consult the written policies of the board of education in determining leaves of absence which are provided by the contract.

Right to Hold Other Employment

The right of a public school teacher to hold employment outside the school system while under contract in the public schools has been the subject of some litigation. Two of the cases pertain to the holding of outside jobs which were either immoral or interfered with the teacher's regular classroom duties, and were prohibited by the courts. In another case, the teacher was prohibited from holding a position as a member of a board of education in the same county in which he

---

[35]State ex rel. Scoggins v. Vernon Parish School Bd., 44 So. 2d 385 (La. 1950).

also held a position as teacher. In the final case, a board ruling preventing teachers from holding two positions in the same school system was sustained.

In the first case, the right of the board to dismiss a teacher because of the type of her outside employment was at issue. In Pennsylvania, a teacher holding a contract under the teacher tenure law of that state acted as a waitress in a restaurant managed by her husband. On certain occasions, she served as bartender after school hours and during summer vacations. In the restaurant, and in the presence of her pupils, she took an occasional drink of beer, served beer to customers, shook dice with customers for drinks, and played and showed customers how to play a pinball machine. She was rated by her superintendent as "43 per cent" competent, a rating of fifty per cent being the passing average rating. She was dismissed by the board on the grounds of incompetency, and she sued for reinstatement.

State law in Pennsylvania provided that a teacher holding a contract under the teacher tenure law could be dismissed only on the grounds of immorality, incompetency, intemperance, cruelty, willful and persistent neglect of duty, and other specified causes. The teacher's argument was that she was illegally dismissed, since her holding an outside job did not come under the specified provisions of the tenure act. Furthermore, her conduct outside the school had no bearing on her competency as a teacher, since it did not pertain to her knowledge of subject matter used in teaching.

The court said that the term incompetency has a common and approved usage, and that its meaning is not limited to lack of substantive knowledge of the subject to be taught. On the question of the teacher's conduct, the court added:

> Is such a course of conduct immoral or intemperate, and does it—in combination with her scholastic and efficiency rating—amount to incompetency? We hold it to be self evident that under the intent and meaning of the act, incompetence is not essentially confined to a deviation from sex morality; it may be such a course of conduct as offends the morals of the community and is a bad example to the youth whose ideals a teacher is supposed to foster and to elevate. Nor need incompetency be confined strictly to overindulgence in alcoholic liquors—temperance implies moderation and a person may be intemperate in conduct without being an alcoholic addict. And so as to incompetency; as we take it, this means under the Act incompetence as a teacher—but does it mean that competency is merely the ability to teach the Three R's?

[We] conclude that it would be "just" to affirm the action
of the board in dismissing the teacher.[36]

A teacher in an Illinois school was under contract to teach agriculture on a twelve-month basis. He became involved in a business venture
in which he sold seed oats, tested soils, advertised and sold fertilizers,
and operated a factory for blending fertilizers. The board of education
sought to determine whether he would teach during the ensuing year,
but he declined to inform the board on this point. He did affirm that
if he sold 500 tons of fertilizer that he would not teach the following
year. The board discharged him on the grounds that (1) his outside
activities interfered with his teaching duties, and (2) the best interests
of the schools would be served thereby.

The teacher sought reinstatement to his former position. In refusing to reinstate him, the appellate court of Illinois cited with approval
an earlier case (Powell v. Board of Education, 97 Ill. 375), in which
the discretionary powers of school boards to dismiss teachers had been
questioned:

> Directors are invested by law with large discretion in all
> matters pertinent to the management of schools and with the
> discretionary powers of officers, whether executive or judi-
> cial; courts have no rightful authority to interfere unless where
> there has been such abuse of their discretion as works palpable
> injustice or injury.[37]

In dealing with the question of whether the outside activities of
the teacher had interfered with his teaching duties, the court said:

> It is peculiarly a province of the Board of Education in
> the exercise of its discretion to determine whether the outside
> activities of the appellant had progressed to such an extent
> as to interfere with the performance of his duties as a member
> of the teaching staff of the educational institution under its
> direction.
>
> The best interest of the schools of the district is the guid-
> ing star of the Board of Education and for the courts to inter-
> fere with the execution of the powers of the board in that
> respect is an unwarranted assumption of authority and can
> only be justified in cases where the board has acted malicious-
> ly, capriciously, and arbitrarily.[38]

---

[36]Horosko v. Mount Pleasant Township School Dist., 335 Pa. 369, 6 A.2d 866
(1939).

[37]Meredith v. Board of Educ. of Community Unit School Dist. No. 7, 7 Ill.
App. 2d 477, 130 N.E.2d 5 (1955).

[38]*Ibid.*

It seems apparent from these leading cases that boards will be upheld in their dismissal of a teacher whose outside work is of such a nature as to make him unfit for the position of teacher, or whose outside activities occupy so much of his time that he "slights" his teaching duties under contract to the board. While it is obvious that teachers may sometimes accept outside employment to supplement their salaries, the board may still release them should such employment substantially interfere with the effective performance of their teaching duties.

In an Arkansas county, one of the members of the county school board was a public school teacher. A statute of that state provided that members of the county board must "not hold any salaried or fee office of the state or any political subdivision thereof." The decision turned upon the word "office." The court said that the position of teacher was not an office within the meaning of the statute, but instead was an employment. The court would not allow the teacher to act as a board member and as an employee of the same school district, but saw no reason why the teacher could not serve as a board member in one district while acting as teacher in another.[39]

The remaining case illustrates a "dual job law" which prohibited teachers in the New York City schools from holding more than one position under the board of education. The court refused to find the law unconstitutional. It said that, although the law might operate harshly on many individuals, "the policy has been expressed by the legislature under this law, and with its wisdom or economics the court on these motions cannot concern itself." The court continued:

> Of the approximately 38,000 teachers employed under the Board of Education, about 1,200 hold more than one teaching position, some of them holding as many as four. The plaintiff teaches both in Day High School and Evening High School. Yet some 5,000 teachers on eligible lists are awaiting appointment. The objective of the challenged law is to spread employment.
>
> Inasmuch as the law applies to all persons of a class, it is not discriminatory. Nor does the law transgress or affect that provision of the Constitution which prescribes merit and fitness as the standard for appointment to the civil service.[40]

---

[39]Maddox v. State, 220 Ark. 762, 249 S.W.2d 972 (1952).

[40]Lapolla v. Board of Educ. of City of N.Y., 172 Misc. 394, 15 N.Y.S.2d 149 (1939).

Workmen's Compensation and Other Insurance

A state may enact a statute requiring that all public employees, including those of a school district, shall be subject to the compensation provisions of the state workmen's compensation act. According to the weight of authority, such statutes are not unconstitutional, in that they divert public moneys for a private or non-school use. Almost without exception, the courts have held that such expenditures are for a "school purpose." In states where such a requirement is mandatory on boards of education, the authority to use the taxing power of the district to raise money to pay workmen's compensation program premiums is generally expressly granted by the state.

The question often before the courts in litigation arising under workmen's compensation laws is whether the injury resulted from a risk or hazard incident to the regular employment of the injured party. For example, in a Kentucky case, an art teacher, laden with art materials, in going from one building to another, was knocked to the pavement by his dog which jumped on him in an overly playful manner. The court ruled that the teacher could not recover, since his injuries did not result from a risk ordinarily or reasonably inherent in or incident to his employment.[41]

In a New Jersey case, the court held that a superintendent of schools was entitled to compensation when he suffered a heart attack while addressing a PTA sponsored dinner meeting. There was considerable controversy in the community over the question of racial integration, the topic of the administrator's address. The court concluded that under the circumstances the superintendent was tense, nervous, and strained. The connection between this condition and his heart attack was found to be causal in nature, and the award of workmen's compensation was affirmed.[42]

Sometimes there is a statutory provision that claims for compensation under the workmen's compensation laws must be filed with the legal authorities by the injured party within a specified period following the injury. In New York, a court refused to permit the filing of a late claim when the claimant alleged he had been physically incapacitated and unable to file the claim within the specified period. The court pointed out that he had, after two weeks in the hospital, been

---

[41]Wilke v. University of Louisville, 327 S.W.2d 739 (Ky. 1959).

[42]McClain v. Board of Educ., City of Woodbury, 30 N.J. 567, 154 A.2d 569 (1959).

able to go to his doctor's office and to attend a workmen's compensation meeting. He had lost his right to recover compensation through *laches* (failure to assert one's rights for an unreasonable and unexplained length of time).[43]

In Louisiana, a teacher who was totally disabled was entitled to full disability compensation within the meaning of the law, even though the board was willing to forbear requiring "performance of such portions of his former duties" as were impossible for the teacher to perform, and to employ him on a full-time basis with the knowledge that he would be confined to his desk for ninety per cent of the time.[44]

In workmen's compensation cases, the state and not the school district is the liable party. In New Mexico, an employee, a janitor who fell from a ladder while repairing school window panes sued the school district for payment of medical expenses incurred through his injury. The supreme court of that state used the following language in denying the claim:

> We feel the school district is a political subdivision of the state created to aid in the administration of education, and subject, in this case, to the immunities available to the state itself. . . . A suit may not be brought against a state institution under the Workmen's Compensation Act without the express consent of the state. . . .

Plaintiff's contention that a school district was a municipal corporation and as such not immune from tort liability was overruled in this case. The award of damages in the lower court was reversed.[45]

The legality of school board purchase of group life or other group insurance for teachers is not clearly defined in most states. In at least one state, such an exercise of board power was declared within the power of the board of education.[46] In some states, boards are required to provide income protection for their employees injured on the job. In the absence of a statute expressly providing for such an expenditure, it is unlikely that the courts would permit boards to pay group insurance premiums for employees of school districts, unless it can be shown that such payment promotes a school purpose. As the practice

[43]Aldi v. Board of Educ. of Central School Dist. No. 1 of the Towns of Rotterdam and Princetown, Schenectady County, 4 App. Div. 2d 921, 167 N.Y.S.2d 125 (1957).

[44]Chase v. Pointe Coupee Parish School Bd., 89 So. 2d 466 (La. 1956).

[45]McWhorter v. Board of Educ. of Tatum Independent School Dist. No. 28, Lea County, 63 N. M. 421, 320 P.2d 1025 (1958).

[46]Nohl v. Board of Educ. of City of Albuquerque, 27 N.M. 232, 199 Pac. 373 (1921).

of group insurance by employers in industry and business spreads, the courts may consider such common practice in the public interest, and allow boards to pay group premiums as a means of competing in the labor market for employees.

Suggested Activities

DISCUSS:

1. What fringe benefits not now generally available to public school teachers should be provided? Why?
2. Why should teachers know their legal rights?
3. Can every fringe benefit for which boards spend money be interpreted as a "school purpose" under the legal meaning of that term?
4. What advice would you give the teacher who has completed an interview with the superintendent of schools, and subsequently signed a contract of employment?

RESOLVED:

1. That referring to teachers as school "employees" is more advantageous to them than as school "officials."
2. That teachers should be allowed to hold outside employment as long as there is no interference with regular classroom duties.
3. That state legislatures should provide more fully for teachers' fringe benefits from state funds than at present.

STATE THE PRINCIPLE OF LAW RELATIVE TO THE:

1. Teacher's right to summer salary.
2. Right to salary when school is closed.
3. Right to duty-free lunch periods.
4. Right of the board to determine teachers' salaries.
5. Right of the board to pay teachers on a merit basis.

CASE STUDY:

Discuss the following problem cases. Decide how you would have ruled on the basis of the principles of law developed in this chapter. Then check your answer by referring to the case in the National Reporter System.

Case # 1. A California school board adopted a rule providing that no salary increments would be paid to any teacher found to be unsatisfactory. A tenure teacher upon whom the board invoked the rule brought suit to require the board to give her a satisfactory rating and pay her the increments to which she would have been entitled had she received the satisfactory rating. The teacher had not been present when the ratings had been presented to the board, nor had she had an opportunity to appear in her own behalf before the board to discuss salary matters.

Heinlein v. Anaheim Union High School Dist., 96 Cal. App. 2d 19, 214 P.2d 536 (1950).

Case # 2. A teacher brought an action for damages against the city board of education for injuries sustained when a fight broke out between two students in the school cafeteria. When the fight began, other students pushed towards it, and in so doing, they pushed the teacher, who fell and hit his head. The teacher was one of four, plus student monitors, assigned to the lunchroom which served over 300 students. The students had received instructions on standards of behavior in the lunchroom, had assigned seats, were limited in their movements in and out, and were given passes if they wished to leave the room.

Diamond v. Board of Educ. of City of N. Y., 171 N.Y.S.2d 703 (City Court 1958).

Case # 3. A teacher who was illegally discharged sued the board for the full amount of his annual salary. Pending the court's decision, he had taken a position at a higher salary in another district.

Coble v. School Dist. of the Town of Metal, 178 Pa. Super. 301, 116 A.2d 113 (1955).

Further Readings

Allen, Ira M. *The Teacher's Contractual Status as Revealed by an Analysis of American Court Decisions* (New York: Bureau of Publications, Teachers College, Columbia University, 1928).

Ballf, Harold P., and Harry A. Ballf. *Pupil and Teacher Security* (Walnut Creek, California: Monument Printing Company, 1960).

Garber, Lee O. *The Yearbook of School Law* (Danville, Illinois: Interstate Printers and Publishers, 1957, 1958, 1959).

Gauerke, Warren E. *Legal and Ethical Responsibilities of School Personnel* (Englewood Cliffs, N. J.: Prentice-Hall, 1959).

Hamilton, Robert R., and E. Edmund Reutter, Jr. *Legal Aspects of School Board Operation* (New York: Bureau of Publications, Teachers College, Columbia University, 1958).

Messick, John D. *The Discretionary Powers of School Boards* (Durham, N. C.: Duke University Press, 1949).

National Education Association. *The Teacher and the Law* (Washington: The Association, 1959), Research Monograph 1959-M3.

_____. *The Teacher's Day in Court: Review of 1959* (Washington: The Association, 1960).

Roe, William H. *School Business Management* (New York: McGraw-Hill Book Company, 1961), Ch. XV, Legal Counsel and the School.

Seitz, Reynolds C. (ed). *Law and the School Principal* (Cincinnati; W. H. Anderson Company, 1961).

Chapter VII

POLITICAL AND PERSONAL RIGHTS
OF TEACHERS

Introduction

Because the public schools teach concepts of freedom and democracy, it is generally assumed that teachers enjoy a considerable measure of personal, political, and academic freedom in their status as teachers. Surprise sometimes accompanies the discovery that teachers as a class often find themselves limited in these respects more so than persons who work in private business and industry.

Teachers are not "second class citizens," however. They have all the rights and immunities accruing to all citizens, plus some rights, such as privileged communication, for example, which the average citizen does not ordinarily possess. The limitations upon political and personal freedom of teachers arise from their unique status as governmental workers, as well as their statutory status under the school laws of the state. Teachers are included in the class with other governmental workers, postal workers, members of the armed forces, and similar workers, and come under specific legislation governing their right to strike and enter into collective arrangements concerning employment. Some of the other rights of teachers are controlled by statutory provisions in the school code. Finally, because teachers contract for personal services, the holding of legislative office may be closed to them, inasmuch as absence from work would serve to breach the contract of employment. Thus, the role of public school teacher can be seen as limiting to some extent the political and personal freedoms which teachers enjoy while holding that position.

The state has provided for a system of public education, and the courts will permit nothing to interfere with its orderly and uninterrupted operation. The board of education, for example, is prohibited from becoming "ham-strung" by engaging in contract agreements with labor unions or other groups; a board may not bargain away the discretion with which the state has clothed it. The teacher, furthermore, may not join organizations which are inimical to the public weal, or which advocate the overthrow of the government by force. Academic freedom cannot be allowed to become license to teach that which is contrary to public policy or in violation of social mores. This chapter deals with some of the problems related to full realization of the political, personal, and academic freedoms of teachers in the public schools of the nation.

Teachers' Constitutional Rights

The first amendment to the Constitution of the United States reads as follows:

> Congress shall make no law respecting an establishment of religion or prohibiting the free exercise thereof; or abridging the freedom of speech, or of the press; or the right of the people peaceably to assemble and to petition the government for a redress of grievances.

A teacher in Pennsylvania was discharged when she was found to be a member of the Communist party. A state statute provided that the contract of a teacher might be terminated for "advocation of or participation in un-American or subversive doctrines." The teacher claimed that her constitutional rights of free speech guaranteed under the first amendment had been violated. Her case reached the Supreme Court of Pennsylvania, which concluded that no constitutional rights of the teacher had been violated. The court said:

> There is no question of the right of free speech involved in this case. Miss Albert is not being penalized in her capacity as a private citizen because of any political, economic or social views she may entertain or any expression she may care to give to those views. The concern here is with her rights as a teacher, and the legislature can certainly prescribe qualifications for teachers in the public schools with respect not only to their academic attainments but also to their moral characters and their loyalty to the state and federal governments.[1]

In effect, the court said that any person who wishes to become a teacher assumes a measure of responsibility for his personal and polit-

---

[1]Appeal of Albert, 372 Pa. 13, 92 A.2d 663 (1952).

ical views. One who works for the state as an employee must come under the rules and regulations which the legislature may reasonably impose upon its employees. Teachers may choose whether they wish to work for the state on these terms or resign and go elsewhere. In any event, they are not deprived of their constitutional rights by a statute limiting membership in an un-American organization.

The question of the teacher's right to freedom of speech was before the United States Court of Appeals for the sixth circuit in 1959. A teacher, Davis, was called to appear before a sub-committee of the House Committee on Un-American Activities investigating Communist methods of infiltration into education. The sub-committee, whose purpose is to collect information only, operated under a set of rules which included the provision that where their answers might lead to self-incrimination, witnesses could plead the protection of the fifth amendment. However, Davis chose to stand squarely on the first amendment, and maintained that his right of free speech protected him in remaining silent. At no time did he claim the protection of the fifth amendment. Because of his refusal to answer questions put to him by the sub-committee, he was convicted of contempt of the Congress of the United States. The court held that the teacher was fully apprised of the object of the inquiry, which was within the power of the committee, and that the questions asked were pertinent to the object of the inquiry. His right to remain silent was superseded by his duty to co-operate with the committee.[2]

In *Barenblatt* v. *United States of America*[3] which arose in 1959, plaintiff, a former college teacher, refused to answer questions as to his membership in and affiliation with the Communist Party before a sub-committee of the House Committee on Un-American Activities. Like Davis, Barenblatt chose to base his defense on the first amendment, maintaining that his right of free speech also entitled him to remain silent. In holding him guilty of contempt of Congress, the Supreme Court of the United States said:

> The congressional power of inquiry, its range and scope, and an individual's duty in relation to it, must be viewed in proper perspective. . . . Of course, broadly viewed, inquiries cannot be made into the teaching that is pursued in any of our educational institutions. When academic teaching-freedom and its corollary learning-freedom, so essential to the well-being of the Nation, are claimed, this Court will always be

---

[2]Davis v. United States of America, 269 F.2d 357 (6th Cir. 1959).
[3]360 U. S. 109, 79 S. Ct. 1081, 3 L. Ed. 2d 1115 (1959).

> on the alert against intrusion of Congress into this constitu-
> tionally protected domain. But this does not mean that the
> Congress is precluded from interrogating a witness merely
> because he is a teacher. An educational institution is not a
> constitutional sanctuary from inquiry into matters that may
> otherwise be within the constitutional legislative domain mere-
> ly for the reason that inquiry is made of someone within its
> walls.[4]

The majority of the Court held that the sub-committee was legislatively authorized to investigate Communist infiltration into the field
of education, and that such authority was not subject to attack because of vagueness. It was held immaterial that the objective of the
committee might have been purely one of exposure.

The fifth amendment to the Constitution of the United States reads
as follows:

> No person shall be held to answer for a capital or other-
> wise infamous crime, unless on a presentment or indictment of
> a grand jury, except in cases arising in the land or naval forces,
> or in the militia, when in actual service in time of war or pub-
> lic danger; nor shall any person be subject for the same offense
> to be twice put in jeopardy of life or limb; nor shall be com-
> pelled in any criminal case to be a witness against himself, nor
> be deprived of life, liberty, or property, without due process
> of law; nor shall private property be taken for public use,
> without just compensation.

The portion of the fifth amendment most often involved in teacher
litigation is the clause "nor shall be compelled in any criminal case to
be a witness against himself. . ." This basic right involves a person's
refusal to testify under oath on the ground that his testimony may
lead to self-incrimination.

May the teacher be discharged from his employment for refusal
to answer questions regarding past Communist Party membership before a congressional sub-committee? A New York City charter provision required that a municipal employee who "took the fifth" would
be automatically dismissed without notice of hearing. In an earlier
hearing, the teacher had cooperated fully in response to similar questions. The earlier testimony was in the hands of the municipal authorities at the time the teacher refused to answer questions about his
membership in the Communist Party. He was dismissed from his teaching position, and he sought determination of the constitutionality of
the charter provision under which he was dismissed. Said the Supreme
Court of the United States, in reinstating the teacher:

[4]*Ibid.*

Appellant argues that § 903 [of the Charter of the City of New York] abridges a privilege or immunity of a citizen of the United States since it in effect imposes a penalty on the exercise of a federally guaranteed right in a federal proceeding. It also violates due process, because the mere claim of privilege under the Fifth Amendment does not provide a reasonable basis for the State to terminate his employment. . . . We do not decide whether a claim under the "privilege or immunity" clause was considered below, since we conclude that the summary dismissal of appellant in the circumstances of this case violates due process of law.

At the outset we must condemn the practice of imputing sinister meaning to the exercise of a person's constitutional right under the Fifth Amendment. The right of an accused person to refuse to testify, which had been in England merely a rule of evidence, was so important to our forefathers that they raised it to the dignity of a constitutional amendment, and it has been recognized as "one of the most vital prerogatives of the citizen." We scored in [earlier cases] the assumption that those who claim this provision are either criminals or perjurers. The privilege against self-incrimination would be reduced to a hollow mockery if its exercise could be taken as equivalent either to a confession of guilt or a conclusive presumption of perjury. As we pointed out in Ullmann, a witness may have a reasonable fear of prosecution and yet be innocent of any wrongdoing. The privilege serves to protect the innocent who otherwise might be ensnared by ambiguous circumstances.[5]

The fourteenth amendment to the Constitution of the United States reads as follows:

All persons born or naturalized in the United States, and subject to the jurisdiction thereof, are citizens of the United States and of the state wherein they reside. No state shall make or enforce any law which shall abridge the privileges or immunities of citizens of the United States; nor shall any state deprive any person of life, liberty, or property without due process of law, nor deny to any person within its jurisdiction the equal protection of the laws.

In a Pennsylvania court, the question before the court was whether a board, in dismissing a teacher on the ground of incompetency for refusal to answer questions about his activities in certain allegedly subversive organizations, had violated the due process clause of the fourteenth amendment. A teacher for twenty-two years in the Philadelphia

---

[5]Slochower v. Board of Higher Educ. of City of N.Y., 350 U.S. 551, 76 Sup. Ct. 637, 100 L. Ed. 692 (1956).

Public School System presented himself at the superintendent's office in response to the latter's request. The superintendent said he had information which reflected adversely on the teacher's loyalty, and he wanted to determine its truth or falsity. The teacher declined to answer the questions put to him by his superintendent, whereupon he was dismissed. In bringing suit for reinstatement, the teacher claimed that his constitutional rights under the fourteenth amendment had been violated. The court could not agree, using the following language:

> By engaging in teaching in the public schools, petitioner did not give up his right to freedom of belief, speech or association. He did, however, undertake obligations of frankness, candor, and cooperation in answering inquiries made of him by his employing Board examining into his fitness to serve it as a public school teacher.[6]

What is the distinction between the *Beilan* case and *Slochower* case, since they appear to be in conflict? In the *Beilan* case, a teacher was held to have been legally dismissed for refusal to answer questions put to him by his superintendent, who was inquiring into the teacher's "competency" to teach. Refusal to respond in the circumstances, said the Court, amounted to incompetency, and constituted legal ground for the teacher's dismissal.

In the *Slochower* case, on the other hand, a teacher was held to have been illegally dismissed for pleading the protection of the fifth amendment before a Congressional sub-committee. The New York City Charter contained a provision that "whenever an employee of the City utilizes the privilege against self-incrimination to avoid answering a question relating to his official conduct, his term or tenure of office or employment shall terminate and such office or employment shall be vacant, and he shall not be eligible to election or appointment to any office or employment under the city or any agency." Slochower was a professor in a college operated by the City of New York. The city charter provision was held to be violative of due process of law. In practical effect, said the Court, taking the fifth under the statute was tantamount to confession. No consideration was given to such factors as the subject matter of the questions, remoteness of the period to which they were directed, or justification for exercise of the privilege. It matters not whether the plea resulted from mistake, inadvertence or legal advice conscientiously given, said the Court, whether

---

[6]Beilan v. Board of Public Educ., School Dist. of Philadelphia, 357 U.S. 399, 78 Sup. Ct. 1317, 2 L. Ed. 2d 1414 (1958).

wisely or unwisely. The heavy hand of the statute falls alike on all who exercise their constitutional privilege, the full enjoyment of which every person is entitled to receive. Such provisions were patently in violation of due process of law, and could not be allowed.

From these and other cases, it appears that the teacher may legally "take the fifth" before a Congressional sub-committee when asked about former activities, but may not legally remain silent when questioned along the same lines by his superintendent of schools.

In another Philadelphia case,[7] a teacher was called upon to answer questions relating to his loyalty put to him by his superintendent. The teacher requested copies of his superior's questions in advance of his meeting with the superintendent, but his request was refused. The teacher then declined to answer any questions put to him by the superintendent. The Supreme Court of Pennsylvania held that a teacher has no right to demand in advance a list of questions to be asked by the superintendent. The teacher who remains silent, said the court, may be held incompetent within the meaning of the state's tenure laws, and may be legally dismissed for refusal to answer questions concerning his loyalty put to him by his superintendent.

Just how free is the teacher to remain silent in such cases? The language used by Mr. Justice Frankfurter in the *Beilan* case *supra* is indicative of the position of the Supreme Court of the United States with respect to this problem. Said Frankfurter:

> The services of two public employees have been terminated because of their refusals to answer questions relevant, or not obviously irrelevant, to an inquiry by their superiors *into their dependability*. When these two employees were discharged, they were not labeled "disloyal." They were discharged because governmental authorities, like other employers, sought to satisfy themselves of the dependability of employees in relation to their duties. Accordingly, they made inquiries that, it is not contradicted, could in and of themselves be made. These inquiries were balked. The services of the employees were therefore terminated.

However, in New York, the Court of Appeals of that state upheld the state commissioner of education in reinstating three teachers, a principal, a school clerk, and a college professor who were dismissed for refusal to identify to the school superintendent other school personnel who belonged, or had belonged, to the Communist Party. The

---

[7]Board of Public Educ., School Dist. of Philadelphia v. Soler, 406 Pa. 168, 176 A.2d 653 (1961).

court held that the commissioner's action was reasonable, in that other methods of investigation were available to the board besides questioning teachers about fellow employees. The objection apparently was not so much to the grounds for dismissal, as to its effect upon the schools. The commissioner maintained, and the court upheld his contention, that such *procedural methods* tended to engender an atmosphere of suspicion and uneasiness in the public schools, and was not to be tolerated.[8]

Academic Freedom

The best known of the academic freedom cases is the famous "monkey trial" of John Thomas Scopes, a Tennessee teacher, who taught his students Darwin's theory of evolution in contravention of a state statute prohibiting the teaching of that subject. The trial attracted nation-wide attention. The famous lawyer, Clarence Darrow, defended Scopes in the trial court and William Jennings Bryan acted for the prosecution. These two colorful and well-known personalities tended to shift the emphasis away from the central question, which was, "Does the state have the power to prohibit by statute the teaching of the theory which holds that man has developed from some pre-existing lower type of animal life?" The trial court held that the state may restrict the teaching of evolution in the public schools, and fined Scopes the sum of $100. The lengthy trial was certainly the most captivating part of the story, but the conviction of Scopes was not the end of it. Clarence Darrow turned the case over to other attorneys, and William Jennings Bryan died a few days after the lower court trial. The question of the constitutionality of the statute was then appealed to the Supreme Court of Tennessee for final disposition. The court upheld the trial court, using the following language:

> The statute before us is not an exercise of the police power of the state undertaking to regulate the conduct and contracts of individuals in their dealings with each other. On the other hand, it is an act of the state as a corporation, a proprietor, an employer. It is a declaration of a master as to the character of work the master's servant shall, or rather shall not, perform. In dealing with its own employees engaged upon its own work the state is not hampered by the limitations of Section 8 of Article 1 of the Tennessee Constitution nor of the

---

[8]Board of Educ. of City of N.Y. v. Allen, 6 N.Y.2d 127, 188 N.Y.S.2d 515 (1959).

Fourteenth Amendment to the Constitution of the United States.[9]

Thus, the court's decision hinged not on the power of the state to control the teaching of certain subjects in the public schools, although it undoubtedly assumed such a power, but rather on the relationship of master and servant. Scopes was an employee of the State of Tennessee, and as such

> He had no right or privilege to serve the state except upon such terms as the state prescribed. His liberty, his privilege, his immunity to teach and to proclaim the theory of evolution elsewhere than in the service of the state was in no way touched by this law.[10]

In blocking further appeal to the Supreme Court of the United States, the Supreme Court of Tennessee noted that the defendant was no longer in the service of the state, and that the case had been prolonged and embarrassing, and thus recommended the entry of a *nolle prosequi* (no further prosecution of the case) to the attorney-general. Thus, the case was terminated. The law still exists on the statute books of Tennessee.

The academic freedom of teachers is further limited in other subject areas. How free, for example, is a teacher to teach about sex? A teacher in a boys' technical high school, who discussed matters relating to sex in his speech classes, was suspended and later discharged. He sued for reinstatement on the grounds that his dismissal had been arbitrary, oppressive, and unreasonable. The court held that the teacher had been legally dismissed.

> Such argument [that the board's action was arbitrary] fails to recognize that the issue is not whether it was improper conduct for relator to discuss sex in his speech classes, but rather whether his handling of this topic was such a violation of recognized standards of propriety as to constitute bad behavior. Thus, if relator's discourses on sex in his speech classes had been conducted in such a manner as to constitute proper conduct in a biology class, they would not automatically have been converted into misconduct warranting discharge by the happenstance that they took place in the speech class, absent any rule of the school authorities prohibiting the same or any specific warnings to relator from the principal or superintendent that sex was not to be a subject of discussion in his speech classes. However, if relator's manner of discoursing on

---

[9]Scopes v. State, 154 Tenn. 105, 289 S.W. 363 (1927).
[10]*Ibid.*

the topic of sex in his speech classes exceeded the bounds of the recognized standards of propriety, we deem that it constituted bad conduct which would warrant a discharge even though there was no express rule prohibiting it and he had received no warning to desist therefrom. As an intelligent person trained to teach at the high school level, relator should have realized that such conduct was improper.[11]

Two judges of the court concurred in the majority opinion (that the teacher had been legally dismissed), but gave as their reason that parents have the right to know that those who teach their children have had special training in presenting the subject matter in question. Not all teachers, the two judges asserted, are competent to teach sex education; only persons properly certificated should be allowed to undertake to teach this delicate subject. Since the plaintiff had no such training, he had acted in excess of his sphere of authority in the classroom, and was therefore legally dismissed.

One further case is noteworthy, because it involves the freedom to teach that which may be called immoral. *Kay v. Board of Higher Education*[12] is interesting in this connection under the heading of academic freedom. The well-known author, Bertrand Russell, had been appointed to the chair of philosophy at City College of New York. His appointment was challenged upon the ground, among others, that Russell was not of good moral character, and his appointment thus violated public policy. The trial court quoted from Russell's writings to the effect that he advocated temporary childless marriages among university students. The court said:

> While this court would not interfere with any action of the board insofar as a pure question of "valid" academic freedom is concerned, it will not tolerate academic freedom being used as a cloak to promote the popularization in the minds of adolescents of acts forbidden by the Penal Law. This appointment affects the public health, safety and morals of the community and it is the duty of the court to act. Academic freedom does not mean academic license. It is the freedom to do good and not to teach evil. Academic freedom cannot authorize a teacher to teach that murder or treason are [*sic*] good. Nor can it permit a teacher to teach directly or indirectly that sexual intercourse between students, where the female is under the age of eighteen years, is proper. This court

---

[11]State ex rel. Wasilewski v. Board of School Directors of the City of Milwaukee, 111 N.W.2d 198 (Wisc. 1961).

[12]173 Misc. 943, 18 N.Y.S.2d 821 (Sup. Ct. 1940), *aff'd*, 259 App. Div. 1012, 20 N.Y.S.2d 1016 (1940).

can take judicial notice of the fact that students in the colleges of the City of New York are under the age of eighteen years, although some of them may be older.[13]

Organizational Membership of Teachers

May the state control the membership of its teachers in organizations which may be listed as "subversive"? It appears that under certain circumstances the state may limit or control teacher membership. Perhaps the leading statute on this point was the Feinberg law enacted by the legislature of the State of New York in 1949. In the preamble of the law, the legislature stated its intent:

> The legislature hereby finds and declares that there is a common report that members of subversive groups, and particularly of affiliated organizations, have infiltrated into public employment in the public schools of the state. . . . The consequence of any such infiltration into the public schools is that subversive propaganda can be disseminated among children of tender years by those who teach them and to whom the children look for guidance, authority, and leadership.[14]

The law charged the board of regents with enforcing the necessary rules to prevent infiltration of subversive teachers into the schools. It required the regents to compile a list of subversive organizations, and to make proved membership in any organization on the list *prima facie* evidence for barring or dismissing an individual from teaching in the public schools of New York. A suit was brought to challenge the constitutionality of the law. On appeal from three lower courts, the case finally reached the Supreme Court of the United States. The question before the Court was, "Did New York's legislation barring from employment in its schools any member of an organization on the 'subversive' list violate the Constitution of the United States?" The Court held that it did not. In a six-to-three decision, the Supreme Court of the United States declared:

> It is first argued that the Feinberg law and the rules promulgated thereunder constitute an abridgement of the freedom of speech and assembly of persons employed or seeking employment in the public schools of the State of New York. . . . It is clear that such persons have the right under our law to assemble, speak, think and believe as they will. . . . It is equally clear that they have no right to work for the state

---

[13]*Ibid.*
[14]N.Y. Education Law § 3022.

in the school system on their own terms. . . . They may work for the school system upon the reasonable terms laid down by the proper authorities of New York. If they do not choose to work on such terms, they are at liberty to retain their beliefs and associations and go elsewhere. Has the State thus deprived them of any right to free speech or assembly? We think not. . . . Past conduct may well relate to present fitness; past loyalty may have a reasonable relationship to present and future trust. . . . A teacher works in a sensitive area in a schoolroom. There he shapes the attitude of young minds towards the society in which we live. In this, the state has a vital concern. It must preserve the integrity of the schools. That the school authorities have the right and the duty to screen officials, teachers, and employees as to their fitness to maintain the integrity of the school as a part of ordered society, cannot be doubted.[15]

In a dissenting opinion, Justice Frankfurter insisted that the case was based on a speculative issue, inasmuch as there existed no concrete situation to be tried. Had a teacher actually been removed, and had the teacher then attacked the constitutionality of the Feinberg law, the result might have conceivably been different, Mr. Frankfurter declared. Nevertheless, the majority of the Court held that the law was not unconstitutional.

In the *Adler* case, teachers were dismissed for *knowingly* belonging to a subversive organization. What of the teacher who belongs *unknowingly* to a subversive group? In a case originating in Oklahoma, the Supreme Court of the United States ruled invalid a state statute which prescribed loyalty oaths for certain public officials and teachers as a violation of the fourteenth amendment. The Court did not reverse its stand taken in the *Adler* case, but found merely that the statutes involved were different. In the *Adler* case, knowingly belonging to an organization on the regents' list resulted in dismissal; in the Oklahoma case mere membership resulted in dismissal. Said the Court in ruling that the Oklahoma statute was unconstitutional:

But membership may be innocent. A state servant may have joined a proscribed organization unaware of its activities and purposes. In recent years, many completely loyal persons have severed organizational ties after learning for the first time of the character of the groups to which they belong. . . . Yet under the Oklahoma Act, the fact of association alone determines disloyalty and disqualification; it matters not

---

[15]Adler v. Board of Educ. of the City of N.Y., 342 U.S. 485, 72 Sup. Ct. 380, 96 L. Ed. 517, 27 A.L.R.2d 472 (1952).

> whether the association existed innocently or knowingly. . . .
> We hold that the distinction observed between the case at bar
> and the Adler case is decisive.[16]

The Feinberg law was upheld because the organizations listed had been afforded notice and given a hearing as to their suspected subversive nature, and were entitled to review. In the Oklahoma law, proof of membership alone resulted in dismissal of the teacher. Such a provision was a denial of the constitutional rights of the teacher, and could not be tolerated.

The Oklahoma case established the principle that it is a denial of due process where the statute penalizes one who innocently joins a group and withdraws when he finds that the organization is subversive. The Oklahoma teachers refused to sign a loyalty oath which stated that they were not affiliated with, and had not been members within the preceding five years of, any foreign political agency, party, organization, association, or group which had been determined by the United States Attorney General or some authorized agency to be a Communist front or subversive organization. Said the Supreme Court of the United States in discussing the efficacy of such a requirement:

> . . . It matters not whether association existed innocently
> or knowingly. To thus inhibit individual freedom of move-
> ment is to stifle the flow of democratic expression and con-
> troversy at one of its chief sources. Indiscriminate classification
> of innocent with knowing activity must fall as an assertion of
> arbitrary power. The oath offends due process.[17]

Mr. Justice Frankfurter in a concurring opinion, said:

> It has an unmistakable tendency to chill that free play
> which all teachers ought especially to cultivate and practice;
> it makes for caution and timidity in their associations by po-
> tential teachers.
> To regard teachers—in our entire educational system, from
> the primary grades to the university—as the priests of our
> democracy is therefore not to indulge in hyperbole. It is the
> special task of teachers to foster those habits of open-minded-
> ness and critical inquiry which alone make for responsible
> citizens, who, in turn, make possible an enlightened and effec-
> tive public opinion.[18]

---

[16]Wieman v. Updegraf, 344 U.S. 183, 73 Sup. Ct. 215, 97 L. Ed. 216 (1952).
[17]*Ibid.*
[18]*Ibid.*

SCHOOL LAW FOR TEACHERS

Loyalty

How widespread is the practice of requiring teachers to sign oaths of loyalty? Teachers in thirty-three states were required by law in 1962 to sign loyalty oaths similar to that in Colorado, which provides:

> I solemnly swear (or affirm) that I will support the Constitution of the State of Colorado, and of the United States of America and the laws of the State of Colorado and of the United States, and will teach, by precept and example, respect for the flags of the United States and of the State of Colorado, reverence for law and order and undivided allegiance to the government of one country, the United States of America.[19]

Some oaths were much longer, and included provisions that teachers shall discharge faithfully the duties of a teacher, teach specific aspects of patriotism, or refrain from teaching overthrow of the government by force. One or two required that the teacher refrain from joining a subversive group while employed as a teacher in the public schools of the state. In three states in 1959, teachers were enjoined from teaching specific theories of government, such as communism or fascism. In twelve states, teachers were specifically forbidden to teach advocating the overthrow of the government by violent means.

The Supreme Court of the United States held unconstitutional a portion of the Florida statutory loyalty oath which related to past and future lending of aid, support, advice, counsel, or influence to the Communist Party. The Supreme Court of Florida ruled that the unconstitutionality of part of the statute, however, did not necessarily condemn the entire statute, and that teachers would be required to execute the oath with the unconstitutional provision eliminated.[20]

The teacher should become familiar with the laws of the state in which he is to teach with respect to loyalty requirements. Since it is well settled that the state may legally require statements of loyalty from its employees, one who wishes to work for the state does so under the terms specified by the legislature thereof.

Teacher's Political Rights

How free is the public school teacher to hold legislative office and engage in political activity? An examination of the few cases on this point reveals that such privileges are not as widely enjoyed among teachers as among other occupational groups.

---

[19]Colo. Rev. Stat. § 123-17-14 (1953).
[20]Cramp v. Board of Public Instr. of Orange Co., 137 So. 2d 828 (Fla. 1962).

Right to hold legislative office. Every qualified citizen duly elected has the *right* to hold legislative office. Where the teacher meets the age, citizenship, residency, and other qualifications, he is entitled to hold office in the legislative branch of the government. The difficulty, however, arises in connection with his absence from the classroom. In practice, the teacher often must choose between serving in the legislature and teaching in the school. An Oregon case is in point.

Article III, section 1 of the Oregon Constitution reads:

> The powers of the Government shall be divided into three separate departments, the Legislative, the Executive, including the administrative, and the Judicial; and no person charged with official duties under one of these departments, shall exercise any of the functions of another, except as in this Constitution expressly provided.

This provision has been held by the highest court of Oregon to preclude teachers from holding legislative office.[21] The court referred to a Supreme Court of the United States ruling to find that separation of powers required that neither branch of government shall be controlled directly or indirectly by another. As a legislator, the teacher was charged with official duties in the legislative department, but in his role as a teacher he was exercising the function of the executive department. The "separation of powers" provision in the constitution was thus upheld.

Article 4, section 19 of the California Constitution provides that:

> No senator or member of the assembly shall, during the term for which he shall have been elected, hold or accept any office, trust, or employment under this state; provided, that the provision shall not apply to any office filled by election by the people.

A California appellate court held that a teacher who is also holding a legislative office does not violate this part of the Constitution of California.[22] The court concluded that a teacher's position is not a public office, but an employment. "One of the necessary characteristics of a public officer," said the court, "is that he perform a public function for the public benefit, and that in so doing he be invested with the exercise of some of the sovereign powers of the state." The teacher did not exercise any of the sovereign powers of the state; the position of teacher was inescapably an employment.

---

[21] Monaghan v. School Dist. No. 1, Clackamas County, 211 Ore. 360, 315 P.2d 797 (1957).

[22] Leymel v. Johnson, 105 Cal. App. 694, 288 Pac. 858 (1930).

But as an employment, was it "under the state"? The court answered in the negative; there was merely a contractual relationship between the board and the teacher. It did not matter that statutes (which were promulgated by the legislature) controlled the duties and privileges of the teacher, because statutes control all types of positions which are traditionally private in nature. The conclusion was that teachers may simultaneously hold legislative office, and the two positions are not incompatible.

Several states have allowed teachers to hold legislative office, while others have taken steps to prevent the holding of such office while the teacher is under a teaching contract.

Right to engage in political activity. The board may not suspend a teacher for a mere rumor that he plans to enter the race for a public office.[23] However, an Indiana court held reasonable a board rule that a teacher, upon filing a declaration of intention to become a candidate for public office, must take a mandatory leave of absence during his political campaign, and during his term of office if elected.[24]

The reason for the latter ruling is clear. Some candidacies are extremely demanding in time and energy, calling for frequent and often continued absence from the classroom. The teacher's contract is one *for personal services* rendered; the law recognizes no substitutes where one contracts for personal services. Failure to perform his part of the contract amounts legally to a breach of contract on the part of the teacher.

Campaigning for another is usually not so time-consuming as campaigning for one's self. However, this privilege may be limited to time outside school hours. A teacher in California was suspended for "unprofessional conduct" after he stated to his students in class, "Many of you know Mr. Golway, what a fine man he is, and that his hopes are to be elected soon. I think he would be more helpful to our department than a lady, and we need more men in our schools. Sometimes your parents do not know one candidate from another; so they might be glad to be informed. Of course, if any of you have relatives or friends trying for the same office (county superintendent), be sure and vote for them." The court upheld the teacher's suspension in the following words:

> It is to be observed that the advocacy before the scholars of a public school by a teacher of the election of a particular

---

[23]Watkins v. Special School Dist. of Lepanto, 194 S.W. 32 (Ark. 1917).
[24]School City of Chicago v. Sigler, 219 Ind. 9, 36 N.E.2d 760 (1941).

candidate for a public office introduces into the school questions wholly foreign to its purposes and objects; that such conduct can have no other effect than to stir up strife among the students over a contest for a political office, and the result of this would inevitably be to disrupt the required discipline of a public school.[25]

A Florida court refused in a recent case in that state to interfere with the teacher's right to engage in political activity engaged in during non-school hours.[26]

Right to Bargain Collectively

There seems to be no reason why teachers and other employee groups in the public schools may not legally organize and bargain in a collective manner with their employer, the board of education. As a matter of fact, teachers have been engaging in this type of activity through their appointed professional committees for many years. In such situations, it is well settled that the board may listen or not as it wishes, accept or reject the proposals which teachers present, and take any action which it considers necessary and proper to the general welfare of the schools. In negotiations involving a board of education, including those pertaining to teachers' salaries and conditions of work, the board, however, will not be permitted to "tie its own hands," since to do so would rob it of its legal prerogative to have the last word concerning all matters pertaining to the schools. A board of education must remain forever free to decide *unilaterally* what is good and best for the children and for the school system in general. This principle of law is illustrated by the words of an Illinois court, which said:

> This court concludes that it is the settled law of this State that public or municipal corporations, as school boards and cities, although free to employ whom they will, cannot by contract, rules or ordinances provide that public work can be performed only by members of certain organizations. This is true whether the organizations in question be trade unions, societies, associations, or any other particular groups of individuals.[27]

The union shop. Besides asserting the right of a board to exercise its discretion at will, the aforementioned case illustrates the principle

---

[25]Goldsmith v. Board of Educ. of Sacramento City High School Dist., 66 Cal. App. 157, 225 Pac. 783 (1924).
[26]Adams v. State ex rel. Sutton, 69 So. 2d 309 (Fla. 1954).
[27]Chapin v. Board of Educ. of the City of Peoria, Ill. Cir. Ct. No. 21255 (1939).

of law governing the union shop in the public schools. The court ruled that the union shop clause amounted to a discrimination between different classes of citizens, *viz.*, those who belonged to the union and hence were eligible for employment, and those who were non-union members and excluded from employment. The court pointed out that labor unions have been held to be lawful organizations, to which there was no objection. However, said the court, for a governmental agency such as a board of education, which is representative of all the tax-payers, to enter into a contract as was involved in this case, has been held to be a discrimination between different classes of citizens, and is therefore illegal and void. Funds expended under such a contract amount to an illegal expenditure of public funds, and a taxpayer may maintain a suit to prevent the board from expending funds in such a manner.[28]

To the same effect was a case which arose in Montana in 1959, in which a board required union membership as a condition to receiving an increase in salary. The court ruled that the board had no authority or power to discriminate between teachers employed by it as to the amount of salary paid to each because of membership or non-member-ship in a labor union. Such a provision, said the court, would be equal to providing that the increased salary shall not be allowed to those who do not affiliate with a certain lodge, service club, church, or political party.[29]

Right to strike. In this country, most employees in private industry are guaranteed the right to strike. This principle originated in the National Labor Relations Act of 1935, and was revised and clarified in 1947. Among the teaching force, however, the right to strike is no-where recognized. Teachers may not include in the bargaining agree-ment a clause that it is permissible for the teachers or other employees to engage in concerted action such as a strike, work stoppage, or collective refusal to enter upon their duties.

This question arose in a Connecticut case in 1951.[30] Some teachers were dismissed because they engaged in a strike. In upholding the dismissal, the court noted that teachers are government employees, and as such have no right to strike. The government is established by and run for all of the people, said the court, not for the benefit of

---

[28]*Ibid.*

[29]Benson v. School Dist. No. 1 of Silver Bow County, 136 Mont. 77, 344 P.2d 117 (1959).

[30]Norwalk Teachers' Ass'n v. Board of Educ. of City of Norwalk, 138 Conn. 269, 83 A.2d 482 (1951).

any person or group. The profit motive, inherent in the free enterprise system, is absent. It should be the aim of every employee of the government to do his or her part to make it function as efficiently and economically as possible. The drastic remedy of the organized strike to enforce the demands of unions of government employees is in direct contravention to this principle, and cannot be allowed.

The Condon-Wadlin Act. In 1947, the Legislature of the State of New York adopted the Condon-Wadlin Act, which prohibited strikes of appointees or employees of the government in New York state. It defined a strike as "the failure to report for duty, the wilful absence from one's position, the stoppage of work, or the abstinence in whole or in part from the full, faithful, and proper performance of the duties of employment, for the purpose of inducing, influencing, or coercing a change in the conditions or compensation, or the rights, privileges, or obligations of employment." Teachers later were brought under the provisions of the law.

The Secondary School Teachers Association of New York, Inc., brought this question before the state court: "May teachers absent themselves from work, in the presence of the Condon-Wadlin Act, to petition the legislature in Albany concerning their rights?" The association proposed to go to the capital *en masse* and consult with members of the legislative and executive branches of the government concerning working conditions and benefits for teachers, as well as educational standards in the secondary school program. Was the Condon-Wadlin Act an obstacle in their way?

The association was contrasting absence from work in contravention of the Condon-Wadlin Act, with the first amendment right to petition the government. The court recognized the superior state interest in an uninterrupted educational system, and held that the statute was constitutional and would be violated by the proposed trip to Albany.[31]

The teachers maintained that school hours conflicted with hours of legislative sessions, making it impossible to petition the government. The court answered that legislative committees hold hearings, and legislators are available at times and places which would present no conflict. The court, however, felt strongly enough about the loss of the teachers' rights to add to its opinion the following:

---

[31]Pruzan v. Board of Educ. of the City of N. Y., 25 Misc. 2d 945, 209 N.Y.S.-2d 966 (Sup. Ct. 1960), *aff'd without opinion,* 9 N.Y.2d 911, 176 N.E.2d 96, 217 N.Y.S.2d 86 (1961).

It is the Court's view that the Act in its present posture is too severe and restrictive and that the unreasonably restrictive aspects thereof [should] be ameliorated to an extent at least sufficient to permit reasonable approved leaves of absence to specific individuals for the purposes set forth in the complaint. The Court commends this view to the Legislature.[32]

The rights of citizens, including teachers, to assemble and speak freely are constitutional rights, and should be zealously guarded, but they must yield when they conflict with a higher public interest. The public interest in an uninterrupted educational system is most important. It may outweigh the constitutional rights of the teacher in certain situations.

Few cases involving the rights of teachers to strike have reached the courts, but it is well established from the legal actions taken that they do not have this right, unless it is specifically provided by law. In 1963, no state had enacted such a law.

Teachers, public employees. Some states expressly allow teachers to organize by means of statutes which pertain generally to all public employees. Wisconsin and New Hampshire have such legislation. In the former, the Wisconsin Employment Relations Board is vested with the power to prevent any interference with organizational and bargaining activities between teachers' groups and the board of education. In New Hampshire, the board may, if it chooses, recognize unions of employees, and make and enter into collective bargaining contracts with unions, so long as there is no loss of the board's discretionary powers involved. The prohibitions in this area seem to be not so much against collective bargaining *per se*, as against the loss of the board's power to decide in the final analysis what is good and right for the schools under its care.

The Supreme Court of Michigan held that teachers are public employees within the meaning of that state's labor laws. The Michigan Labor Mediations Board is clothed with authority to mediate grievances of teachers when petitioned to do so. There seems to be a growing tendency among teachers' groups to seek collective bargaining or representative negotiation as a means of obtaining better salaries and conditions of work. This procedure for settling conditions of employment has recently become acceptable to relatively few boards of education.

---

[32]*Ibid.*

National Labor Relations Act. Prior to the passage of the National Labor Relations Act in 1935, the courts consistently upheld boards in prohibiting teachers and other school employees from joining labor unions. In Chicago in 1917, and in Seattle in 1930, board rules against union membership were upheld in the courts. In the Chicago case,[33] the rule was upheld because "it was inimical to proper discipline, prejudicial to the efficiency of the teaching force, and detrimental to the welfare of the public school system." Union members were not to be employed, and if teachers violated the rule, they were subject to dismissal. Said the court:

> No person has the right to demand that he or she shall be employed as a teacher. The board has the absolute right to decline to employ or to re-employ any applicant for any reason whatever or for no reason at all. . . . The board is not bound to give any reason for its action. . . . Neither the Constitution nor the statute places any restriction upon this right of the board to contract, and no one has any grievance which the courts will recognize simply because the board of education refuses to contract with him or her. Questions of policy are solely for the determination of the board, and when they have once been determined by it the courts will not inquire into their propriety.[34]

In the Seattle case, membership was prohibited in the American Federation of Labor or its locals. Any prospective teacher was required to sign a declaration of non-membership. The court found that the rule was not in violation of the fourteenth amendment to the Constitution of the United States, because refusal to employ "is not a denial of a constitutional right of a person to follow his chosen profession."[35]

With the announced federal public policy favoring collective bargaining in the National Labor Relations Act, boards exhibited a more lenient attitude towards membership in teachers' organizations of all kinds, even though teachers were not covered by the Act. Under the provisions of this public law, the employer is required to respond to the request of the representative group for a conference, to bargain in good faith, and to reduce to writing the terms of the agreement when compromise has been reached. Although the NLRA specifically excludes public employees, some state laws do otherwise. The effect has been to provide a framework through which negoti-

---

[33]People ex rel. Fursman v. City of Chicago, 278 Ill. 318, 116 N.E. 158 (1917).
[34]*Ibid.*
[35]Seattle High School Chapter No. 200 of the AFT v. Sharples, 159 Wash. 424, 293 Pac. 994 (1930).

ations by teachers' groups may be instituted with the board, and by which agreements on conditions of work may be hammered out. Although dissimilar from negotiations with private employers, and without the coercive power of strike action, this framework affords a means of arriving at compromises necessary to the improvement of the teaching profession.

Right to non-membership. May a board of education require membership in a professional teachers' organization as a condition of inclusion in the salary schedule? This question was before a Missouri court in 1961. The board of education of the Riverview Gardens school district adopted a resolution that each teacher on the salary schedule must join the local, county, state, and national professional organizations specified, failure of which would preclude the person from benefits "derived through the salary schedule, and place such person outside the salary schedule." Magenheim, a teacher, brought suit to test the right of the board to enforce such a resolution. He cited an earlier Montana case[36] in which it was held that the board had no right to require *union* membership as a condition of employment. The court could not agree with the teacher.[37]

The two cases were not the same, said the court. In the Montana case, union membership *was required*, since failure to join the union resulted in discharge of the teacher. In the case at bar, plaintiff Magenheim was *not required* to meet the conditions stated in the board resolution, and might remain outside the salary schedule if he chose to do so. The rule included the provision that teachers employed by the district who did not choose to meet the conditions stated for compensation under the salary schedule were entitled to negotiate individually with the board in arriving at their rate of compensation.

The court, in holding the rule reasonable and a valid exercise of board power, used the following language:

> The Legislature of this State has given Boards of Education the broad power "to make all needful rules and regulations for the organization, grading and government in their school district." In the teaching profession, as in all professions, membership in professional organizations tends to increase and improve the interest, knowledge, experience and overall professional competence. . . . Such membership affords an opportunity for self-improvement and self-development on

[36]Benson v. School Dist. No. 1 of Silver Bow County, 136 Mont. 77, 344 P.2d 117 (1959).

[37]Magenheim v. Board of Educ. of the School Dist. of Riverview Gardens, 347 S.W.2d 409 (Mo. 1961).

the part of the individual member. It is the duty of every school board to obtain the services of the best qualified teachers, and it is not only within their power but it is their duty to adopt rules and regulations which seek to elevate the standards of teachers and the educational standards within their district.[38]

Some states have adopted statutes outlawing clauses in teachers' contracts requiring membership in any specific organization as a condition of contracting. The latter seems to be the wiser course to be followed in school board-teacher negotiations.

Right to Speak and Write

A teacher is sometimes placed in the precarious position of having to make statements which can be construed as defaming the reputation of another. To allow the teacher to carry out the proper function of teaching, the law recognizes that the teacher must be free to state candidly his opinions, observations, and beliefs. There is a tacit recognition that the responsibilities of a teacher to his pupils, to his superiors, and to the public, demand a well-defined limit of free communication without threat of liability. Certain types of statements, when made by one who is not a teacher, may tend to hold a pupil or colleague up to ridicule, and he may be held accountable. As may be expected, the teacher, under certain circumstances, has a qualified privilege of communication. The right of free speech guaranteed by the first amendment to the federal constitution has never meant the unrestricted right to say what one pleases at all times under all circumstances.

It is of primary importance to the teacher to recognize the limitations of the privilege, *i.e.*, which statements fall within the area of protection and which do not. Unfortunately, there is a dearth of authority on this subject, which limits the scope of this account to an examination of the general rules on the law of defamation. The few cases in the field will also be examined.

Defamation of character. One who writes or speaks disparagingly of another or who spreads false or damaging rumors may be held guilty of defamation of character. The definition of defamation of character is "the offense of injuring a person's character, fame, or reputation by false and malicious statements. The term includes both libel and slander."

---

[38]*Ibid.*

Communication about another, whether written or oral, is called *publication.* When the defamatory words are published in written form, they are *libelous;* when verbally published, they are *slanderous.* Libel and slander are torts against the person of another, and an action will lie where the words spoken or written constitute accusations relating to criminal activities, certain loathsome diseases, mental disorder, unchastity, or other statements resulting in damage to another.

A teacher as a public employee owes a duty to the public. When a teacher makes a publication which is prompted by a duty owed another, the statement is generally *privileged,* if made in good faith and without malice. Any statement, however, which is false or motivated by malice removes the privilege, and subjects the communicating party to liability.

What defense has the teacher against a charge of defamation of character? One defense, of course, is that the communication was *privileged.* Still another defense is *truth,* but although truth is a defense, even the truth can prove defamatory if not published with good intentions and toward justifiable ends. School people should not feel that because they speak the truth, and enjoy a measure of privilege, publication of certain information about others is permissible.[39]

In order that the truth may be known, the courts have set up a protection for those whose duty it is to divulge information about others. Publication may be either *absolutely* or *qualifiedly* privileged. The former applies to judges, legislative personnel, and executive members of government in the proper discharge of their duties. It is never applicable to teachers, who come within the province of the second classification, that of qualified or conditional privilege.

Thus, a school principal who, in his administrative duties and in good faith, provides information about a teacher, is protected by the law of privileged communications, even though the information may be false. Unless actual malice and knowledge of the falsity of the statement is shown, the principal is protected in the line of duty. But the teacher who speaks ill of another teacher may not claim a privilege, inasmuch as his communication does not arise out of his teaching responsibilities. Similarly, where his communication goes beyond "fair criticism," one who impugns the character of another may be held answerable if malice can be proved by the person injured.

An otherwise actionable defamatory statement may be allowed if the plaintiff has *consented* to its publication. Obviously, in cases

---

[39]Forsythe v. Durham, 270 N.Y. Supp. 141, 200 N.E. 674 (1936).

affecting pupils, this consent would come from the parent or guardian, since children may not know what they are doing when giving consent of publication, although it is conceivable that the consent may sometimes be implied. Where the words can be shown *not defamatory in nature*, there is no question of liability, and in such a case, there is no issue of privilege. These constitute the most commonly utilized defenses of the teacher against a charge of defamation of character.

Since all defamation of character cases turn on the rule of reasonableness, it is difficult to declare unequivocally in advance what may constitute defamation in any given set of circumstances. Teachers, counselors, and principals should be doubly careful to avoid abuse of privileged communications in the discharge of their duties.

Communications by teachers about pupils. Teachers are often asked to provide a character analysis of their pupils. One teacher, who knew that his register would go to the clerk of the board, and was in fact read to the other board members, made the following notation in the school register immediately preceding the plaintiff-student's name: "Drag all the time; ruined by tobacco and whiskey." The teacher admitted the falsity of the statement, but maintained that the statement was protected by the qualified privilege because he believed the truth of the statement at the time of publication. Since there was no malice present, the teacher contended the statement fell within the conditioned privilege.

The court could not agree with the teacher. It was determined that the teacher deviated from the procedure necessary to do his job effectively. Since defamatory statements in his register were beyond the teacher's strict line of duty, the court concluded that such statements were not privileged and within the normal ambit of immunity.[40]

Similarly, a California court held that publication concerning a student in a newspaper by a teacher in a normal school was not privileged, but was false and malicious. The newspaper account read:

> By her conduct in class, by her behavior in and around the building, and by her spirit, as exhibited in numberless interviews, she has shown herself tricky and unreliable, and almost destitute of those womanly and honorable characteristics that should be the first requisites in a teacher.[41]

The principle of law governing slander was spelled out by a Kentucky court in 1913:

---

[40]Dawkins v. Billingsley, 69 Okla. 259, 172 Pac. 69 (1918).
[41]Dixon v. Allen, 69 Cal. 527, 11 Pac. 179 (1886).

> Words are slanderous or actionable *per se* only in cases where they are falsely spoken and (1) impute the commission of a crime involving moral turpitude for which the party might be indicted and punished; (2) impute an infectious disease likely to exclude him from society; or (3) impute unfitness to perform the duties of an office or employment; or (4) prejudice him in his profession or trade; or (5) tend to discredit him.
>
> In all other cases spoken words are either (a) not actionable at all or are only actionable (b) on proof of special damage.[42]

Finally, the courts have ruled that there is no privileged communication where the teacher, superintendent, or board of education act *outside* their powers. In California, the Educational Code contained a provision that no teacher, principal, employee, or governing board should give out any personal information concerning any minor pupil enrolled in the school, except under certain limited circumstances. Nevertheless, the board sent a special announcement through the mails to many members of the general public, a portion of which read as follows:

> At a special public meeting to be held Tuesday, November 24, 1959, in the Caruthers High School gymnasium at 7:30 P. M. the Caruthers High School Board of Trustees, the administration, teachers and sponsors of the Los Angeles Band trip will bring the public in full focus of the serious violation of manners, morals, and discipline that occurred in Los Angeles as the direct result of interference by the Elder and Fries boys who are now suspended from school.[43]

The mother of one of the boys brought action asserting libel on the part of the board and administration of the school. The case turned on whether the action of the board was ministerial or discretionary. Said the court:

> Government officials are liable for the negligent performance of their ministerial duties, but are not liable for their discretionary acts within the scope of their authority. It is the plaintiff's contention that all matters in which discretion is not allowed are ministerial acts; that the prohibition expressed in section 10751 of the Education Code constitutes a mandatory, hard and fast rule; and that violation of that section eliminates the doctrine of sovereign immunity as far as the defendant trustees are concerned. With this we agree.[44]

---

[42]Spears v. McCoy, 155 Ky. 1, 159 S.W. 610 (1913).
[43]Elder v. Anderson, 23 Calif. Rptr. 48 (1960).
[44]*Ibid.*

School boards have only such authority as is specifically granted by the legislature, said the court, and boards must act at all times within the scope of this authority. The court continued:

> We think it is clear that no immunity exists for discretionary acts if the acts complained of are beyond the course and scope of the duties of the school trustees. But here we find more than a good faith mistaken action. In this case, defendant trustees violated a code section prohibiting dissemination of personal information concerning pupils, and thus stepped outside the protection of their office.[45]

Communications between board and superintendent. May a county superintendent and the district attorney be held liable in damages to a district school superintendent for their acts insofar as they are related to the superintendent's fitness to hold the position? A California court had this question before it in 1961. Lipman, the superintendent of the elementary district, asserted that the three trustees had made disparaging remarks concerning her, stating that she was dictatorial, operated a "rubber stamp board," was overpaid, suppressed facts from district employees, and engaged in shady dealings involving district moneys. The court in its verdict made a distinction between acts of the district, acts of the school trustees individually, and acts of the school officials, in this case the county superintendent and the district attorney. Concerning the liability of the school board, acting as a unit, the court said, "The district is immune from tort liability for the alleged acts of the trustees within the scope of their authority."[46]

With respect to the acts of the trustees individually, the court held that the plaintiff could bring suit against the three trustees on the ground that their statements to newspaper reporters and others "would obviously make it difficult and burdensome for plaintiff to perform her contractual obligations." In making these statements, the trustees were not within the ambit of the immunity rule, and cause of action existed against them as individuals.

The county superintendent and district attorney were acting within the scope of their powers in making investigations concerning the plaintiff's fitness to hold her position. "The district attorney has a duty to conduct all prosecutions for public offenses," said the court, "and to give his opinion to county and district officers." His actions

---

[45] *Ibid.*
[46] Lipman v. Brisbane Elementary School Dist., 55 Cal. App. 2d 244, 359 P.2d 465 (1961).

did not, therefore, constitute defamation of character within the general meaning of that term.

Communications from one teacher about another. There is generally no privilege where one teacher falsely charges another with incompetency. In Philadelphia, plaintiff and defendant were principals of the only schools in the city where the Haven system of shorthand was being taught. The two schools were rivals. Plaintiff's school was called "Haven College." Defendant, in full possession of the facts, published the statements that her school was the only authorized Haven College; that another teacher was using the name without authority; and that the author of the system recommended the defendant's teaching, but could not recommend such other teacher. The court held that the publication was libelous on the grounds that an innuendo was created that plaintiff was incompetent to teach the Haven system of shorthand, and was using the name "Haven College" without authority.[47]

On the other hand, the report of a principal to his superintendent concerning the work of a teacher under his supervision is conditionally privileged, and in the absence of express malice is not actionable, however false and unfavorable it may be. A Brooklyn principal reported that a teacher was generally efficient, but was "careless" in her blackboard work. The teacher brought action to recover damages from the principal for libel. The court held that the principal's publication was privileged and no libel existed. Said the court:

> The report indeed is but the common, ordinary affair of modern school life. Its good faith has not been successfully impugned. It bears no obvious imprint of malice. It is not unkind in tone. It is not unjust in substance. It was not inspired by ill will. It has wrought no financial harm.
>
> It was clearly the duty of the defendant Best as principal of the school in which the plaintiff teacher teaches, to note and to record her work and his opinion of her capacity and skill, and no offense attaches to an unfavorable expression which is believed to be truthful and honest. Moreover, the charge of carelessness is not libelous, as might be a charge of unskillfulness or general incapacity. History furnishes many instances of genius wasted by a life of carelessness and indifference. The plaintiff is not necessarily injured thereby.[48]

Communications from third parties about teachers. Parents of pupils, as well as pupils themselves, have a right to complain to the

[47]Price v. Conway, 134 Pa. 340, 19 Atl. 687 (1890).
[48]Walker v. Best, 107 App. Div. 304, 95 N.Y. Supp. 151 (1905).

proper authorities about a teacher's conduct. If the statements are made in good faith, although they have no basis in fact, they are not actionable in the absence of express malice. Charges touching the character of a teacher which are *known* to be groundless, however, are not privileged communications.[49]

A New York jury awarded a teacher $100,000 in damages after the defendant was found guilty of circulating to approximately sixty persons a libelous statement to the effect that the teacher was a malicious liar. Since the teacher enjoyed a fine reputation, and did not lose his job as a result of the statements, the court reduced the award of the jury to $50,000, but indicated an award of $100,000 "might well be sustained" where "the libel found circulation through the medium of a metropolitan newspaper." The court emphasized that, although the libel was circulated to the limited extent of sixty copies, serious consequences can result from a malicious defamation.[50]

Statements charging a teacher with immoral conduct with his pupils, published in a magazine of wide circulation in one region of the United States, were libel *per se*. The article contained pictures and a detailed description of the teacher's alleged relations with school students, an attack with a hatchet and pistol on a pastor, and of his resignation from a prior teaching position following charges of improper relations with students. The jury concluded that the publications had been made and the information therein was false. They returned a verdict of damages in the amount of $67,500, which was reduced to $45,000, to compensate the teacher for the injury and to punish the publishing company.[51]

Right to Work

It is well settled that no person has an inherent right to be employed as a teacher in the public schools. The courts have consistently agreed that the teacher's status, despite possession of a teaching certificate, or the attainment of permanent tenure, is an employment and not an office. Neither does meeting the additional qualifications of loyalty, age, moral character, experience, and passing prescribed examinations work to effect such a right to a position in the public schools.

On the other hand, a person may not be refused a position on the basis of his race, creed, color, or national origin alone. Since World

---

[49]Decker v. Gaylord, 35 Hun. 584 (N.Y. 1885).
[50]Foerster v. Ridder, 57 N.Y.S.2d 668 (Sup. Ct. 1945).
[51]Johnson Publishing Co. v. Davis, 271 Ala. 474, 124 So. 2d 441 (1960).

War II, the courts have enunciated several significant pronouncements with respect to the teacher's right to be employed. The general tenor of these decisions is to the effect that distinctions in employment or non-employment of persons on these bases alone are in violation of the due process and equal protection clauses of the fourteenth amendment to the Constitution of the United States.

Since the earliest beginnings of our nation, states and municipalities have consistently sought to forbid various types of discrimination based on race or creed. In recent years, the most effective means to curb discriminatory practices has been the so-called *fair employment practices act*. By 1961, twenty states had such legislation, administered in each instance by specialized state-level commissions. The purpose of such legislation is to provide opportunities for minority groups to secure adequate employment, and to attempt to create public attitudes which reject discriminatory practices. Even pre-employment inquiries, advertising, and statements by an employer or employment agency which directly or indirectly express a policy of discrimination are prohibited in most states. Here the law extends beyond discrimination, as it is commonly understood, and forbids certain expressions of prejudice.[52]

Anti-discrimination law. Representative of the current anti-discrimination laws in the twenty states are those in the State of Colorado, enacted in 1957. The essence of these statutes is that it shall be a discriminatory or unfair employment practice for an employer, whether public or private, to refuse to hire, to discharge, promote or demote, or to discriminate in matters of pay against an individual, otherwise qualified; or, for an employment agency to refuse to list and properly classify, or refuse to refer such person to a known available job; or for a labor organization to refuse such person full membership rights solely because of race, creed, color, national origin or ancestry, all as the case may be.[53]

To accomplish the objectives of the act, the state anti-discrimination commission is empowered to make studies to determine the existence, causes, character, and extent of discrimination in employment, and to conduct educational programs and receive complaints alleging violations of the act. Where probable causes for complaint exist, the commission is empowered to effect a settlement by conference, conciliation, and persuasion. When conciliation fails, the commission may

[52]68 Harv. L. Rev. 685.
[53]*Second Annual Report of the Colorado Anti-Discrimination Com.,* (1955-1956), p. 17.

call a public hearing on the complaint. The hearing is conducted in much the same manner as a trial. Where the commission finds that a discriminatory or unfair employment practice has been committed, it is empowered to issue a cease and desist order, and to order employment or reinstatement. If an order of the commission is ignored, the commission may apply to the district court for enforcement. On the other hand, any person or organization allegedly aggrieved by an order of the commission is entitled to judicial review of his alleged aggrievance in due time.

Several complaints have been filed by school teachers with the anti-discrimination commission, but only two complaints have fallen short of conciliation and compromise by the efforts of the parties involved. The two cases requiring a public hearing were complaints against the same school district alleging discriminatory employment practices against Negro applicants. The commission ruled that the complaints were meritorious, and issued cease and desist orders to the school authorities involved.

Rights involved. Fair employment practices legislation points up the clash between two basic rights—the normal freedom of an employer to choose whom he will to work for him, as opposed to the right of an individual to be free from arbitrary restrictions on his work opportunity on bases other than his individual merit or qualifications. The latter right transcends the former as seen in the following statement of the Supreme Court of the United States:

> The main proposition advanced by the defendant is that his enjoyment upon terms of equality with all others in similar circumstances of the privilege of pursuing an ordinary calling or trade is an essential part of his rights of liberty and property as guaranteed by the Fourteenth Amendment. The court assents to this general proposition as embodying a sound principle of constitutional law.[54]

The courts will not, however, interfere in the exercise of the board's discretion on employment practices, unless it can be shown that the board has been discriminatory in its deliberations; that is, discrimination must be on the basis of race, color, or creed, rather than on the basis of the individual's qualification. This may not be easy to prove. Two cases will serve to illustrate how the courts have ruled in matters of this kind.

In decreeing that Negro school teachers may recover damages for being the victims of discriminatory wage scales, notwithstanding the

---

[54] Powell v. Pennsylvania, 127 U.S. 678, 8 Sup. Ct. 1257, 32 L. Ed. 253 (1888).

fact that they had accepted employment at the pay scale offered, the Supreme Court of Virginia announced a significant doctrine applicable to all vocations:

> . . . they are qualified school teachers, and have the civil right, as such, to pursue their profession without being subjected to discriminatory legislation on account of race or color. It is no answer to say that the hiring of any teacher is a matter resting in the discretion of the school authorities. Plaintiffs, as teachers qualified and subject to employment by the state, are entitled to apply for positions and to have the discretion of the authorities exercised lawfully and without unconstitutional discrimination as to the rate of pay to be awarded them, if their applications are accepted.[55]

Thus, the courts will protect the worker against *undue* discrimination while at the same time protecting the right of the board to choose within certain limits whom it will employ to teach in the public schools.

To the opposite effect was a 1959 case which arose in Missouri. In Moberly, in that state, the schools were integrated in 1955. The Negro school was permanently closed, resulting in the need for fewer public school teachers. The contracts of four of 98 white teachers and the contracts of all eleven Negro teachers were not renewed. Eight of the latter, who contended that they had more education or more experience, or both, than some of the rehired white teachers, brought action seeking a declaratory judgment, injunction, and damages against the board of education on the ground that their discharge was due to racial discrimination. The board denied the allegation, contending instead that re-employment was "on the basis of merit, determined by the Superintendent from the applicant's qualifications, training, experience, *personality and ability to fulfill the requirements of the position.*" (Emphasis supplied by the court.) The emphasized portion of the standard presented the trouble, because it represented the ground upon which the board relied for discharge. The board contended that the teachers who were employed were superior in the realm of personality and ability. The eight teachers who were dismissed challenged the criterion of re-employment as arbitrary and discriminatory, and a denial of their constitutional rights before the law.

The court could not agree with this contention of the teachers.

---

[55]Alston v. School Bd. of City of Norfolk, 112 F.2d 992 (4th Cir. 1940); *cert. denied,* 311 U.S. 693 (1940).

The trial court said that the teachers had presented no proof of discriminatory abuse of the authority of the board. On appeal, the Supreme Court of the United States declined to review the case, thus upholding the finding of the lower court.

The burden of proof of discriminatory employment practices rests with those aggrieved, said the trial court. This is a rigorous requirement, which in the instant case was not met.[56]

Teacher's Right to a Redress of Grievances

The statutes of nearly every state outline the procedure for appeal from a decision of the board of education to other authority, usually the county superintendent, county board of education, state superintendent, or state board of education. In some states, all steps in the power hierarchy may be involved when the teacher appeals to higher authority for adjudication of a board rule or decision. In other states, the statutes may call for original appeal to the lower courts. In only a few states is there no statutory provision for appeal from a board decision.

Unless expressly prohibited, appeal is available from board decisions directly to the lower courts. Courts, however, will not upset decisions of boards of education unless there has been an abuse of the discretionary power. To do so would be to substitute the judgment of the court for that of the board. It is only where the jurisdiction or the right of the board to act is in question that the courts will intercede, or where there is some question that the board acted in good faith, or in the best interest of the schools. Usually at issue in these latter cases is the question of whether the statute under which the board acted is constitutional. The courts will recognize the teacher's rights, but it will not interfere in the normal operation of the schools where the board acts in good faith and within its powers.

New York is perhaps the only state in which the teacher must choose between appealing board decisions to the chief state school officer, or taking the matter to court. When the choice is to utilize the state commissioner's office, the courts will bar further appeal through the judicial branch, unless evidence of unfairness exists. The rule almost completely precludes appeal from the commissioner's of-

---

[56]Brooks v. School Dist. of City of Moberly, Missouri, 267 F.2d 733 (Mo. 1959).

fice to the courts, since it is generally assumed that administrative decisions are reasonable *per se*.[57]

Appeal to the appropriate state school officials is usually much less costly than to the courts. Some courts will not hear a case unless appeal has gone through certain preliminary steps, *i.e.*, an exhaustion of available administrative remedies. Reference to the school code in the state where the teacher works will clarify the grievance machinery available to the teacher who is not satisfied with a decision of the board of education.

Suggested Activities

Case Study:

Discuss the following cases, then refer to each case under the appropriate citation.

Case # 1. A high school principal voluntarily administered a fund out of which choir robes, athletic equipment, and aids for classroom instruction were purchased. He failed to keep a full and accurate accounting, although he readily admitted this was one of his duties. Some parents brought action for an accounting and sought to enjoin the board from continuing to employ the principal in the school system on the ground of an alleged unfitness. Is the question of defendant's unfitness one for the courts or for the board to decide?

Betterson v. Stewart, 121 S.E.2d 102 (S.C. 1961).

Case # 2. A father sought through mandamus to compel the board to disclose the contents of his son's cumulative records, charging concealment. The board had the policy, generally followed today, of keeping parents informed of the pupil's progress, without specific disclosure of such information as the child's I. Q. test results, anecdotal records, and the like. There was no statute either granting or denying this right, but the Commissioner had ruled earlier that parents had such a right. Is the father entitled to full disclosure of the son's school cumulative record?

Van Allen v. McCleary, 211 N.Y.S.2d 501 (Sup. Ct. 1961).

Case # 3. Plaintiff was employed for one year as a teacher in the Detroit Public Schools. After the defendant, a superintendent of the public schools, refused to recommend the plaintiff for reappointment, the defendant gave his permission to the publication of the alleged libelous article explaining his position in the matter. The article contained no charges of wrong-doing, but simply was a defense to the question of the propriety of his conduct in failing to recommend the plaintiff for re-employment.

Under the circumstances, did the defendant enjoy a qualified

---

[57]Gable v. Raftery, 65 N.Y.S. 2d 513 (Sup. Ct. 1945).

privilege to express his criticisms of the plaintiff in order to vindicate himself?

O'Connor v. Sill, 60 Mich. 175, 27 N.W. 13 (1886).

Case # 4. A prospective employer made inquiry about a former student, and the principal replied, mistakenly but in good faith, that the student had been expelled and arrested for the theft of a typewriter. Is the principal answerable in damages for misinforming the would-be employer?

Tyler Commercial College v. Lattimore, 12 S.W.2d 680 (Tex. 1928).

Further Readings

Chafee, Zechariah. *The Blessings of Liberty* (Philadelphia: Lippincott, 1956), Ch. VII, The Right Not To Speak.

Edwards, Newton. *The Courts and the Public Schools* (Chicago: University of Chicago Press, 1955), pp. 473-474.

Gauerke, Warren E. *Legal and Ethical Responsibilities of School Personnel* (Englewood Cliffs, N. J.: Prentice-Hall, 1959), pp. 178-181.

MacIver, Robert M. *Academic Freedom in Our Time* (New York: Columbia University Press, 1955).

National Education Association. *The Teacher and the Law* (Washington: The Association, 1959), Research Monograph 1959-M3.

————. *The Teacher's Day in Court* (Washington: The Association, 1960), Research Report 1960-R5.

Remmlein, Madaline Kinter. *School Law, Second Edition* (Danville, Illinois: Interstate Printers and Publishers, 1962), Ch. 8, Defamation of Character.

Seitz, Reynolds (ed). *Law and the School Principal* (Cincinnati: W. H. Anderson Company, 1961), NOLPE Series, Ch. 8.

————. "School Boards and Labor Unions," *American School Board Journal* (August, 1960).

Section Four

TEACHER RESPONSIBILITY
AND LIABILITY

Pupil Discipline and Control

*Teacher Liability for
Pupil Injury*

Dismissal of Teachers

Chapter VIII

PUPIL DISCIPLINE AND CONTROL

Introduction

The discipline and control of pupils has changed considerably from the earliest days of our nation's history, when children were required by law to submit to the will of the parents, no matter how harsh and unreasonable such discipline might be. The colonists were responsive to the Biblical admonition, "Children, obey your parents," and were fearful lest parental authority should be impaired by a lack of respect for the parental will. Hence, a rebellious son could legally be put to death by his father, and a child who cursed and struck a parent might be similarly punished. Although neither of these severe laws was ever invoked, there were numerous cases of record prior to 1650 in which children were publicly whipped or otherwise exposed to scorn for disobedience to parental control.

Colonial parents, particularly the father, ruled the family with almost complete authority. An early Massachusetts law charged that parents should instruct their children "in some honest lawful calling, labour, or imployment" under pain of fine or imprisonment. The law further provided that parents should assume responsibility for the "moral upbringing and ultimate marriage" of their offspring. Instruction was mandatory and consisted of reading, writing, and ciphering, but above all, included instruction leading to salvation by means of Bible reading, catechism, public worship, and continuous religious teaching.

In 1699, Cotton Mather published a tract entitled *A Family Well-Ordered*, which had a tremendous impact on control and disciplining of children. Mather visualized fear, obedience, discipline, and absolute authority as essential ingredients of the upbringing of children, both in the church and in the home. Later, Mather's ideas were included in the *New England Primer*, which next to the Bible became the most widely read book in America for over one hundred years. Between 1700 and 1850, more than three million copies of the primer were used, and its teachings provided the foundation for the treatment of children in state-supported schools during the formative years of our system of public education.

Elaborating on the concept of original sin, Mather contended that children were born in iniquity, and thus were creatures of hell, death, and wrath, possessed of corrupt natures which must be subdued. A child misbehaved because of an evil spirit within him. Discipline, therefore, was retribution imposed on the child in an attempt to "beat the devil out of him." But parents were forbidden to whip the child in anger. The use of the rod was *for the child's salvation!* The responsibility of the parent was to keep the child in rein, rebuking and restraining him when necessary as one of the duties of parenthood. Subsequently, discipline and control of children passed through several stages, such as fitting the punishment to the crime, or removing the child from the society of his friends to protect society and the offender. More recently, earlier concepts of discipline became tempered by a desire to *prevent* misbehavior, maladjustment, and crime through a positive approach, emphasizing wholesome activities and the acquisition of self-control on the part of the child.

The chief seat of instruction in the colonies was the home; early governments assumed little responsibility for teaching the young, except to provide by law that education was specifically the task of the parents. After the adoption of the federal constitution, states began to provide for the establishment of public schools as a part of their constitutional responsibility. Under the new state systems of education, control of children for educational purposes gradually shifted from the parents to public school teachers. With the adoption of early compulsory attendance laws, the child was required, unless taught by other means, to attend the public schools. This arrangement involved the surrender by parents of their children into the care and keeping of the public school teacher. New legal relationships were created, which will now be examined to determine the right of the modern teacher to control and discipline pupils under his jurisdiction.

In Loco Parentis

As education shifted gradually from the home to the state school system, courts of law were called upon to define the relationship of the teacher standing in place of the parent. The legal term, *in loco parentis*, has come to have a legal meaning in the common law, based upon the courts' description of the relationship which exists between teacher and pupil in the public schools.

In loco parentis, as applied by the courts and developed over the years, provides that the teacher may exercise *only* those powers which are just, proper, and necessary for the welfare of the child under the circumstances. As a substitute for the parent, the teacher's authority is less broad than that of the parent, because his control is limited to situations within his jurisdiction and responsibility *as a teacher*. The parent, on the other hand, retains control of such parental prerogatives as the determination of the manner and mode of moral and religious training of the offspring, and the type of medical treatment which the child shall receive. Since these are not educationally-connected prerogatives, they are outside the authority of the teacher to determine. The teacher, in the *in loco parentis* relationship, may control the pupil in matters relating to school and education only, but this control extends to pupils outside school hours when the good name and respect of the school's authority are involved.

What are the limitations upon the teacher acting in place of the parent? As a parental substitute, the teacher is subject first of all to the standard of *reasonableness* in all actions involving pupil discipline and control. The question asked by the court is, "Might a reasonable parent act thusly under similar circumstances in controlling the child?" The assumption is that the parent has the best interest of the child at heart; no less a standard is required of the teacher. When the answer to the question is in the affirmative, courts are reluctant to interfere in the exercise of the teacher's discretion, so long as he acts within the scope of his authority.

In addition to the rule of reasonableness, state statutes, and rules and regulations of boards of education limit the powers of the teacher to control and discipline pupils. The board can rule, for example, that the teacher may not inflict corporal punishment, or that if corporal punishment is inflicted, it shall only be in the presence of another adult. The teacher's control is to that extent thus limited by the board ruling. If not restricted by rule or law, and his demands are not unreasonable, the teacher has the common law right to direct how and when each pupil shall attend to his appropriate duties, and the manner in which the pupil shall conduct himself.

Much of the control and disciplining of pupils falls within the common law. It is virtually impossible for the legislature, or indeed the board of education, to deal with the control of each individual child; it devolves upon the teacher to exercise his judgment in matters of this nature. There are few statutes relating to pupil control; the teacher must decide when, to what extent, and how control must be exercised. The rule to remember is that the teacher, standing in place of the parent, has that authority which a reasonable parent might exercise under similar circumstances, unless there is a board rule or statute limiting that authority.

The teacher's discipline of a pupil under his care must, in order to be reasonable, take into account the age, sex, size, strength, and general health of the pupil. Disciplinary action which may be considered reasonable for a boy of ten might not be reasonable for a girl of twelve.

Finally, the right to control pupils and discipline them is counterbalanced by the *prohibitions* incident to the protection of the best interests of the child. Thus, a teacher may not use inhumane and barbaric treatment, mental cruelty, or excessive force in administering school rules. Courts will assist the teacher in enforcing reasonable school rules in a reasonable manner, but they will not condone malice, anger, arbitrary, or capricious actions on the part of the teacher in controlling his pupils.

Right to Control Pupils Outside School Hours

A teacher may discipline a pupil for an act committed outside school hours when the act tends to destroy respect for the school or one of its staff. In an early Vermont case, a boy returned to his home, then was sent to fetch a cow. While passing the teacher's home, the boy, in the presence of another student, made a disparaging remark to which the teacher took exception. When school opened the next morning, the teacher gave the boy a whipping. In an action against the teacher for assault and battery, the parents contended that the teacher had exceeded his authority. With this contention the court could not agree. Said the court:

> Where the offense has a direct and immediate tendency to injure the school and bring the master's authority into contempt, as in this case, when done in the presence of other scholars and of the master, and with a design to insult him we

think he has the right to punish the scholar for such acts if he comes again to school.[1]

To the same effect was an early case which arose in Iowa. Said the Supreme Court of Iowa, in ruling on a suit involving truancy of a pupil who was suspended by the board:

> The view that acts, to be within the authority of the school board and teachers for discipline and correction, must be done within school hours, is narrow, and without regard to the spirit of the law and the best interest of our common schools.[2]

Similarly, the authority of the board to prohibit children from patronizing a certain cafe was challenged. A rule stipulated that no child, while in school, should be allowed to enter the restaurant adjoining the school grounds. The school operated a lunch room which served meals at reasonable cost to school pupils. When two children persisted in visiting the cafe, they were suspended by the principal. In bringing suit for their reinstatement, the father insisted that the rule was unreasonable, in that it was for the sole purpose of encouraging the children to buy food from the school lunchroom. The court decided that the rule was reasonable.

> If the school lunch is to be successful, then all children who purchase their noon meal may be required to do so from the school lunchroom. The regulation appears to be for the common good of all children attending this school.[3]

An interesting Connecticut case arose when three boys abused two small girls at the home of one of the boys on their way home from school after school hours. All were pupils in the same school. The principal summoned the boys and told them of the offenses charged against them. The boys admitted their guilt, whereupon the principal administered a moderate punishment to each of them. The parents of one of the boys brought action to recover damages from the principal for assault and battery because the acts of the boys were outside the authority of the school. The court pointed out that the conduct of the boys tended to demoralize the school children and to interfere with the efficient conduct of the school. In upholding the principal, the court said:

> Examination of the authorities clearly reveals the true test of the teacher's right and jurisdiction to punish for offenses

---

[1]Lander v. Seaver, 32 Vt. 114 (1859).
[2]Burdick v. Babcock, 31 Iowa 562 (1871).
[3]Casey County Bd. of Educ. v. Luster, 282 S.W.2d 333 (Ky. 1955).

not committed on the school property or going and returning therefrom, but after the return of the pupil to the parental abode, to be not the time or place of the offense, but its effect upon the morale and efficiency of the school, whether it in fact is detrimental to its good order, and to the welfare and advancement of the pupils therein. . . . Correction will usually be sought in vain at the hands of parents; it can only be successfully applied by the teacher. . . . It is observed that while the plaintiff had reached his home after school, his victims had not. This is an important fact, even if the rule claimed by plaintiff should be upheld as a general statement.[4]

A Michigan court held that a girl who smoked cigarettes on the streets and aired her defiance of the school authorities in the public press might legally be suspended, although such actions were performed outside regular school hours.[5]

On the other hand, once the child is remitted to the custody of the parent following the school day, and no defiance of the school's authority is involved, it appears that the board may not enforce a school rule limiting the freedom of pupils out of school. A Missouri board adopted a rule against high school students attending social parties during the school year outside school hours. In declaring that the board did not have the authority to make and enforce such a rule, the Supreme Court of Missouri said:

> The directors of a school district are invested with the power and authority to make and execute all needful rules and regulations for the government, management and control of such school children as they may think proper, not inconsistent with the laws of the land. Under the power thus conferred, the directors are not authorized to prescribe a rule which undertakes to regulate the conduct of the children within the district, who have a right to attend the school, after they are dismissed from it and remitted to the custody and care of the parent or guardian.[6]

From these and other cases, the principle has been established that a board of education may legally control pupil conduct deleterious to the welfare, reputation, or good order of the school, even though such conduct occurs outside school hours and off school property. Where there is no deleterious effect, and the children have been remitted to the custody of the parents, school authorities may not regulate pupil conduct after school hours and off school premises.

---

[4]O'Rourke v. Walker, 102 Conn. 130, 128 Atl. 25, 41 A.L.R. 1308 (1925).
[5]Tanton v. McKenney, 226 Mich. 245, 197 N.W. 510, 33 A.L.R. 1175 (1924).
[6]Dritt v. Snodgrass, 66 Mo. 286 (1877).

The Law Governing Pupil Attendance

Compulsory attendance laws are common to all the states, and one might expect that very few problems related to pupil attendance would arise. This area of the law, however, continues to be one of the fertile areas of litigation in spite of the controlling statutory framework. Questions which continually come before the courts are indicative of the unsettled conditions related to this problem: Under what conditions may instruction of children in the home excuse attendance at the public or private school? May a child be admitted to the public school at an earlier age than that stipulated by the board of education? Is a board rule requiring vaccination as a prerequisite to admission a legal exercise of board power? May the board assign pupils to attend a school far from home in contravention of the wishes of the parents? These and many other related questions continually arise to plague the teachers and administrators, and many of these issues reach the courts of the land.

Compulsory attendance. The authority of the state to enact compulsory attendance laws has been frequently challenged, but consistently upheld. Such laws became necessary when the state, rather than the parents, assumed responsibility for the education of all the children of all the people. Under compulsory attendance statutes, parents are required to relinquish custody of their child during certain specified years in order that minimum educational standards may be attained, and an enlightened citizenry may be provided, an essential ingredient of our American form of government. Penalties are assessed where parents fail, during the compulsory attendance age of the child, to relinquish him for educational purposes, unless other arrangements are made for his education. The age range of compulsory school attendance varies from state to state, but generally includes the elementary and in some states the high school years.

Perhaps the most famous of the cases concerned with compulsory attendance was the so-called Oregon case described in Chapter I. The legislature of that state enacted a statute requiring that children between the ages of eight and eighteen attend the public schools only. The Supreme Court of the United States held the Oregon statute unconstitutional on the ground that it interfered with a basic constitutional right of parents and guardians to direct the upbringing of their children as they choose.

> The fundamental theory of liberty upon which all governments in this Union repose excludes any general power of the

State to standardize its children by forcing them to accept instruction from public teachers only. The child is not the mere creature of the State; those who nurture him and direct his destiny have the right, coupled with the high duty, to recognize and prepare him for additional obligations.[7]

The law providing for compulsory attendance must be a reasonable one, and reasonably enforced. Children who live at a great distance from school, where transportation is not provided, or who are ill, or mentally unable to profit by their attendance in the public school, may not be held truant when they do not comply with compulsory attendance laws in most jurisdictions. If certain dangers exist, *e.g.*, where it is necessary for children to cross a railroad track, school attendance cannot be required, and the parents cannot be held guilty of failure to comply with the attendance law. Of course, when parents maintain that the child has been kept out of school for sufficient reason, the sufficiency of the reason is a matter for the court. For example, because of their religious beliefs, which forbade music and dancing, the parents of a fourth-grade child in the state of Washington withdrew her from public school without permission of the school authorities. The court held that the parents were subject to the penalties of the compulsory attendance laws, and had no legal justification for violating positive law.[8]

Home instruction. Where legislatures permit, the child may be instructed at home. As a rule, a parent who provides substantially the same education the child would receive in the public school is considered to have complied with the requirements of the compulsory attendance law. In the case of a private tutor, the child may be receiving "substantially the same" education as that provided in schools outside the home, and no questions are asked. However, in those instances in which the parents undertake to instruct the child themselves, the courts are not so liberal.

In the *Shoreline* case above, the parents were instructing their fourth-grade daughter at home, but the court ruled that such instruction was "not equivalent" to that which the child would receive in a public or private school.[9] In California, *equivalency* is defined by statute, and consists of instruction in study and recitation for at least

---

[7]Pierce v. Society of Sisters, 268 U.S. 510, 45 Sup. Ct. 571, 69 L. Ed. 1070, 39 A.L.R. 468 (1925).

[8]State ex rel. Shoreline School Dist. No. 412 v. Superior Court, 55 Wash. 2d 177, 346 P.2d 999 (1959).

[9]*Ibid.*

three hours a day for 170 days each calendar year by a private tutor or other person, in the several branches of study required to be taught in the public schools of the state. Furthermore, the tutor or other person must hold a valid state credential for the grade taught. This statutory provision would ordinarily exclude most parents from avoiding the compulsory attendance law through the medium of home instruction, unless one or the other was a certificated teacher, or the couple could afford a private tutor. Furthermore, the courts are becoming more particular about what constitutes equivalency with the result that home instruction must in fact be of equal quality to that offered in the public schools in order to exempt the parents from the compulsory attendance statutes.

Entrance age. Some of the states have statutory provisions barring from admittance into the public schools any child who has not reached a specified age by a certain calendar date. This "cut-off" date may be September 1, November 1, or any other date which the legislature may adopt. The great mobility of population within the states and from state to state has formed the rationale for these laws, and the right of the state legislature to enact statutes of this type is unchallenged. Where such legislation exists, boards of education have no discretion in the matter of entrance age, but must comply with the statutory provisions. However, in those states having no entrance age legislation, local boards may legally adopt "cut-off dates" which specify the age requirements for children entering kindergarten or first grade for the first time.

A board rule of this nature was tested by the Supreme Court of Montana in 1960. There a board adopted the rule that a child, in order to be enrolled in the kindergarten, must be five years of age on or before October 31 of the year of entry, or six by that date for entry into the first grade. If the child's birthday fell between November 1 and 15, he might be admitted on the basis of certain test results. The parents of a child who was six on November 18 sought through mandamus to compel the board to admit their child to the first grade in September. The child missed the mandatory cut-off date for entrance into the first grade by only three days, when the test clause was considered.

The petition of the parents was denied. The Supreme Court of Montana held that the board might legally set a date after which no child would be admitted to that particular term of school. Practical difficulties would arise were children to be admitted immediately upon reaching the state's constitutional school age of six years. The court refused to admit the child, reasoning that (1) she might actually suffer detriment from late admittance, inasmuch as she would be behind her classmates in her studies, and (2) she would be admitted the following September "in the ordinary course of schooling while she was still six years old."[10]

Vaccination. The Supreme Court of the United States has twice decided that a compulsory vaccination law is within the power of the state to enact, and that under such legislation this power can be exercised regardless of an epidemic.[11] The states, under their broad police powers, may legislate concerning the health, safety, morals, and general welfare of the people. The compulsory vaccination rule has been interpreted as a legal means by which the public health may be safeguarded. The state, furthermore, may delegate to municipalities, school boards, and similar public bodies the authority to determine under what conditions health regulations shall become operative. Thus, school officials may enforce a rule which says that all pupils must be vaccinated as a condition of entry or re-entry into the public schools even in the absence of an epidemic, provided statutory authority exists. In the absence of such statutory authority, the state's power to require vaccination usually cannot be exercised except in case of an epidemic.

There seems to be a lack of agreement, however, among state courts as to what constitutes an epidemic. For example, the Supreme Court of Pennsylvania upheld as reasonable a rule excluding all pupils who would not undergo a vaccination against smallpox, even though the rule was based only on a rumor.[12] On the other hand, courts in Michigan, Illinois, and Wisconsin have refused to give the board such broad powers.[13]

Compulsory vaccination rules have been attacked on the ground that they violate the constitutional rights of the child, but the courts consistently hold that this position is tenuous. The state requirement which seeks to protect the health, safety, and welfare of all the people of the state supersedes the rights of the individual citizen, and one's

---

[10]State ex rel. Ronish v. School Dist. No. 1, 348 P.2d 797 (Mont. 1960).

[11]Jacobson v. Massachusetts, 197 U.S. 11, 35 Sup. Ct. 358, 49 L. Ed. 643 (1905); Zucht v. King, 260 U.S. 174, 43 Sup. Ct. 24, 67 L. Ed. 194 (1922).

[12]Duffield v. School Dist. of Williamsport, 162 Pa. 476, 29 Atl. 742 (1894).

[13]Mathews v. Board of Educ., 127 Mich. 530, 86 N.W. 1036 (1901); LaBaugh v. Board of Educ., 122 Ill. 572, 52 N.E. 850 (1890); Adams v. Burdge, 95 Wis. 390, 70 N.W. 347 (1897).

constitutional rights are not violated by such a rule. Nor does the fact that a parent may conscientiously object to vaccination on religious grounds relieve the child of the duty to be vaccinated prior to admission to the public schools. The school board is not prohibited from requiring compulsory vaccination merely because of differences of opinion on the subject.

What is the effect of keeping a child out of school where it violates the state compulsory attendance law? This question was before the court in New York.[14] A parent was convicted in a magistrate's court for failure to send his son to public school in violation of the compulsory attendance law. The boy had been in attendance, but was excluded for non-vaccination. The father urged that the exclusion constituted valid reason why he should not comply with the provisions of the compulsory attendance act. The court held that such exclusion was not a sufficient defense to save the father from prosecution by the state for violation of the educational attendance law of New York. Failure to send his child to a private school or to any school other than the public school was evidence of lack of good faith on the part of the parent, the court asserted.

Similarly, where a parent objected to vaccination on religious grounds, he could not use the defense that he offered to send his son to school unvaccinated, but the board refused to receive him. The court held that a direct provision for vaccination with a penalty for refusal to submit, is valid, and a parent may be forced to comply, or suffer the consequences.[15]

Right to assign pupils. The courts will not interfere with the implied power of the board of education to adopt reasonable rules governing admission and assignment of pupils within the district. Ordinarily, pupils attend the school nearest their residence, but it is well settled that this is not an inherent right. If a school is crowded, the board may assign pupils to another school not so conveniently located. A pupil has no legal right to attend a particular school within a district merely because he lives in the district, or because his parents desire his attendance at a specific school.

In Iowa, the parents of a handicapped child refused to send the child to an ungraded school to which the child had been assigned. Because the school was considered the "dumb school," and because the child was sensitive, the parents contended that attending the special

---

[14]People v. Ekerold, 211 N.Y. 386, 105 N.E. 670 (1914).
[15]State v. Drew, 89 N.H. 54, 192 Atl. 629 (1937).

education classes might embitter the child against attendance at any educational institution. The board, however, refused to assign the child to another school. The Supreme Court of Iowa held that the board had acted entirely within its authority in assigning the child as it did, and that failure of the parents to send the child where assigned constituted a violation of the compulsory attendance laws.[16]

Under very special conditions, parents may withdraw their children from school without penalty, even though they provide no home instruction or do not enroll the children in a private school. In a New York City case in 1958, the court upheld the parents under the following circumstances. Two Negro children were withdrawn by their parents from a predominately Negro and Puerto Rican school because, compared with the white schools, the school to which the children were assigned offered educationally inferior opportunities for learning. Discriminatory staffing of the two schools with teaching personnel having qualifications inferior to those possessed by most other teachers in the system, according to the parents, denied their children equal educational opportunities in violation of their rights under the equal protection clause of the fourteenth amendment.

Said the court, in upholding the parents' right to disregard the compulsory attendance law under these conditions:

> The Board of Education has no moral or legal right to ask that this court shall punish parents, or deprive them of custody of their children, for refusal to accept an unconstitutional condition which exists in the schools to which the Board has assigned their children.[17]

Under the circumstances, the parents could not be made to instruct their children at home, or enroll them in a private school. It was the duty of the school officials to provide adequate schools and instructors if they expected the compulsory attendance laws to be observed.

Right of the board to charge fees. One characteristic of American public education is that it is *free*. Most of the states have constitutionally provided for a system of public education in which all children of school age may be educated gratuitously. The question then arises whether schools which charge incidental or special fees still come within the constitutional provisions that the schools shall be free to the children of the state. The courts are not in complete agreement on this question.

---

[16]State v. Ghrist, 222 Iowa 1069, 270 N.W. 376 (1936).
[17]In re Skipwith, 14 Misc. 2d 325, 180 N.Y.S.2d 852 (1958).

In a leading Alabama case, the court made a distinction between fees for incidental purposes, and a general tuition fee, holding that the former were permissible, while the latter was not.[18] In Oklahoma, a student who refused to pay a non-returnable $2.50 fee which was used to support student literary societies, the college paper, men's and women's athletic associations, and the like at a state college was ordered admitted by the court. The court ruled that such fees were proper, but that they may not be charged as a condition of admittance to a state-supported school.[19]

To combat the problem of failure to complete the high school course in the usual four-year period, the school board in a North Dakota high school district adopted a rule requiring students to pay tuition after completing four years of attendance at high school. The Supreme Court of North Dakota enjoined enforcement of the rule on the ground that it violated a state constitutional provision that the public schools should be free, open, and accessible to all children "over six and under twenty-one years of age."[20]

Similarly, an Arkansas court knocked down a board rule requiring pupils to pay a registration fee as a condition of admittance to the public schools.[21] From the cases, it would appear that a board may not legally charge registration fees, but may, under certain conditions, collect fees for breakage, lockers, the cost of special courses, and the like, so long as they are not prerequisite to admission into the public schools.

Enforcement of School Board Rules and Regulations

Board powers are said to be (1) those specifically *enumerated* in the statutes, (2) those which may be reasonably *implied* from the nature of the enterprise, or (3) those which are necessary to the good order of the school. Inasmuch as comparatively few pupil-discipline statutes exist, the control of pupils and their punishment for violations of school rules are held to be powers implied or necessary on the part of the board and its employees. Many boards today have found it desirable to include rules pertaining to pupil punishment and control

---

[18]Shirey v. City Board of Educ. of Fort Payne, 94 So. 2d 758 (Ala. 1957).

[19]Connell v. Gray, 33 Okla. 591, 127 Pac. 417 (1912).

[20]Batty v. Board of Educ. of City of Williston, 67 N.D. 6, 269 N.W. 49 (1936).

[21]Dowell v. School Dist. No. 1, Boone County, 220 Ark. 828, 250 S.W.2d 127 (1952).

in the written policies of the board. Where these exist, the teachers and administrators should become familiar with the policies of the board, and abide thereby. However, even in the presence of written disciplinary policies, there exists a broad area of teacher discretion in matters relating to pupil punishment.

The following pages contain information about corporal punishment of school pupils, assault and battery, suspension and expulsion, control of married pupils, and other topics related to the orderly control of pupils in the public schools. The student will notice no dearth of cases illustrative of the potential problems of teachers which arise from the need to control and discipline pupils under the jurisdiction of the school.

Corporal punishment. Law dictionaries define corporal punishment as *physical* chastisement, such as whipping, as distinguished from fines, imprisonment, and other types of punishment. As a general rule, unless prohibited by statute or board ruling, the teacher has the power to inflict corporal punishment upon his pupils. This power is accorded the teacher for two reasons: one, because it is necessary to control the class for instructional purposes, and two, because the teacher, standing in place of the parent, is responsible for the training of the child in acceptable behavior. It is interesting to note that the number of corporal punishment cases which reach the courts has been declining in recent years, due, no doubt, to newer psychological concepts on the part of teachers, and to clearer delineation of the role of the teacher in controlling pupils.

The power to administer corporal punishment exists as a privilege growing out of the *in loco parentis* relationship, but is not without its limitations. A teacher is not justified in inflicting corporal punishment on a pupil to enforce an unreasonable rule, to pursue a course of study forbidden by his parents, or to compel him to do something which the parent has requested that he be excused from doing. The privilege is further limited to "reasonable" punishment; there must be a logical relationship between the act which brought about the punishment and the severity of the punishment itself. Children may not be expected to act like adults. The teacher should take into account that pupils, particularly the younger ones, will make mistakes occasionally, and teachers must accordingly adjust the punishment. The power to administer corporal punishment is a valuable asset to any teacher, but the courts will not allow an abuse of the power on the pretense that "the pupil brought it on himself."

The decision to use corporal punishment is at the discretion of the teacher, in the absence of laws or board rules which limit the teacher's exercise of this power. Only one state, New Jersey, has a statute strictly prohibiting the use of corporal punishment by pupil school teachers. In nearly all the states, however, local boards have enacted policies which define the teacher's right to inflict corporal punishment. Usually, such policies do not wholly prohibit corporal punishment, but establish specific procedures for the exercise of this power.

The majority of court cases relating to corporal punishment have come about when the teacher is charged with assault and battery, but some of the cases have dealt with dismissal of the teacher on the grounds of misuse of corporal punishment. Courts have been inclined to decide in favor of the teacher, unless there was evidence of malice, brutality, or permanent injury to the pupil. Nine states have indirectly sanctioned corporal punishment by placing the teacher beyond reach of a suit for assault and battery when using physical force upon a pupil, unless immoderate punishment is involved.

In states where the law is silent on the matter, the courts have developed criteria by which to determine whether corporal punishment administered by the teacher is "reasonable." While the circumstances surrounding each case are controlling, the courts will hesitate to interfere with the teacher's right to administer corporal punishment if it is:

1. Not prohibited by statute;
2. For the good of the child, and administered in good faith and without malice;
3. Not cruel and excessive, nor performed with an instrument which leaves permanent mark or injury;
4. Performed under the *in loco parentis* relationship;
5. Suited to the age, sex, size, and physical strength of the child;
6. Conducive to the general welfare of the school;
7. In proportion to the gravity of the offense; and
8. Not performed to enforce an unreasonable rule.

Assault and battery. "To be guilty of an 'assault and battery,'" said one court, "a school teacher must not only inflict on the pupil immoderate chastisement, but he must do so with legal malice or wicked motives, or he must inflict some permanent injury."[22] This ruling would seem to indicate that the teacher will be given "the

---

[22]Suits v. Glover, 260 Ala. 449, 71 So. 2d 49 (1954).

benefit of the doubt" in most corporal punishment cases, but the courts will quickly condemn unreasonable and cruel punishment. The burden of proof is with the plaintiff, but the teacher may be asked to show that he exercised discretion and judgment in determining the necessity for corporal punishment, and that the punishment inflicted was reasonable.

In one of the cases noted earlier in this chapter, the parents of three small boys who annoyed two girls off school property brought suit against the principal of the school for assault and battery. The principal had punished the boys by striking the hand of each eight times with a flat stick two feet long and over one-half inch thick, used in the school for that purpose only. The court, however, refused to agree with the contention of the parents that the punishment was unreasonable or excessive. The acts of the boys, said the court, were detrimental to the good order and best interest of the school, and the punishment was reasonable and proper, even though the acts for which punishment was administered occurred off school property.[23]

Similarly, the parents of a boy brought suit against two teachers for alleged excessive punishment of the youth. A dime had disappeared, and the teachers suspected the boy of having taken it from a window ledge. When the boy denied knowledge of the lost coin, the two teachers searched his pockets but failed to find the dime. Because he resisted, the teachers administered slight punishment in the search. The court refused to hold the teachers liable for assault and battery.[24]

In at least one case, a court has ruled that relatively severe punishment may be inflicted without legal penalty. In Ohio, a teacher paddled a boy six to fifteen times with a medium-sized paddle. As a result, the child's buttocks were vividly discolored black and blue for about five days. The court, in refusing to hold the teacher liable, ruled that punishment is not excessive if it does not produce a lasting or permanent injury, or if the plaintiff fails to prove that the punishment was administered with spite, hatred, or revenge.[25]

In another case, however, the result was quite different when the principal of an elementary school ordered a disobedient ten-year-old boy to come into his office. Because the pupil resisted, the principal dropped him to the floor, and knelt and sat upon the boy to subdue

---

[23]O'Rourke v. Walker, 102 Conn. 130, 128 Atl. 25, 41 A.L.R. 1308 (1925).

[24]Marlar v. Bill, 181 Tenn. 100, 178 S.W.2d 634 (1944).

[25]State v. Lutz, 113 N.E.2d 757 (Ohio 1953).

him. The third grade boy, who was small for his age, weighed 89 pounds; the principal weighed 190. The court ruled the principal had exercised unreasonable force in disciplining the boy, and held him liable for the injuries which the pupil sustained.[26]

Fists and a piece of flooring were considered improper instruments for disciplining a fifteen-year-old pupil, and their use constituted proper ground for discharge of the teacher in a 1940 Arkansas case. The first whipping was administered to the student for telling a riddle, and the second whipping on the same day was for throwing a paper wad at the teacher. These acts on the part of the pupil, especially the last one, said the court, justified the teacher in inflicting reasonable punishment on the pupil, but he was not justified in inflicting excessive or cruel punishment.[27]

In Louisiana, a principal on permanent tenure whipped a twelve-year-old boy with a piece of sash cord, assigning as the reason therefor the pupil's absence from school without permission. Testimony revealed that the boy was severely bruised, and that three weeks passed before the skin was completely healed. The court held that the board had acted within its authority in dismissing the principal, although the latter had tenure under the laws of the state.[28]

An Iowa pupil was in poor health, and her father requested that she be allowed to attend school only in the forenoon. The class in algebra was offered in the afternoon. When the girl failed to appear for her algebra class, the teacher whipped her with a four-foot whip, although the girl insisted that her father had "excused" her from taking the class. The parents brought suit against the teacher for assault and battery.

In upholding the parents and ruling that the teacher was indeed guilty of assault and battery, the Supreme Court of Iowa enunciated the leading principle of law relating to the use of corporal punishment to compel a pupil to take a certain subject:

> If a pupil attends school it must be presumed he submits himself to the rules. We are unwilling to sanction the rule that a teacher may punish a pupil, as in this case, for not doing something the parent has requested the pupil be excused from doing. The remedy in such case is not corporal punishment, but expulsion.[29]

---

[26]Calway v. Williamson, 130 Conn. 575, 36 A.2d 377 (1944).
[27]Berry v. Arnold School Dist., 199 Ark. 1118, 137 S.W.2d 256 (1940).
[28]Houeye v. St. Helena Parish School Bd., 223 La. 966, 67 So. 2d 553 (1953).
[29]State v. Mizner, 50 Iowa 145 (1878).

Suspension and expulsion. The right of the board to suspend or expel a pupil is implied in the grant of power to establish public schools, and will not be interfered in by the courts unless there appears to be an abuse of the board's power or an individual's constitutional rights must be protected. Pupils who do not maintain a required academic standard may be dropped from school so long as the board acts in good faith, the rule setting the academic standards is a reasonable one, and the rule is reasonably applied. (But the Supreme Court of Minnesota held that a board acted arbitrarily in dismissing as academically deficient a college student without first giving the student notice or a hearing.[30] Many state statutes or board rules require a hearing at the time of suspension or expulsion, so it is important that the parent of the child be promptly notified by the teacher or school administrator when a pupil is suspended or expelled.[31])

A board has the power to dismiss a pupil for offenses which are detrimental to the general good order and welfare of the school, even though no specific rule is violated. In a leading Missouri case the court held that the board was not without power to expel a boy for general misconduct even though it had not adopted a rule covering the matter.[32] Boards have also been held to have acted within their power in expelling pupils for disrepect toward the board and its policies,[33] for using face paint and powder,[34] and for being tardy without sufficient excuse.[35]

A distinction is noted between *suspension* and *expulsion* when applied to public school pupils. The former refers to temporary removal from the school pending later action of the board of education. Often this is desirable because a time may elapse before the board will meet, or the teacher or principal may merely wish to provide a "cooling off period" before allowing the pupil to return to school. It seems well settled that teachers and administrators may legally *suspend* a pupil pending final disposition of his case by the board. The power to *expel* a pupil, however, rests entirely with the board, in the absence of a statute to the contrary. Suspension is thus seen as a temporary measure employed legally by teachers and administrators, while expulsion is

---

[30]Gleason v. University of Minn., 104 Minn. 359, 116 N.W. 650 (1908).

[31]Flory v. Smith, 145 Va. 164, 136 S.E. 360 (1926).

[32]Crain v. Hamilton, 42 Mo. App. 24 (1890).

[33]State ex rel. Dresser v. District Bd. of School Dist. No. 1, 135 Wis. 619, 116 N.W. 232 (1908).

[34]Pugsley v. Sellmeyer, 158 Ark. 247, 250 S.W. 538, 30 A.L.R. 1212 (1923).

[35]King v. Jefferson City School Bd., 71 Mo. 628 (1880).

of more permanent nature, and exclusively within the power of boards of education. From the cases, it seems unlikely that expulsion will be upheld by the courts beyond the beginning of the ensuing year of school following the year in which the expulsion takes place except in most unusual circumstances.

A Kansas court held that a pupil who refused to salute the flag, because of a religious belief taught him by his parents, and who was expelled from school, had been illegally dismissed.[36] Similarly, a California court ruled that a school board which expelled a pupil for refusal to take part in a prescribed dancing class had violated the pupil's constitutional right of freedom of religion, since the parents' religious beliefs were violated by dancing. The court noted that the trustees could lawfully prescribe dancing as a part of the curriculum, but that, where a child's religious beliefs were violated, it was unreasonable and violative of the child's rights to compel him to take the class or face expulsion.[37]

From these and similar cases, the principle is clear that a pupil may not be corporally punished for refusal to take a prescribed course, nor can he be expelled because of refusal when a constitutional right is violated. The parents have the right to request that the child be excused from participating in subjects to which they object on religious grounds, but this right is not unlimited. The parent is required to show that his request is reasonable under the circumstances. For example, an Oklahoma school board had a rule that all pupils should take grammar. A father requested that his children be excused from taking the course, but he gave no reason for his request. The court refused to interfere in the enforcement of the rule.[38]

Boards have been restrained by the courts from expelling pupils for accidentally destroying school property,[39] for failure to pay a monthly fee,[40] for marriage,[41] and for failure to remain at home and study between seven and nine o'clock in the evening.[42] Whenever a question arises as to whether the power of the school authorities to

---

[36]State v. Smith, 155 Kan. 588, 127 P.2d 518 (1942).

[37]Hardwick v. Board of School Trustees of Fruitridge School Dist., Sacramento County, 54 Cal. App. 696, 205 Pac. 49 (1921).

[38]Crews v. Johnson, 46 Okla. 164, 148 Pac. 77 (1915).

[39]Holman v. Trustees of School Dist. No. 5, 77 Mich. 605, 43 N.W. 996 (1889).

[40]Williams v. Smith, 192 Ala. 428, 68 So. 323 (1915).

[41]McLeod v. State, 154 Miss. 468, 122 So. 737, 63 A.L.R. 1161 (1929).

[42]Hobbs v. Germany, 94 Miss. 469, 49 So. 515 (1909).

make a certain rule or regulation is reasonably within the scope of the power conferred on them by law, the question is subject to inquiry by the courts.

The remedy for wrongful expulsion is a writ of mandamus to compel the board to readmit the child. There is a possible additional remedy, an action for damages, but ordinarily courts will not hold the board collectively or the board members individually liable for damages, unless dismissal is shown to be willful or malicious or in contravention of a state-granted right. The cases in which damages have been assessed against boards of education for wrongful expulsion are not numerous. Indeed, it would be almost impossible to induce laymen to serve on boards of education if they were made insurors of the legality of their acts.

In Alabama, however, where a pupil was excluded from school in violation of a state-granted right, both the board and the teacher were held accountable in damages. The state legislature had provided that all pupils might attend the public schools free of charge. A pupil refused to pay a tuition fee levied by the board, and was expelled from school. In holding the teacher and the board liable, the court said:

> Appellant acted under the direction of the school board; but he must be charged in law with a knowledge of the unlawful character of his act. As a joint tort-feasor with the school board, he is liable, notwithstanding their direction in the premises. There can be no innocent agency in the commission of an act upon its face unlawful and tortious.
> . . . [the teacher] deprived appellee [child] of a valuable right or privilege which by law and without price is extended to all the children of the state.[43]

Regulation of the personal appearance of pupils. Although relatively few cases have been adjudicated on the subject, the courts have generally agreed that local boards are invested with sufficient authority to regulate the dress and personal appearance of pupils. In 1923, a school board in the state of Arkansas adopted a rule prohibiting pupils from wearing transparent hosiery, low-necked dresses, or any style of clothing tending toward immodesty in dress, or the use of face paint or cosmetics. A high school girl who used talcum powder on her face was suspended from school until she consented to abide by the rule. She sued for a writ of mandamus to compel the board to readmit her. The case finally reached the Supreme Court of Arkansas.

---

[43]Williams v. Smith, 192 Ala. 428, 68 So. 323 (1915).

That court refused to overrule the board, maintaining that the latter body was more familiar with local conditions, and therefore in a better position to decide whether the rule was a reasonable one. Said the court:

> We are unwilling to say, as a matter of law, that a local condition might not exist which would make a rule of this character desirable in aid of the discipline of the school, and we therefore decline to annul it, for we will not annul a rule of the kind unless a valid reason for doing so is made to appear; whereas, to uphold it we are not required to find a valid reason for its promulgation.[44]

A North Dakota court ruled that a board was acting entirely within its authority in regulating the wearing of metal heel-plates on the ground that the use of such plates injured the floors and caused noise and confusion in the schoolroom.[45] Similarly, the Supreme Court of Mississippi upheld the right of the board to require pupils in the public schools to wear a prescribed uniform, even when visiting public places away from the school.[46]

To the opposite effect was a ruling by an Iowa court, in which the board withheld the graduation certificate of a girl who refused to wear a cap and gown at commencement exercises. Said the Supreme Court of Iowa, in holding that the rule was unreasonable:

> The wearing of a cap and gown on commencement night has no relation to educational values, the discipline of the school, scholastic grades, or intellectual advancement. Such a rule may be justified in some instances from the viewpoint of economy, but from a legal viewpoint, the board might as well attempt to direct the wearing of overalls by the boys and calico dresses by the girls.[47]

May a pupil be required on pain of expulsion to attend a physical education class and wear the prescribed female outfit against an objection that such brief attire offends her religious principles? In Alabama, a high school girl was suspended for refusal to wear a prescribed uniform in her gymnasium class. Her parents, in a suit for reinstatement, contended that wearing the uniform subjected the girl to immodest display in contravention of their religious beliefs. The court held that the girl could be required to attend the class, but that

---

[44]Pugsley v. Sellmeyer, 158 Ark. 247, 250 S.W. 538, 30 A.L.R. 1212 (1923).
[45]Stromberg v. French, 60 N.D. 750, 236 N.W. 477 (1931).
[46]Jones v. Day, 127 Miss. 136, 89 So. 906, 18 A.L.R. 645 (1921).
[47]Valentine v. Independent School Dist. of Casey, 191 Iowa 1100, 183 N.W., 434 (1921).

she could not be required to wear the prescribed outfit and engage in exercises which would be immodest in ordinary apparel.[48]

Requiring pupils or their parents to pay for damage to school property. A decided increase in juvenile delinquency and vandalism focused the attention of school authorities on the problem of whether a pupil, or his parent or guardian, can be required to pay for damage to school property resulting from the acts of the child. The common law principle is that the pupil may not be suspended for defacing school property on condition that he pay for the damage before being allowed to return to school. Enforcement of the rule requiring a child to "settle for the damages" before he will be allowed back in school might result, according to one court, in depriving a poor child of the right to a common-school education.[49]

Said the Supreme Court of Iowa in dealing with the problem:

> It would be very harsh and obviously unjust to deprive a child of education for the reason that through accident and without intention of wrong he destroyed property of the school district. Doubtless a child can be expelled from school as a punishment for breach of discipline or for offences against good morals, but not for innocent acts.[50]

Court cases involving injury to school property by pupils are few in number, but the decisions seem to be in agreement that boards of education may not require pupils to pay for school damages occasioned by negligence or carelessness, unless there is a specific statute imposing such liability. New Jersey and South Dakota are states which impose liability upon the *parent or guardian* of a pupil who cuts, defaces, or otherwise injures school property, and there have been some cities in which liability was imposed under certain circumstances. Under the New Jersey law, which provides that the parent shall be liable to the full extent of the damage, the parents of a boy who set fire to a school building were held liable for the sum of $344,000![51]

Parental knowledge of the whereabouts of the boy was not an issue in the case, but in another case involving damages it was ruled

[48]Mitchell v. McCall, 143 So. 2d 629 (Ala. 1962).

[49]Holman v. School Trustees of Avon, 77 Mich. 605, 43 N.W. 996, 6 L.R.A. 534 (1889).

[50]Perkins v. Independent School Dist. of Des Moines, 56 Iowa 476, 9 N.W. 356 (1880).

[51]Palmyra Board of Educ. of Borough of Palmyra in County of Burlington v. Hansen, 56 N.J. Super. 567, 153 A.2d 393 (1959).

that parents who knew of their son's propensity for causing damage might be held liable for the child's acts on the grounds that their prior knowledge constituted assent and participation on the part of the parents. Under these conditions, the parents were held negligent and required to respond in damages.[52]

The number of states having specific statutes requiring parents to assume responsibility for acts of their children is not large, but will probably increase. In those states which have no such legislation, parents are not liable for damage to school property by their minor children simply because of the parent-child relationship, although it is apparent that the child is personally liable for injury he may cause to another, as if he were an adult. Should the child hold property in his own name, and be held liable for injury to another, his property may be taken to satisfy the damages involved. For all practical purposes, then, unless the child holds property in his own right, a suit against a minor for tort or property destruction damages is wholly empty. Even in cases where the parents own substantial property, and are held liable for acts of their minor child, an award of a large judgment in damages could well serve to force the parents into bankruptcy.

What is the legality of teacher-collected fines and fees? May teachers "fine" students who damage or destroy school property? Unless authority for such teacher action rests in the state statutes or board rules and regulations, the practice would be entirely without legal sanction because the school property is generally state property held in trust by the board of education. The teacher has no right to take it upon himself to collect any fines or fees.

Pupil marriages. Since World War II, the average age at which young people marry has gradually fallen. It is not uncommon for college students to marry, and the trend is toward marriage in the high school years. Faced with the married pupil problem, boards of education have sought solutions through the enforcement of rules and regulations for those who marry while still in school.

May a board of education legally exclude from school a pupil who is married? The courts are not in agreement on this point. In an early case which arose in Kansas, the supreme court of that state ruled that a girl who had married and was mother of a child could not be excluded on that basis alone. Every child has the right under the constitution of the state to attend school, the court declared, unless his or

---

[52]Ryley v. Lafferty, 45 F.2d 641 (N.D. Idaho 1930).

her moral standards are detrimental to the other students. Said the court:

> Other than the fact that her child was conceived out of wedlock, no sufficient reason is advanced for preventing her from attending school. Her child was born in wedlock, and the fact that her husband may have abandoned her should not prevent her from gaining an education which will better fit her to meet the problems of life.[53]

It seems reasonable to assume that a married pupil might stand in as much, if indeed not more, need of an education than the pupil who remains unmarried.

To the argument that unmarried pupils associating with married pupils in the public schools might be demoralized, a Mississippi court responded:

> Marriage is a domestic relation highly favored by the law. When the relation is entered into with correct motives, the effect upon the husband and wife is refining and elevating, rather than demoralizing. Pupils associating in school with a child occupying such a relation, it seems, would be benefited instead of harmed.[54]

However, where marriage may be detrimental to the good order and discipline of the school, it appears that a board may be upheld in excluding from school a person on the basis of marriage alone. In Tennessee, in a county high school system containing four high schools, the four principals thereof petitioned the board to adopt a resolution excluding anyone who was married, on the ground that student marriages had led to a general deterioration of discipline. The board adopted such a resolution, and a girl of eighteen was denied the right to attend school and graduate with her class. Her father-in-law brought suit to have her reinstated, citing the *McLeod* case in support of his contention that the girl had been illegally dismissed. The case eventually reached the Supreme Court of Tennessee.

After pointing out that "expert" testimony (that of the four high school principals) was to the effect that pupil marriages "influenced" the other pupils, the court went on to say:

> Boards of education, rather than courts, are charged with the important and difficult duty of operating the public schools. So, it is not a question of whether this or that indi-

---

[53]Nutt v. Board of Educ. of City of Goodland, Sherman County, 128 Kan. 507, 278 Pac. 1065 (1929).
[54]McLeod v. State ex rel. Miles, 154 Miss. 468, 122 So. 737 (1929).

vidual, judge or court considers a given regulation adopted by the Board as expedient. The court's duty, regardless of its personal views, is to uphold the Board's regulation unless it is generally viewed as being arbitrary and unreasonable. Any other policy would result in confusion detrimental to the progress and efficiency of our public school system.[55]

The court, in refusing to interfere with the board rule in question, pointed out that the principals' testimony was to the effect that, at least for a limited amount of time, the married students' presence in the school had a deleterious effect on the morale and efficiency of the other students. Because of this, it appeared reasonable to suspend *temporarily* a student who married during the school year.

On the question of the *McLeod* case, which was used as an argument by the plaintiff, and which was to the effect that students may not be excluded from school on the basis of marriage alone, the court had this to say:

> Whatever else may be said of that case it is distinguishable from the instant case by the fact that the resolution there adjudged unreasonable, hence void, expelled such marrying students *permanently* from the public schools (emphasis supplied).[56]

May a board of education legally exclude a female married high school student on the grounds that she is pregnant? In at least one case, the court ruled that it may. In Ohio, a board barred a sixteen-year-old student from attending high school for this reason, although they permitted her to continue her studies at home and receive credit. In an action seeking readmission, the girl maintained that the action of the board was unreasonable, and *ultra vires* the power of the board to enact. The common pleas court of Butler County,[57] however, refused to reinstate the student, even though an Ohio law required children between the ages of six and eighteen to attend the public schools. The board was within its rights, said the court, and the rule was not unreasonable. Under its terms, the rule permitted school attendance by married students, but specifically barred those who were pregnant. It appears that a board rule barring pregnant students from school will be upheld so long as the board acts in a manner not punitive to the student, and provides for a continuation of the student's education.

---

[55]State v. Marion County Bd. of Educ., 202 Tenn. 29, 302 S.W.2d 57 (1957).
[56]*Ibid.*
[57]State v. Chamberlain, 174 N.E.2d 539 (Ohio 1962).

229

Participation in athletics. In Texas, a board adopted the rule that married boys were barred from participating in athletic programs because parents were "up in arms" about married students being allowed to participate alongside those who were unmarried. There were 62 married students in the district whose school activities were thus limited to classroom work only.

A boy of sixteen, who had married a girl of fifteen, brought suit to test the reasonableness of the rule. He attacked the rule on the grounds that it was arbitrary, unreasonable, and in restraint of his constitutional rights. With his contention the Civil Court of Appeals of Texas could not agree.[58] The court pointed out that the right to marry is subject to certain limitations. In the case of eligibility for the athletic team, the pupil was subject, along with all others, to certain restrictions, such as physical condition and scholastic achievement. It was reasonable, said the court, for the board to require that students, in order to participate in athletics, should also be single rather than married. The fact that the boy lost a chance at a college athletic scholarship was not such a right as the law will protect.

To the same effect as *Kissick* was an interesting case which arose in Michigan. A local board, fearful lest high school student marriages would get out of hand, first considered an expulsion policy, but rejected the idea as too severe. Subsequently, the board adopted a rule that boys who married would be denied the right to participate in inter-scholastic athletics as a "punishment." Two boys who were denied the right, both model students according to the superintendent, brought suit to set aside the board ruling. The lower court sustained the action of the board, and the case finally reached the Supreme Court of Michigan. That august body was evenly divided, 4-4 on the question, thus indirectly upholding the decision of the lower court. Three of the judges who supported the board wrote:

> It necessarily follows that those in charge of said school must be allowed to judge and determine the propriety of allowing married students to participate in the playing of football on the high school team. It is manifest that those in charge of the schools, and not the courts, are better qualified to determine when and under what circumstances a student may be allowed to play football under the banner of the high school team. Students were not prevented from obtaining an educa-

---

[58]Kissick v. Garland Independent School Dist., 330 S.W.2d 708 (Tex. 1959).

tion. They were merely denied the right to play on the high school football team.[59]

An Indiana court similarly held that the right of pupils to attend the public schools and receive education does not include the right to participate in inter-scholastic athletics. In the latter case, the question of marriage was not involved.[60]

Control of secret societies. The courts have consistently upheld legislation prohibiting membership in secret societies in the public schools. Some states have enacted statutes limiting the general participation privileges of students who are members of secret societies, while others outlaw secret societies entirely. In Michigan, for example, a statute declares that:

> It shall be unlawful for any pupil of the elementary school and the high school of the public schools or any other public school of the state comprising one or all of the 12 grades in any manner to organize, join or belong to any high school fraternity, sorority or any other secret society. . . . Every such fraternity, sorority and secret society as herein defined is declared an obstruction to education, inimical to the public welfare and illegal.[61]

Oregon is a state with similar legislation. Despite the law, secret fraternities continued to flourish in the city of Portland. The school board, in an attempt to control mounting apprehension among the school staff, adopted a resolution directing the school superintendent to suppress secret societies which he considered inimical to the best interests of school pupils. A number of pupils and parents attacked the resolution on the ground that it was unreasonable. The Supreme Court of Oregon upheld the board, and ruled that the resolution was reasonable and proper.[62]

Similar resolutions have been sustained in Iowa,[63] California,[64] Mississippi,[65] and Illinois.[66] In the presence of a state statute controlling

---

[59]Cochrane v. Board of Educ. of Mesick Consolidated School Dist., 360 Mich. 390, 103 N.W.2d 569 (1960).

[60]State ex rel. Indiana High School Athletic Ass'n v. Lawrence Cir. Ct., 162 N.E.2d 250 (Ind. 1959).

[61]Mich. School Code § 15.3921.

[62]Burkitt v. School Dist. No. 1, Multnomah County, 195 Ore. 471, 246 P.2d 566 (1952).

[63]Lee v. Hoffman, 182 Iowa 216, 166 N.W. 565 (1918).

[64]Bradford v. Board of Educ. of City and County of San Francisco, 18 Cal. App. 19, 121 Pac. 929 (1912).

[65]Waugh v. Board of Trustees of the Univ. of Miss., 237 U.S. 589, 35 Sup. Ct. 720, 59 L. Ed. 1131 (1915).

[66]Smith v. Board of Educ., 182 Ill. App. 342 (1913).

secret societies, the courts are in complete accord that local boards may legally exercise reasonable powers delegated to them under the statutes.

Not so clearly defined, however, is the right of a board to adopt a rule controlling secret societies within the school in the *absence* of a state statute giving them that authority. While the majority of cases support the principle that such a rule is within the authority of the local board, in one case a Missouri court restrained the board with these words:

> No rule should be adopted which attempts to control the conduct of pupils out of school hours after they have reached their homes which does not clearly seek to regulate actions, which, if permitted, will detrimentally interfere with the management and discipline of the school.[67]

The court held that a board rule denying participation privileges to fraternity members was unreasonable, on the grounds that this was *ultra vires* the power of the board, and not designed to regulate detrimental interferences with school discipline. The case is noteworthy since it appears to be the only one in which a court has denied a local board the right to control secret societies in the public schools.

The weight of authority is represented in a 1945 case which arose in Texas. A board resolution denied pupils belonging to secret societies the right to participate in athletic, military, literary, and similar school activities, although the meetings of the secret societies were held outside school hours, off school property, and with parental consent. The court upheld the right of the board to adopt such a resolution, on the strength of evidence that membership in secret societies tended to destroy discipline and scholarship.[68]

In an almost identical case, the Columbus, Ohio, school board, in line with a state law to that effect, limited the extracurricular activities of known members of secret societies. Some parents sought to enjoin the enforcement of the resolution. In denying injunctive relief, the court said:

> Regulation 10.22 [the resolution] has a criminal counterpart in Section 2923.35, Ohio Revised Code. This statute is found in the Code chapter entitled "Crimes Against Society Not Otherwise Classified." That statute imposes a fine of ten

---

[67]Wright v. Board of Educ. of St. Louis, 295 Mo. 466, 246 S.W. 43 (1922).
[68]Wilson v. Abilene Independent School Dist., 190 S.W.2d 406 (1945).

to twenty-five dollars for each offense of any pupil in our public schools who shall organize, join or belong to a fraternity, sorority or *other like society* composed of or made up of pupils of the public schools. The Columbus Board of Education clearly adopted Regulation 10.22 as being a less onerous modus operandi than that of attaching a minor criminal record to many students under its jurisdiction as a sort of pre-commencement gift, free but not without charge; and, we believe, it is to be commended for its moderation.[69]

Right to withhold diploma. Is the pupil who completes the requisite courses and possesses the necessary qualifications for graduation legally entitled to the diploma? It appears from the few cases on this point that he is, except in extreme cases. Denial of the diploma for infractions of school rules is looked upon with disfavor by the courts. In one case, a senior girl who had completed all the other requirements for graduation was accused of cheating on a final American History examination and denied a diploma. The court held that the evidence of cheating was insufficient, and ordered the board to issue the diploma.[70] Similarly, we noted earlier that refusal to wear the required cap and gown at commencement exercises was ruled insufficient reason for denial of the diploma by an Iowa court.[71]

The right of the board to deny the diploma will not be interfered with unless there is evidence of unreasonableness on the part of the board. Should any doubt exist, it will be resolved in favor of the pupil. However, where a student passed his final examinations but became involved in a "scrape" and was denied a diploma, the court refused to interfere.[72]

Constitutional Rights v. Police Power

The struggle for proper balance between the rights of the individual and the power of the state is as old as organized government:

> Men think that what is just is equal; and that equality is the supremacy of the popular will; and that freedom means the doing what a man likes. In such democracies every one lives as he pleases, or in the words of Euripides, "according to his

---

[69]Holroyd v. Eibling, 188 N.E.2d 208 (Ohio 1961).

[70]Ryan v. Board of Educ. of City of Eureka, 124 Kan. 89, 257 Pac. 945 (1927).

[71]Valentine v. Independent School Dist. of Casey, 191 Iowa 1100, 183 N.W. 434 (1921).

[72]People ex rel. O'Sullivan v. New York Law School, 68 Hun. 118, 22 N.Y.S. 663 (1893).

fancy." But this is all wrong; men should not think it slavery to live according to the rule of the constitution; for it is their salvation.—Aristotle

In American society, as in perhaps no other place has this struggle been more dramatic or pronounced than in the people's schools, for it is this agency alone which touches the children of all the people. The story of how individual freedom has been maintained under our form of "police power" statehood is an interesting and informative one, and should be understood by every American teacher.

The police power of the state is designed to limit individual rights where these rights must be controlled for the common good. The power to control individual rights for the general welfare is rightfully the prerogative of the legislative branch of government, but it is not a prerogative of the legislature to determine the extent of this power. Exactly where the power of the state to limit individual freedom ends, and the rights of the individual to act "according to his fancy" begins are properly questions for the courts to decide. In matters affecting the constitutional rights of citizens, the Supreme Court of the United States is the final arbiter.

If a person feels that his constitutional rights are being denied or unreasonably limited, and relief is not available through appeal to the state courts, he may carry his case to the highest Court of the land. If the Court decides that the state has exercised its powers in a reasonable way and for the protection of the health, welfare and morals of the general public, the statute in question will be declared constitutional. If, on the other hand, there is an undue violation of the personal or property rights of the individual, the statute will be declared unconstitutional, and the state's power curtailed.

In cases involving balance between the power of the state and the right of the individual, the Supreme Court of the United States will determine whether the state has acted within its authority in promoting some common good which supersedes the individual's constitutional rights. In the past, the Supreme Court has limited even rights guaranteed by the Constitution of the United States, where it was shown that such limitation was necessary to the public health, morals, comfort, and general welfare of the people of the state.

Speaking of this responsibility of the Court, Justice Frankfurter said, in part:

> A grave responsibility confronts this Court whenever in course of litigation it must reconcile the conflicting claims of liberty and authority. But when the liberty invoked is liberty

of conscience, and the authority is authority to safeguard the nation's fellowship, judicial conscience is put to its severest test. Of such a nature is the present controversy.[73]

At issue in the *Gobitis* case was a fundamental individual right, that of refusing to salute the flag as a condition of school attendance. The Minersville school board ruled that children should salute the flag each day on pain of expulsion. The children of Gobitis, who were members of Jehovah's Witnesses, refused to do so, and were expelled. The father brought suit to enjoin the board from enforcing the rule in question.

The issue before the court was whether the board could make the flag salute a condition of school attendance. In ruling that the board had such a right, the Court said, "It mocks reason and denies our whole history to find in the allowance of a requirement to salute our flag on fitting occasions the seeds of sanction for obeisance to a leader."[74] The Court based its decision on the theory that the state may require the flag salute as a means of achieving national unity and patriotism.

The three years following the decision saw many expulsions (mostly of the Witnesses) for refusal to submit to the flag salute requirement. Certain misgivings among the Justices arose, and in a 1943 case, the Supreme Court reversed the *Gobitis* decision, and ruled in favor of Jehovah's Witnesses. The later decision was generally received more favorably than the first. In holding that a state rule requiring all students to salute the flag and recite the pledge of allegiance as a condition of school attendance violated the first amendment, the Court decided that the rule was one "which invades the sphere of intellect and spirit which it is the purpose of the first amendment of our Constitution to reserve from all official control."[75]

In 1962, in the case of *Engle v. Vitale,* the issue of the state's ability to compose a prayer that would be recited by all children in the public schools of New York was before the Supreme Court of the United States. That Court said:

> ... The constitutional prohibition against laws respecting an establishment of religion must at least mean that in this country

[73]Minersville School Dist. v. Gobitis, 310 U.S. 586, 60 Sup. Ct. 1011, 84 L. Ed. 1375 (1940).

[74]*Ibid.*

[75]West Virginia State Board of Educ. v. Barnette, 319 U.S. 624, 63 Sup. Ct. 1178, 87 L. Ed. 1628 (1943).

it is no part of the business of government to compose official prayers for any group of the American people to recite as part of a religious program carried on by government.

. . . The First Amendment was added to the Constitution to stand as a guarantee that neither the power nor the prestige of the Federal Government would be used to control, support or influence the kinds of prayer the American people say—that the people's religions must not be subjected to the pressures of government for change each time a new political administration is elected to office. Under that Amendment's prohibition against governmental establishment of religion, as reinforced by the provisions of the Fourteenth Amendment, government in this country, be it state or federal, is without power to prescribe by law any particular form of prayer which is to be used as an official prayer in carrying on any program of governmentally sponsored religious activity.[76]

Again, in 1963, the Supreme Court considered the scope of the provision of the first amendment concerning religion when companion cases presented the issues in the context of state action requiring that schools begin each day with reading from the Bible and the saying of the Lord's Prayer. The Bible reading was done in the schools without comment and the student could absent himself from the classroom or elect not to participate in the exercises. Nevertheless, the Court held these religious exercises were in violation of the first amendment, the purpose of which is to secure religious liberty in the individual by prohibiting any invasion thereof by civil authority. In this area, the court said that the state must take a position of "wholesome neutrality"; it can neither favor religion nor show hostility to religion.[77]

Parental Right to Control Children at School

May a parent legally direct his child to disregard school rules, and may the child thus escape the effect of school rules where the parent objects to their enforcement? In a North Dakota case, the parents of a high school boy objected to a school rule that pupils should not wear metal heel-plates to school. The boy knew of the rule, but

---

[76]370 U.S. 421, 82 Sup. Ct. 1261, 8 L.Ed.2d 601 (1962).

[77]School Dist. of Abington Township, Pa. v. Schempp, and Murray v. Curlett, 83 Sup. Ct. 1560 (1963).

insisted that his parents had directed him to disregard it. Said the Supreme Court of North Dakota in ruling that the board was entirely within its rights in insisting that the rule be obeyed:

> In most instances, the right of the parent is paramount, but sometimes the interests of the public generally require that the parent shall give way. The trial court found, and we think rightly, that under the circumstances there was no abuse of authority and the rule was proper and reasonable. Plaintiff [parent] argues that if such a rule may be enacted and enforced, then other rules may be enacted and enforced, and thus the school board enabled to prescribe absolutely the apparel that children must wear in order to enjoy the privileges of the school. But the plaintiff overlooks the safeguard of reasonableness which must always be considered.[78]

Commenting on whether children may act in violation of a reasonable school rule at the direction of their parents, the court had this to say:

> No rule or regulation could be enforced, provided the parent directed the pupil not to observe it. So we hold that the action of Murray [the boy], though taken at the command of his parents, constituted insubordination within the meaning of that term as used in the statute.[79]

In California, some parents objecting to their daughter's participation in a dancing class, sought to enjoin the board from enforcing the rule that children must attend the class or face expulsion. The court held that the school officials could lawfully prescribe dancing as a part of the curriculum, but could not enforce attendance at the class of those who objected to dancing on religious grounds. Said the court:

> Neither the state nor a school board has the right to enact a law or regulation the effect of which will be to alienate in a measure the children from parental authority along lines looking to the building up of the personal character and the advancement of the personal welfare of the children, where the views of the parents are not offensive to the moral well-being of the children nor inconsistent with the best interests of society.[80]

Finally, it seems clear that parents retain a measure of control over their offspring, even though the law requires them to relinquish the

---

[78]Stromberg v. French, 60 N.D. 750, 236 N.W. 477 (1931).
[79]*Ibid.*
[80]Hardwick v. Board of School Trustees of Fruitridge School Dist., Sacramento County, 54 Cal. App. 696, 205 Pac. 49 (1921).

child to the state for instructional purposes. Parental control is most clearly defined in the areas of who shall treat the child medically, whether the child shall be submitted to psychiatric testing, and to what extent the child shall be free of school-sponsored religious orientation. Evidence indicates that parents tend to retain a large measure of legal control in each of these three areas: medical treatment, psychiatric testing, and the religious training of their children.

Suggested Activities

CASE STUDY:

Discuss the following cases, giving reasons for your position. Then refer to the case as cited.

Case #1. A boy of fifteen, who had a reputation for misbehavior, created a disturbance in the school detention room, whereupon the teacher took him firmly by the arm and led him from the room. Outside the room in the hall, the boy clenched his fists, assumed a belligerent attitude, and uttered a vulgar remark to the teacher. Believing the boy intended to strike him, the teacher slapped the boy across the face with the back of his hand.

The district had a rule that a principal might administer corporal punishment only in the presence of a teacher. Suit was brought by the parents of the boy on the grounds of assault and battery. Under these circumstances, would you assume that the teacher would be found guilty of the charge?

Andreozzi v. Rubano, 145 Conn. 280, 141 A.2d 639 (1958).

Case #2. Students driving automobiles to high school were required to park them in a parking lot upon arrival and to leave them there until dismissal time, unless given special permission by school officials. A high school girl, in violation of the rule, parked her car one block from school, and drove the car to return home for lunch each noon. The principal discovered the ruse, and suspended the girl subject to further action of the board. Her father sued to enjoin the board from expelling her, insisting that the rule was void and outside the board's power to enact. Evidence brought out the fact that student drivers endangered the safety of the public near the school. Did the board abuse its discretion in adopting the rule in question?

McLean Independent School Dist. v. Andrews, 333 S.W.2d 886 (Tex. 1960).

Case #3. Trustees of a state university adopted a resolution banning social groups having national affiliations. Students so affected sought through injunction to prevent the trustees from enforcing the rule, on the grounds that it violated the due process clause, encroached upon their rights of assembly, etc. What would the courts rule under these circumstances?

Webb v. State Univ. of N. Y., 125 F. Supp. 910 (N.Y. 1954).

Further Readings

Eastmond, Jefferson. *The Teacher and School Administration* (Boston: Houghton Mifflin Company, 1959), pp. 126-127.

Edwards, Newton. *The Courts and the Public Schools* (Chicago: University of Chicago Press, 1955), Ch. XXII, Discipline and Punishment of Pupils.

Haskins, George. *Law and Authority in Early Massachusetts* (New York: Macmillan Company, 1960), Ch. V.

Messick, John D. *The Discretionary Powers of School Boards* (Durham, N. C.: Duke University Press, 1949), Ch. XV.

National Education Association. "Corporal Punishment," *Research Bulletin* (October, 1958), pp. 88-89.

Spurlock, Clark. *Education and the Supreme Court* (Urbana: University of Illinois Press, 1955), pp. 100-107.

Vedder, Clyde. *The Juvenile Offender* (New York: Random House, 1954).

Chapter IX

TEACHER LIABILITY FOR
PUPIL INJURY

Torts

A civil (not criminal) wrong committed against the person or property of another independent of contract is called a *tort*. The word derives from English law, and is so called because it is *twisted*, or crooked, and contrary to that which is right and straight. A civil action will lie against one who commits a tortious act against another, causing a direct invasion of his person, reputation, or property. Thus, one who negligently drives his automobile through a plate glass window commits a tort against the one who owns the window, and the courts will allow the injured party to recover damages. Injuring the property of another is a civil wrong, not a criminal act, although intentional torts, wilful or wanton in nature, such as assault and battery, may also be considered criminal. Tortious conduct may be misfeasance, malfeasance, or nonfeasance resulting in breach of a duty owed to another.

Similarly, one who causes injury to the reputation of another by speaking or writing false statements may be held accountable in tort for his actions, even though he may plead his right of free speech under the constitution. Libel (a written statement tending to damage a person's reputation) and slander (a spoken statement to the same effect) are examples of actionable torts, that is, tortious conduct for which an action at law may be instituted to right the wrong.

The legal test of a tortious act is (1) the existence of a legal *duty* of one person to another, (2) a *breach* of that duty, and (3) a *causal link* between the breach and the distress of the injured party.

As a matter of law, the courts will ask the following three questions whenever a person alleges that a tort has been committed against him:

1. Did the defendant owe the plaintiff a duty?
2. Was there a breach of the duty owed?
3. Was the breach the proximate cause of the plaintiff's injury?

For example, where the teacher has been charged with failure to provide proper supervision, and a child is injured, the court will first seek to determine whether the teacher owed the pupil a duty to provide supervision. This question, insofar as teachers and pupils are concerned, is usually answered in the affirmative. Second, was there a breach of the duty owed, that is, did the teacher unjustifiably fail to provide a reasonable degree of supervision? Finally, was the breach of duty the proximate cause of the injury—did the pupil's injury result because of lack of supervision? Where all three answers are affirmative, the teacher may be held liable in damages for injuries to those under his care and keeping.

Tort Liability of Public School Districts

It is well settled that a school district is not liable for the negligent acts of its agents, servants and officers, unless its immunity has been modified or abrogated by the legislature. This so-called *doctrine of sovereign immunity* was established in antiquity with the dictum that "the King can do no wrong." Under this common law principle, the governments of England and several European countries were held immune from the payment of damages to persons injured as a result of the activities of governmental agencies. Although the doctrine of sovereign immunity has largely disappeared in those countries from which it was adopted, it was accepted wholeheartedly in this country, and remains in a vast majority of the states as the common law rule.

Very few legislatures have attempted to abrogate the common law immunity of local school boards. Only New York, Washington, California, Illinois, and to a limited extent North Carolina and New Jersey have provided by law for a waiver of sovereign immunity. In those states, school districts may be held liable under certain conditions for the negligence of their officers and employees. In most of the other states, the doctrine of non-liability applies. There is a trend, however, notably in Wisconsin,[1] Minnesota and Pennsylvania, for the courts to

---

[1]Holytz v. City of Milwaukee, 17 Wis. 2d 26, 115 N.W.2d 618 (1962).

denounce the theory of sovereign immunity and hold school districts liable for their torts. This trend will, in all likelihood, continue.

Two arguments have been advanced to support the theory of non-liability of school districts for their torts. The first argument rests on the concept that schools perform a governmental function, namely, education of the young, and hence are not liable because, as involuntary agents of the state, they perform a necessary service imposed upon them by law. The service is without profit and for the general good of the state. As "mere agents of the state," so the argument goes, school districts should enjoy the same immunity from suit without consent as that afforded the sovereign state. This is the best known and most often quoted theory underlying non-liability of school districts from tort action.

The validity of this argument has been seriously questioned. Schools today are big business. Many of the functions which schools perform are not purely *governmental* in nature, nor do they relate directly to educational pursuits. Large spectator gatherings, such as at athletic events sponsored by the schools, for which an admission fee is charged, can hardly be considered "governmental functions." Injuries incurred by spectators under these conditions should be directly answerable in damages by the schools, critics of this argument maintain. The injured party should not be made to suffer loss on the ground that the schools are performing a purely governmental activity.

In the majority of states in which the common law rule of non-liability of school districts has not been abrogated by the legislature, school districts are not held liable for injuries caused by the negligence of their officers and employees while engaged in a *governmental* function, but may be liable if they engage in a *proprietary* function and injury results. The problem before the courts in these cases centers on the distinction between governmental and proprietary functions. The distinction must be found in the factual situation and it is no simple matter in each case to determine whether the board has engaged in a governmental (educational) function or a proprietary (non-educational) function.

In a 1960 case which arose in Virginia, a school board permitted the use of a school auditorium by a non-school group for a concert. A patron attending the concert was injured when she fell on a "slick and slippery floor." The injured party brought suit for damages against the school district, maintaining that the leasing of the auditorium amounted to a proprietary function, and that the school district was therefore liable in tort.

The court could not agree with this contention, and ruled that leasing the auditorium for a concert was a governmental rather than a proprietary function, since it tended to stimulate and foster the interest of pupils and the public, and promote the efficiency of the schools. The fact that a lease was involved did not constitute a proprietary function, and the board was not held liable.[2]

On the other hand, in a case which arose in Arizona, the court ruled that by renting its stadium to two other districts for a football game, in effect the district had entered the real estate business. The district was held liable for an injury to a spectator because of the board's involvement in a proprietary function.[3]

Various standards for deciding whether a school is engaged in a proprietary function have been applied by the courts. In a case which reached the Supreme Court of Pennsylvania, that court held that an activity may be proprietary in nature if the school is not required to perform it, if it can be carried out by a commercial agency, or if it is used as a means of raising revenue. In the Pennsylvania case, a child had been injured while participating in a summer recreation program, a function which the court said amounted to a proprietary activity. The school district was held liable for the injury.[4]

A second argument supporting school district immunity is the *trust fund theory;* it is based on the contention that school districts have no monies out of which to pay damages. The property which schools possess is held in trust by local boards of education to be used solely for educational purposes. School boards have no power to raise money for the payment of judgments against them unless permitted to do so by the legislature. Furthermore, according to this argument, the payment of judgments arising out of tort actions would be an illegal diversion of public funds, and could conceivably bankrupt the district and greatly hamper the educational program. For reasons of convenience, therefore, it is better to invoke the doctrine of immunity and avoid the risks of illegal diversion of funds and bankruptcy of the district. This argument was utilized by the courts in school injury cases in this country between 1860 and 1896, and is often combined with the sovereign immunity doctrine by courts today in their decisions.

---

[2]Kellam v. School Bd. of City of Norfolk, 202 Va. 252, 117 S.E.2d 96 (1960).
[3]Sawaya v. Tucson High School Dist., 78 Ariz. 389, 281 P.2d 105 (1955).
[4]Morris v. School Dist. of Township of Mount Lebanon, 393 Pa. 633, 144 A.2d 737 (1958).

The trust fund theory evidently results in harshness in its application. Critics of the theory maintain that no person should be made to bear the burden of injuries arising out of the tortious conduct of a school district on the pretext that *there are no funds from which to pay damages.* They point out that liability insurance is available to guarantee that the educational program of the school district will not be jeopardized.

Local boards in most states are now permitted to appropriate money for the payment of liability insurance premiums. Even in those states in which the law is silent on the legality of such an appropriation, and where the common law principle of non-liability of school districts is the rule, many boards of education are purchasing liability insurance and in many cases "save harmless" insurance for their employees, even though the appropriateness of the expenditure may be challenged. In California, a plan similar to workmen's compensation, which protects pupils and the general public from financial loss occasioned by school injuries, is under serious study.[5]

Liability of the School's Employees

The immunity from tort liability which school districts generally enjoy does not extend to the district's employees. The individual employee may be held liable for torts arising out of his own negligence. Even though the district is not liable under the doctrine of *respondeat superior* (by which the master must answer for the wrongs of his servant), each teacher, bus driver, custodian, principal, and superintendent is held accountable, either singly or severally, for injuries caused *by his negligence.* The injured party, failing to have a cause of action against the school district, may seek relief by instituting suit against the employee.

Negligence. Negligence is defined as the omission to do something which a reasonable man, guided by those considerations which ordinarily regulate human affairs, would do, or the doing of something which a reasonable and prudent man would not do. In cases involving the possibility of negligence, the courts have generally sought to determine what a reasonable and prudent man would have done under the circumstances, then apply this norm to the acts of the person alleged to have acted negligently. Negligence is thus viewed

---

[5]Harold P. Ballf and Harry A. Ballf. *Pupil and Teacher Security* (Walnut Creek, California: Monument Printing Company, 1960), Ch. VI.

as the failure to use such care and caution as a *hypothetically* reasonable and prudent person would ordinarily have exercised under the same or similar conditions.

A case in point arose in a New York school. In a physical education class, the instructor permitted two husky boys untrained in the sport of boxing to fight through one round and part of another while he sat in the bleachers. One of the boys was fatally injured, and the parents brought suit for recovery of damages against the instructor. Said the court, in holding that the instructor was negligent and personally liable for the injury:

> It is the duty of a teacher to exercise reasonable care to prevent injuries. Pupils should be warned before being permitted to engage in a dangerous and hazardous exercise. These young men should have been taught the principles of defense if indeed it was a reasonable thing to permit a slugging match of the kind which the testimony shows this contest was. The testimony indicates that the teacher failed in his duties in this regard and that he was negligent, and the plaintiff is entitled to recovery.[6]

Under the doctrine of *in loco parentis*, in which the teacher stands in place of the parent in implementing the state's instructional function, the teacher has certain rights—the right to control pupils under his care and to discipline them within legal limits, the right to receive the respect due the tutorial position, and the right to control the class for the good of the school. But these rights are accompanied by duties—to protect the health, safety, and welfare, and to promote the moral guidance of the students under his supervision. Since the teacher is expected to act as a prudent person would act under the circumstances, *foreseeability* is an important aspect of negligence cases. If there is a known hazard, the teacher is expected to instruct the students thoroughly as to the dangers involved. Failure to furnish ordinary precautionary instruction constitutes negligence on the part of the teacher. When accidents occur, and personal injury to students results, the teacher should be able to prove in court that proper instruction was given to provide student safety.

It is sometimes said that the study of negligence is the study of the mistakes a reasonable man might make. The law considers what would be blameworthy in the average man, the man of ordinary intelligence and prudence, and determines liability by that standard.

---

[6]LaValley v. Stanford, 272 App. Div. 183, 70 N.Y.S.2d 460 (1947).

Thus, no teacher is expected to be clairvoyant, because the average man of ordinary intelligence and prudence cannot foresee everything in the future. All that is expected of the teacher is that he shall exercise those considerations which ordinarily regulate the conduct of human affairs in each instance. The reasonable man, and the teacher acting in a reasonable manner, are capable of making honest mistakes and errors of judgment. The teacher is expected to act not from the facts as they are but from the facts as they reasonably appear to him at the moment.

Generally, the determination of negligence is for the jury, and it seems that in these cases negligence is what a jury of twelve laymen say it is. Since it would be presumptious to charge the teacher with never making a mistake, the jury in its non-expert status, has the task of interpreting whether the defendant, under the circumstances, acted as the reasonably prudent person would have acted under the same or similar circumstances. Hence, it is not always easy to predict under what circumstances juries will consider the teacher's actions negligent, and under what circumstances they will exonerate the teacher.

Teacher Liability for Inadequate Supervision

Parents have entrusted their children to the public schools for instructional purposes as the compulsory attendance laws direct. The law anticipates that the children will be protected and their best interests looked after by those in charge. Sometimes children are injured at school; the question then becomes is the teacher liable? The adequacy of teacher supervision is not always easy to determine. The following cases will serve to illustrate the principles of law which apply where the question is whether supervision was adequate.

In a leading case originating in Washington, the supreme court of that state concisely expressed the principle of law applied almost universally by the courts. The school children rigged a teeter-board across the playground swing, and a child was injured when he fell from the board. The parents brought suit against the teacher, maintaining inadequate supervision. In sustaining a charge of negligence against the teacher, the court said:

> If the teacher knew it [that pupils used the teeter-board as they did], it was negligence to permit it, and if she did not know it, it was negligence not to have observed it.[7]

---

[7]Bruenn v. North Yakima School Dist. No. 7, 101 Wash. 374, 172 Pac. 569 (1918).

In a California case, a teacher was held liable for an injury to a pupil where proper supervision, said the court, might have prevented the accident. The school shop was noisy, so the shop teacher took his class to the lawn outside the classroom. The boys sat in a semi-circle around the teacher. One boy started to flip a home-made knife into the ground. This went on for about thirty minutes, when finally the knife hit a student's drawing board, was deflected upward, and injured the eye of another boy so severely that the eye had to be removed. Although the teacher testified that he did not know of the knife throwing, the court said that there was evidence that he knew or should have known about it. Said the court:

> The evidence tending to prove that the knife throwing had been going on for thirty minutes plus the teacher's own testimony that the students were facing him and were all plainly visible and that he looked up frequently and viewed them to give them a chance to ask questions, would, we think, warrant the jury to infer that he did observe these knife throwing activities or that he was inattentive and careless in failing to observe such an activity which was going on over such an extended period of time.[8]

The standard of supervisory conduct on the part of the teacher is that prudence and care which the normal parent might exercise under the same or similar conditions. In Detroit, a teacher of nature study allowed the children to care for certain plants. An eight-year-old girl was directed by the teacher to water some plants in an adjoining room. The child, with the teacher's knowledge, took a chair on which to stand while watering the plants. The child fell from the chair and was severely cut on a broken milk bottle in which she had been carrying water. The Supreme Court of Michigan ruled that the teacher had not been negligent in her duty to the pupil. Said the court:

> There was nothing in the nature of the act itself or the instrumentalities with which plaintiff was permitted to perform the act which would lead a reasonably careful and prudent person to anticipate that the child's safety or welfare was endangered in the performance of the act. The mere fact that an accident occurred, and one that was unfortunate, does not render defendant liable.[9]

A teacher may not assume, however, that the mere fact that "it was an accident" will absolve him of a charge of negligence. Where

---

[8]Lilienthal v. San Leandro Unified School District, 193 Cal. App. 2d 453, 293 P.2d 889 (1956).
[9]Gaincott v. Davis, 281 Mich. 515, 275 N.W.2d 229 (1937).

a known hazard exists, the teacher has the duty of *foreseeing* the danger, and preventing an accident before it occurs. For example, a boy in an auto mechanics class was welding an automobile gasoline tank, when the tank exploded, killing one of the boys and seriously injuring another. The teacher was held negligent for lack of proper supervision of the activity.[10] To the same effect was a case arising out of an accident which occurred in a chemistry class when the teacher was demonstrating the production of explosive gases. An explosion occurred and a student was permanently injured. In holding the teacher liable for negligence, the court pointed out that the teacher knew of the dangerous nature of the chemicals, and should therefore have exercised greater precaution in conducting the experiment.[11]

Sometimes a pupil suffers an injury while the teacher is absent from the classroom. The question then arises whether the absence of the teacher renders him liable for the injury. Courts seek a causal relationship between the teacher's absence and the injury; for a charge of negligence to lie, the teacher's absence must be the proximate cause of the injury. Where the injury is perpetrated by another student, however, the absence of the teacher may not be considered the proximate cause. Two New York cases will serve to illustrate this point.

In the first case a teacher was temporarily absent from the classroom for the purpose of storing instructional materials, a routine task forming part of her usual duties. The pupils were unruly, and one student was injured when another student threw a pencil intended for a classmate. The classmate ducked and the pencil permanently injured the first pupil's eye. The teacher was absent from the classroom for more than an hour. Nevertheless, the court said that the absence of the teacher from the classroom was not the proximate cause of the injury.[12]

Said the Court of Appeals of New York:

> Whether [tossing the pencil] was done mischievously and heedlessly or wantonly and willfully, or with the serious purpose of returning the pencil to its owner, it was the act of an intervening third party which under the circumstances could hardly have been anticipated in the reasonable exercise of the teacher's legal duty toward the plaintiff. . . . a teacher may be

---

[10]Butcher v. Santa Rosa High School Dist., 137 Cal. App. 2d 481, 290 P.2d 316 (1955).

[11]Damgarrd v. Oakland High School Dist., 212 Cal. App. 316, 298 Pac. 983 (1931).

[12]Ohman v. Board of Educ. of City of N. Y., 300 N. Y. 306, 90 N.E.2d 474 (1949).

charged only with reasonable care such as a parent of ordinary prudence would exercise under comparable circumstances. Proper supervision depends largely upon the circumstances attending the event but so far as the cases indicate there has been no departure from the usual rules of negligence. . . . There is no proof of similar accidents, nor can anyone seriously contend that a pencil in the hands of a school pupil is a dangerous instrumentality. This is one of those events which could occur equally as well in the presence of the teacher as during her absence.[13]

The most definitive case to date on the subject of the adequacy of supervision is the second case in point. Although the case arose out of an incident which took place in a private school, the principle of law is equally applicable to public schools. The facts of the case are as follows. The pupils were required to report to their classroom at 8:30. One morning, when almost all of the pupils were present at the appointed time, the teacher was not present to supervise them. The children were noisy, and some of them were milling around the classroom. At 8:45 the bell rang for the commencement of classes; the teacher was still absent. One of the boys pulled out a knife, and began to brandish it about. This activity went on for five or ten minutes, when suddenly, without provocation, he stabbed another boy in the hand. The guardians of the injured boy brought suit against the school to recover damages for the injury.

As a defense, the school officials maintained that "an intervening party," *i.e.*, the boy with the knife, was the proximate cause of the injury, and not the absence of the teacher from the classroom. In support of their case, the officials cited several cases[14] in which plaintiffs were not permitted to recover for the allegedly negligent acts of teachers.

The court ruled that the parents could recover. In the cases cited by defendants, the *instrumentalities* causing the injuries complained of were not of a dangerous variety—a pencil, a ball, a finger, or a piece of glass. The case was different where a knife with a three-inch blade was involved. This was clearly *a dangerous instrumentality*, and any reasonably alert teacher would have perceived that it might be danger-

---

[13]*Ibid.*

[14]Ohman v. City of New York, 300 N.Y. 306, 90 N.E.2d 474 (1949); Mauer v. Board of Educ. of City of New York, 294 N.Y. 672, 60 N.E.2d 759 (1945); Clark v. City of Buffalo, 288 N.Y. 62, 41 N.E.2d 459 (1942); Berner v. Board of Educ., 286 N.Y. 174, 36 N.E.2d 100 (1941); Graff v. Board of Educ., 258 App. Div. 813, 15 N.Y.S.2d 941, affd. 283 N.Y. 574, 27 N.E.2d 438 (1940); Kaufman v. City of New York, 30 Misc.2d 285, 214 N.Y.S.2d 767 (1961).

ous to other pupils. Also, in the cases cited, there was a difference in the *time element*. In the earlier cases, there had been an instantaneous action of a momentary nature. In the case at bar, there was a "buildup" resulting in pupil injury. The boy brandishing the knife was clearly visible to all the pupils in the room. The conduct of the pupils would have been obvious to the teacher if he had been present. The teacher would have had sufficient time within which to take steps to protect the pupils and prevent the occurrence of the incident causing the injury. Therefore, the teacher's absence from the room was the proximate cause of the injury, and the school was liable for the damages.

Said the court:

> Whether the act was done intentionally or accidentally does not matter. What matters is whether a teacher, if present, could have anticipated the act in the reasonable exercise of his duty toward the plaintiff, and whether a teacher could have anticipated the unprovoked conduct of a boy whose act was not sudden and impulsive. The court therefore holds that the teacher's absence from the classroom was the proximate cause of the injuries resulting from the stabbing of the plaintiff by a classmate. There was legal causation between the failure to provide supervision and the injury to the plaintiff. It is true that the efficient cause of the plaintiff's injury was the wrongful act of an intervening third party, a mischievous boy. However, under all the circumstances here—*the dangerous instrumentality, the warning period of five to ten minutes*—the stabbing of the plaintiff was an act which could have been reasonably foreseen by a teacher if he were present in the classroom. It was an act which could easily have been anticipated in the reasonable exercise of the teacher's legal duty to each classmate. The third party act was not an event which could occur *equally* as well in the presence of the teacher as during his absence. The act producing the injury might have been prevented by the presence of the teacher (emphasis supplied by the court).[15]

The teacher is not expected to exercise extraordinary or unremitting supervision; he cannot continuously keep under his eye all the students in his care, and sometimes accidents occur when the teacher is "looking in the opposite direction." In such cases, if the *general supervision* is held to be adequate, no negligence attaches.[16] The principle of law

---

[15]Christofides v. Hellenic Eastern Orthodox Christian Church of New York, 33 Misc. 2d 741, 227 N.Y.S.2d 946 (1962).

[16]Nestor v. City of N. Y., 211 N.Y.S.2d 975 (Sup. Ct. 1961); Lopez v. City of N. Y., 4 App. Div. 2d 48, 163 N.Y.S.2d 562 (1957).

upon which the adequacy of supervision rests is the question whether, if the teacher *were* present, it would have been necessary for him to take positive steps to prevent the injury. The principle is illustrated by another New York case. There a student was injured between classes while going from one part of the building to another. Said the court, in holding the teacher guiltless:

> The conduct of the students while proceeding from a classroom on the fourth floor of the school building to a classroom on the fifth floor was not so unruly or disorderly that if the teacher had been at her post instead of conversing with another teacher in the hall nearby she would have been required to take some positive action to restore order. No actionable negligence has been established. To hold defendant liable in the circumstances here disclosed would be tantamount to imposing an insurer's liability.[17]

Teachers will do well to minimize the number of times they must be absent from their posts, inasmuch as such absences may amount legally to failure to provide adequate supervision.

Defenses Against Charges of Negligence

The teacher is not without defenses when charges of negligence are leveled at him. He may use one or a combination of the following defenses:

1. The teacher *acted without negligence* and as the reasonably prudent person would have acted under the circumstances. Although it is not always easy to determine what this means, the defense of denial of any negligence may be sufficient. A more positive approach is to assert that instruction in the hazards involved had been given the students, or that proper precautions had been taken to protect the students' health and safety.
2. The student *assumed* the risk. In certain school activities, such as athletic events, there are inherent and obvious risks. The student is assumed to know the risks involved, and thus assumption of risk falls upon the student when he enters the activity. This is the same as saying that some school activities are much more dangerous than others, and that the teacher should not assume all the risk in activities of more than ordinary danger.
3. The student contributed to the injury. The defense of *contributory negligence* is based on the contention that even though the

---

[17]Sanchick v. Board of Educ. of the City of N. Y., 172 N.Y.S.2d 748 (1958).

teacher was negligent, there was a lack of ordinary care on the part of the person injured, which contributed to the injury, and constituted an element of negligence without which the injury would not have occurred. However, the contributory negligence in such cases must be shown to be a proximate cause of the injury.

4. There was *comparative negligence*. A few states have adopted the doctrine of comparative negligence, in which the teacher's and student's negligence are ruled to be mutually contributory to the injury. The damages in such cases are pro-rated on the basis of whether the negligence of each party was slight, ordinary, or gross. Thus, a teacher might be held to be only slightly negligent, in which instance the injured party would be required to carry the major portion of the burden of the injury. While this principle has general acceptance in foreign countries, it has not been widely accepted in the United States.

5. The injury was the result of an *unavoidable accident*, and nothing that the defendant could have done would have prevented it. Since an accident is an event which occurred without fault, carelessness, or want of proper circumspection on the part of the defendant, a charge of negligence will ordinarily fall before it.

6. It was an *act of God*, and was the direct, immediate, and exclusive operation of the forces of nature, uncontrolled or uninfluenced by the power of man, and without human intervention. No amount of foresight would have prevented the occurrence, and defendant is innocent of causality.

In defense of teachers, it should be emphasized that school employees cannot guarantee that no student or spectator will be injured as a result of their acts. Sometimes accidents happen even though the most elaborate precautions are taken. But the law does not require superhuman foresight or vigilance; it requires only reasonable and ordinary precautions on the part of teachers and other employees of the school. In other words, it requires only those precautions which the reasonably prudent person would observe under the circumstances. When these have been observed, the teacher has done all that the law requires. For courts to hold otherwise would constitute a premise that teachers are insurors of their students, a position wholly inconsistent with the basic laws of equity and justice.

Let us turn now to an examination of some of the cases in which teachers have been charged with negligence. Student assumption of risk and contributory negligence, the more common defenses, will be treated in some detail in the pages immediately following.

Student assumption of risk. A defense of the teacher against tort liability action is that the student *assumes the risk.* The age, sex, and size of the child, and the type of activity in which he is participating are controlling matters of fact which determine whether the teacher may be held negligent. The standard required of a pupil is that he exercise the same degree of care as the normal child of the same age, intelligence, and experience ordinarily would exercise under the same conditions. If the child fails to exercise the required standard of care, his conduct may bar recovery from a negligent teacher. Ordinarily, larger and older children are expected to act in such a way as to avoid the ordinary dangers.

A case in point resulted when during rehearsal for an operatic production, a student was directed by a professor of the college to make a "haughty" exit from the stage without looking down. The student, a young lady of college age, protested because she had to step down twenty inches from the stage to the auditorium floor after her exit. She was told that she would lose her role if she did not comply. In making the exit as directed, she fell and injured her ankle, and brought suit to recover damages for personal injuries. The court held that the student could not recover. She had failed to exercise reasonable care for her own safety, and must *share the risk* even though she was under the direction of the professor. Her complaint was dismissed.[18]

Athletic activities each year produce a large number of student injuries, many of which result in litigation. The courts have rather consistently pointed out that the student who participates in a sport assumes some risk, and have tended to be lenient in interpreting the negligence of the coach, so long as that individual acts in good faith. A fifteen-year-old boy, who was "uncoordinated" and inexperienced, was injured in a regularly scheduled game when tackled by two larger boys simultaneously. The boy's neck was broken, resulting in permanent injury. When he reached the age of twenty-one, the boy brought an action for damages. The complaint charged that the boy's team was "overmatched," and that the boy had received insufficient coaching.

---

[18]Verduce v. Board of Higher Educ., City of N.Y., 9 App. Div. 2d 214, 192 N.Y.S.2d 913 (1959).

The court noted that it was normal for one team to be superior to another in the game of football, even when the teams were in the same athletic league. Said the court:

> Although complaint alleges that the Vale team contained "large" and "rough" boys, there is nothing to negative the idea that the Nyssa team also contained large and rough boys, albeit inexperienced. It is our opinion that the allegations do not describe a breach of duty on the part of the school district or of its agents or servants. . . .
>
> The playing of football is a body-contact sport. . . . There is no other way to play it. No prospective player need be told that a participant . . . may sustain injury. That fact is self-evident.[19]

Contributory negligence. Contributory negligence has been defined as "the want of ordinary care on the part of the person injured, or on the part of another whose negligence is imputable to him, which combined and concurred with the defendant's negligence, and contributed to the injury as a proximate cause thereof, and without which the injury would not have occurred."[20] When the negligence of a student contributes to his own injury, he is precluded from recovery against the teacher unless the act took place in one of the few jurisdictions applying the comparative negligence doctrine. In cases involving contributory negligence, younger children are not held to the same high standards of conduct as are older youth and adults. The teacher of younger children should exercise a greater than ordinary amount of care, since younger children are unpredictable in their actions.

The question of whether the injured party contributed to his injury may be an issue for the jury to decide. A ten-year-old girl was excused by her teacher to go to the playground during the noon recess. The child was playing alone, when she fell from the top of some baseball bleachers which were six tiers high. The playground was unsupervised at the time. Action was brought against the district for damages on the ground that the teacher, an employee of the district, was negligent. The lower court set aside the jury's verdict in favor of the plaintiff and dismissed the case, whereupon the plaintiff appealed. On appeal, the verdict was reversed, and the defendant in turn appealed. The higher court held that the question of whether the child had

---

[19]Vendrell v. School Dist. No. 26C Malheur County, 376 P.2d 406 (Ore. 1962).
[20]Henry C. Black. *Black's Law Dictionary* (St. Paul: West Publishing Company, 1933), p. 1231.

contributed to her own injury through negligence, and whether the district had failed to provide proper supervision were rightfully factual issues for the jury to decide.[21]

The age at which a minor child is presumed to have sufficient capacity to be sensitive to danger and to have power to avoid it is not clear. One jury might fix the age at 14, and another at 18, and another at 20. Three cases will serve to illustrate this principle of law. A boy of fifteen was granted permission to use the chemistry laboratory with others in order to set up apparatus for the day's lesson. While engaged in this pursuit, without the supervision of a teacher, the boy made gunpowder which exploded and injured one of the students. The textbook did not include lessons in mixing gunpowder, and there had been no classroom instruction on this subject. The court held that there was no negligence on the part of the school, and that it was the boy's negligence which was the proximate cause of the accident.[22]

An eight-year-old boy was injured when he fell from the back of a bus in the school yard. The boys were in the habit of swinging up onto the back of the bus when it pulled into the school yard to load the children for passage. Evidence tended to show that the accident happened before the bus reached the point in the school yard where the students were to board it. There was no evidence to show unusual knowledge or training with reference to the hazard of this sort. Nonetheless, the court held that a sense of danger from impact with a moving bus is not wanting in a school child of eight years of age. The child was held to have contributed to his injury.[23]

Finally, the right foot of a boy aged twelve was injured from coming in contact with the rear wheels of a bus through an opening in the floor of the bus. The other children had been sticking their feet through the hole for amusement but had ceased to do so when the plaintiff stuck his foot through the hole and against the rear tire of the bus. The father of the boy, in an action for damages against the bus driver, maintained that the accident was the result of carelessness and negligence on the driver's part in that he allowed the hole in the bus' floor to remain open and dangerous to the passengers. The driver

---

[21]Decker v. Dundee Central School Dist., 4 App. Div. 2d 1008, 167 N.Y.S.2d 666 (1957).

[22]Moore v. Order Minor Conventuals, 164 F. Supp. 711 (W.D. N.C. 1958).

[23]Weems v. Robbins, 243 Ala. 276, 9 So. 2d 882 (1942).

averred that the boy was injured solely through his own contributory negligence. In upholding the bus driver, and ruling that the boy had been contributorily negligent, the court said:

> At the time of the accident, plaintiff's son was twelve years of age. Judging from the answers given by him to questions while on the witness stand, he is at least of average intelligence, if not above the average. This being true, he was capable of contributory negligence and under the law should be held responsible for such acts on his part.
>
> The record does not clearly establish any negligence on defendant's part, but, conceding that such was proven, it is obvious that the boy's own imprudence in putting his foot into the opening was the proximate and contributing cause of the accident and consequent injuries.[24]

Said the court in the *Moore* case:

> From these and other approved authorities the principle is deduced that an infant, so far as he is personally concerned, is held to such care and prudence as is usual among children of the same age, and if his own act directly brings the injury upon him, while the negligence of the defendant is only such as exposes the infant to the possibility of an injury, the latter cannot recover.[25]

Liability Waivers

Sometimes the school administration may require written parental consent before permitting a student to participate in certain school activities, such as athletic programs, field trips, and the like. In relieving the teacher or the school of tort liability, these parental permission slips have little legal value. The parent cannot abrogate his responsibility for the safety of the child by "signing it away." The teacher, standing *in loco parentis*, has assumed a legal duty to protect the health, safety, and welfare of the student, and cannot therefore alter or abrogate it merely by obtaining the consent of the parent.

The only value of the permission slip, in addition to its public relations worth, lies in the knowledge that the parent knows of the activity, and has indicated a willingness for his child to participate in it. Conversely, the absence of the permission slip indicates that the parent does not wish his child to participate. But even when the consent slip has been properly signed, and returned to the teacher, the presence

---

[24]Gilcrease v. Speight, 6 So. 2d 95 (La. 1942).

[25]Moore v. Order Minor Conventuals, 164 F.Supp. 711 (W.D. N.C. 1958).

of the slip does not absolve the teacher of his responsibility to exercise the usual care in protecting the welfare of the child. Legal action can still be instituted against the teacher for his negligence by the child in his own right.

The same principle of law applies to waivers, by which the parent relinquishes some right or claim intentionally. Because some games are dangerous, participants in these games may be asked to obtain parental waivers exonerating the school or teacher of any responsibility for personal injuries incurred while participating. It is well settled that a parent, merely because of the parental relationship, cannot waive or release any claim accruing to his child for personal injury resulting from the negligence of another. The most that a parent can waive by signing a waiver or release is his own right to bring suit for medical costs or other expenses which result to the parent from the pupil injury. The child may still sue for the injuries he has sustained. In some instances, the injured student has brought suit after reaching his majority.

It is the policy of each state to determine limitations of time within which an action at law or suit in equity can be maintained. The *statutes of limitations* among the states are by no means uniform. One state may require that actions based in tort must be brought within one year from the time of the injury; another state may enact legislation that will limit the time to two, three, or more years. Such statutes are founded on the belief that valid claims should not be neglected and that timely actions will suppress fraudulent claims that might arise long after facts have become obscure, evidences are lost, and witnesses have moved away. In many states, the statute of limitations does not run against infants, but will begin to run once the child attains his majority. Thus, an action may be brought against a teacher, for his negligence resulting in injury to a student, many years after the occurrence of the tortious conduct.

School Safety Patrols

Systematic safety education as a part of the regular school curriculum appeared during the 1920's. The need was not so much to cut down the rate of accidents in schools, as to allow teachers to make a planned attack upon the accidents arising from traffic conditions and the unnecessarily high accident rate in homes, playgrounds, factories, swimming pools, and on the highways. The school safety patrol was a technique adopted to familiarize pupils with safety, and to give them some practice in exercising safety precautions during school hours. Types of school safety patrols included those for playground, building, fire drill, school bus, and street traffic instructional purposes. Despite the wide use of school patrols, there appears to be no case to come before the courts involving pupil injury while on patrol duty. Therefore, consideration of the legal aspects of school safety patrols must be based upon general principles.

It is well settled that school districts should not assign pupils to duties which are adult tasks, or which place pupils in unnecessarily hazardous positions. Neither should the school assign pupils to patrol territory outside the limits of the school's property. Such territory is the rightful dominion of the civil officers, and schools would be in a compromising position should suit for pupil injury arise under these conditions.

Boards of education may legally make reasonable rules and regulations for the control and management of the schools, including rules for the formation and assignment of school safety patrols, unless expressly prohibited by statute. Boards must determine for themselves whether the possible educational values of patrol operation justify the risk of accident and the possible blame for injury to pupils which might result. The complete absence of cases on this subject would seem to indicate that many boards have been justified in deciding that the educational values were worthy of the risk.

Because of the alleged dangers inherent in school patrol operation, a few states have adopted legislation protecting the school and its employees from liability for pupil injury incurred during school patrol operations. Such legislation provides that (1) claims for damages must be filed within a short period of time, usually ninety days following the accident, (2) the school district is held liable if negligence on the part of its employees is proved, and (3) the district may legally expend public funds for the purchase of liability insurance to cover its employees in schools where patrols are maintained.

Field Trips

Field trips under the supervision of the school have become important features of modern school curricula. Once the field trip consisted of a walk to a park, zoo, or museum. Such relatively short trips presented little if any real danger to the pupils. It was not until field trips included visits to hazardous and distant places that litigation concerning them arose. No case has been found in which it was sought to hold the teacher or principal liable for pupil injury while on a field trip. All of the reported cases were instituted by the injured child or his parents against the *agency visited* wherein the injury occurred.

The courts have had little difficulty in developing rules to govern recovery in cases involving injury to pupils under the direction of a teacher on visits to agencies outside the school. They have consistently ruled that recovery depends upon whether the pupils are on the premises solely for their own benefit, or whether the host organization also derives some substantial benefit from the visit. If the pupils alone benefit, and the host organization derives little if any benefit, the pupils are said to be *licensees*. The host organization owes no care to such visitors other than to make certain that no dangerous "trap" is set for them. Licensees visit the host organization more or less at their own peril, insofar as the host organization's liability is concerned. An early case which arose in Maryland is in point.

The principal of a high school in Baltimore requested and obtained permission from a power plant in that city to bring a class of thirty boys to tour the plant. A guide from the company conducted the tour, but midway through it he excused himself because he had to return to work. He invited the principal and class to continue their tour of the plant. This the class did, without the services of the guide. Near the conclusion of the visit, one of the boys fell into a vat of boiling water in a dimly-lighted portion of the plant. Suit was brought by the injured boy against the company for damages sustained in the fall. The court refused to hold the company liable. The class were *licensees*, present on the premises for their own benefit and pleasure. While not trespassers in a legal sense, they escaped that category only because they had temporary permission to visit the plant for their own edification. If any negligence was apparent, said the court, it was in taking thirty boys at one time into a building filled with dangerous machinery!

The legal standing of licensees was explained by the court thusly:

> We have found no support for any rule which would protect those who go where they are not invited, but merely with express or tacit permission, from curiosity or motives of private convenience, in no way connected with business or other relations with the occupant. . . . appellant was not in any manner invited or induced by any act of the appellee to visit its power house, but he went there solely for his own personal benefit and pleasure, and he must take the consequences, unfortunate though they may be. . . . So a licensee who enters on premises by permission only, without any inducement being held out to him by the owner or occupant, cannot recover damages for

injuries caused by obstructions or pitfalls. He goes there at his own risk, and enjoys the license subject to its concomitant perils.[26]

While *licensees* visit the host organization at their own peril, the case is different if the host stands to gain some benefit from the visit. Under these circumstances, the pupils are considered *invitees,* and the organization owes reasonable care for their safety. A case adjudicated by a Missouri court will serve to illustrate the difference.

The host organization in this case was a combined bakery and creamery in Kirksville which served a large trading area. One of its windows carried a sign saying "Inspection Invited." The company acted as host to several high school classes, including the one in which a girl was injured when she inserted her hand into an ice crushing machine. The girl's hand and arm were so badly mangled that amputation was necessary. Her suit against the host company for damages was successful. The court held that the relationship of the girl was that of an *invitee,* rather than a licensee. The fact that the company annually was host to several other classes, and that the sign "invited" people to visit the plant made the company legally liable, since it received advertising benefits from such tours.[27]

Of course, the teacher must exercise reasonable care in conducting the tours even though the class comes under the category of invitees. The teacher may be held liable for injuries to students on field trips where his negligence is the proximate cause of the injuries. Instead of conducting the tour himself, the teacher should request that some member of the host organization lead the group while on the premises. A court might hold that taking a large group of immature pupils into unfamiliar and dangerous places alone constitutes negligence on the part of the teacher.

Administrators and teachers should plan carefully for field trips in the full realization that pupil injury may result. Students should be adequately chaperoned while away from school. While it is not easy to determine what constitutes adequate supervision on these trips, it is certain that the adequacy of oversight must stand the test of reasonableness. This would indicate that the number and ages of the children would to some extent determine how many adults should accompany the group.

---

[26]Benson v. Baltimore Traction Co., 77 Md. 535, 26 Atl. 973 (1893).

[27]Gilliland v. Bondurant, 332 Mo. 881, 59 S.W.2d 679 (1933).

The teacher may obtain personal liability insurance from a reputable company. While insurance will not guarantee immunity from suit, it will insure that the teacher, even in winning, will not suffer severe financial loss in defending himself against charges of negligence.

Errands. The practice of sending pupils on errands beyond the boundaries of school property is fortunately on the decline. The possibilities of student injury are greatly increased away from the school's familiar surroundings. Furthermore, it is well settled that a teacher may be held liable for injuries to a pupil on errands, or to third parties on whom the pupil inflicts injury. On an errand under the direction of the teacher, the pupil is legally an *agent* of the teacher, and the laws of agency apply.

No doubt a jury would hold it reasonable to send a pupil on an errand within the school, where no danger to the child is apparent, but would hold otherwise if the errand took the pupil into dangerous areas outside school boundaries. Pupils should be sent on errands away from the school only in an emergency, and only then when an adult is not available. The most mature and dependable pupil should be chosen for this purpose.

Transportation in Privately Owned Cars

Sometimes a teacher uses his private car to transport pupils to athletic contests, music festivals, and similar meetings. In court action involving pupil injury under such conditions, the courts have consistently ruled that the teacher may be held liable for damages while transporting school pupils, even though the trip is a regular part of the teacher's duties. An Idaho case will illustrate the application of this principle of law.[28]

A high school coach requested and obtained the use of another teacher's car to transport members of the football team to a game in a neighboring town. While driving the car, the coach missed a curve, went down an embankment, and severely injured one of the boys riding in the car. Suit was brought for damages against the owner of the car, on the ground that the coach, as an agent of the owner, had acted in a negligent manner. The death of the coach shortly after the accident may have had something to do with the plaintiff's decision to seek damages from the owner-teacher.

The jury found that the coach had been negligent, and ordered the car owner to respond in damages for the boy's injuries. Idaho is

---

[28]Gorton v. Doty, 57 Idaho 792, 69 P.2d 136 (1937).

a state in which a *guest statute* exists—that is, state legislation provides that one who rides with another on invitation without payment for the ride ordinarily may not recover for injuries caused by the simple negligence of the driver. The Idaho "guest statute" is typical of similar legislation in many other states. Enacted in 1931, the portion of the statute dealing with the subject of tort liability of automobile owners who invite guests to ride with them reads as follows:

> *Liability of motor owner to guest.*—No person transported by the owner or operator of a motor vehicle as his guest without payment for such transportation shall have a cause for damages against such owner or operator for injuries, death or loss, in case of an accident, unless such accident shall have been intentional on the part of the said owner or operator or caused by his intoxication or his reckless disregard of the rights of others.[29]

The Idaho statute further charges the owner of a motor vehicle with liability where any person other than the owner using or operating the vehicle with the permission, expressed or implied, of the owner results in an injury to another in the motor vehicle. The question in the case above was whether the boys riding with the coach came within the classification of "guests" in the car, because if they did, they would have no grounds for damages, except where the operator was intoxicated or was so grossly negligent as to be tantamount to a reckless disregard of the rights of his passengers. The court, however, said that the boys were not "guests" within the meaning of the statute, because they had been instructed by the coach to ride in this particular vehicle on the school-sponsored trip, and held the driver-coach was an *agent* of the teacher-owner. The latter was held liable in the amount of $5,000 for the injury.

Teachers should use extreme caution in using their own or others' cars for transportation of school pupils. When in doubt about the potential liability to accrue in case of injury, the teacher should consult an attorney.

Medical Treatment of Pupils

The weight of legal authority supports the principle that school boards may employ a nurse, and provide physical examinations for pupils. The extent of the board's power seems to be that of examination and diagnosis only; a board may not provide *treatment* for pupils in

---

[29] Idaho Code § 49-1401.

the public schools as a part of the regular school program. Treatment is, under most circumstances, the prerogative of the parents. In the absence of an emergency, school personnel are not permitted to substitute their judgment for that of the parent in matters related to how a given medical condition should be treated.

When a child becomes ill at school, or is injured, it is the duty of the teacher to call the school nurse, or the child's parents for medical treatment by the family physician. Failure to provide promptly for the child's safety may result in a charge of negligence against the teacher. However, under no circumstances should the teacher attempt medical treatment of any more than a first-aid nature, and then, only in case of an emergency. In a Pennsylvania case, an attempt by two teachers to render medical treatment to a child in the absence of an emergency was held to render them liable where the treatment given was harmful to the pupil.

A ten-year-old boy had an infection on the little finger of his right hand, but the condition did not prevent him from playing baseball during the noon recess. Two teachers detained the boy after school for the purpose of giving him medical attention. One heated a pan of water to the boiling point and with the assistance of the other, immersed the boy's hand in the water for about ten minutes. The boy's hand was permanently disfigured. The parents brought suit against the teachers for damages. The court held that the teachers were liable, pointing out that even though they stood *in loco parentis*, there was nothing in this relationship to justify their "exercise of lay judgment, such as a parent may, in the matter of treatment of injury or disease suffered by a pupil." Said the court:

> Defendants were not acting in an emergency. The defendants were not school nurses and neither of them had any medical training or experience. Whether treatment of the infected finger was necessary was a question for the boy's parents to decide.[30]

In *Duda v. Gaines*,[31] a New Jersey court also pointed out that the teacher or principal stands *in loco parentis* to the child for the treatment of injuries only in case of an emergency. The court stated that there is no emergency in the absence of proofs from which it is reasonably inferable that the decision whether to secure medical aid and the choice

---

[30]Guerrieri v. Tyson, 147 Pa. Super. 239, 24 A.2d 468 (1942).
[31]12 N.J. Super. 326, 79 A.2d 695 (1951).

of the physician cannot safely await parental determination. The teacher should not substitute his opinion about the seriousness of the injury or the selection of a doctor for that of the parent.

Some schools ask parents to fill out a card indicating the doctor to be called in case of an emergency. Only if the doctor indicated is not available, and the parent cannot be contacted should another doctor be summoned, and then only in case of an emergency. The courts will protect the parental right to choose under what circumstances the child shall be treated, and who shall be summoned to treat him. If no person with medical training is available, the teacher should make the child comfortable and send for the parent. If the parent is not readily available, the nearest doctor should be summoned. Under no circumstances should the teacher send a seriously ill or injured pupil home without proper escort, or without first ascertaining that the parent is at home.

Similarly, the teacher should not render a pupil to a public clinic for psychiatric help without parental consent. The same rule of parental right applies in the treatment of mental and emotional disorders as applies to referrals for medical reasons. Parents have a right to maintain the custody of their child, which right extends to their moral and religious upbringing and their medical treatment. Mental disorders are not of an emergency nature, and ordinarily the teacher would not be justified in referring a student on psychiatric grounds alone. Of course, the teacher should be in close touch with the parents when matters of a mental or emotional nature arise. Under no circumstances should the decision to refer the child to a psychiatrist be undertaken by the teacher or principal without parental consent.

Avoidance of Tort Liability

Increasing school enrollments following World War II led to the construction of larger and larger school units, some of which enroll as many as two to three thousand pupils in a single building. The question of whether a school board may be held liable for allowing so many pupils to congregate in one place has not been judicially determined. Since school districts enjoy an immunity from their torts in most states, it is quite likely that plaintiffs would bring suit against the school personnel—the principal, teacher, bus driver, or other school employee—where the possibility of negligence exists. In fact, many of the cases related to pupil injury in schools are of this nature.

One major administrative problem where large numbers of school children are brought together in close proximity is how to organize and coordinate the school in such a way that hazards are reduced to a minimum, and that general supervision is adequate at all times. This is a tremendous, continuous task involving administrators, teachers, bus drivers, lunchroom workers, and the custodial staff, as well as children themselves. The safety of pupils and the general public should be a matter for continuous study and discussion by the board and all employees of the district. The law assumes that children are in a "safe place," and has charged school personnel with the responsibility of foreseeing accidents and taking positive steps to avoid them.

Inasmuch as the question of tort liability of the school district and its employees rests almost exclusively on the element of *foreseeability*, the importance of careful staff planning to make the school a safe place for pupils cannot be overemphasized. Regularly scheduled inspection tours of the buildings, school equipment, and grounds are helpful in this regard. Any defects should be reported promptly. The use of the defective and dangerous equipment should be prohibited until repairs are made. Trash and wastepaper should be emptied daily, and areas under stairs maintained free from litter and potential fire hazards. Fire drills should be scheduled on a regular basis and close cooperation should be established between the school and fire and health departments.

Some states have provided by statute for facility and equipment inspections by outside agencies, such as the state department of education or the state industrial commission. In the absence of such legislation, the school staff should cooperatively plan frequent inspections to assure that corridors, stairs, shops, and the like are free from dangerous conditions where pupil injury might result. Heating, lighting, and ventilating systems should be checked regularly. The courts might well rule that failure on the part of the school staff to maintain the building in a safe condition constitutes negligence on the part of the members individually and severally. Teachers are especially vulnerable in those states, actually the great majority of the fifty states, in which the rule of sovereign immunity is in effect. However, some school boards are obtaining liability insurance at public expense to cover instances where suit is brought because of the negligence of school personnel for pupil injury.

"Save harmless" legislation. Five states have adopted statutes requiring or permitting boards of education to come to the aid of school

personnel who are found liable for damages in pupil injury cases. Four of the five states require boards to protect and *save harmless financially* the teacher who has been required to respond in damages for his negligence in the line of duty. One state permits boards to protect the teacher financially if the board so chooses.

Connecticut is one of the states in which it is mandatory that boards "save harmless" teachers who are liable for damages. Said a court of that state in interpreting the intent of the law:

> Obviously, the General Assembly felt that a school teacher should be held harmless from the burden of paying damages for certain acts of civil misconduct on his part and that this burden should be transferred to the taxpayers.[32]

The principle underlying the Connecticut law is sound. The teacher who must pay damages for a single mistake in conduct may be saddled with a judgment for the remainder of his professional life or be forced into bankruptcy proceedings. The growing complexity of the educational enterprise indicates that the number of pupil injury cases will doubtless increase. In the interests of school morale, boards will find it increasingly expedient to save harmless those who are "taking the risks" in classrooms throughout the land. State associations of school boards should therefore urge the enactment of mandatory save harmless legislation in their states. Teachers' associations can do no less.

Suggested Activities

DISCUSSION:

1. What precautions should the principal and teachers observe in planning and conducting field trips?
2. What are the similarities and differences between the legal role of the teacher in relation to pupil injury and that of the parent?
3. What areas in the modern school plant are of special danger to students? What precautions should be taken by the school staff to insure that the school is a "safe place" for students in each area?

RESEARCH:

Consult the education code of your state or the state in which you plan to teach to determine the number and nature of statutes relating to pupil injury.

RESOLVED:

1. The number of states abrogating the common law rule of governmental immunity for school districts should increase.

---

[32]Swainbank v. Coombs, 19 Conn. Supp. 391, 115 A.2d 468 (1957).

2. Principals and teachers should be held personally and severally liable for damages arising from their negligent acts.

SUMMARIZE:

1. The defenses of the teacher against charges of negligence.
2. The major principles of law related to
   (a) school safety patrols
   (b) field trips
   (c) errands

VOCABULARY:

1. Distinguish between
   (a) Licensees and invitees
   (b) Governmental v. proprietary functions
   (c) Mandatory v. permissive legislation
   (d) Save harmless and guest statutes
2. Define
   (a) Tort
   (b) Negligence
   (c) Foreseeability
   (d) Known hazard
   (e) Liability waiver
   (f) Doctrine of governmental immunity

CASE STUDY:

Case #1. In Kansas, a public school custodian burned out a tree stump on the school grounds, but left the fire unextinguished and unattended. Some boys played on the grounds, and one of them, a boy of six, stepped into the live coals and suffered severe foot burns. The parents of the boy sought damages in a joint suit against the board and custodian.

Was the board liable due to the alleged negligence of one of its employees? Was the custodian liable because of his own negligence?

Rose v. Board of Educ. of Abilene, 184 Kan. 486, 337 P.2d 652 (1959).

Case #2. The parents of a deceased girl brought suit against the director of guidance and counselling in a Wisconsin state college, to recover damages for the alleged wrongful death of their daughter. The girl had committed suicide about six weeks after the counselor, who had given her various tests, had suggested that the interview series be terminated. Plaintiffs alleged negligence on the part of defendant because he failed to provide proper guidance for the girl, and failed to advise the parents of the true mental state and condition of their daughter.

Is a school counselor negligent for the suicide of a student under his guidance? What are the rules relating to suicide in a wrongful death action?

Bogust v. Iverson, 10 Wisc. 2d 129, 102 N.W.2d 228 (1960).

Further Readings

Ballf, Harold P., and Harry A. Ballf. *Pupil and Teacher Security* (Walnut Creek, California: Monument Printing Company, 1960), Ch. 5.

Florio, A. E., and G. T. Stafford. *Safety Education* (New York: McGraw-Hill Company, 1956).

Garber, Lee O. *Handbook of School Law* (New London, Conn.: A. C. Croft, 1954), pp. 89-93.

Hamilton, Robert R. *Legal Rights and Liabilities of Teachers* (Laramie, Wyoming: School Law Publications, 1956), Ch. III.

National Education Association. "School Patrols," *Research Bulletin* (February, 1950).

———. "The Pupil's Day in Court," Research Report 1960-R6 (April, 1960).

———. "The Teacher's Day in Court," Research Report 1960-R5 (April, 1960).

———. "The Teacher and the Law," Research Monograph 1959-M3 (September, 1959).

Seitz, Reynolds C. (ed). *Law and the School Principal* (Cincinnati: W. H. Anderson Company, 1961), Chs. 3 and 6.

Schultz, Raymond E. *Student Teaching in the Secondary Schools* (New York: Harcourt, Brace and Company, 1959), Appendix C "The Law's View of the Teacher."

Chapter X

DISMISSAL OF TEACHERS

Dismissal in General

The word *dismissal* refers to the termination of the teacher's services by a board of education prior to the lawful expiration date of the contract. It applies to the tenure teacher as well as to the probationary teacher, so long as the action is taken prior to the end of the contractual period. It does not apply to refusal of a board to renew the non-tenure teacher's contract; such non-renewal does not constitute dismissal in the legal sense of the word. In general, dismissal in legal terminology is interchangeable with such other terms as released, discharged, let go, let out, terminated, and removed from the position of teacher. While there are obvious differences of meaning in these terms, they are essentially the same when applied to teacher dismissal, *viz.*, removal from the position of teacher in the public schools prior to the lawful end of the contractual period of employment.

The right of the board to dismiss teachers is a correlative function of its right to employ them. This right must be exercised, however, in a reasonable manner and within the limitations of any existing legal framework—the contractual agreement, statutory and constitutional limits, and other legal barriers. A teacher's contract of employment includes the implied power of the school board to dismiss the teacher who fails to competently and loyally perform all reasonably assigned duties and to act in an exemplary manner. There is, of course, sometimes great difficulty in determining what teacher action constitutes cause for dismissal. An examination of the state statutes and court cases reveals a wide range of causes for which teachers may be legally dismissed from their positions—incompetency, immorality, neglect of duty, lack of cooperation, unprofessional conduct, and disloyalty, to name a few.

Said the Supreme Court of Indiana, in passing on an early case involving the dismissal of a public school teacher:

> Now, if a teacher proves to be incompetent, and unable to teach the branches of instruction he has been employed to teach, he has broken the agreement on his part, and the trustees are clearly authorized to dismiss him from such employment.[1]

The term "good cause" implies that the basis for dismissal is reasonable, and that it is related to the general welfare and governance of the school system. It may also be influenced somewhat by surrounding conditions. Shortly after Pearl Harbor, a Chicago teacher was dismissed for conduct unbecoming a school teacher in the public schools. She had written a letter to a former student, who had failed to register under the Selective Service Act, congratulating him on his "courageous and idealistic stand," and stating that "you and others who take the same stand are the hope of America." The teacher was fully aware that all male persons between the ages of 20 and 45 who had not previously registered were required under the law to register —nevertheless, she wrote the letter. Consequently, the board dismissed her. She sought through court action to be reinstated to her position, asserting that her actions were not "cause" for her removal. The court held otherwise. Said the court:

> The remaining consideration is whether the charges, finding and report constitute "cause," within the meaning of the statute, as rendering plaintiff unfit to be a teacher in the public schools of Chicago. . . . Plaintiff argues that this letter did not constitute cause for removal, to which defendants reply that it is for the Board to determine what constitutes cause. . . . It will be noted that when the charges were preferred against plaintiff by the superintendent, the United States was engaged in a war with Japan. . . . Certainly it was incumbent upon teachers, who mould the minds of the young, to display the proper patriotic attitude. . . . We think the board was fully justified in finding that the teacher writing such a letter ought not to be permitted to continue as a teacher in the public schools, and having jurisdiction of plaintiff as an employee

---

[1]Crawfordsville v. Hays, 42 Ind. 200 (1873).

of the board, it had the right to determine whether her conduct constituted cause for dismissal.[2]

The Chicago teacher was "on tenure" and could be dismissed only
after a legal hearing, which the board provided. Courts will make a
distinction between dismissal in the case of the tenure teacher and
the one employed on a temporary basis. The tenure law is the measure
of the board's power in dismissing tenure teachers. In cases involving
dismissal of temporary, probationary, or substitute teachers, however, the board often has wider latitude. Failure to renew the contract
of the probationary teacher is not considered dismissal in the sense
that it is actionable at law; mandamus will not lie to compel the board
to reinstate the non-tenure teacher in the absence of a statute to the
contrary. The non-tenure teacher is re-employed at the pleasure of
the board, and the board need not give its reasons for non-renewal
of an annual contract, unless required by law to do so.

A possible exception to the above rule of law arises when the contract in question is that which will place the teacher on permanent
tenure in the district. It is generally held that the teacher, when refused tenure status by board action, is entitled at least to an explanation
if not a hearing. A board is required to act in good faith, and not
from passion, prejudice, or caprice. Where the teacher has been allowed to continue for the term of probation, and is then suddenly
refused the right to enter upon tenure status, the courts will question
the good faith of the board in refusing to renew the teacher's contract.

Board Limitations in Dismissal

A board cannot disregard controlling statutes in dismissing the
temporary teacher. A Colorado case serves to illustrate this principle
of law. In that state, a statute provided that "no teacher shall be dismissed without good cause shown, and such teacher shall be entitled
to receive pay for services rendered."[3] A non-tenure teacher entered
into a contract to teach for the school year 1958-59. On January 30,
1959, the president of the board advised the teacher in writing that his
contract was terminated and that he was dismissed. Contending that
his dismissal was improper and that no good cause had been shown,
the teacher brought suit for the balance of his annual salary.

The district court rendered a decision for the teacher, whereupon

---

[2]Joyce v. Board of Educ. of Chicago, 325 Ill. App. 543, 60 N.E.2d 431;
certiorari denied 327 U.S. 786, 66 Sup. Ct. 702, 90 L. Ed. 1013 (1945).
[3]Colo. Rev. Stat. §123-17-1 (1953).

the board appealed to the Supreme Court of Colorado. Said the court, in upholding the decision of the lower court and ruling in favor of the teacher:

> There was no "good cause shown" for the dismissal of Thomas; no specific charges were ever filed against him; no notice of any pending charges was ever served upon him; and no hearing was ever held in compliance with the contract of employment, the statutes of Colorado, and the adjudicated cases decided by this court over a long period of time. . . . While we do not mean . . . [that a formal trial is necessary], still we think that good cause shown means specific accusation, notice, evidence of the charge before the board in its official capacity, and an opportunity to the teacher to be heard and refute the charge.[4]

The *Thomas* case illustrates that the board must take into account not only the controlling statutes, but also the common law principle that the non-tenure teacher may legally be entitled to a hearing in the absence of a prescribed procedure for dismissal. The courts will hesitate to allow the summary dismissal of a teacher without good cause shown. At common law, there exists an implied right on the part of the teacher to be presented with the charges against him, and an opportunity given to be heard in his own defense. Where this right has not been limited by statute, the teacher is generally held to be entitled to a hearing.

Where the board reserves in its rules and regulations the right to dismiss the teacher prior to the end of the contractual period, such reservations of power are controlling. A teacher who was employed under a contract containing a provision that she might be dismissed on thirty days' notice at the pleasure of the board, was dismissed prior to the commencement of her work. She was ruled to have been legally dismissed.[5]

In other jurisdictions, however, the courts may not support this principle of law. A teacher in Kansas signed a contract providing that she would hold her position for one year, "unless sooner removed by vote of the board." After teaching six months, the teacher was removed for alleged cruelty to pupils. She was not allowed a hearing. She contended that the board could remove her only after a hearing, *i.e.*, she could be removed for cause only. The teacher was allowed to retain her position.[6]

---

[4]School Dist. No. 38, El Paso County v. Thomas, 363 P.2d 700 (Colo. 1961).
[5]Dees v. Board of Educ., 146 Mich. 64, 109 N.W. 39 (1906).
[6]Board of Educ. v. Cook, 3 Kan. App. 269, 45 Pac. 119 (1896).

The teacher is also subject to controlling statutes in contracting. A 1957 act of the Alaska territorial legislature provided that school boards might employ teachers and issue contracts any time after January 1, but must notify teachers in writing of nonretention on or before March 15. Responding to a form inquiry from the board in January, 1959, a teacher indicated, by crossing out the words "do not," that he did desire to remain in his teaching position for the ensuing year 1959-1960. The board thereupon elected the teacher on March 10, 1959; at no time did the board give notice of nonretention. A contract was duly issued, but since it had not been returned by April 22, the date indicated by the board, the board notified the teacher in writing that his teaching position had been declared vacant. The teacher returned the signed contract on September 8, 1959, but the board refused to recognize it. The teacher then brought suit to compel the board to recognize him as a teacher in the district.

The Supreme Court of Alaska said that by not giving the teacher notice of nonretention prior to March 15, as required by law, the board had waived its right to urge any of the "causes" specified in the law. But the rights acquired by the teacher did not divest the board of the right to require that he enter into a written contract within a reasonable time. The board had the right, said the court, to require the teacher to either accept or reject the contract by April 22. The teacher's failure to return the signed contract by that date created legal grounds for assumption by the board that he had rejected or abandoned the contract.[7]

Dismissal of the Tenure Teacher

Approximately three-fourths of the states have enacted so-called *tenure legislation,* which affords a special type of protection to those who are "on tenure status." Since the tenure law is the measure of the board's power, the board terminating the contract of a tenured teacher must observe completely the controlling statute *in all respects* to succeed in dismissal proceedings. The manner and mode of dismissal are controlling; any deviation, however slight, from the prescribed procedure will be prohibited by the courts, and the teacher's rights protected.

Tenure statutes usually contain, among other things, two provisions relating to the dismissal of the tenure teacher. These two provisions relate to (1) *specific charges* upon which the teacher on tenure

---

[7]Swick v. Seward School Board, 379 P.2d 97 (Alaska 1963).

may be dismissed, and (2) a *specified procedure* to be followed where there is just cause for dismissal.

List of charges. Contained in the tenure act is a list of specified causes upon which the board must base its contract cancellation procedures. For example, the tenure law may provide that cancellation of an employment contract with a tenure teacher may be made for "incompetency, cruelty, negligence, immorality or other sufficient cause. . ."[8]

Where the grounds for dismissal are specified in the statute, dismissal is possible on those grounds, and those only. The list of causes is considered exhaustive, and dismissal on grounds other than those specified in the statute will not suffice. The board is thus faced with deciding upon which of the grounds specified in the act it wishes to base its case when dismissing a tenure teacher. Should the list prove too narrow, and the board attempt to discharge the teacher under the clause "or other good and just cause," the courts will often interpret this clause to mean essentially the same type of cause as those specifically enumerated in the earlier portion of the statute.

Similarly, a New York statute provided that teachers could be removed after trial on charges of gross misconduct, insubordination, neglect of duty, or general inefficiency. The Board of Education of the Borough of Brooklyn adopted a resolution which provided that female teachers who married would be subject to dismissal. Under this by-law, a female teacher was dismissed. The teacher sought by mandamus to compel the board to reinstate her. The court ruled that the list of causes for dismissal was exclusive, and that the board by-law was in conflict with the tenure provisions of the city charter.[9]

Prescribed procedure. Besides choosing a cause for dismissal contained specifically in the act, the board must follow carefully prescribed procedure in dismissing the tenure teacher. Such procedure usually relates to the service of notice on the teacher, right of the teacher to request a hearing, right to be represented by counsel, and the provision of a hearing at which testimony shall be taken under oath. Most tenure legislation spells out in minute detail the steps to be followed by the board in dismissing the tenure teacher. If the board omits some of the procedure, or performs it in a manner other than that prescribed, its attempt at dismissal will result in failure.

Nor may the board circumvent the law by merely "going through

---

[8]Illinois School Code, Ch. 122 § 10-22.4 (1961).
[9]People ex rel. Murphy v. Maxwell, 177 N.Y. Supp. 494, 69 N.E. 1092 (1904).

the motions" of a prescribed procedure. A Michigan law provided that cancellation of a tenure teacher's contract should be preceded by a hearing, at which testimony under oath was required. A teacher so situated requested a public hearing, and indicated that about 100 friends and witnesses would be present. The board, however, chose to hold the meeting in a room which had only twenty-four seats in addition to the seats at the table occupied by the board.

There were no seats available to the teacher's friends and witnesses, and it was impossible for any of them to gain entrance to the room. A request was made to the board to adjourn the meeting to an adjoining larger room, but the request was refused. Following the hearing, the teacher was discharged. He appealed to the state tenure commission to compel the board to reinstate him. In granting his request the commission noted:

> It is the opinion of the Tenure Commission that the hearing held before the Controlling Board on April 10, 1947, was not a proper public hearing and the rights of Rehberg to such a hearing as provided by statute were not respected and provided for.[10]

The school board appealed the case to the Michigan Supreme Court, which agreed with the Tenure Commission. Said the court, in ordering reinstatement of the teacher:

> It should be noted that the issue of whether Clark Rehberg had a fair hearing before the school board does not in any way control the issue of whether or not he should have been discharged as a teacher. This issue should be passed upon by the state Tenure Commission, which found as a fact that Clark Rehberg had not been accorded a fair and impartial hearing. In our examination of the record we find that there was substantial and competent evidence to support its finding of fact, and we affirm its decision on this issue.[11]

Reasons for Dismissal

The large amount of litigation pertaining to dismissal of teachers poses a problem when one wishes to generalize from the available court cases. The best plan seems to be that of arranging the cases into categories: dismissal for insubordination, for immorality, unprofessional conduct, incompetency, and the like. For clarity of understand-

---

[10] Rehberg v. Board of Educ. of Melvindale, 345 Mich. 731, 77 N.W.2d 131 (1956).
[11] *Ibid.*

ing, therefore, as well as for purposes of extracting leading principles of law relating to teacher dismissal, the following pages contain a categorical analysis of the cases related to the dismissal of public school teachers.

Insubordination. Teachers are required to obey reasonable rules and regulations of the board of education. It makes no difference whether the rules were in force at the time of original employment; the teacher is obliged to follow whatever *reasonable* rules the board may from time to time adopt. While a *definition of insubordination in the abstract* is not possible, it is usually thought of as the willful refusal of the teacher to obey reasonable rules and regulations of the board.

One who is continually disobedient and disdainful of constituted authority may "wear out the patience" of the employing officials, and be dismissed on the basis of insubordination. In a leading case in California, a teacher-principal who flouted the authority of the board, and referred to the members as "henchmen" was dismissed. Her dismissal was upheld when the Supreme Court of the United States refused to review the case. Her contention was that she had been denied the privilege of free speech, a defense she used in the lower court. But the high Court ruled, in effect, that she had been guilty of insubordination, and had been legally dismissed.[12]

In Oklahoma, a teacher was assigned to teach the fourth and fifth grades. She agreed to the assignment and taught for four days, whereupon without authority or consent, she took over the seventh grade and advised the superintendent that she would teach only that grade. She refused, even after consultation with the superintendent, to resume her work in the fourth and fifth grades. The district board dismissed her for insubordination. Her dismissal was upheld in the courts. The court said her failure "to observe the rules and regulations of the district board," a provision she had agreed to in the contract, constituted a breach of contract on her part.[13]

However, it is equally well settled that a teacher is not obliged to obey an *unreasonable* rule of the board. The question of whether a rule is reasonable is, of course, a matter for the courts to decide. In one case, a board rule requiring the teacher to perform janitorial services was held to be an unreasonable exercise of board power.

---

[12]Board of Educ. of City of Los Angeles v. Swan, 41 Cal. App. 2d 546, 261 P.2d 261 (1953).
[13]Consolidated School Dist. No. 4, Bryan County v. Millis, 192 Okla. 687, 139 P.2d 183 (1943).

Also, the board may limit its ability to dismiss a teacher by prior action or agreement. This may be illustrated by two cases, one in Nebraska, the other in Montana. In the Nebraska case, a board attempted to discharge a teacher for insubordination and incompetency during the life of a valid contract. The contract, which had several months to run, contained a provision that it could be terminated only by mutual agreement or operation of law. The teacher brought suit for the balance of her salary under the contract. The court held that she had been illegally discharged, because the board had contracted in such a way that it could remove the teacher under the conditions stipulated in the contract only. The board's failure to dismiss under one of the stipulated conditions had resulted in an unlawful dismissal of the teacher.[14]

The Montana case involved an infraction of a rule of the superintendent of schools. One would normally suppose that a teacher as an employee of the district would be subject to the rules laid down by the superintendent of schools. The Montana board assumed as much in dismissing a teacher for lack of cooperation with the superintendent. The latter claimed that the teacher failed to obey rules laid down by him, and that she complained about taking her turn staying at school during the noon hour. In Montana, lack of cooperation is not one of the statutory grounds for dismissal of a teacher. The court ruled that the teacher had been illegally dismissed; although the contract provided that the teacher should be subject to the laws of the State of Montana and the rules and regulations of the board of trustees, it was nowhere mentioned that she should be subject to rules laid down by the superintendent of schools.[15]

A Wisconsin board invited a teacher to a board meeting with the purpose of requesting his resignation. Aware of the board's intentions, the teacher refused to attend the board meeting. In his absence, the meeting was held and the board voted to terminate his contract even though there were three months remaining on it. The ground chosen for dismissal was "insubordination," since the teacher had refused to attend the meeting, and had told the clerk he "could go to hell." The teacher sought adjudication of his discharge in the courts.

The court ruled in favor of the teacher. Although a board might terminate a teacher's contract for insubordination, mere refusal to attend a meeting of the board did not constitute an insubordinate act. Said the court, in ruling that the teacher had not been legally dismissed:

[14]Greer v. Chelewski, 162 Neb. 450, 76 N.W.2d 438 (1946).
[15]Hovland v. School Dist. No. 52, 128 Mont. 507, 278 P.2d 211 (1954).

The proof indicates that the disrespectful remarks were provoked by the defendant's representatives. It does not appear that the defendant, the public or the pupils were prejudiced thereby. We are not impressed with the defendant's position on this appeal that had the plaintiff appeared at the meeting, he might have been afforded an opportunity to explain his demeanor during the two day period after he had been advised that his resignation would be expected. However, as is manifest, he was summoned only for the purpose of resigning and saving face; his failure to be present was not insubordination and cannot react to the detriment of his rights.[16]

Immorality. No clear definition is possible of those acts on the part of the teacher which may amount to immorality, and hence constitute grounds for dismissal. In interpreting the meaning of the term immorality, the courts have been known to hold teachers to a stricter definition than is usually applicable to the acts of other citizens. The reason for this is obvious; the teacher is an example for the youth of the community, and his conduct is expected to be above reproach. Any deviation from the *mores* of the local community, or the accepted standard of behavior in its society, may subject the teacher to dismissal for immorality or moral turpitude.

It is not necessary for the teacher to be found guilty of an immoral act; it is only necessary that the teacher's reputation be such as to embarrass the board. Since a teacher's reputation in the community is of prime importance, a board may dismiss a teacher who "has a bad reputation," even though he may not be found guilty of a specific wrongful act.

A school superintendent was indicted for adultery, and the board dismissed him for immoral conduct. The adultery verdict against the superintendent was later legally set aside, but the court held that the board might dismiss him nonetheless. His usefulness had been destroyed by the notoriety received in the other trial. The court pointed out that not only good character, but good reputation are essential to the greatest usefulness of a teacher in any position.[17]

In a case which arose in Kentucky, a male teacher was dismissed for entering a building at night with some young ladies without turning on the lights. Although the young man and the ladies testified that no misconduct took place, and the objects they entered the building to obtain were clearly visible by moonlight, the verdict was in favor

---

[16]Millar v. Joint School Dist. No. 2, Village of Wild Rose, 2 Wis. 2d 303, 86 N.W.2d 455 (1957).

[17]Freeman v. Town of Bourne, 170 Mass. 289, 49 N.E. 435 (1898).

of the board. The court stated that the board is the best judge of whether or not a teacher's conduct is so questionable as to set a bad example before the pupils. Where the board is of the opinion that the effectiveness of the teacher has been lowered, the court ruled that it should not interfere in the legitimate exercise of board discretion.[18]

"Drinking within the boundary of the schoolhouse and also offering such to the students" provided the grounds for dismissal of a Wyoming teacher. The teacher charged that he had been illegally dismissed, and sued for the salary due him. Said the Supreme Court of Wyoming, in ruling in favor of the board:

> . . . Even charges of or reputation for immorality, although not supported by full proof, might in some cases be sufficient ground for removal. Not merely good character but good reputation is essential.[19]

Hamilton[20] stated that, when the teacher enters the teaching profession, he legally surrenders a measure of his freedom of action. A teacher may legally be free to be immoral, so long as he violates no law, but he is not legally or educationally free to be a teacher and engage in immoral conduct.

Sometimes the statute specifies that the teacher may be dismissed for "gross inefficiency or immorality." Just what constitutes *gross* immorality is not entirely clear. A West Virginia court, in ruling on the use of the word "gross" before the word immorality, pointed out that instead of meaning great and excessive, the word means willful, flagrant, or shameless conduct, which shows a moral indifference to the wishes of the respectable members of the community. It may be any act on the part of the teacher which offends the moral sense of the community, presents a bad example for the youth thereof, or is contrary to the standards of the teaching profession.[21]

Unprofessional conduct. No hard and fast rule exists with regard to which actions of a teacher may constitute unprofessional conduct. As the *mores* of society change, obviously the standards by which a teacher's actions are judged will change also. What may have been unprofessional conduct at one time and place may well be accepted practice at another time and place. It seems possible that not all unprofessional conduct would be immoral, but some of it may well be.

---

[18]Gover v. Stovall, 237 Ky. 172, 35 S.W.2d 24 (1931).

[19]Tracy v. School Dist. No. 22, Sheridan County, 70 Wyo. 1, 243 P.2d 932 (1954).

[20]Robert R. Hamilton. *The Bi-Weekly School Law Letter* (December 23, 1954), p. 87.

[21]Moore v. Strickling, 36 W. Va. 515, 33 S.E. 274 (1899).

The suspension of a teacher in California for advocating before his public school class the election of a candidate to public office was upheld by the court.[22] In another case, a conscientious objector, who stated that she would not support her country in resisting invasion, was dismissed for unprofessional conduct. The court refused to intervene.[23]

Another teacher's dismissal for unprofessional conduct was upheld by the court in a California case where the evidence revealed that the teacher had falsified class attendance records, marking students present when in reality they were absent. The fact was that if the enrollment in the adult typing class taught by the defendant fell below a certain number, the class would be discontinued, and the teacher would be out of a job. To insure the continuation of the class, the teacher had falsified the attendance records. The court held that the teacher had been legally dismissed.[24]

In Illinois, a teacher was dismissed for appearing on the streets in an intoxicated condition, for arousing unfavorable publicity, and because she was the subject of talk in the community. In upholding her dismissal, the court noted that there was no question of her competency as a teacher, but that her outside actions were grounds for her dismissal. Said the court:

> It is plain the dismissal was not simply because plaintiff had consumed intoxicants. It is the opinion of the court that a teacher is something of a leader to pupils of tender age, resulting in admiration and emulation, and that the Board might properly fear the effect of social conduct in public not in keeping with the dignity and leadership they desired from teachers.[25]

Incompetency. Another grounds for dismissal of a teacher under both the common law or statutes in all the states is incompetency. It is not always clear what constitutes incompetency, since the fact that the teacher holds a valid certificate is considered *prima facie* evidence of competence before the law. The burden of proof in incompetency proceedings rests with the board of education. There is a presumption of competency at the time of the issuance of the

[22]Goldsmith v. Board of Educ. of Sacramento City High School Dist., 66 Cal. App. 157, 225 Pac. 783 (1924).

[23]McDowell v. Board of Educ. of City of N.Y., 104 Misc. 564, 172 N.Y. Supp. 590 (1918).

[24]Board of Educ. of San Francisco v. Weiland, 179 Cal. App. 2d 808, 4 Calif. 286 (1960).

[25]Scott v. Board of Educ. of Alton, 20 Ill. App. 2d 292, 156 N.E.2d 1 (1959).

certificate. That the teacher is not now competent is not conclusive until supporting evidence is presented by the board.

The corollary of this is also true: when a teacher accepts a teaching position, by implication he serves notice that he has the capacity to do the job effectively. The competency extends to subject matter, the control of pupils under his care, and to his role as a good example for children. If the teacher fails in these particulars, he may be dismissed. The line between competency and incompetency is not clearly drawn, and depends upon the circumstances in each case.

In the *Horosko*[26] case cited in an earlier chapter, a teacher who worked in a beer garden was discharged on the grounds of incompetency, inasmuch as the *type of work* caused her to lose the respect of the community and her pupils. She had been given a rating of "43 per cent competent" by the county superintendent; a rating of 50 per cent was the passing or average rating. The court ruled that the combination of her outside work and low rating constituted legal basis for dismissal on the grounds of incompetency.

There is also an implied *physical competency* on the part of the teacher. The question before a Pennsylvania court was whether a teacher became *incompetent* because of her pregnancy. There was no question of the teacher's ability to perform her educational tasks; the question was whether, by reason of her physical condition, she became incompetent. Evidence was presented that the teacher had been neglectful of her duties, and had been absent frequently. The Supreme Court of Pennsylvania ruled that incompetency may extend to the physical inability of the teacher to perform her duties, as well as to her educational and professional qualifications. The teacher's dismissal on the ground of incompetency was upheld.[27]

The courts will not usually find that one or two minor defects in the work of the teacher can be construed as incompetency. There must be a persistent quality which "strikes at the heart of the contract." The incompetency must be of such a nature as to render the overall work of the teacher ineffective. But it is not necessary that the teacher possess the *highest* qualifications in order to be retained. Said the Supreme Court of Illinois on this subject:

> It may be that the evidence fails to show the highest possible qualifications, or a talent for his profession equal to the most eminent and successful teachers. But the law requires no such qualifications; it only requires average qualification

---

[26] 335 Pa. 369, 6 A.2d 866 (1939).
[27] Appeal of School Dist. of City of Bethlehem, 347 Pa. 418, 32 A.2d 565 (1943).

and ability, and the usual application to the discharge of the duties of a teacher to fulfill his contract.[28]

In California, the Los Angeles school board dismissed a permanent teacher for incompetency, basing its charges on a lack of knowledge of subject matter, failure to organize courses of study, lack of control over pupils, and failure to cooperate with colleagues. The teacher contended that the charges set forth in the complaint failed to give *sufficient definiteness* as to enable him to prepare a defense. Said the Supreme Court of California, in ruling for the board and against the teacher:

> . . . Section 5.652 [of the school code] requires that the notice specify the "nature" of the alleged incompetency with sufficient particularity to furnish the employee an opportunity to correct his faults. It is not required that any particular facts or episodes be set forth in the Notice. Defendant was given sufficient notice of the charges against him to enable him to overcome his deficiencies if he had the ability and desire to do so. Counsel for plaintiff aptly suggests that the governing board notified defendant to study more, plan more, control his temper, be more polite, be more cooperative, and be more self-controlled. The notice was a sufficient compliance with section 5.652 of the School Code. According to the charges contained in the complaint, defendant did not profit by the admonition contained in the notice. In our view, the complaint states a cause of action.[29]

Neglect of duty. Like several other good causes, neglect of duty cannot be clearly and categorically defined. In an Illinois case cited earlier, outside employment of the agriculture teacher which tended to interfere with his teaching duties constituted sufficient neglect in the opinion of the court to warrant the teacher's dismissal.[30] Serious illness may render the teacher incapable of performing his regular duties. In California, a teacher who became the victim of sarcoidosis was absent from school for long periods of time. The board dismissed him on the ground that he was neglecting his teaching duties. The court upheld the board, noting that the teacher's affliction made it necessary for him to be absent from duty more often than the normal person.[31]

---

[28]Neville v. School Directors of Dist. No. 1, 36 Ill. 71 (1864).

[29]Board of Educ. of City of Los Angeles v. Ballou, 21 Cal. App. 2d 52, 68 P.2d 389 (1937).

[30]Meredith v. Board of Educ. of Community Unit School Dist. No. 7, 7 Ill. App. 2d 477, 130 N.E.2d 5 (1955).

[31]Riggins v. Board of Educ., 144 Cal. App. 2d 232, 300 P.2d 848 (1956).

In New York City, a court held that a teacher who was absent for the purpose of bearing a child could be dismissed by the board on the ground of neglect of duty. The reasoning of the court was that her absence under these circumstances might be of such length as to confer jurisdiction on the board to remove her, whereas the board did not have this jurisdiction because of mere absence alone.[32] From these and other cases, it appears that the courts will attempt to discover whether the absence was of such duration as to breach the contract, not whether the absence was unavoidable.

May the teacher employ a substitute, or does failure to perform the work *personally* constitute neglect of duty? In an early case in point, the court ruled that a teacher does have the right to employ a substitute, but this right is not unlimited.[33] The teacher may not use this method to extend her vacation period, for example. The court noted that the test of neglect of duty was whether or not the absence was *avoidable*. If it is clearly unavoidable, and of short duration, the courts will not permit the dismissal of the teacher for neglect of duty.

A Colorado teacher was visiting in Europe, and missed the boat which would have permitted her to arrive at her post in time for the opening of school. Her unavoidable delay did not serve to terminate the contract, said the court.[34] Similarly, a Kentucky teacher who was prevented by floods from reaching her teaching station was judged not to have breached her contract. The board could not legally dismiss her for neglect, inasmuch as the delay was unintentional and unavoidable.[35]

To the same effect was a case in California where the court ruled that an unavoidable delay in reporting back to work after a brief vacation did not constitute sufficient basis for the teacher's dismissal on the ground of neglect of duty. The teacher had been employed in the district for more than twenty years. He had worked diligently, sometimes without pay, for the promotion of the summer school, and other similar projects. Leaving a note on the principal's desk, he absented himself from the job, and went deer hunting, giving the impression that he was absent on account of illness. Much to his

---

[32]People ex rel. Peixotto v. Board of Educ. of City of N.Y., 82 Misc. 684, 144 N.Y. Supp. 87 (1913).

[33]School Directors v. Hudson, 88 Ill. 563 (1878).

[34]School District No. 1 of Jefferson County v. Parker, 82 Colo. 385, 260 Pac. 521 (1927).

[35]Turner v. Hampton, 30 Ky. L. Rep. 179, 97 S.W. 761 (1906).

dismay, he was "snowed in" while on the hunting trip, and reported back to school later than he had anticipated.

The board deducted $96.00 from his salary, and dismissed him. The Supreme Court of California, in a three-to-two decision, refused to uphold the board in its action. Said the court:

> That the defendant was guilty of a measure of deception may not be doubted and his conduct was reprehensible when measured by the high standards of his profession. But whether the Legislature intended that all deception, however slight, should result in dismissal is doubtful. A judicial question is thus presented. The trial court having the responsibility in the premises, chose to relieve the defendant [teacher] from the rigorous result of his misconduct and we are disposed not to disturb its judgment in this respect.[36]

In dismissing teachers, the board must not act hastily, nor in an arbitrary or capricious manner, no matter how well convinced it may be that the teacher is not "working out." By so doing, a board may inadvertently act in such a manner as to render its decision ineffective and void. A school board in Minnesota sought to discharge a non-tenure teacher for several minor "discrepancies" in her work. In a letter addressed to the teacher, and signed by all members of the board, the following sentences appeared:

> Miss Kuehn.
>
> We, the school board, hereby give you notice that you have by all means, not lived up to your contract, as you have agreed too. [sic]
> You have been told at different times that your teaching school was not satisfactory.
> You have not followed your rules and school regulations according to laws.
> You have not put in your school classes, you have left out classes days and days.
> You have not put in full hours at school which is required of law for teachers to do.
> Therefore we expel you as a teacher of District 70.
> Yours truly,
> (Signatures of the board members)[37]

No hearing was provided for non-tenure teachers in the Minnesota statute, and the teacher was given no hearing. The teacher sued for

---

[36]Midway School Dist. of Kern County v. Griffeath, 29 Cal. App. 2d 13, 172 P.2d 857 (1946).

[37]Kuehn v. School Dist. No. 70, Goodhue County, 221 Minn. 443, 22 N.W.2d 220 (1946).

the balance of her salary under the contract, on the grounds that the action of the board had been arbitrary and capricious.

The case was tried before a jury. The court instructed the jury that if it found that the action of the board had been arbitrary and capricious or in bad faith, it should find for the plaintiff teacher. The jury found for the teacher, whereupon the board moved for a new trial. The trial was denied, "since in dismissing a teacher the board acted in a quasi-judicial capacity." The court held that the plaintiff was entitled to a notice and hearing before dismissal. The action of the board in not proceeding in this matter was lacking due process of law, and was arbitrary and capricious.

Said the Supreme Court of Minnesota, in dealing with the appeal:

> The statute did not provide a process for the release of a non-tenure teacher "for cause." However, even though no manner of procedure is set out in the statute for the guidance of the school board, a teacher is, nevertheless, entitled to notice of charges made against him and a fair hearing before an impartial board.[38]

Generally, a letter alone will not serve to dismiss a teacher. The case does not deal with the question of whether a teacher is entitled to a reasonable time to "make up any deficiencies in her work"; however, it may well be argued that the board should be in close enough communication with teachers so as to render it unnecessary to summarily dismiss them. Most teachers, if given the opportunity, will attempt to improve themselves, when it is clear that the board is acting in good faith.

Marriage. Theoretically, legislatures could enumerate many causes for dismissal of teachers, among them the marriage of a female teacher. Curiously, marriage has not been generally included in statutes bearing on the dismissal of teachers for cause. Neither has it been implied through the "elastic clause" of the statutes, that part which covers "other good and just cause." It is doubtful whether, in this day and age, a legislature would intend that the teacher who became married during the life of the contract should be dismissed for her marriage *per se*, unless her contract contained such a provision.

Boards of an earlier era often included in their rules and regulations a provision that marriage of women teachers would automatically terminate their services. Such a rule was challenged in the presence of a statute which said that "teachers placed upon the permanent list

---

[38] *Ibid.*

shall continue to serve until dismissed in the manner herein provided, but such rules shall be reasonable and for the good of the schools." The year was 1915. Said the court in ruling that the teacher could not be dismissed solely on the basis of marriage:

> The act of marriage, however, does not of itself furnish a reasonable cause. . . . The reason advanced for the rule adopted is that after marriage a woman may devote her time and attention to her home—rather than school. . . . It is impossible to know in advance whether the efficiency of a woman teacher will become impaired because of marriage, and a rule which assumes that all persons do become less competent because of marriage is unreasonable because such regulation is purely arbitrary. If a teacher is just as competent and efficient after marriage, a dismissal because of marriage would be capricious. If a teacher is neglectful, incompetent, and inefficient, she ought to be discharged whether she is married or whether she is single.[39]

Similarly, where the statute provided that teachers could be dismissed for certain specified causes, the court held that inasmuch as marriage of a female teacher was not included in the causes for dismissal, discharge of a teacher for marriage alone was illegal.[40]

What is the effect of a board rule that marriage of a woman teacher shall constitute grounds for her dismissal adopted *after* the teacher has been employed? Apparently, the courts, although in conflict on certain aspects of the subject, are in substantial agreement that a marriage rule adopted after the teacher has been employed does not apply to that particular teacher. This is especially true for tenure teachers. However, where the teacher agrees to the stipulation that her marriage shall constitute a termination of the contract, the courts are in agreement that the board may legally dismiss her for marriage alone.[41]

The Supreme Judicial Court of Massachusetts ruled that it is within the power of the school board to decide against employing married teachers in the public schools, although this policy should be gradually introduced in order not to cause hardships. Furthermore, said the court, the board may provide by contract that when the single teacher marries, her contract is automatically terminated. There is

---

[39] Richards v. District School Bd. for School Dist. No. 1, 78 Ore. 621, 153 Pac. 482 (1915).

[40] Jameson v. Board of Educ. of Union Dist., 74 W. Va. 389, 81 S.E. 1126 (1914).

[41] Taggart v. School Dist. No. 52, Carroll County, 339 Mo. 223, 96 S.W.2d 335 (1936).

one exception, however, to this rule. When the teacher can show that she must support herself, or other dependents, the rule may be considered unreasonable, and therefore unenforceable.[42]

Justifiable decrease in teaching positions. America's population is a mobile one, and shifts in pupil population may sometimes leave the board with an abundance of teachers. When school districts are consolidated, the result may be that there are more teachers than needed at the moment. Within statutory limits, the courts hold that teachers may be dismissed "in the best interests of the schools, and of the resulting economies."

However, the board must follow the statute exactly in making reductions in the teaching staff. The statute is the measure of the board's power in the matter. A court will very closely examine dismissals related to a decrease in teaching positions. If there is evidence of fraud or misconduct on the part of the board, the court will intervene.

An appellate court of Illinois refused to allow the dismissal of eleven tenure teachers upon the loss by the district of certain territory through reorganization. An Illinois statute provided that teachers might be dismissed because of a justifiable decrease in the number of teaching positions. The discharges were made upon the grounds of the loss of the territory, rather than upon the attempt by the board to reduce the number of teachers, a cause which they might just as well have stated. Failure to follow the controlling statute rendered the action of the board unenforceable.[43]

The courts are in agreement that when a board reduces the number of teaching positions, it must begin by retaining those teachers who have the greatest amount of seniority in the district. Teachers on tenure must be retained, while those on a probationary or temporary basis shall be dismissed first. Clearly, the board must act at all times in an honest, straightforward manner, and with complete candor. The courts will allow no usurpation of the teachers' rights to fair treatment in the presence of an oversupply of teachers. Nor will the courts allow a board "to pick on a teacher" in an arbitrary and capricious manner through the abolition of his position.

Such a case arose in Louisiana, where discharge because of reduction in teaching positions does not exist as a statutory cause for dis-

---

[42]Houghton v. School Comm. of Sommerville, 306 Mass. 542, 28 N.E.2d 1001 (1940).

[43]Hankenson v. Board of Educ. of Waukegan Township, 10 Ill. App. 2d 79, 134 N.E.2d 356 (1956).

missal. A supervisor of classroom instruction was dismissed by the board on the grounds that the position was no longer needed, and that it should be abolished. There was evidence that the board was trying to "get at" the teacher by abolishing his position. In a subsequent court action, the supervisor was successful in recovering back pay. The court stated that the supervisor was entitled to a position of equal rank, if such were available. In any event, he was entitled to a salary equal to that which his service with the district warranted, even though he was relegated to lesser rank; he could not be dismissed.[44]

Subversion. One who would overthrow a government would undoubtedly begin by gaining control of the means of education. Because of the close relationship between public education and national security, public interest has been aroused lest subversive groups infiltrate the school system and work from within to undermine the government. The result has been the adoption of statutes designed to control subversive activities in most of the states. Signing a loyalty oath, for example, is required in three-fourths of the states, and in many local school districts. Several of the states have enacted laws pertaining to teacher dismissal for association with so-called communistic organizations, and such legislation has been upheld in several of the states. In Chapter VII, these laws were considered in detail, and will be merely summarized here.

In New York, the Feinberg law required the state Board of Regents to list organizations which it found were communistic in nature. Anyone who was a member of a listed organization could be dismissed, and membership alone constituted evidence of disqualification for public office. In dismissing teachers on the membership list of organizations, school boards were upheld by the court, which said that teachers may work for the school system only so long as they comply with reasonable rules laid down by the school authorities. Persons who work in the public schools do so on the terms stipulated by the legislature, not on their own terms.[45]

The Supreme Court of the United States ruled that a teacher who refused to testify before a Congressional sub-committee and was subsequently dismissed, had been illegally discharged.[46] On the other

---

[44]Dugas v. Ascension Parish School Bd., 228 La. 80, 81 So. 2d 817 (1955).

[45]Adler v. Board of Educ. of City of New York, 342 U.S. 485, 72 Sup. Ct. 380, 96 L. Ed. 517, 27 A.L.R.2d 472 (1952).

[46]Slochower v. Board of Higher Education of the City of N. Y., 350 U.S. 551, 76 Sup. Ct. 637, 100 L. Ed. 692 (1956).

hand, the teacher who refused to answer questions put to him by his superintendent concerning his past memberships in certain organizations was legally dismissed for refusal to so testify.[47]

Miscellaneous reasons. The statutes may provide that a teacher shall be dismissed or required to retire when a certain specified age is reached. In Colorado, for example, tenure protection ceases past the age of sixty-five years, "unless or until the teacher has had at least one year's notice in writing from the employing board or committee that his employment will be terminated."[48] The effect of this type of legislation has been to place the teacher after age sixty-five on an annual contractual basis, instead of a tenure basis. In Ohio, the local board may, as of the thirteenth day of June of any year, terminate the contract of a teacher who has reached the age of seventy, or who will attain the age of seventy on or before the following thirty-first of August.

In both of these states, when the super-annuated teacher is in good health and able to perform his teaching duties to the board's satisfaction, there is nothing to prevent the board from employing him on an annual basis as long as the board desires.

Courts have upheld board rules providing that the teacher sit for a national examination, pass a physical examination including chest x-ray, and live in the school district. In the absence of statutory restraint, a board may likewise employ only married teachers, and refuse to employ those who are associated with labor unions. However, boards may not require a religious test of applicants, nor extract political promises from teachers. Hamilton and Reutter[49] pointed out that there is often a tremendous difference between an *unwise* and an *illegal* school board rule. A rule may be unwise without being necessarily illegal. Relief from an illegal rule is to test it in the properly constituted courts of the land, whereas there may be little if any relief from an unwise rule of the board of education.

Remedies of the Teacher Wrongfully Dismissed

When a teacher is wrongfully dismissed, he may recover damages to the extent he has suffered damages by his dismissal. In this respect, recovery is comparable to that afforded through breach of any com-

---

[47]Beilan v. Board of Public Educ., School Dist. of Philadelphia, 357 U.S. 399, 78 Sup. Ct. 1317, 2 L. Ed. 1414 (1958).

[48]Colo. Rev. Stat. § 123-18-9 (1953).

[49]Robert R. Hamilton and E. Edmund Reutter, Jr. *Legal Aspects of School Board Operation* (New York: Teachers College, Columbia University, 1958), p. 49.

mercial contract. Under the law of contracts, the injured party is protected to the extent that he will be restored to the relative position he would have occupied had the contract not been broken. Thus, where the teacher is unable to obtain other employment, his damages may extend to the full amount of the breached contract. However, the teacher is expected to make a reasonable effort to obtain other employment in his chosen field pending the outcome of the case. Any money earned in another position may be credited toward damages due him by the offending board of education. Hence, the teacher wrongfully dismissed is entitled only to a reasonable amount, usually the actual amount of his monetary losses in damages from the board.

The *mitigation of damages principle* has been clearly stated by the Supreme Court of Oklahoma. Said that body in dealing with the problem:

> The measure of plaintiff's recovery in an action for breach of contract for employment is *prima facie* the sum stipulated to be paid by the employer for the services, but it is subject to reduction in such sums as the plaintiff has earned or might with reasonable diligence have earned during the period by securing other employment of a similar character, but the plaintiff is neither required to allege nor prove that he has been unable to secure other employment. The burden is upon the defendant to plead and prove in mitigation of damages that the plaintiff has, or might with reasonable diligence have, obtained profitable employment during the remainder of the term.[50]

The burden of proof that the teacher has failed to mitigate damages thus is seen to rest with the board of education. Furthermore, a teacher is not obliged to accept a lower position, nor one which is outside the field of education, in order to mitigate damages; nor is he required to accept a position in a distant community from that in which he lives.

In a Pennsylvania case, a teacher was illegally discharged. He then obtained employment in another district at a salary higher than that provided under the original contract. In awarding the teacher nominal damages of $1.00, the Supreme Court of Pennsylvania noted:

> . . . Improper dismissal is a breach of contract for which the employee may recover damages. Damages are the loss suffered by one person by reason of a breach of contract on the part of another, and if the school teacher received the same

---

[50]School Dist. No. 60 of Ellis County v. Crabtree, 146 Okla. 197, 294 Pac. 171 (1930).

compensation for his work during the period of improper dismissal as he would have received if he had continued in the position from which he was improperly dismissed, he has suffered no damages except such as may arise from matters following other elements than loss of salary.[51]

What relief has the teacher who is illegally dismissed *before* being allowed to enter upon his duties? Apparently, a teacher who is qualified may not be discharged on the ground of incompetency before rendering any services. An early Michigan case illustrates the basic reasoning underlying this principle. Said the Supreme Court of Michigan, in discussing the rights of the teacher wrongfully dismissed:

> When a master rescinds a contract of service before the time agreed for the commencement of such service, the servant has his choice of two courses—he may consider and treat the contract as rescinded, or he may treat it as still existing, and tender performance at the proper time. The same reasoning does not apply to a rescission before the time fixed for the service to commence as does to a discharge from service. In the latter case the servant is presumed to be out of employment and it is clearly his duty to accept other similar employment; but in the former case he is not presumed to be out of employment and cannot, therefore, in reason, be required to seek other employment to cover the future period. If, however, as in the case of teachers, they are taking their vacation for rest and recreation, they cannot legally be called upon to abandon these, and seek employment for the coming year. Plaintiff was therefore justified in notifying the defendant that she would insist upon her contract, and be ready at the proper time to perform it.[52]

A teacher may be discharged before entering upon performance of his contract, however, if he is immoral or generally unfit for his role as a teacher, but it is incumbent upon the board to justify its action by proof that dismissal was because of such immorality or unfitness.[53]

The teacher illegally discharged should, of course, include all expenses incurred in obtaining other employment. For example, a teacher was discharged on December 31, 1904, for failure to obtain a first grade county certificate, although she held a certificate valid in any school of the state. She immediately obtained a position in another school district some distance away in the same state, and brought

---

[51]Coble v. School Dist. of Township of Metal, 178 Pa. 301, 116 A.2d 113 (1955).

[52]Farrell v. School Dist. No. 2 of Township of Rubicon, 98 Mich. 43, 56 N.W. 1053 (1893). Also, Gardner v. North Little Rock School Dist., 161 Ark. 466, 257 S.W. 73, (1923); Watkins v. School Dist., 194 S.W. 32 (Ark. 1917).

[53]Argenta School Dist. v. Strickland, 152 Ark. 215, 238 S.W. 9 (1922).

suit against the board for the balance of her contract. The state supreme court ruled that she had been illegally dismissed, and entered judgment against the board for the actual damages sustained by the teacher. But in listing her expenses, the teacher forgot to include the cost of moving her dependent mother and sister to the new school district. The court said that failure to include the moving expenses as a part of the total expense sustained precluded recovery of this item on the part of the teacher, inasmuch as such expenses must be specially pleaded in order to be recovered.[54]

The teacher wrongfully dismissed is required to utilize proper channels in obtaining relief. Where administrative machinery is provided, it is generally necessary for the teacher to exhaust the administrative remedies available to him before recourse to the courts can be had. This principle may be illustrated by a Kansas case in which a period of ten days was allowed for appeal to the county superintendent following the dismissal of a teacher. A discharged teacher failed to appeal to the proper official within the allotted time limit, but instead brought suit for reinstatement by the board. The court dismissed his case, maintaining that parties who have not first exhausted their legal administrative remedies may not bring suit in the courts for a redress of their grievances.[55]

The teacher wrongfully discharged may initiate an action in damages, or bring an action for reinstatement. Or the teacher may request damages for the time he is illegally suspended, and sue for reinstatement to his former position. Whatever his decision, he is not entitled to sit idly by and recover his salary. He is expected to make reasonable effort to obtain other employment in his chosen field in the meantime. He may, through *laches*, entirely lose his right to be reimbursed if he "sits on his hands."

Boards of education, being composed of laymen unfamiliar with the law, are not always aware of the legal procedures required in dismissing teaching personnel. Thus, the board may fail in its attempt to "fire the teacher" because of some flaw in the dismissal procedures employed. Three cases will serve to illustrate what may happen when boards act outside the proper legal procedure.

In Illinois, a teacher was dismissed for un-remediable defects in his teaching. The court ordered him reinstated to his former position, ruling that the teacher's alleged defects were causes which *were*

---

[54]School Dist. No. 3 in Clear Creek County v. Nash, 27 Colo. App. 551, 140 Pac. 473 (1914).
[55]Moore v. Starkey, 185 Kan. 26, 340 P. 2d 905 (1959).

remediable, and that the board's findings that they were not remediable was against the manifest weight of evidence. Under the tenure law, the plaintiff was entitled to notice in writing and an opportunity to remedy defects before he could be legally discharged.[56]

To the same effect was an Arizona case. A discharged teacher sued for reinstatement on the grounds that she had been denied an opportunity to cross-examine the witnesses who appeared against her at the hearing. The court upheld her claim. Said the court:

> The overwhelming weight of authority holds that for an administrative body, conducting a quasi-judicial hearing, to preclude the individual concerned from cross-examination of witnesses appearing against him denies him due process of law.[57]

Finally, the charges may be so general in nature as to preclude clear definition, and lead to the teacher's reinstatement. Such a case arose in Louisiana in 1959. A list of eleven causes had been given by the board for the teacher's discharge. These were couched in such general terms that the court reinstated the teacher, using the following language:

> . . . [The charges against plaintiff teacher] are couched in general language. They do not specify definite acts; neither do they state the number of times the dereliction of duty was committed, nor specify the dates on which infractions occurred. Nothing is itemized or pin-pointed. . . . We find that the charges against plaintiff are not supported by substantial evidence as factually required.[58]

Right of the Teacher to Resign

The foregoing cases describe some of the aspects of termination of a teaching contract *by the board of education*. But in all contracts, there are at least two parties to the contractual arrangement. Hence, the teacher, for one reason or another, may wish to terminate the contract through *resignation*.

The general rule governing resignations is that the one who resigns must do so under such limitations as the statutes and the terms of the contract impose. Where, for example, the statute provides that thirty days' notice must be given by either of the parties for termination, twenty days' notice will not suffice to effect termination.

---

[56]Hauswald v. Board of Educ. of Community High School Dist. No. 217, Cook County, 20 Ill. App. 2d 49, 155 N.E.2d 319 (1958).
[57]Forman v. Creighton School Dist. No. 14, 87 Ariz. 329, 351 P.2d 165 (1960).
[58]Lewing v. De Soto Parish School Bd., 238 La. 43, 113 So. 2d 462 (1959).

Furthermore, one who resigns must direct and tender his resignation *to the person or persons* who have the power to fill the vacancy created by the resignation. Thus, a board member who resigned to the board president, when the law provided for the filling of vacancies by the county superintendent, was ruled to have failed in his effort to resign.

In effect, a resignation is an *offer* by the teacher to terminate the contract. The contract remains in effect, however, until the resignation is accepted by the board. Usually, this means that the board must meet in a legally-called meeting, and by a majority vote agree to accept the resignation as tendered. It is well settled that a teacher may withdraw a resignation without penalty if the board has not acted upon it. Said a court in stating the general principle of resignation and acceptance:

> The tender of a so-called "resignation" by a teacher under contract to teach in a district school, being a mere offer to effect a mutual rescission of a contract of employment, is not binding on either party to the contract until its acceptance by her employer, assembled as a board, and may be withdrawn at any time before such acceptance takes place.[59]

When the teacher resigns, however, and his resignation is legally accepted, he may not then change his mind and claim his former position. He has tendered, and the board has accepted, his offer of rescission; there has been a meeting of the minds, and the courts will leave the two parties as they are found.

Such a case arose in New Jersey. A tenure teacher of some twenty-five years' service in the Camden Public Schools was invited to attend a meeting "to talk the situation over." Present at the meeting were her principal, the superintendent of schools, and the president of the school board. The meeting was a stormy one, and the teacher became quite upset. Twice she threatened to resign, and twice the superintendent cautioned her to wait until Monday. Adamant, she wrote out her resignation, which was addressed to the superintendent, signed it, and in his absence, deposited it on the clerk's desk.

A special meeting of the board had been planned for some time prior to the conference with the teacher. Accordingly, on the same evening, the board met in special session and accepted the teacher's resignation. The next day, the teacher noticed a newspaper story relative to the meeting of the board. She sought to get in touch with

---

[59]LeMasters v. Board of Educ. of Grant Dist., 105 W. Va. 81, 141 S.E. 515 (1928).

the superintendent, but he was unavailable. Thereupon, she dispatched a night letter to the board, stating that she was rescinding her resignation. The board refused to reinstate her, and she brought action to compel the board to restore her to her former position.

The plaintiff contended that she had not intended to resign, that she did so only to provoke a discussion by the board of her status. Furthermore, she contended that the resignation was null and void, inasmuch as it was addressed to the superintendent, rather than to the board. She also argued that the resignation was the "product of fraud, coercion and duress," and that it was accepted by the board at a special session, and was therefore beyond the purpose of the meeting.

The Supreme Court of New Jersey rejected all of the teacher's contentions, including the argument that she had not really intended to resign. The court said:

> We find no merit in appellant's contention that the document she wrote, signed and left at the superintendent's office was in fact not a resignation. Our conclusion flows not only from the unequivocal language used in the above quoted written resignation, but the record shows that the proposal originated with her and, as noted, that she expected that the school board might accept it or reject it.[60]

It is clear from this and similar cases that the teacher who does not wish to resign should hesitate before tendering a resignation. Once the board has accepted the offer, the contract is, in effect and in fact, terminated.

Not all "resignations" are as unequivocal as that in the preceding case. Sometimes the question of *what constitutes a resignation* arises. Of course, the resignation must be sufficiently definite in its clarity as to effect an offer on the part of the teacher to void the contract. A case which arose in Missouri best illustrates this principle of law. A school superintendent became critical of the way a teacher maintained discipline. Just before Christmas, he informed the teacher that his services were no longer needed. At the direction of the superintendent, but under protest, the teacher turned in his keys and picked up his certificate. After the holidays, he returned to school and offered to work, but the superintendent said other arrangements had been made, and the teacher was no longer needed. The board did not formally dismiss him, so the teacher sued for the balance of his contract.

---

[60]Evaul v. Board of Educ. of City of Camden, 65 N.J. Super. 68, 167 A.2d 39 (1961).

The teacher's suit was successful. The court said that the act of turning in his keys, and picking up his certificate had not constituted an abandonment of the teacher's contract, since it was done under the direction of the superintendent, the teacher's superior. His willingness to work and his presence in the school were evidence of his intention to fulfill his part of the contractual arrangement.[61]

It is not unusual to include in the contract document the conditions under which a teacher may legally resign. Certain specific penalties, liquidated damages, may be provided for where a teacher terminates the contract prior to its legal termination date. Some state statutes provide that a teacher who resigns is required to forfeit a part of his annual salary to the board of education as liquidated damages. Supposedly, this is to protect the board against loss occasioned by the additional cost of finding another teacher.

Suspension

A distinction should be observed between *suspension* and *dismissal* when applied to teacher-board relationships. It is well settled that the board may suspend the teacher-employee pending a hearing. Suspension amounts to advising the teacher to "stand by" while the legal machinery is set in motion. But suspension is not tantamount to dismissal. In the latter, the teacher's contractual association with the board is terminated entirely, whereas in the former, there is the possibility that the contract may be continued.

The question may arise, "Is the teacher entitled to salary under contract during suspension?" A taxpayer might say that he is not, advancing the argument that since the teacher is not rendering a service, the board may not expend public moneys for work that is not performed. In a case which arose in Kansas, the court ruled that a tenure teacher who was suspended pending a legal hearing was entitled to salary under the terms of the contract, even though her contract was later legally terminated by the board. The board had warned the teacher to improve her work, or face dismissal. When no improvement was evident, the board suspended her, and later a hearing was held at which she was discharged. The court did not rule on the right of the board to pay the teacher, but in asserting that she was entitled to salary while suspended, the court, in effect, ruled that the board does have such a right.[62]

---

[61]Parker v. School Dist. of Valley Park, 325 S.W.2d 59 (Mo. 1959).
[62]Million v. Board of Educ. of Wichita, 181 Kan. 230, 310 P.2d 917 (1957).

Power of Boards to Assign and Transfer Teachers

Boards of education may enforce compliance with rules and regulations necessary to the general governance of the schools. Such rules and regulations must stand the test of reasonableness; the teacher is not required to obey an unreasonable rule of the board. Hence, a teacher cannot be required to perform service of a kind other than that provided for in the contract. The teacher is not required to do janitorial work or perform tasks different in nature from those specified in the contract. Refusal to perform non-teaching duties is not grounds for dismissal.[63] However, failure to follow an assignment may constitute adequate grounds for dismissal.[64]

Whether a teacher may be discharged for refusal to obey a board rule involving work other than that already being performed, or different from that specified in the contract, is *a matter of fact* to be decided by the courts. The board's power to transfer or reassign teachers rests upon the rule of reasonableness, and must pass the further test of "work substantially the same" as that for which the original agreement was made.

Courts have consistently ruled that assignment of a teacher to perform work essentially different from that which he was employed to perform is equivalent to dismissal. Said the Supreme Court of Iowa, in deciding that a teacher could not be transferred from her position as a teacher in the intermediate grades to a position in the high school, or face discharge:

> When a servant is wrongfully discharged, he is not bound to accept new employment from the same master, unless (1) the work is in the same general line as that of the first employment, and (2) the offer is made in such a manner as that its acceptance will not amount to a modification of the original agreement. . . . The law would not . . . compel [the teacher] either to make a new agreement with [the school board] or lose all her rights under the old one. If plaintiff had accepted the offer as alleged to have been made, and found herself incompetent for the new work, she would have been liable to discharge under the new agreement, and her rights under the other would have been lost. The offer, as set up, does not constitute a defense in whole or in part.[65]

---

[63]School Dist. No. 25 of Blaine County v. Bear, 106 Okla. 172, 233 Pac. 427 (1925).

[64]Consolidated School Dist. No. 4, Bryan County v. Millis, 192 Okla. 687, 139 P.2d 183 (1943).

[65]Jackson v. Independent School Dist. of Steamboat Rock, 110 Iowa 313, 81 N.W. 596 (1900).

Because the board may not know in advance to what particular position it may be necessary to assign the teacher, contracts of employment may be drawn to allow the board more latitude in transferring teachers within the system. If the teacher agrees to work where the board assigns him, he is, of course, bound by the contract, and may be assigned work anywhere within the system at the board's discretion.[66]

In transferring teachers, a board cannot be allowed to act in a manner inconsistent with fairness and good judgment, or in an arbitrary or unreasonable manner. This principle is best illustrated by a case which arose in Tennessee. A statute of that state provided that a county superintendent, on the approval of the county board of education, might transfer teachers from one location within the county school system to another. A county superintendent presented a recommendation that all teachers be reemployed in the positions which they had held during the previous year. The board refused to follow the recommendation, and instead adopted a "slate" of its own transferring 80 of the 200 teachers in the system. This was done over the protest of the county superintendent. The tenure teachers affected sought an injunction restraining the board of education from transferring them.

The court could not agree with the teachers that the transfer could not be accomplished legally in the absence of joint action by the superintendent and the county board of education. Here, the court said, the board had not only the right but the responsibility of deciding whether or not teachers should be transferred. The consent of the county superintendent was not necessary to legal transfer.

In stating what has come to be the generally accepted relationship between the board and superintendent, the Supreme Court of Tennessee used the following language:

> The duties of the superintendent are highly important but they do not with respect to essential features of school management override the authority of the school board. Naturally the superintendent's advice will be given much consideration, but the ultimate responsibility and the finality as to choice rests with the school board. It may act on its own sound judgment as to what is required by the public welfare, and

[66]Alexander v. School Dist. No. 1 in Multnomah County, 84 Ore. 172, 164 Pac. 711 (1917); Underwood v. Board of Public Educ. for City of Savannah and Chatham County, 25 Ga. App. 634, 104 S.E. 90 (1920).

contrary to advice from any source, even from the superintendent of schools. The school board is still the master and not the servant.[67]

However, the power of the board is not without limitation. Where it can be shown that the board acted in an arbitrary or capricious manner, the court will not allow teacher transfer. In the *Yoakum* case, some teachers were transferred as far as forty miles from their homes, and others had to travel over mountains and to places difficult to reach in bad weather. Therefore, the court held that the board had acted in a capricious and arbitrary manner. Said the court:

> While unquestionably the school board along with the superintendent was given the right, the latitude and discretion of assigning and transferring teachers within the school system this must be done *for the good of the schools* (emphasis supplied). The teacher should be dealt with considerately . . . [and] the best interests of the school must be intended. Where it is shown that there is an arbitrary or capricious use of power being exercised by those in authority the courts will not tolerate the use of this power.[68]

Is transfer from a high school principalship to the corresponding position in a junior high school a demotion? A case which arose in Louisiana[69] was based upon this question. A tenured high school principal was transferred to a junior high school principalship, a transfer which he contended amounted to a demotion. The lower court ruled that he had no cause for action, inasmuch as a junior high school principal may receive a larger salary, enjoy greater prestige, and have more pleasant duties and a higher status than a senior high school principal. The transfer was not a demotion in the opinion of this court. On appeal, however, the Court of Appeals of Louisiana reversed the lower court, using the following reasoning:

> The tenured teacher is protected from disturbance not only by change in salary, but also by transfer to unpleasant duties, or duties not of the "particular type of teaching position or status which the teacher has attained." For a school board could thus indirectly accomplish the removal of a tenured teacher from the school system, although unable to do so directly by proven charges.[70]

---

[67]Tennessee v. Yoakum, 297 S.W.2d 635 (Tenn. 1957).
[68]*Ibid.*
[69]Verret v. Calcasieu Parish School Bd., 85 So.2d 646 (La. 1956).
[70]*Ibid.*

Suggested Activities

SUMMARIZATION:

Summarize the principles of law applicable to dismissal of the following teachers:

1. The tenure teacher
2. The non-tenure teacher
3. The teacher who is insubordinate
4. The teacher who is subversive

ROLE PLAYING:

Choose a case from this chapter to illustrate a point of law related to dismissal of teachers. Dramatize the case utilizing roles for several members of the class. Refer if necessary to the case as cited in the National Reporter System in completing the roles.

RESOLVED:

That the competency which a board may expect of the teacher extends not only to the subject matter and the control of pupils, but also to the good moral character and reputation of the teacher.

COMPARISON AND CONTRAST:

Distinguish between

1. Breach of contract and legal dismissal
2. Legal and illegal dismissal of teaching personnel
3. Suspension and dismissal

RESEARCH:

What are the grounds for dismissal of the tenure teacher in the state in which you intend to teach? What is the procedure which boards must follow in legally dismissing a tenure teacher?

CASE STUDY:

Case # 1. A ruling of the board of education in San Francisco provided that when a teacher who had been ten years or more in the district was absent on leave for three months or longer, he would be entitled to return to a position equal to or better than the one which he had left. A teacher-principal earning $175 per month took a leave for one semester. Upon her return, she was transferred to the position of principal in another school at $100 per month. She appeared at the school where she was formerly the principal, ready and willing to assume her responsibilities, but the superintendent refused to reinstate her to her former position. She sought reinstatement through mandamus action. Did the board have the power to remove the principal from her former position, and transfer her to a position of lower rank? Is mandamus the proper remedy, or should she resort to an action for damages, as for a breach of contract?

Kennedy v. Board of Educ., 82 Cal. 483, 22 Pac. 1042 (1890).

Case # 2. A teacher was dismissed and the school closed because of lack of funds. The budget included enough money to cover all school expenses including the teacher's salary, but not all taxes were collected. The teacher brought suit to compel the payment of the balance of the annual salary. Is the teacher entitled to the unpaid balance of her salary? What is the principle of law upon which you base your answer?

Rudy v. Poplar Bluff School Dist., 30 Mo. App. 113 (1888).

Further Readings

Burrup, Percy E. *The Teacher and the Public School System* (New York: Harper and Brothers, 1960), Ch. 6.

Carr, William D. "Selected Aspects of the Legal Status of the Public School Teacher in Oklahoma," (Stillwater: Oklahoma State University, 1959), unpublished doctoral dissertation, 133 pp.

Education Court Digest (Emmanuel Bund, publisher, 1957-date).

Edwards, Newton. *The Courts and the Public Schools* (Chicago: University of Chicago Press, 1961), Ch. XVII.

Garber, Lee O., et al. *The Law and the Ohio Teacher* (Danville, Illinois: Interstate Printers and Publishers, 1956).

Hamilton, Robert R. *Legal Rights and Liabilities of Teachers* (Laramie, Wyoming: School Law Publications, 1956).

Messick, John D. *The Discretionary Powers of School Boards* (Durham, N. C.: Duke University Press, 1949).

National Education Association. "The Teacher and the Law," Research Monograph 1959-M3 (September, 1959).

Remmlein, Madaline Kintér. *School Law, Second Edition* (Danville, Illinois: Interstate Printers and Publishers, 1962).

Seitz, Reynolds C. (ed). *Law and the School Principal* (Cincinnati: W. H. Anderson Company, 1961), Ch. 10.

EMERGING CONCEPTS OF SCHOOL LAW

The Student Teacher
in Legal Theory

Chapter XI

THE STUDENT TEACHER

IN LEGAL THEORY

Introduction

The state requirement that persons must have had a specified number of college hours for initial teacher certification is of fairly recent origin in this country, having largely developed since 1900. By 1930, most of the states had begun to require supervised student teaching as a part of the teacher certification requirement. In that year, ten of the states had statutes providing for the establishment of campus laboratory schools and another nine states had off-campus model schools in cooperation with public school systems. After World War II, the rise of the student teaching movement was rapid, and the practice continues to receive widening acceptance as a necessary and essential aspect of the teacher-preparation program in all states.

History of Student Teaching

The local school committee in colonial America examined "those who would teach," and when it found a suitable candidate, it issued him a certificate. Little concern was shown for academic preparation at the college level. The candidate's religious orthodoxy and ability to control "the bigger boys" meant more to the committee than did a college transcript evidencing educational studies in depth. Indeed, because transcripts and college placement papers had not yet come into general usage, the committee often was unable to establish the candidate's preparation level, or whether he had had any formal schooling at all. The candidate was generally expected to provide personal references in the form of letters from pastors or former school committees, but even these were often considered unnecessary.

Formal preparation for teachers was hit-and-miss, consisting generally of attendance at the "common" school, followed by one or two years at the Latin grammar school or academy. If the supply of teachers was limited, the school committee in colonial times might waive the school attendance requirement. This condition gradually led state general assemblies to enact legislation restricting the power of local boards to issue certificates; in some instances the state university was given this prerogative. Eventually, local authority to certificate teachers was withdrawn; certification became the exclusive function of the state. Among the statutory standards which states enacted was one that required persons seeking a teaching license to undergo a certain amount of student teaching as a part of their preparation. Some type of field experience as a prerequisite to teacher certification is now either common practice, or is being considered for adoption in all of the states.

The public schools were in existence long before the states began the practice of requiring student teaching. School districts were locally controlled, and almost entirely supported by local means. Many schools were small in size, often one-room, poorly equipped, and inadequately financed. To superimpose a system of student teaching upon such a base was difficult at the outset. Local school boards were unsure of their authority to use schools for student teaching purposes. In addition, colleges lacked liaison with local boards, and were misunderstood in their attempts to provide field experiences for student teachers. Not infrequently, there was opposition from teachers' groups.

Several factors hastened the acceptance of student teaching as a general practice following World War I. Perhaps the most important of these were the state efforts to overcome the provincialism of local boards and establish normal schools and laboratory schools as a part of the state's educational system. A second factor was professional teachers' groups, which helped promote the idea of the need for student training in actual teaching conditions. The rapid growth of knowledge, and the constant change accompanying the Scientific Revolution further emphasized that longer periods of time were necessary in which to prepare teachers for the complexities of a modern society. The success of internships in medicine, dentistry, and law encouraged educators to adopt student teaching as a technique in preparing teachers following World War II.

The legality of a statute which requires that a person do supervised student teaching to obtain a teacher's certificate is not now generally believed to be open to question. The legislature, in prescribing student teaching for initial certification has, by fiat, imposed upon its educational system a mandate to prepare teachers in a certain manner, and in no other, and the courts have been reluctant to interfere with the intention of the legislative body, unless there is evidence of abuse of the state's power.

Character of Student Teaching Changing

Early practice had the student teacher spending perhaps an hour a day in the classroom and the remainder of the time on the college campus. Thus, the student teaching portion of the total class load was comparatively small. The intention was to give the student a glimpse of the world of teaching, without actually giving him the responsibilities subsequently thought necessary for adequate preparation. Emphasis was on the student *proving* himself in teaching; the classroom situation merely opened the way for the student to take his problems to the supervising teacher and the college coordinator. The majority of such early-day student teaching was done in on-campus laboratory schools.

Today, student teaching is taking on new dimensions. Many of the teachers' colleges, if indeed not the state legislatures themselves, require the student to do practice teaching full-time for a period ranging from six to eighteen weeks. The experience often follows one or more periods of supervised observation in classroom techniques at various grade levels. The scope and depth of the experience have increased to include larger amounts of experimentation and demonstration. Because of the rapid rise in student teacher enrollments, colleges can accommodate only a small proportion of all students in laboratory schools. The majority of student teaching today is done in off-campus situations, most of it in the classrooms of the public schools.

The trend toward a required fifth year of college preparation, with increased amounts of student teaching and internship for initial certification of teachers, is evident. Standard practice in the future, if present tendencies continue, may include one full year of professional internship for beginning teachers. The larger numbers of students, engaged in longer and more intensive field experience, will multiply the possibilities of legal problems arising out of the student teacher relationship. That relationship now is legally nebulous and precarious. In most of the states, student teachers go unrecognized and without particular status in the law. Similarly, the status of regularly certificated teachers and principals in the student teaching situation is not well defined.

It is the purpose of this chapter to explore the legal theory underlying student teaching, and to clarify the rights and liabilities of those preparing for initial certification by this means. The legal rights and liabilities of the critic teacher in the current student teacher situation will also come under consideration.

Authority to Permit Practice Teaching

In the usual student teaching arrangement, the college student-teacher-coordinator assigns the student to a regularly certificated supervising (critic or master) teacher, who acts as a guide and confidant to the teacher-to-be. It is customary practice for the cooperating principal also to be involved in the arrangement. This team of educators assists the student in the necessary observation and planning incident to his role as a prospective teacher. Part of the plan is to allow the student to take over the class and, under the direction of the critic teacher, actually engage in the teaching function.

A number of legal questions immediately come to mind. Since the public schools are obviously for the benefit of the pupils attendant therein, may a board of education legally enter into an agreement in which the critic teachers, usually employees of the public school district, *instruct* student teachers? What is the legal status of the student teacher? The law in most states directs that the one in charge of pupils must be a properly certificated teacher. To what extent may the board delegate its authority to control the schools to another agency, in this case the teacher-training institution?

School boards are creatures of the state, and derive their powers from the state level of government. The power of the school district to contract is only such as is conferred by statute expressly or by fair implication.[1] In the absence of a statute specifically conferring upon the board the authority to enter into a student teacher agreement, what has been the attitude of courts in the matter? The number of

---

[1]Schofield v. School Dist. No. 113, 105 Kan. 343, 184 Pac. 480, 7 A.L.R. 788 (1919).

court cases is small, but the cases have a consistency from which one may generalize that the board may enter into such an agreement so long as *it does not barter away its right of discretion.*

One of the earliest cases arose in Illinois in 1906. A local school district had a contract with the state normal school in which the two, acting concurrently, furnished critic teachers, who were paid in part by the school district. The school board and the board of control of the state normal school jointly exercised control over certain schools in which practice teaching was carried on. The Supreme Court of Illinois declared the contract void on the ground that the local board could not legally delegate to another body the authority and discretion vested in it by law. Said the court:

> It is apparent from the bill that these critic teachers are employed not to instruct the pupils in the public school branches, but to perfect the student teachers of the university in the art of teaching, while the latter are endeavoring to teach the pupils of the common school for the experience thereby afforded. The attempt is to merge two schools into one. The student teachers of the university, without compensation, are practice teaching in the grades of the public schools which are being used by the university as practice schools, and the critic teachers supervise and instruct, not the pupils in the common schools, but the students of the university. The public school board is without authority to employ teachers to perform the duties of the critic teachers. It follows therefore that the contract is void, and that the payment of those teachers out of the funds of the public school is an unlawful diversion of the public money. The complaining taxpayer is injured, and he may have an injunction to prevent the appropriation of the school fund to this purpose.[2]

Said the court further, "Pedagogy has no lawful or proper place in the curriculum of the common schools. As well might law or medicine be found there."[3]

The development of student teaching might not have been possible had the *Lindblad* precedent been allowed to control later practice. Apparently, the court's objection to the contract hinged on two arguments: (1) the local board was delegating some of its power to another body, thus divesting itself of final discretion in matters relating to its control over the public schools, and (2) public money was

---

[2]Lindblad v. Board of Educ. of Normal School Dist., 221 Ill. 261, 77 N.E. 450 (1906).
[3]*Ibid.*

being diverted from its intended use for public school pupils to the benefit of university students, a violation of the stewardship principle.

These objections were disposed of in a 1914 case concerned with a practice teaching arrangement in West Virginia, which set the precedent for later cases, and led to utilization of the local board-university contract now standard practice in several of the states. Under the West Virginia plan, the State Board of Regents of the state colleges furnished the pay for certain critic teachers in the model school, and in addition provided the sum of $1,600, which was paid to the other teachers, representing payment for part-time services rendered student teachers. In return, the local board permitted the use of the Fourth Ward School as a site for observation and practice for the students of the Fairmont State Normal School. An injunction was sought to restrain the board from carrying on a model school in cooperation with the normal school. The Supreme Court of Appeals of West Virginia ruled that the contract was legal. Pointing out that local boards have "exclusive control of the schools within the district" plus the power to "establish and maintain such schools as may be for the best interest of the district," the court said:

> Deeming it to be for the best interests of the district to provide a school or department of practice in teaching for such of the young people residing in the district as desire to qualify themselves thoroughly for the profession of teaching, as in the other cases supposed, the board has made such provision, and, in doing so, seems clearly to have acted within its legal powers. To that body alone, so long as it transgresses no positive law, is left the determination of the question: What educationally is for the best interest of the district?[4]

Two related questions came up for consideration in the *Spedden* case and are worthy of note here. Contentions were made by plaintiffs that student teaching worked a hardship on the pupils, and infringed upon their legal rights. With these contentions the court could not agree.

> The use of the pupils of a public school, as subjects of practice in teaching, by student teachers, under the immediate, direct, and personal control of their regularly employed teachers, and in the regularly prescribed course of study of such pupils, involves no invasion or violation of their legal rights.[5]

[4]Spedden v. Board of Educ. of Independent School Dist. of Fairmont, 74 W. Va. 181, 81 S.E. 724 (1914).
[5]*Ibid.*

To the contention by plaintiffs that school boards might employ only "competent" teachers, and that student teachers did not fall within this category, the court declared:

> The law requires the employment of competent teachers, but there is no express exclusion of assistant or under teachers. The student teachers are not employed, they receive no compensation, nor have they a particle of authority in management or control. While they are dealing with the classes, the regularly employed, competent teachers stand over them to see that the recitations are heard and instruction given according to their own judgment, will and discretion. This involves no delegation of their powers. It is a mere departure or variation in method, which in the opinion of some people is unwise and inefficient, and, in the opinion of others, efficient and helpful.[6]

Finally, with respect to the authority of the board to establish the department in question, in spite of the objections of townspeople, the court declared:

> There may not have been sufficient cause, in the judgment of the majority of the citizens of the district, for the establishment of the department in question, and, if there was, possibly a better system or plan might have been devised; but both questions were nevertheless matters for determination of the board, not the courts nor the citizens.[7]

To the same effect as *Spedden* was an Iowa case which arose in 1919. The arrangement was much like that in the *Spedden* case, calling for critic teachers to be paid from district funds for less than full-time wages, the difference being supplied by the college for so much of their time as was given to their work as critic teachers. The board surrendered no right nor delegated any authority to the college to act for it in the control of the schools, hence this point was not at issue. Some taxpayers brought action to restrain the board from allowing anyone to teach in the public schools except persons legally certificated. After naming several duties and powers of local boards, the Supreme Court of Iowa used these words:

> These are but a few of the multifarious duties required and power conferred upon the district and its board of directors, and for any and all acts fairly within their scope the directors are answerable to no other tribunal than the people,

---

[6]*Ibid.*
[7]*Ibid.*

who elected them to that trust and can replace them by others, if they so express their will at the polls.[8]

To the charge that uncertificated persons were "teaching" in the public schools, the court declared:

> It is doubtful, however, whether the statute prohibiting the employment of uncertified teachers has any application to a case where the person in question does no more than render gratuitous temporary or incidental assistance to a competent and duly certified teacher, who has the room and pupils in her immediate charge and control. It is certainly neither unknown nor reprehensible practice for a responsible teacher in charge of a school or department to call upon bright and promising students or pupils to assist her in some phase of the work of instruction, nor is she open to just condemnation if in so doing she is actuated more by a desire to encourage and develop the capacity of such young persons than by any pressing need of assistance in her work.[9]

Statutory Provision for Student Teaching

It is now well settled that so long as there is no delegation of discretion and the board acts within its powers and in a reasonable manner, it may enter into a contract with a college or university to provide facilities for the conduct of student teaching in the public schools, even though there is no statutory authority for such a contract. A few of the states have left nothing to chance, however, and have enacted statutes providing for contractual agreements between school districts and state colleges. The California Education Code of 1959 reads in part as follows:

> The governing board of any school district may enter into agreements with a state college, the University of California, or any other university or college accredited by the State Board of Education as a teacher education institution, to provide teaching experience through practice teaching and to provide for supervised field experience in the public schools in such areas as may be called for in the requirements of the various authorized credentials for public school service to students enrolled in teacher curricula of such institutions. Any such agreement may provide for the payment for the services rendered by the school district of an amount not to exceed the actual cost to the school district of the services rendered

---

[8]Clay v. Independent School Dist. of Cedar Falls, 187 Iowa 89, 174 N.W. 47 (1919).
[9]*Ibid.*

or such agreement may provide for the rendering of services to the school district of a value not to exceed the actual cost to the school district of the services rendered to the district. The Director of Education and the Regents of the University of California are hereby authorized to enter into such agreements with the governing board of any school district as to any state college, and the University of California, respectively.

All funds received by the governing board of a school district shall be paid by it into the county treasury to the credit of the general fund of the district.[10]

A similar statute passed by the Legislature of Pennsylvania provides that it shall be lawful for the board of trustees of any college and the board of directors of any school district to enter into an agreement, by which all or part of the pupils of the school district may be instructed in the training school of the college upon terms mutually agreeable to the board of trustees and the school board involved. The statute further provides:

It also shall be lawful for the board of trustees of any college and the board of school directors of any district or districts to enter into an agreement, upon terms mutually satisfactory, in accordance with which all or part of the classes of such district or districts may be available for practice teaching facilities for the students of such college. Such actions of the school district or school districts and the boards of trustees of such colleges shall be entered respectively upon the minutes of the respective boards and must be approved by the Superintendent of Public Instruction. The board of trustees of any college may provide for the transportation of students of the college to and from the place or places where such practice teaching facilities are available.[11]

Arizona law provides that every teacher training school established in connection with the state colleges shall be a part of the public school system, and a branch of the public schools of the school district within which the training school is located. The teacher training school shall be under the supervision and management of the board of regents. All teachers in the school, except the principal, shall be employed by the board of regents and the trustees of the school district in which the training school is located, acting jointly.

The school district is required to pay toward the expense of the teacher training school an amount equal to one-half of the school money which it is entitled to have appropriated to it from the state.

---

[10]Cal. Educ. Code § 1095 (1959).
[11]24 Pa. Stat. Ann. § 20-2006 (1949).

The board of regents and the trustees of the school district jointly prescribe rules and regulations governing admission and attendance at the training school for pupils living within the school district. In all other matters, the training school shall be governed by the laws and regulations relating to public schools.[12]

The Arizona law is unique among the states, inasmuch as the courts have consistently held that teachers' colleges do not constitute a part of the public school system. Where the constitution of the state provides that public school funds shall be utilized for the use of pupils in the public schools, the legislature is without power to transfer such funds for the use of a model school in connection with a state teachers' college.

The legislature of Washington passed a statute establishing model schools in each of the teachers' colleges of the state, and instructing the state superintendent of public instruction to apportion to the support of the model school such part of the common-school funds as the local district would have been entitled to if the children attending the model school had attended the public schools. The Supreme Court of Washington restrained the enforcement of the statute on the ground it violated the state constitution.[13] Similar cases in other states support this principle.[14]

Student Teacher Certification

Does the student teacher have the authority to teach, even temporarily, without a certificate where the law is silent on the matter? Apparently he does, so long as he receives no compensation for his teaching. It is universally held that a board may not pay over public moneys to one who lacks the license to teach; the prohibition is not so much against unqualified persons in the schools, as against the illegal disbursement of funds from the public treasury. Only one state, California, has seen fit to authorize the issuance of a temporary certificate to student teachers. Such a practice has certain advantages: (1) the status of the student teacher is legalized and clarified, (2) legal responsibility for one's action is more clearly defined, and (3) any doubt that the student teacher has authority to control the class is dispelled.

---

[12]Ariz. Rev. Stat. § 15-901-3 (1939).

[13]School Dist. No. 20 v. Bryan, 51 Wash. 498, 99 Pac. 28 (1909).

[14]State Female Normal School v. Auditors, 79 Va. 233 (1884); Gordon v. Cornes, 47 N.Y. 608 (1872).

The California Education Code of 1959 provides for student teacher certification in the following language:

> 13158. The superintendent of schools of each county shall issue to persons in training for the teaching service *preliminary certificates of a temporary character.* [Emphasis supplied.]
>
> 13159. A preliminary certificate shall be issued to the holder of a recommendation from a state college, the University of California, or any private university or college accredited by the State Board of Education to train teachers. The certificate shall specifically authorize the holder to do student teaching and to do supervised field experience in such areas as may be called for in the requirements of the various authorized credentials for public school service without salary from district funds, and no student teaching or supervised field experience may be performed without such a certificate. The holder shall be deemed a certificated employee of the district with respect to acts performed by him at the direction, suggestion, or consent of the certificated employees under whose supervision and control the holder performs his duties whether or not such duties are performed entirely in the presence of the employees of the district assigned to supervise the holder.
>
> 13160. Practice teaching shall be of the same kind in the same grades, classes, or types of schools as specified in the recommendation.
>
> 13161. No preliminary certificate shall be granted for a period exceeding two years, nor shall the superintendent of schools collect a fee therefor.[15]

Another section of the California code permits the school board to reimburse student teachers for travel costs accruing from their work in vocational agriculture.[16]

In Arizona, special teacher training schools were established in connection with the schools of the local district in which the college was located. Students in the college might, under rules prescribed by the board of regents of the college, teach in the training schools without being certificated teachers.[17]

The purpose of some state legislation pertaining to student teachers is to protect and "save harmless" the teacher from possible court actions against the critic teacher or the student teacher while engaged in the education of teachers. To that end, the legislature of the state of Connecticut enacted a statute providing that each board of edu-

---

[15]Cal. Educ. Code § 13158-13161 (1959).
[16]Cal. Educ. Code § 13553 (1959).
[17]Ariz. Rev. Stat. § 15-901 (1939).

cation shall protect and save harmless any member of the board, or any teacher, employee, or any other school-connected person from financial loss and expense, including legal fees and costs, if any, arising from any claim, demand, suit or judgment by reason of negligence which results in bodily injury to another person. The save harmless clause extends also to accidental damage or destruction of property belonging to another while in the discharge of the employee's duties within the scope of his employment. The student teacher is covered by the following words in the law:

> For the purposes of this section, the term "teacher" shall include any student teacher doing practice teaching under the direction of a teacher employed by a town board of education or by the state board of education.[18]

Liability of Student Teacher for Tort

When the student teacher has charge of a class, and an injury to a pupil occurs, who may be held liable for the damages? No case has arisen in a state in which the doctrine of governmental immunity applies. Two cases involving the liability of student teachers have arisen, both of them in New York, which is a state in which school districts are held liable for the negligent torts of their employees. In 1939, a seventh grade pupil at the Cortland State Normal School, an institution maintained and controlled by the state, was a member of a class in physical education in the laboratory school. The course was mandatory, and a student teacher, a junior in college, was in charge of the class. One of the required exercises for all pupils was one known as the headstand. The student teacher directed a student to do the headstand. In complying, the student suffered a dislocated vertebra, and presented a claim against the state to recover damages on the ground that the school authorities were negligent.

The court was unwilling to assert that the injury was "an unavoidable accident." In holding that there had indeed been negligence the court said:

> That the school authorities, for whose acts the state is answerable, were negligent is not even a debatable question. They compelled a child of tender years to participate in a dangerous exercise without any attempt to comply with the rule relating to supervision adopted by the Board of Regents. It is no answer to say that even if properly supervised the

---

[18]Conn. Gen. Stat. Ann. § 10-235 (1959).

child might have been injured. We are also convinced that the state was grossly negligent in requiring immature children to perform a headstand. It seems to us that anyone with any sense of intelligence would anticipate grave danger to result from such a performance. If children are forcibly taken from their parents and guardians by the state and compelled to perform such fantastic and perilous antics as the headstand then the state should be held strictly to account for the safety of the children. Compelling children, especially young girls, to stand on their heads and turn somersaults as part of their education is distinctly unique and novel. Perhaps our notions on the subject of education are outmoded but the view that exercises such as these form a necessary part of education impresses us as being absurd.[19]

Judgment in the amount of $3,000 was entered for the plaintiff student against the state as a result of the injury sustained. One judge dissented, maintaining that the amount of the judgment was excessive, since it represented more than the actual cost of medical treatment for the student.

The second case involved an injury to a high school senior who sought admission to college. As a prerequisite for admission, certain mental and physical tests were administered to the applicants. The professor in charge of the tests enlisted the aid of several senior college students, one of whom administered the tests while another recorded the results. While performing one of the tests, the plaintiff received a serious injury to her left knee. The professor in charge of the tests was not present at the time of the accident.

The court found that the Courtland State Teachers College owed the claimant a duty of reasonable care in the conduct of the tests to which she was required to submit to gain consideration of her application for admission to the college. It was also the court's ruling that if the test had been administered to the plaintiff by or under the direct supervision of a qualified and experienced tester, the accident would not have occurred. Said the court, in awarding judgment for the claimant and against the State of New York in the amount of $7,500:

> The New York State Board of Regents requires that in order to teach physical education a teacher "must have completed a four-year approved high school course followed by four years of academic and professional training leading to a degree or its equivalent as approved by the Commissioner of Education." A similar standard of care, competence and super-

---

[19]Gardner v. State, 256 App. Div. 385, 10 N.Y.S.2d 274 (1939).

> vision should be required in the administration of the physical fitness index tests. There is no persuasive proof that Patrick [the senior student] had himself received sufficient instructions in the administration of the leg lift test, that he was aware that the test could be dangerous, or that he had sufficient experience to anticipate or recognize any evidence of strain, overexertion or erroneous technique on the part of the person to be tested. It is extremely doubtful that the claimant received proper instructions from Patrick on how to take the test. She was not instructed to do any warm up exercises prior to the taking of the test, a procedure recommended by the experts.[20]

While the amount awarded by the court was more than the actual medical expenses incurred, the court felt that the permanent injury sustained by the claimant, and the fact that she would be precluded from engaging in physical contact sports in the future, or pursuing a career as a physical education instructor, entitled her to the excess amount above actual expenses. Judgment was accordingly directed in favor of the plaintiff and against the State of New York.

The absence of reported cases involving student injury which occurred when the student was under the direction of a student teacher in a state in which the immunity doctrine applies leaves the student of school law to conjecture concerning liability for such injury. It is without doubt that the student teacher would be liable for any injury resulting from his negligence. Of course, the same defenses that are available to a regularly certified teacher are also available to a student teacher. The fact that no case of this kind has been reported may be taken as indicative of the care with which student teachers have conducted their classes.

It seems reasonable to assume that if injury did come to a student in a class situation controlled by a student teacher, any resultant litigation might be brought against the critic teacher or the school administrator as well as the negligent student teacher. The liability of the critic teacher or the administrator would rest on the facts of the particular case—that is, to the extent the critic teacher remained legally responsible for the conduct within the classroom even while the student teacher took charge of the learning activity, and whether the school administrator had relieved the critic teacher of his responsibility or had negligently placed the student teacher completely in charge. The language of the courts quoted earlier in this chapter suggests that the critic teacher retains complete charge of the class

---

[20]Brittain v. State, 200 Misc. 743, 103 N.Y.S.2d 485 (1951).

and remains primarily responsible at law for everything that occurs within the classroom. For this reason, a critic teacher should not leave the classroom, even when the instruction is being provided by an apparently competent student teacher, unless he has been authorized to do so by the school administrator.

It is generally believed that student teachers will profit most from their practice teaching if they are sometimes given the complete freedom and responsibility generally enjoyed by the regular teacher in the classroom. Because most state legislatures and boards of education have not specifically provided for such unsupervised student teaching, the critic teacher is not free to abandon his legal responsibility and liability for the conduct of the class.

Legal Rights of the Student Teacher

Kolson has pointed out that no matter how hard the university and school district employees may try to remedy the situation, a basic difference exists between actual teaching and student teaching.

> It cannot be denied that the student teacher does not have complete authority. She is "second boss" and it does not take children long to come to this conclusion. Since "no man can serve two masters," the children give first loyalty to the regular teacher.[21]

The result is that children find there is someone who symbolizes authority but does not have the power or legal right to make misbehavior unprofitable. This person, who is above them but below the regular teacher, is the student teacher. Lacking legal authority, the student teacher must establish by careful planning and professional performance a classroom atmosphere that will not only let the children know the limitations of acceptable behavior, but that will challenge the children to act in an exemplary manner.

Haines stated:

> Legally, the student teacher has no authority in the classroom. He should not punish a child; he does not promote or fail pupils. He has, however, the responsibilities of a teacher, within the areas of his functioning, without the authority or professional status. For some students, it is difficult to sense when to take a stand with pupils and when to defer to the teacher's judgment.[22]

[21]Clifford J. Kolson. "The Student Teacher and Discipline," *Peabody Journal of Education* (November, 1957), pp. 156-159.
[22]Aleyne Clayton Haines. "Role Dilemmas in Student Teaching," *Journal of Teacher Education* (December, 1957), p. 367.

The student teacher should avoid creating any situation which might eventually involve legal entanglements. The courts would no doubt construe the student teacher's legal rights as very limited in a case concerning pupil discipline.

The members of the student teaching team have a professional obligation to the student teacher, inasmuch as the latter's legal status is obscure. Said Martin,[23] in discussing the role of team members in assisting the student teacher to control the class:

> The principal, too, has a key role in this matter. The teacher needs to know that she has support if needed. The principal who tells his teachers that classroom discipline is within the confines of the classroom walls is shirking his duty.

The board of education likewise has a leading role in assisting the student teacher:

> Since the school board is the policy making body of any district, it should have policies regarding discipline; *and* the teacher should know what the policy is. Similar to the pupil-teacher relationship, the teacher can experience security only by knowing where she stands, her rights, responsibilities, and obligations. Board policy must be consistent.[24]

But it is the critic teacher who best understands the students in his classroom and who can render the greatest assistance to the student teacher in matters of pupil discipline. He can set the tone for student conduct, anticipate problems, and helpfully suggest workable procedure for the student teacher.

What are some of the other areas involving the rights of student teachers? Does the student teacher have the right of privileged communication as does the regular teacher? It is well settled that certificated teachers may report with immunity certain information concerning pupils which might be damaging to the pupils' reputations. What of the student teacher in like circumstances? Do the same rules of reasonableness, good faith, and lack of maliciousness apply to the student teacher as they do to the regular teacher? The courts have had no case of this nature before them for adjudication.

Sometimes the student teacher is asked to substitute for the regular teacher. May the student teacher be used in this way? If so, may he be paid for his services? May the board expend public funds for

---

[23]John E. Martin. "Discipline, the Student Teacher's Nemesis," *Educational Forum* (January, 1961), pp. 213-214.
[24]*Ibid.*

payment to one who lacks the certificate? The student teacher should be aware that no claim attaches against the board for teaching services rendered by one without the teaching license. No vested right can ever accrue to the benefit of the certificateless teacher, no matter how long he may teach, or how much the board may appreciate his work.

Finally, what is the legal right of a student teacher who receives injury during student teaching? In California, a student teacher was injured while engaged in student teaching in a public school of that state. The question was whether she was entitled to compensation from the district under the state's workmen's compensation act. The legislature of California provided that

> The holder [of a preliminary certificate] shall be deemed a a certificated *employee* (emphasis supplied) of the district with respect to acts performed by him at the direction, suggestion, or consent of the certificated employees under whose supervision and control the holder performs his duties whether or not such duties are performed entirely in the presence of the employees of the district assigned to supervise the holder.[25]

Under this statute, the student teacher contended that she was entitled, as an *employee* of the district, to compensation for her injury. The Supreme Court of California agreed and upheld a ruling of the State Industrial Accident Commission to that effect. It should be remembered that California certificates student teachers temporarily while they are engaged in the student teaching function.[26]

To the opposite effect was an Illinois case[27] in which a senior student in a boys' private school received an injury while supervising boys on a boating expedition. The court refused to hold that the senior student was an employee of the district. It is unlikely that the courts in most of the states would hold that there was an employer-employee relationship in the usual student teaching situation.

Suggested Activities

CASE STUDY:

Case # 1. A student of junior high school age was injured in the gymnasium while a student teacher was in charge; the critic teacher was absent from the room at the time. A boy charged into a wall

---

[25]Cal. Educ. Code § 13159 (1959).

[26]State Compensation Ins. Fund v. Industrial Accident Comm'n of Cal., 22 CCC 212.

[27]Todd School for Boys v. Industrial Accident Comm'n, 412 Ill. 453, 107 N.E.2d 745 (1952).

while dribbling the basketball in an intra-mural game, and received a concussion. The state in which the accident occurred was one in which school districts are not held liable for torts arising out of the actions of their employees or agents. Is the student teacher liable for the student's injury?

Case #2. A student teacher completed student teaching, but was advised by the college supervisor that he would not make a satisfactory teacher. The state was one in which student teaching is required as a qualification for certification. Is the student teacher legally entitled to certification even though in the opinion of the college authorities he will not make a satisfactory teacher?

Case #3. In a junior high school social studies class, a boy created a disturbance, and the student teacher kept him in after school. The detention was with the knowledge and consent of the critic teacher, who was present after school but not at the time that the punishment was meted out. Is the student teacher legally liable for disciplining the pupil in this particular way?

DISCUSSION:

1. In what ways is student teaching legally similar to regular teaching; in what ways different?
2. How do you think student teaching will be carried on fifteen years from now? 25 years?

RESOLVED:

1. That the student teacher should be considered an employee of the district while engaged in student teaching.
2. That the student teacher should be certificated temporarily while doing student teaching.
3. That the student teacher should be allowed to receive pay for services rendered outside the regular student teaching function.

SUMMARIZE:

1. The state laws relating to student teaching in the state in which you will do your student teaching.
2. The rights and responsibilities of student teachers in most of the states.
3. The comparative apprenticeship and internship rights and responsibilities among the other professions with that of the student teacher.

Further Readings

Edwards, Newton. *The Courts and the Public Schools* (Chicago: University of Chicago Press, 1955), pp. 157-159.

Haines, Aleyne C. "Role Dilemmas in Student Teaching," *Journal of Teacher Education* (December, 1957), pp. 365-368.

Kolson, Clifford J. "The Student Teacher and Discipline," *Peabody Journal of Education* (November, 1957), pp. 156-159.

Martin, John E. "Discipline, the Student Teacher's Nemesis," *Educational Forum* (January, 1961), pp. 213-214.

Mead, A. R. "Legal Status of Laboratory Schools and Teacher Education Practices," *Journal of Teacher Education* (December, 1957), pp. 356-364.

Schultz, Raymond E. *Student Teaching in the Secondary Schools* (New York: Harcourt, Brace and Company, 1959), pp. 360-393.

Seitz, Reynolds C. (ed). *Law and the School Principal* (Cincinnati: W. H. Anderson Company, 1961), Ch. 9.

Tieszen, D. W., and Charles M. Foreman. "Student Teaching—Some Legal Considerations," *Journal of Teacher Education* (June, 1961), pp. 216-218.

APPENDIX

*Literature and Organizations
in School Law*

LITERATURE AND ORGANIZATIONS
IN SCHOOL LAW

Current Status of School Law

Said Garber, in discussing the emergence of school law as an
evolving discipline in 1959:

> It may be said that up to about 1930 school law was in its
> infancy. By 1940, it had reached adolescence. Today it is
> attaining adulthood. As a field for the training of administra-
> tors, it has at last the same respectability accorded such other
> fields as business management and school finance.[1]

One might add, hopefully, that the same acceptance should very
soon be accorded school law as a study in the preparation of all of
tomorrow's teachers. Reports on the scope and extent of the study of
law in teacher preparation are often incomplete or in conflict. A
growing general interest in school law, however, is evidenced in
increased legal literature, activity, and organizational development
that should be of interest to all students of school law.[2]

The literature. Most of the early writings in the field of school
law, never extensive in scope, are now out of print. Nevertheless, an
increased activity in this area has been apparent since 1950, and bids
well to continue. Noteworthy among the newer books are those by

---

[1]Lee O. Garber. "School Law in Retrospect," *The Yearbook of School Law*
(Danville, Illinois: Interstate Printers and Publishers, 1959), pp. 157-171.

[2]See "Is School Law in Tune with the Times?" by E. C. Bolmeier. *Yearbook of
School Law* (Danville, Illinois: Interstate Printers and Publishers, 1962), pp. 185-
198.

Gauerke[3] and Remmlein[4] in the textbook field, and Rezny and Remmlein in legal research.[5]

A series of yearbooks entitled the *Legal Problems of Education Series,* published in 1958, 1959, and 1961, under the auspices of the National Organization on Legal Problems in Education is worthy of the attention of the serious student of school law. These books relate to the work of the school superintendent,[6] the principal,[7] and existing forms of school laws.[8] The series is an excellent general reference for the student, inasmuch as the contributors include most of the leading writers in the field of school law today.

Another general reference in the growing literature of the field is *The Yearbook of School Law* series,[9] which was begun in 1933 by Dr. M. M. Chambers and has become an annual publication. In 1950, after a brief pause in publication, the project was revived under the editorship of Lee O. Garber of the University of Pennsylvania, a prolific writer as well as one of the leading authorities in this fast-developing discipline.[10]

The student is directed to the yearbooks for current trends in school law since 1933.[11] In the present book, references for further reading are listed at the conclusion of each chapter for the use of the student. In addition, a rather extensive bibliography is provided in Rezny and Remmlein.[12]

School law at the state level. Initially, state departments of education exercised a *regulatory* function over the public schools, but this exercise has largely given way in recent years to the *leadership*

---

[3]Warren E. Gauerke. *Legal and Ethical Responsibilities of School Personnel* (Englewood Cliffs: Prentice-Hall, 1959), 302 pp.

[4]Madaline K. Remmlein. *School Law, Second Edition* (Danville, Illinois: Interstate Printers and Publishers, 1962), 346 pp.

[5]Arthur A. Rezny and Madaline K. Remmlein. *A Schoolman in the Law Library* (Danville, Illinois: Interstate Printers and Publishers, 1962), 64 pp.

[6]Robert L. Drury (ed). *Law and the School Superintendent* (Cincinnati: W. H. Anderson Company, 1958), 339 pp.

[7]Reynolds C. Seitz (ed). *Law and the School Principal* (Cincinnati: W. H. Anderson Company, 1961), 266 pp.

[8]Madaline K. Remmlein and Martha L. Ware. *An Evaluation of Existing Forms of School Laws* (Cincinnati: W. H. Anderson Company, 1959), 253 pp.

[9]Lee O. Garber. *The Yearbook of School Law* (Danville, Illinois: Interstate Printers and Publishers, 1933 to date).

[10]See Lee O. Garber. *Law and the School Business Manager* (Danville, Illinois: Interstate Printers and Publishers, 1957), 331 pp.

[11]For example, see "Annotated Bibliography of Recent Studies in School Law" in *The Yearbook of School Law, 1962,* pp. 210-221.

[12]Rezny and Remmlein, *op. cit.,* pp. 61-64.

function. While state departments spend considerable time in advising local school authorities and legislators on existing and proposed school laws, it remains the primary function of the state department to carry out the wishes of the legislature with respect to education. This task is accomplished in many states through a state board of education, a state educational commissioner, or both. Rules and regulations of state departments of education have the force and effect of law, and the departments are charged with the interpretation of such laws to local officials and others. In many states, the state department compiles and distributes the state educational laws, and calls upon the attorney-general to interpret a point of law in the event of confusion. In others, the state department may be called upon to draft proposed legislation when asked by the legislature or state board of education to do so.

In 1961, the United States Office of Education reported that with but few exceptions, the organization at the state level was not entirely adequate for handling the day-to-day legal problems arising within the states, much less permit state departments of education to make contributions to the literature of school law. This was due in part to a shortage of qualified legal personnel in state departments of education for this purpose.[13]

School law in colleges and universities. Collegiate courses in school law are of comparatively recent development. As late as 1900, there were no courses of any kind at the college level to prepare school administrators for the job of administering the schools. In that year, Teachers College, Columbia offered two courses for prospective administrators, and by 1950 more than 300 colleges and universities had entered the field. Administration courses today number well into the thousands. The study of school law at the college level began for administrators in 1922, when Professor Newton Edwards offered such a course at the University of Chicago, but other colleges were slow in introducing school law into their curricula.

In 1955, a questionnaire was sent to 81 teacher-training institutions to determine the extent of school law education offered by each. Seventy institutions returned questionnaires, of which 56 reported offering a separate course in school law. Eleven others reported they offered no separate course, but that units on legal theory were included in related courses for administrators. In both cases, however, school

---

[13]M. A. McGhehey. "Research and Reporting Activities in Legal Problems of Education," (Washington: U. S. Office of Education Bulletin #OE-23011, 1961), p. 10.

law was open to graduate students only, since but two institutions reported school law was required of teachers at the undergraduate level.

School law courses were reported under a variety of titles, and included a wide range of content. In only a few institutions did the school of education report a working arrangement with their college of law. Furthermore, there was an almost complete lack of courses devoted to the study of research techniques in the field of school law.[14] Only a handful of states have seen fit to require school law of teachers for initial certification. Garber[15] reported that most courses in this field for teachers were, until recent times, "more or less superficial."

Organizations. The school law field was slow to organize on the national level, despite a growing interest in the subject by national groups. The necessary impetus was given organization in 1954 by the Kellogg Foundation, which sponsored a successful law conference at Duke University as a part of the Cooperative Program in Educational Administration (CPEA). Subsequent to the conference, the National Organization on Legal Problems of Education (NOLPE) was formed, and within a decade had more than 300 members, chiefly from among school administrators, attorneys interested in school law, school board members, and educational administration professors. Mention has already been made of the three NOLPE yearbooks,[16] which have been instrumental in stimulating growth of interest in the subject of school law. NOLPE annually sponsors a two-day conference for the discussion of current legal problems in education.

Publications. As organizations develop, as the literature in school law receives wider attention, and as state and national educational groups realize the importance of having teachers well informed in their legal rights and responsibilities, school law will assume its full stature in the curricula of teacher training institutions and teacher in-service programs.

The following publications relating to school law are noteworthy:

Association for Student Teaching. *Teacher Education and the Public Schools* (Dubuque, Iowa: William C. Brown Company, 1961), 291 pp.

Bolmeier, E. C. "Directions in School Law," *American School Board Journal* (December, 1959), pp. 33-35.

---

[14]National Education Association. "Your College and School Law," (Washington: The Association, 1955), 17 pp.

[15]Lee O. Garber. "School Law in Retrospect," *Yearbook of School Law, 1959* (Danville, Illinois: Interstate Printers and Publishers, 1959), p. 162.

[16]Drury, Seitz, and Remmlein and Ware, *op. cit.*

————. "Is School Law in Tune with the Times?" *Yearbook of School Law*, 1962, pp. 185-198.

————. "Teacher and School Law," *Elementary School Journal* (December, 1954), pp. 209-218.

Eastmond, Jefferson N. *The Teacher and School Administration* (Boston: Houghton Mifflin Company, 1959), Ch. 5—The Teacher and the State, pp. 93-112.

Jones, Rolland W. "The Legal Rights and Legal Liabilities Involved in Pupil-School Relationships in the Colorado Public Schools," (Denver: University of Denver, 1961), unpublished doctoral dissertation, 189 pp.

National Education Association. *The Teacher and the Law* (Washington: The Association, September, 1959), Research Monograph 1959-M3, 92 pp.

Overholser, Winfred. *The Psychiatrist and the Law* (New York: Harcourt, Brace, 1953), 147 pp.

Reutter, E. Edmund, Jr. "Essentials of School Law for Educators," *Teachers College Record* (May, 1958), pp. 441-449.

Schultz, Raymond E. *Student Teaching in the Secondary Schools* (New York: Harcourt, Brace and Company, 1959), Appendix C—The Law's View of the Teacher, pp. 360-393.

Thayer, V. T. *The Role of the School in American Society* (New York: Dodd, Mead and Company, 1960), 530 pp.

INDEX OF CASES CITED BY STATE

A

Alabama, 195, 217, 219, 223, 224-25, 226, 256
Alaska, 275
Arizona, 126, 244, 295
Arkansas, 162, 182, 217, 221, 222, 293

C

California, 61, 74, 104, 118-19, 121, 145-46, 148-49, 165, 181-83, 191, 192-93, 223, 231, 237, 248, 249, 278, 282, 284, 286, 302, 323
Colorado, 60, 61, 62-63, 65, 82, 85-87, 89, 144, 274, 285, 294
Connecticut, 184-85, 209-10, 220-21, 238, 267

D

Delaware, 97, 99-100, 146-47
District of Columbia, 129

F

Florida, 141, 180, 183

G

Georgia, 300

I

Idaho, 227, 262-63
Illinois, 24, 26, 101, 129, 133, 149-50, 151, 161, 183-84, 187, 214, 231, 273, 282, 284, 285, 289, 295, 311, 323
Indiana, 48, 51, 90-91, 92, 99, 101, 121, 122-23, 126, 128, 142, 150, 151, 182, 231, 272
Iowa, 88, 89-90, 131-32, 209, 215-16, 221, 225, 226, 231, 233, 299, 314

K

Kansas, 28, 148, 223, 228, 233, 268, 274, 294, 298, 310
Kentucky, 47, 62, 73, 91-92, 163, 191-92, 209, 281, 285

L

Louisiana, 26, 28, 47, 116, 157, 159, 164, 221, 256-57, 290, 295, 301

M

Maryland, 236, 260-61
Massachusetts, 27, 50, 142-43, 214, 280, 288
Michigan, 20, 21, 186, 200-01, 210, 214, 223, 226, 231, 248, 274, 277, 293
Minnesota, 61-62, 111-12, 115-16, 123, 129, 130-31, 222, 286-87
Mississippi, 92, 223, 225, 228, 231
Missouri, 87, 97-98, 100-01, 188-89, 198-99, 210, 222, 232, 261, 288, 298, 303
Montana, 122, 130, 184, 188, 213-14, 279

N

Nebraska, 64-65, 84, 279
New Hampshire, 15-16, 215
New Jersey, 26, 133, 134, 143, 163, 226, 264, 297
New Mexico, 124, 131, 164
New York, 26-27, 120, 147, 154, 162, 163-64, 166, 170-71, 173-74, 176-79, 185-86, 190, 194, 195, 200, 215, 216, 233, 235-36, 238, 246, 249-50, 251-52, 254, 256, 276, 282, 285, 290, 316, 319, 320
North Carolina, 87, 256, 257
North Dakota, 217, 225, 236-37

O

Ohio, 91, 125-26, 220, 229, 232-33
Oklahoma, 104, 179, 191, 217, 223, 278, 292, 299
Oregon, 24, 25-27, 152, 181, 211-12, 231, 254-55, 288, 300

P

Pennsylvania, 27, 61, 89, 97, 116-17, 141, 149, 155, 157-58, 160-61, 166, 168, 172-73, 194, 197, 214, 234-35, 236, 244, 264, 283, 291, 293

S

South Carolina, 200
South Dakota, 88

T

Tennessee, 141-42, 152, 174-75, 220, 228-29, 301
Texas, 151, 201, 230, 232, 238

U

Utah, 151

V

Vermont, 208-09
Virginia, 124, 198, 222, 244, 316

W

Washington, 187, 212, 247, 316
West Virginia, 27, 235, 281, 288, 296, 312
Wisconsin, 175-76, 214, 222, 242, 268, 280
Wyoming, 281

INDEX OF TOPICS

A

Academic freedom, 174-77
Academies, 19-20, 308
Accreditation
  agencies in, 76-77
  defined, 55, 75-77
  value of, 76
Agents
  and employees, 4, 139
  in automobile injury, 262-63
  of the state, 243, 324
  of the teacher, 262
  negligence of the, 254-55
Alcott, William A., 68-69
Allen, Ira M., 83
American legal system
  court action
    defined, 38
  courts
    federal, 34-36
    juvenile, 37
    state, 37-38
  law
    common, 32-33
    defined, 31
    finding the, 46-50
    judge-made, 33
    sources of, 31-33
    types of, 32-33
Annual contract, 113, 120, 273
Assault and battery, 208-09, 218, 219-21, 238
Attorney-general, 85-86, 99
Automobiles, 3, 4, 238, 262-63

B

Bible reading, 236
Boards of Education
  and breach of contract, 105-07, 273-74
  and certification, 308
  and contracting, 84-87, 97-98, 111-ff.
  and flag salute, 223, 235
  and immunity doctrine, 242-45
  and married students, 227-29
  and method of dismissal, 274, 276-77, 279, 286-87, 289
  and mitigation of damages, 292
  and mode of contracting, 97-98
  and parents, 236, 238
  and retirement, 118-19
  and school patrols, 259
  and student health, 263-64
  and student teachers, 310
  and tenure, 111-12, 118-19, 122-ff.
  colonial, 93-95
  implied powers of, 103-04, 271
  liability of, 267
  limitations
    in delegation of authority, 311
    in dismissing teachers, 273-76, 288, 289, 294-95
  minutes of the, 92
  powers of, 9-11, 217, 235
  responsibility
    to pay minimum salaries, 152-53
  rights
    to assign pupils, 215-16
    to bargain collectively, 183-84
    to charge fees, 216-17
    to charge tuition, 217
    to communicate, 193-94
    to control secret societies, 231, 233
    to dismiss personnel, 111-12, 125-29, 155-56, 271-73, 280-81
    to fix salaries, 140-44
    to provide leaves of absence, 153-54

to purchase insurance, 164-65, 245
to reduce salaries, 143-44
to regulate student dress, 224-26
to transfer teachers, 122-ff., 144, 299-301
to withhold diploma, 225, 233
rules and regulations
enforcement of, 217-18
in control of pupils, 207, 210, 213, 215
incorporated in contracts, 99-102, 147
limiting athletic participation, 230-31
special meetings of, 86-87
tort liability of, 224
ultra vires acts of, 84, 125, 229, 232
written policies of, 94, 218
Burrup, Percy, 70

C

Caps and gowns, rules governing, 225, 233
Certification
as a personal privilege, 58, 61
as a prerequisite to employment, 58, 62-63
as a prerequisite to salary, 58, 63-64, 65
by local boards, 68-70
colonial, 68, 307-08
confusion concerning, 56
court cases on, 57
defined, 55-56
examinations for, 60, 68-71
grandfather clauses, 72
history of, 68-71
hopeful signs, 72
legal framework underlying, 57
limitations of the, 57-59
need to improve, 72
number of, 57
of student teachers, 316-18, 324
preparation for, 71-72
purposes of, 66-67
qualifications for, 59-61
reciprocity in, 72
research in, 56
revocation of, 74-75, 105-07
right to a certificate, 59-61, 68-69, 73-75
state and, 73-75, 106

sub-standard, 71-72
Chambers, M. M., 330
Common school
as seen by Jefferson, 13-14
defined, 13
in history, 68-69
in the law, 21-23
Communications
between board and superintendent, 193-94
by teachers about pupils, 191-93
from one teacher to another, 194
from third parties to teachers, 194-95
privileged, 190
Compulsory attendance, 211-12
Condon-Wadlin Act, 185-86
Contracts
annual, 113-14
and fraud, 88-90
and superintendent, 85
automatic, 98, 101, 127
binding, 89-90, 103-07, 128
board powers in, 84-85, 141
board rules read into, 95, 100-02
breach of, penalties for, 105-07
capacity to, 83
comprehensiveness of, 89
considerations under, 91-92, 94-95
continuing contract, 97-98, 101, 113-14, 124-29
contractual relationship, 82-ff.
defined, 82
duties under, 94, 148-49
early colonial, 23, 93-95
earmarks of good, 102-03
elements of valid, 82-93
eligibility to, 83
executory, 92
impairing the obligations of, 127, 143
implied, 63, 88
"jumping," 106-07
legislation and, 97-98, 120
manner and mode of, 86, 97-98
offer and acceptance, 87-88
of today, 95-96
outside influences affecting, 95-102, 147, 150
provisions in, 98
ratification of, 103-04
renewal of, 104-05, 113, 124-26
sample, 96

short form of, 96
teacher's, 81-ff., 111-ff.
terms of the, 92-93
voidable, 65, 103-04
written, 88, 94, 104
Corporal punishment
limitations on, 218-19
use of, 207, 218-19
v. expulsion, 221
County superintendent, 85, 193-94, 300
Court decisions
in contracting, 102
in determining rights of individuals, 234
Court system, 34-38
Cubberley, Ellwood, 12, 19

D

Damages,
liquidated, 298
mitigation of, principle, 292
Dancing, 212, 223, 237
Dartmouth College case, 15-16
Defamation of character
by teacher, 189
defined, 189
Dismissal of teachers
before entering upon duties, 293
for "cause," 125, 175-76, 184-85, 272, 274, 287
for immorality, 280-81
for incompetency, 74, 155-56, 171-72, 272, 279, 282-84, 293
for insubordination, 278-80, 299
for justifiable decrease in teaching positions, 198-99, 289-90
for lack of cooperation, 279
for marriage, 125, 276, 287-89
for miscellaneous reasons, 64, 160-62, 291
for neglect of duty, 161, 284-87
for subversion, 168-69, 177-79, 290-91
for unprofessional conduct, 182-83, 272, 281-82
in general, 124-27, 271-73
of a tenure teacher, 124-29, 275-77
District attorney, 193-94
Districts, school
as quasi-corporations, 10
established, 10

immunity of, 11
size of, 308
Douglas, Lawrence M., 57
Duties of teachers
in damages, 224
in loco parentis, 206-08, 246
in tort, 241-42, 245-ff., 257-58
to answer questions, 169-70
to be ethical, 106-07
to be loyal, 180, 290
to conduct themselves well, 194-95
to follow board rules, 278
to fulfill contract, 106-07, 299-301
to make up lost time, 150-51
to protect pupils, 266
under contract, 105-07, 148-49

E

Edwards, Newton, 24, 331
Employees
as agents, 4, 139
teachers as, 138-39, 186
welfare rights of, 137-ff.
Epidemic
exclusion of pupils on basis of, 214
Errands, 262
Extra-curricular activities, 262-63

F

Federal government
amendments, 18-19
land grants, 17-18
Feinberg law, 177-79, 290
Field trips, 259-62
invitees, 261
licensees, 260
Fifth Amendment, 169-70, 172-73
Fire drills, 266
First Amendment, 18-19, 168-69, 235-36
Flag salute, 223, 235
Flower, Enoch, 22, 23
Fourteenth Amendment, 18, 171-75, 236
Franklin, Benjamin, 19

G

Garber, Lee O., 330, 332
Gauerke, Warren, 70

H

Habeas corpus, 17
Haines, Aleyne, 321
Hamilton and Reutter, 291
Hansen, Kenneth, 12, 23
Harvard, 13-14
Hazards, 4, 246, 248-49, 250, 256-57, 266
Higher education, 14-16
High schools, 19-21
Home instruction, 212-13
Huggett and Stinnett, 56

I

Immunity doctrine, 242, 265
Incompetency, 74, 155-56, 171-72, 272, 279, 282-84, 293
In loco parentis, 206-08, 218-19, 246, 257, 264
Insubordination, 278-80, 299
defined, 278

J

Jefferson, Thomas, 14, 15
Jehovah's Witnesses, 235

K

Kalamazoo case, 20-21
Kolson, Clifford, 321

L

La Bue, Anthony, 68
Laches
defined, 164
loss of rights through, 294
Law; *see* School Law
Leaves of absence, 101
Legislation
and contracting, 97
and student teachers, 309, 314-16
attendance, 213
guest statute, 263
school patrols, 258-59
tenure, 114, 275-76
Liability
avoidance of, 265-67
defenses against, 252-57
for improper supervision; *see* Supervision
in privately owned cars, 262-63

insurance against, for teachers, 262
of school's employees, 245-47
of teachers, 241-42, 245-ff.
under guest statute, 263
waivers of, 257-58
Libel, 190, 241
Litigation
needless, 8
possibility of, 310

M

Mandamus
defined, 73
use of, 74
Mann, Horace, 69
Marriage, pupil, 227-29
Martin, John. E., 322
Maternity leave, teacher, 155-58
Mather, Cotton, 205-06
Merit pay, 144-47
Minimum salary laws, 152-53

N

National Labor Relations Act, 184-87
National Reporter System, 47-50
Negligence
and third parties, 249-50
assumption of risk, 252, 254-55
comparative, 253
contributory, 252-53, 255-57
defenses against, 252-57
defined, 245
in training student teachers, 24
of the teacher, 246-ff.
Negroes, 24, 27-29, 123-24, 142, 197-98, 216
New England Primer, 206
Normal schools, 69
Nuisance, 4

O

Oaths and affirmations, 180, 290

P

Parental rights
and compulsory attendance, 216
and home instruction, 212-13
and pupil punishments, 220-21, 225
and school rules, 236-38
to control children at school, 210, 215-16, 236-38

to determine medical treatment, 263-65
Parents
  colonial, 205-06
  objections, 212, 215, 223, 231
  penalties assessed against, 211
  required to pay for damages to school property, 226-27
  waiver of liability, 257-58
Parol evidence
  in clarifying contract, 88-89
Patrols, pupil, 258-59
Police power
  and constitutional rights, 233-36
  and vaccination, 214
  defined, 66
Political office
  teachers' right to hold, 101
Prayers, 235-36
Pregnancy of pupils, 229
Pregnancy of teachers, 283
Probationary period, 120-22
Professional growth of teachers, 7-8
Proximate cause, 4
Psychology
  and the law, 7
Pupil discipline and control
  colonial, 205-06
  constitutional rights, 312
  dress of, 224-26
  entrance age of, 213-14
  injuries to, 241-ff.
  medical treatment, 238, 263-65
  outside school hours, 208-10
  participation in athletics, 230-231
  suspension and expulsion, 222-224
Pupils
  and corporal punishment, 218-19
  and dress, 224-26
  and fees, 216-17
  and flag salute, 223
  and secret societies, 231-33, 238
  assumption of risk, 254-55
  attendance, 211-15
  marriages of, 223, 227-29
  minor, and torts, 255-57
  safety of, 246, 247, 256-ff., 266

R

Remedies
  for wrongful expulsion, 224
Resignation, of teachers, 295-301

Retirement benefits
  denial of, 131-35
  eligibility under, 131
  right of teacher to, 129
Rezny and Remmlein, 330
Roach, Stephen F., 140

S

Safety patrols, 258-59
Salaries
  extra pay for extra work, 147-49
  merit pay, 144-46
  minimum, 141, 144
  miscellaneous rights to, 149-52
  reduction of, 143-44
  right of board to fix, 140-42
  right to increments, 151
  salary schedules, 142-44
  when paid, 146-47
Save harmless legislation, 219, 266-67
School districts
  defined, 10
  exemption from liability, 11
School law
  and universities, 331-32
  at state level, 330
  current status of, 329
  literature in, 329-30
  organizations in, 332
  why study? 5-8
School system
  and immunity doctrine, 242-45
  and Thomas Jefferson, 14-15
  establishment and maintenance of, 9
  evolving, 11-12
Secret societies, 231-33
Slander, 190, 191-92
  defined, 241
State department of education, 99-100, 266, 330-31
State government
  and academic freedom, 174-77
  and contracts, 97-98
  and union membership, 189
  education a state function, 8-11
Statutes
  governing dismissal, 274-75
  guest, 4, 263
  inspection, 266
  of frauds, 88
  of limitations, 258
  save harmless, 266-67

Student teachers
  and communications, 322
  as employees, 323
  authority to discipline pupils, 321-23
  authority to permit, 310
  certification of, 316-18
  character of, 309-10
  history of, 307-08
  legal rights of, 321, 323
  liability of, 318-21
  right to collect on injury, 323
  statutory provisions for, 314-16
Superintendent
  and dismissal of pupils, 230-31
  and dismissal of teachers, 198-99, 272, 278, 279, 291
  and libel, 192-94
  and maternity leaves, 156
  and teacher resignations, 296-98
  dismissal of the, 91, 280
  powers of the, in contracting, 85
  reports of, 69
  right to question teachers, 171-74
Supervision
  tort test of, 242-52
  unremitting, 251-53
  when adequate, 247-ff., 255-57
Supreme Court
  and education, 23-29
  and individual rights, 234
  and vaccination, 214
  appeals to the, 34-35
  Dartmouth College case, 15-16
  Oregon case, 25-26, 211-12
  prayers in schools, 235-36
  racial segregation, 27-29
  released time, 26-27
  retirement, 129
  Slaughter-house cases, 24
Suspension of teachers, 298-301

T

Teachers
  in loco parentis, 206-08
Teacher's rights
  to academic freedom, 175-76
  to administer corporal punishment, 219
  to a hearing, 277
  to appeal board decisions, 124-29
  to bargain collectively, 167
  to breach contract, 105-07
  to communicate, 167, 175-76
  to constitutional rights, 168-74
  to continuing contract, 104-05, 120-24
  to control pupils, 205-ff., 236-38
  to damages, 291-92
  to duty-free lunch periods, 153
  to employee welfare benefits, 137-ff.
  to employ substitute, 285
  to engage in political activity, 182-83, 185-86
  to extra pay for extra work, 147-49
  to freedom from cancellation, 120-22
  to freedom from transfer, 144
  to freedom of speech, 175-76
  to fringe benefits, 151-52
  to hold legislative office, 181-82
  to hold outside employment, 159-62
  to keep memberships secret, 169-74
  to leaves of absence, 153-ff., 284-85
  to marry, 276
  to minimum salary, 141, 144, 152-53
  to non-membership, 188-89
  to organizational membership, 177-79
  to redress of grievances, 199-200, 185-86
  to reinstatement, 291-95
  to rescind resignation, 296-97
  to resign, 295-98
  to retirement benefits, 129-35
  to salary increments, 151
  to speak and write, 169, 175-76, 186, 189-95, 278
  to strike, 167
  to tenure, 122-ff.
  to treat children medically, 263, 265
  to union membership, 187-88
  to work, 183-89, 195-99
  to workmen's compensation, 163-65
Teacher welfare
  importance of, 138
  teacher disability, 164
  teacher injury, 163
  teachers are employees, 138-39
Tenth Amendment, 19
Tenure
  courts and, 116

defined, 116
guarantees under, 117-18
purposes of, 114-19
validity of, 120
Thomas, Wesley E., 102-03
Tort
  avoidance of, 265-67
  defined, 241
  legal test of, 241-42
  liability of school districts, 242, 245
  liability of school employees, 245-ff., 257, 262-63

U

Union shop, 183-84
U. S. S. R., 8, 55

V

Vaccination, 214-15
Vested rights, 127, 130, 133
Volunteer, 62

W

Workmen's compensation, 163-65